Sustainable Resource Management

Dedication
To Roma and Fiona – those whom I hold most dear

Sustainable Resource Management

Reality or Illusion?

Edited by

Peter N. Nemetz

University of British Columbia, Canada

Edward Elgar
Cheltenham, UK • Northampton, MA, USA

Published by
Edward Elgar Publishing Limited
Glensanda House
Montpellier Parade
Cheltenham
Glos GL50 1UA
UK

Edward Elgar Publishing, Inc.
William Pratt House
9 Dewey Court
Northampton
Massachusetts 01060
USA

A catalogue record for this book
is available from the British Library

Library of Congress Cataloguing in Publication Data

Sustainable resource management : reality or illusion? / edited by Peter N. Nemetz.
   p. cm
Includes bibliographical references and index.
1. Sustainable development. I. Nemetz, Peter N., 1944–
HC79.E5S86496 2006
333.72—dc22   2006012550

ISBN 978 1 84542 594 4

Printed and bound in Great Britain by MPG Books Ltd, Bodmin, Cornwall

Contents

Contributors

EDITOR

Peter N. Nemetz, Professor of Strategy and Business Economics, Sauder School of Business, University of British Columbia

AUTHORS

Miguel A. Altieri, Professor, University of California, Berkeley

Ray Anderson, Chairman and CEO, Interface Inc.

Jean-Philippe Barde, Head, National Policies Division, Environment Directorate, OECD

Nils Axel Braathen, National Policies Division, Environment Directorate, OECD

Ratana Chuenpagdee, Associate Professor, Department of Geography, Memorial University of Newfoundland

Ronald Colman, Executive Director, Genuine Progress Index Atlantic

Clyde Hertzman, Professor, Department of Health Care and Epidemiology, UBC, Former Director for the Program in Population Health, Canadian Institute for Advanced Research

J.P. (Hamish) Kimmins, Professor, Faculty of Forestry, UBC

Jane Lister, Institute for Resources, Environment & Sustainability, University of British Columbia

Brian J. McLean, Director, Office of Atmospheric Programs, U.S. Environmental Protection Agency

Daniel Pauly, Director, Fisheries Centre, UBC

William E. Rees, Former Director, UBC School of Community and Regional Planning, Co-creator of The Ecological Footprint

Robert Repetto, Professor in the Practice of Economics, Yale School of Forestry & Sustainable Development

Burton Richter, Paul Pigott Professor in the Physical Sciences, Stanford University; Director Emeritus, Stanford Linear Accelerator Center; Nobel Laureate, Physics

Roger A. Sedjo, Resources for the Future, Washington, DC

Anthony R.E. Sinclair, Professor, Former Director, Biodiversity Research Centre, UBC

W.G.B. Smith, Environment Canada

David T. Suzuki, Professor Emeritus, Department of Zoology, UBC

PART I

Introduction and overview

Introduction

Humanity's conceptualization of the global environment has changed radically in the four decades since the publication of Rachel Carson's *Silent Spring* (1962). In many respects, there has been a fundamental transformation within the sciences, social sciences and humanities with the emergence of such critical disciplines as ecology, environmental ethics and, more recently, ecological economics. Underlying this remarkable disciplinary change has been a dramatic paradigm shift – from humanity as dominant over, yet independent of, the natural environment, to humanity as one, albeit important, element of a complex interrelated array of ecological entities. This reformulation of humanity's place in the global ecosystem crystallized in 1987 with the publication of the Bruntland Report (WCED, 1987) and the articulation of the concept of sustainable development.

Defined simply as 'development which meets the needs of the present without compromising the ability of future generations to meet their own needs', the concept of sustainable development has spurred a vast amount of interpretative research literature which has focused on its implications across a broad range of human activities and academic disciplines. Beguilingly simple in its phraseology, sustainable development has created an extraordinary intellectual challenge – first, to define it operationally and, second, to generate metrics to assess change both toward and away from it.

At the heart of sustainable development is the concept of systems theory – that all elements of a system are interrelated and that the whole is greater than the sum of its parts. In simplest terms, sustainable development encompasses three subsystems. It is based on the analogy of a three-legged stool, requiring the simultaneous achievement of sustainability in three disparate spheres: economic, ecological and social. In the last category, sustainable development must address both intragenerational and intergenerational equity; that is, issues of empowerment and distributional equity not only among the current inhabitants of the earth, but also across generations yet to be born. Several critical conceptual threads run throughout studies of sustainability:

1. a distinction between qualitative and quantitative changes in the utilization of our technology and natural resource base (that is *development* versus *growth*). Central to operationalizing this distinction are technological advances which may permit us to raise our standard of

3

living without increasing the throughput of resources – a process commonly referred to as 'dematerialization';

2. a focus on social justice, stability and empowerment with particular emphasis on reducing poverty and maintaining an adequate quality of life for all global inhabitants;

3. borrowing from principles of business sector accounting, a direct or indirect articulation of the concept of *natural* capital – where maintenance of a constant natural capital stock (including the renewable resource base and the environment) yields an indefinite stream of output or 'income'. At its core is the proposition that the current generation must leave its descendants a stock of capital no less than is currently available. Implicit in this proposition is that we must, to the best of our ability, live off the 'interest' on this capital stock and not draw it down. If part of this capital is consumed, it must be replaced by substitute capital. The ability to achieve this goal hinges on which of two alternative definitions is adopted: 'weak' sustainability or 'strong' sustainability.

    Under the weak sustainability constant capital rule, we can consume some of our natural capital (in the form of environmental degradation, for example) as long as we offset this loss by increasing our stock of man-made capital. In contrast, under the strong sustainability constant capital rule, there is no perfect substitution among different forms of capital. Some elements of the natural capital stock (such as life-support services) cannot be replaced by man-made capital. To implement either of these concepts requires the ability to distinguish more accurately among the various forms of capital (natural, human and physical). Without more accurate measures of these forms of capital, we cannot make the right decisions;

4. a concept known as the 'precautionary principle' which states that one cannot wait for definitive scientific proof of a potential threat to the global ecosystem before acting, if that threat is both large and credible (Harremoes et al., 2002). The underlying theory is based on scientific principles, largely associated with the work of ecologists such as C.S. Holling (1978), that ecosystems under stress do not necessarily adjust slowly and steadily, but may jump suddenly between alternative equilibrium states, some much less hospitable for human activity than others. The import of this theory is that by the time one recognizes or begins to feel the tangible effects of certain types of ecological threats, it may be too late to reverse their effects (see for example, NRC, 2002).

    The application of the precautionary principle to the threat of global warming can be modeled using the economic methodology of game theory pioneered by Von Neumann and Morgenstern (1944). Figure I.1 presents a simple 2×2 decision matrix which represents

	Player #1 (in this case, society) Possible actions	Player #2 (in this case, unknown states of nature)	
		Global warming is NOT occurring	Global warming is occurring
	We assume global warming is occurring and act on it	Generally unproductive investment COSTS: significant BENEFITS: marginal	COSTS: significant BENEFITS: we can slow or possibly reverse the damage
	We assume global warming is NOT occurring and do nothing	COSTS: none BENEFITS: none	COSTS: enormous BENEFITS: none

Figure I.1   Decision matrix for global warming

5

two states of nature (global warming is/is not occurring) and two possible courses of action (act/not act). Each of the four matrix cells
entails markedly different 'payoffs'. Given the enormous costs of
non-response to global warming, a 'maximin' strategy is warranted,
where society (here denoted as Player #1) chooses a course of action
which minimizes potential losses. Acting on the assumption that
global warming is occurring may entail significant opportunity costs
if global warming is not occurring, but avoids the potentially catastrophic consequences of not acting if in fact global warming is
occurring.

WHERE ARE WE NOW?

The recently published United Nations Millennium Ecosystem Assessment Report is perhaps the most comprehensive analysis to date of the
state of the global ecosystem. The report's multiple volumes paint a startling and relatively dismal picture, summarized in four major findings
(WRI, 2005, p. 1):

- Over the past 50 years, humans have changed ecosystems more rapidly and
  extensively than in any comparable period of time in human history, largely
  to meet rapidly growing demands for food, fresh water, timber, fiber, and
  fuel. This has resulted in a substantial and largely irreversible loss in the
  diversity of life on Earth.
- The changes that have been made to ecosystems have contributed to substantial net gains in human well-being and economic development, but these
  gains have been achieved at growing costs in the form of the degradation of
  many ecosystem services, increased risks of nonlinear changes, and the exacerbation of poverty for some groups of people. These problems, unless
  addressed, will substantially diminish the benefits that future generations
  obtain from ecosystems.
- The degradation of ecosystem services could grow significantly worse during
  the first half of this century and is a barrier to achieving the Millennium
  Development Goals.
- The challenge of reversing the degradation of ecosystems while meeting
  increasing demands for their services can be partially met under some scenarios that the MA has considered, but these involve significant changes in
  policies, institutions, and practices that are not currently under way. Many
  options exist to conserve or enhance specific ecosystem services in ways that
  reduce negative trade-offs or that provide positive synergies with other
  ecosystem services.

These observations stand in stark contrast to the economic, political and
social optimism of the immediate post World War II period, when new

multinational institutions, the Marshall Plan, and rapidly expanding international trade and development promised an era of increasing affluence and limitless possibilities for the international community of nations. What changed so dramatically in so few decades?

The Worldwatch Institute's *2006 State of the World Report* (Flavin and Gardner, 2006, pp. 18, 21) concludes that 'the twentieth-century resource-intensive development path is a dead end' and that this western model is 'simply not capable of meeting the growing needs of the more than 8 billion people in the twenty-first century'. The model of growth that western industrialized nations have implemented has not only failed to detect and report signals of ecological stress and decline, but also, in many instances, conveyed misleading and erroneous economic signals.

The near universally accepted standards of progress and competitive well-being – gross domestic product (GDP) and GDP per capita – have only recently been subjected to serious re-examination. In his overview of the OECD's 2006 document entitled *Economic Policy Reforms. Going for Growth*, Jean-Philippe Cotis (2006) asks 'how reliable a measure of overall welfare is GDP?' He concludes that GDP suffers from many shortcomings: 'It does not incorporate environmental degradation, nor the value of leisure. Neither does it take into account the influence on well-being of income distribution. By using GDP per capita as an indicator of well-being, you always run the risk of adopting a reductionist approach.'

The OECD considers a number of alternative indicators, complementing several existing attempts to create measures of well-being which can lead toward, rather than away from, sustainability (Daly and Cobb, 1994; Serageldin, 1995; Colman, Chapter 16, this volume). Herman Daly (1999, pp. 6–7) has captured the essence of the problem we face in attempting to evaluate the state of the world with standard measures of macroeconomic performance:

> The notion of an optimal scale for an activity is the very heart of microeconomics. . . . Yet for the macro level, the aggregate of all microeconomic activities . . . there is no concept of an optimal scale. The notion that the macroeconomy could become too large relative to the ecosystem is simply absent from macroeconomic theory. The macroeconomy is supposed to grow for ever. Since GNP adds costs and benefits together instead of comparing them at the margin, we have no macro-level accounting by which an optimal scale could be identified. Beyond a certain scale, growth begins to destroy more values than it creates – economic growth gives way to an era of anti-economic growth. But GNP keeps rising, giving us no clue as to whether we have passed that critical point!

While it now appears that the western industrialized world may have chosen a questionable metric to assess its performance, there is little doubt that our economic systems have pursued the maximization of this measure with awesome efficiency. The process of globalization in the last half century has entailed the construction of a complex and highly interconnected international system of finance and trade which has made possible the remarkable growth of GDP and GDP per capita on every continent except Africa. How sustainable is this international system? The creation of this complex system has come at a cost/risk which cannot be easily reduced. To borrow from Charles Perrow (1984), author of *Normal Accidents*, which focuses on the nature of complex modern technologies, we have created a 'tightly coupled system' which is extremely vulnerable to both economic and ecological shocks originating anywhere within the international community. In simplest terms, we have traded system resilience for efficiency.

Recent examples of these risks include the Mexican Peso crisis in 1995; Thailand's financial crisis in July 1997 (referred to at the time as the 'Asian Flu'); and the 'near meltdown' of the international financial system following the near collapse in September 1998 of Long Term Capital Management with an exposure in excess of $1.25 trillion. Of even greater concern are the international economic consequences from a potential global avian flu pandemic which originated in East Asia (BMO Nesbitt Burns, 2005; Bloom et al., 2005). As the BMO Nesbitt Burns report observes:

> This would be the first pandemic since East Asia became integrated into the global economy. The new globalism that has become one of the greatest sources of strength for the world's financial and commodity markets would become their greatest vulnerability. . . . The economic and societal effects of a pandemic, even a moderate one, are so severe that businesses and consumers need to join the medical and scientific community in creating a crisis and management plan.

In fact, the seeds of the current threats to global ecological and economic viability significantly predate the post World War II period. The advent of the Industrial Revolution in the late eighteenth and early nineteenth centuries marked a significant turning point in human history. At the risk of oversimplification, it is possible to conclude that this epoch event dramatically changed humankind's utilization of the global resource base. The Industrial Revolution marked the transition from a principal reliance on the global renewable resource base to the large-scale exploitation of non-renewable resources, most notably fossil-based energy sources. This transition and new focus on fossil fuels has tended to mask but not change the fundamental fact that renewable resources are not only essential to human survival but many are also capable of exhaustion.

Garrett Hardin (1968), in his classic article 'The tragedy of the commons', theorized why renewable resources could face exhaustion from rational profit-maximizing decisions taken by individual economic actors. In fact, the situation is more complex, as what Hardin described as 'common property resources' were in fact 'open access resources'. Traditional community-based institutional safeguards have existed in many parts of the world to preserve common property resources. Unfortunately, many of these safeguards have been eroded by a broad range of factors, including mounting population pressure, loss of local control to national governments, and increased resource demands. Indeed, globalization and international trade have played a pivotal role in the over-exploitation of local resources.

It was observed earlier that the post World War II process of global industrialization and wealth accumulation was facilitated, if not created, by international flows of capital, goods and services. It has been conventional wisdom that international trade is unambiguously beneficial for all participants and that this positive effect extends to the state of the environment among trading nations as well. The neo-classical view in economics is that trade will improve the environment for two reasons: (1) according to David Ricardo's theory of comparative advantage, trade increases wealth as measured by GDP per capita, and (2) as wealth increases, pollution and risks in general tend to decrease. The mantra of this philosophy is: 'a rising tide lifts all boats'.

We already know that increasing GDP and GDP per capita do not necessarily imply that we are better off (for example, consider the contrast between traditional GDP and newer measures of national well-being). We also know that the nature of pollution and risk change as economies grow (see Smith and Ezzati's (2005) concept of the 'risk transition') and that we face far greater risks to the global ecosystem now than ever before. In fact, while we have indeed observed increases in GDP and GDP per capita as international trade has increased in the post World War II period, the relationship between this economic growth and the quality of the environment is much more complex than it first appears.

In a recent article in the journal *Ecological Economics*, Nobel Laureate Kenneth Arrow and other distinguished academics, including Robert Costanza, Partha Dasgupta, C.S. Holling and David Pimental (1995), state that: 'National and international economic policy has usually ignored the environment', and that 'The environmental consequences of growing economic activity may be very mixed'. They conclude that:

> economic liberalization and other policies that promote gross national product growth are not substitutes for environmental policy. . . . Abrupt changes can seldom be anticipated from systems of signals that are typically received by

decision-makers in the world today. Moreover, the signals that do exist are often not observed, or are wrongly interpreted, or are not part of the incentive structure of societies. This is due to ignorance about the dynamic effects of changes in ecosystem variables (for example thresholds, buffering capacity, and loss of resilience) and to the presence of institutional impediments, such as lack of well-defined property rights. Economic growth is not a panacea for environmental quality; indeed, it is not even the main issue. What matters is the content of growth – the composition of inputs (including environmental resources) and outputs (including waste products).

With respect to the claim made by conventional economic theory about the beneficial effects of international trade on wealth, there is indisputable evidence that in most of the countries of the world (Africa is the general exception), GDP and GDP per capita have been increasing for the last 60 years. Two general observations are possible: (1) the First World is increasing the wealth gap over the Third World; however, there is still increasing wealth among most developing nations, and some of these countries (such as China) have established an outstanding track record in annual economic growth; but (2) the gain in wealth as measured by GDP per capita has not been distributed equitably. In fact, there is evidence that some lower income groups in countries which have opened up to free trade have become further impoverished. Many of these poorest groups have relied on marginal agriculture to sustain themselves with food and essential supplemental income from the sale of their agriculture produce. When free trade opens their borders, there is frequently a flood of inexpensive manufactured and subsidized agricultural goods against which they cannot compete. The result is further impoverishment and an increased tendency of locals to fall back on the consumption of local environmental goods (such as fuelwood) in order to survive.

A recent study by the Carnegie Endowment for International Peace (2003, pp. 5–6) on the economic and environmental impact of NAFTA on Mexico suggests that this phenomenon is happening in the southern, most impoverished regions of the country. The report concludes, in part, that:

- NAFTA has not helped the Mexican economy keep pace with the growing demand for jobs. While there has been an increase of 500 000 jobs in manufacturing from 1994 to 2002, the agricultural sector, where almost a fifth of Mexicans still work, has lost 1.3 million jobs since 1994.
- Real wages for most Mexicans today are lower than they were when NAFTA took effect. However, this setback in wages was caused by the peso crisis of 1994–1995 – not by NAFTA. That said, the productivity growth that has occurred over the last decade has not translated into growth in wages.
- The Mexican government estimates that annual pollution damages over the past decade exceeded US$36 billion per year. This damage to the environment is greater than the economic gains from the growth of trade and of the economy as a whole. More specifically, enactment of NAFTA accelerated

changes in commercial farming practices that have put Mexico's diverse ecosystem at great risk of contamination from concentrations of nitrogen and other chemicals commonly used in modern farming.

● Mexico's evolution toward a modern, export-oriented agricultural sector has also failed to deliver the anticipated environmental benefits of reduced deforestation and tillage. Rural farmers have replaced lost income caused by the collapse in commodity prices by farming more marginal land, a practice that has resulted in an average deforestation rate of more than 630,000 hectares per year since 1993 in the biologically rich regions of southern Mexico.

While utilitarian theory suggests that nations with increased per capita wealth resulting from trade are unambiguously wealthier because resources can, *in theory*, be transferred intra-nationally in the Third World from the 'winners' to the 'losers' and still leave everyone better off, the creation of significant numbers of economically disenfranchised people in developing countries *in practice* creates major sources of political and social instability as well as potentially serious environmental degradation. The risks associated with this 'collateral damage' of globalization have been the subject of discussion in such important forums as the annual meeting at Davos, Switzerland of many of the world's political and business leaders (*New York Times*, 2000a and 2000b).

The second critical question concerning the role of international trade focuses on the impact of trade on the environment and local renewable resource base. There is emerging evidence to suggest that in many Third World countries liquidation of natural capital is masquerading as increases in wealth. Exposure of local renewable resource streams to high prices and high demands of the international marketplace may lead to the serious diminution or destruction of the renewable resource base in the medium to long term. Local historical institutional controls which have maintained these resource streams are under increased pressure from commercial interests or central governments.

A cogent example of the potential impact of trade on the environment has emerged in the last decade with respect to China's forests. After several years of horrendous flooding attributed to massive deforestation of watersheds, China has embarked on a major program of reforestation and controls or bans on logging. Nevertheless, China has a steadily increasing need for wood products as it industrializes and as its emerging middle class develops a taste for western-style wooden housing. In addition, China has become the dominant world player in the production of plywood; a title it has assumed from the USA and Indonesia. While China is trying to protect its forest resource base, it is endangering the forest base of many of its trading partners through both legal and illegal trade in roundwood. Illegal logging in the tropics is a disaster of major proportions threatening the survival of the great tropical forests, and a significant proportion of it is being driven by international markets.

A tentative conclusion with respect to trade and the environment is that trade can and does increase wealth among trading partners. This wealth accumulation, however, may be accompanied by increasing inter-national and intra-national income disparities. Trade may be a necessary but not sufficient vehicle for protecting the environment. In fact, it can lead to serious environmental degradation without the proper local, national and international economic, political and social controls. These preconditions are non-trivial and may be very difficult to achieve in practice.

BOOK OUTLINE

Much of the sustainable development literature is ultimately concerned with humanity's production, use and disposal of natural resources. The focus is bifaceted: achieving a rate of resource utilization which will not only guarantee the requirements of future generations, but also will ensure that this rate will not damage or destroy the ecological system in which human activity is embedded. As such, this volume focuses on the complex interrelationship of humankind and the natural resources it uses to survive and flourish, and whether humanity is managing these resources in a sustainable manner. The remainder of this volume is divided into three parts: (1) three case studies which reflect innovative policy and strategic initiatives toward the goal of sustainable development within both the corporate and public sectors; (2) a sector-by-sector analysis of specific opportunities and challenges within the resource domains of energy and global climate, human health, fisheries, agriculture, biodiversity and forestry; and finally (3) a group of chapters which consider the broader and more complex conceptual issues which must be addressed if sustainable development is to be achieved. These issues include how national economic and corporate activity is to be measured and assessed and, perhaps most important, whether humanity is itself capable to making the changes necessary to guarantee its own survival.

Central to much of the discussion which ensues in this volume are issues which are fundamentally economic in nature – what is the appropriate rate of resource extraction? What are appropriate prices for natural resources, and can they be implemented? And which models of resource ownership and business production and organization are truly functional from the perspective of sustainable development? In this regard, ecological economics has much to contribute. The foundations of this discipline rest on a simple philosophical premise: that the economic system is embedded in the ecological system, cannot function without it, and is ultimately subject to the same laws and constraints which apply to natural systems.

Throughout this volume, one can witness, on the one hand, the spark of human ingenuity and invention which holds out a promise of success and, on the other hand, the mindsets, myths and new conventional wisdom which characterize the emerging domain of sustainable development and which pose a daunting and potentially insurmountable challenge to its achievement. It is the conclusion of this volume that while progress has indeed been made, the issues underlying sustainable development are far more complex than has been generally realized. Indeed, it is possible to offer the tentative hypothesis, drawn from the contributions herein, that nothing short of a revolution in the way we produce goods and services, the way we structure our corporate decision making, and the way we view our relationship with the natural environment will guarantee the achievement of sustainable development. Central to this is a realization that many of the reigning beliefs that guide our actions today must be critically re-examined, challenged and, if necessary, rejected and replaced. Each contribution to this volume engages in just such a challenge to the tenets of current conventional wisdom.

REFERENCES

Arrow, Kenneth, Bert Bolin, Robert Costanza, Partha Dasgupta, Carl Folke, C.S. Holling, Bengt-Owe Jansson, Simon Levin, Karl-Goran Maler, Charles Perrings and David Pimentel (1995), 'Economic growth, carrying capacity, and the environment', *Ecological Economics*, **15**, 91–5.
Bloom Erik, Vincent de Wit and Mary Jane Carangal-San Jose (2005), 'Potential economic impact of an avian flu pandemic on Asia', Asian Development Bank (ADB) ERD Policy Brief No. 42, Manila.
BMO Nesbitt Burns (2005), *An Investor's Guide to Avian Flu*, www2.bmo.com/bmo/files/news%20release/4/1/Avian%20Flu.pdf.
Carnegie Endowment for International Peace (2003), 'NAFTA's promise and reality: lessons from Mexico for the hemisphere', www.carnegieendowment.org/pdf/files/NAFTA_Report_Intro.pdf, ChapterOne.pdf, ChapterTwo.pdf, ChapterThree.pdf.
Carson, Rachel (1962), *Silent Spring*, reprinted (2002) New York: Houghton Mifflin.
Cotis, Jean-Philippe (2006), 'Going for growth one year on', 7 February, OECD.
Daly, Herman E. (1999), *Ecological Economics and the Ecology of Economics. Essays in Criticism*, Cheltenham, UK and Northampton, MA, USA: Edward Elgar.
Daly, Herman E. and John B. Cobb (1994), 'Appendix: "The index for sustainable economic welfare"', in *For the Common Good. Redirecting the economy toward community, the environment, and a sustainable future*, Boston: Beacon Press.
Flavin, Christopher and Gary Gardner (2006), 'China, India, and the New World Order', *State of the World 2006*, The Worldwatch Institute, pp. 3–23.
Hardin, Garrett (1968), 'The tragedy of the commons', *Science*, **162**, 1243–48.

Harremoes, Poul et al. (eds) (2002), *The Precautionary Principle in the 20th Century. Late Lessons from Early Warnings*, London: Earthscan for the European Environment Agency.

Holling, C.S. (1978), 'Myths of ecological stability: resilience and the problem of failure', in C.F. Smart and W.T. Stanbury (eds), *Studies in Crisis Management*, Montreal: Butterworth & Co.

National Research Council (NRC) (2002), *Abrupt Climate Change. Inevitable Surprises*, Washington, DC: National Academy Press.

New York Times (2000a), 'At trade forum, Clinton pleads for the poor', 30 January.

New York Times (2000b), 'Davos forum opens with qualified exuberance', 28 January.

Perrow, Charles (1984), *Normal Accidents. Living With High-Risk Technologies*, New York: Basic Books.

Serageldin, Ismail (1995), 'Sustainability and the wealth of nations: first steps in an ongoing journey', preliminary draft, Washington, DC: World Bank, 30 September.

Smith, Kirk R. and Majid Ezzati (2005), 'How environmental health risks change with development: the epidemiologic and environmental risk transitions revisited', *Annual Review of Environment and Resources*, **30**, 291–333.

Von Neumann, J. and O. Morgenstern (1944), *The Theory of Games and Economic Behaviour*, Princeton, NJ: Princeton University Press.

World Commission on Environment and Development (WCED) (1987), *Our Common Future*, Oxford: Oxford University Press.

World Resources Institute (WRI) (2005), *Ecosystems and Human Well-Being. Synthesis*, Millennium Ecosystem Assessment, Published for the United Nations.

PART II

Some successes on the road to sustainability

Introduction

All of the conceptual problems which have faced the achievement of traditional environmental policy represent a subset of the challenges which the goal of sustainable development must address. Foremost among these have been the economic inefficiency of command and control regulatory systems, and the presence of taxation systems which distort incentives or even create disincentives for environmental protection. Pioneering policy research and implementation has been conducted on both sides of the Atlantic with respect to both of these keystone problems. Chapter 1 by Brian McLean of the US Environmental Protection Agency describes the successful development and application of a market for, and trading in, permits for SO_2 emissions from the utility industry throughout the United States. The results of this policy shift toward economic incentives to protect the environment have been remarkable. As McLean states:

> When the full SO_2 reductions are achieved in 2010, a significant benefit to public health is expected because of the reduction in airborne fine particulate matter, much of which is due to sulfates. Monetized benefits, from the entire Acid Rain Program (both SO_2 and NO_x) are estimated at $122 billion annually. . . . In stark contrast to the benefits of the emissions reductions is the cost of compliance. . . . When the Acid Rain Program was being considered by Congress in 1989 and 1990, the estimated cost of the program ranged from over $4 billion per year to over $7 billion per year. But four years after its enactment, an audit of the program by the US General Accounting Office concluded that the cost of full implementation was likely to be closer to $2 billion per year. More recent estimates have placed the cost closer to $1 billion per year.

The success of the cap and trade program for sulphur dioxide has demonstrated the applicability of this concept to a range of other critical air pollutants, including nitrogen dioxide and greenhouse gases (GHG) such as carbon dioxide. Provisions for trading in CO_2 emissions are incorporated in the terms of the Kyoto Protocol and private sector offsets such as tree planting or the creation of ecological reserves in the Third World have already been undertaken by several companies in North America and Japan.

It is important to note, however, that despite the success of the US cap and trade program for SO_2, market permits for air pollutants are not universally applicable. There are generally four criteria required to render a pollutant amenable to a regional, national or global trading regime: (i) relative homogeneity of physical and chemical properties, (ii) relatively low toxicity, (iii) susceptibility to diffusion by medium to long-term airborne transport, and (iv) fairly homogeneous distribution.

The problem of non-spatial homogeneity of even a physically and chemically homogeneous pollutant was first recognized and modeled in the 1980s by Caltech scientists for the greater Los Angeles airshed (Case et al., 1982). The potential for 'hotspots' generated by topographical and meteorological conditions may require the utilization of either pre-specified limitations on industrial plant emissions or the development of transfer coefficients which capture the inter-regional differences in pollutant impact. The current US government's interest in establishing a marketable pollutant system for mercury discharges, especially from coal-fired power plants, is a cogent example of a pollutant which fails to meet most of the criteria essential for this type of program to succeed.

One of the most powerful tools available in the economic armory available to government for influencing corporate behaviour, including environmental impact, lies in the tax code. At least four key elements are essential to the utilization of the tax code to promote sustainable development: (1) a fundamental shift in the tax base from 'goods' to 'bads'; that is, the design of a consistent and comprehensive system of taxation which encourages activities and the production of goods and services consistent with sustainability while discouraging goods and services inconsistent with sustainability; (2) tax 'neutrality' which permits governments to undertake a reasonably short-term process of taxation restructuring without engendering resistance from the private sector over issues of equity; (3) the creation of a taxation system which does not diminish or extinguish its own revenue stream as it induces positive responses among private sector economic actors; and (4) the necessity of coordinating policies among national governments to avoid artificially impeding economic competitiveness. The remarkable track record of the European states of the OECD is outlined by Jean-Philippe Barde and Nils-Axel Braathen of the OECD's Environmental Directorate in Chapter 2. Barde and Braathen describe the intricacies of the move toward the adoption of ecological, or 'green' tax reform in this jurisdiction by focusing on achievements to date and challenges which remain. They conclude that:

> In the context of growing environmental challenges, both nationally and internationally, environmentally related taxes are now recognized as an environmentally effective and economically efficient policy instrument. As a matter of fact, virtually all OECD countries are using such taxes to a larger or lesser extent, while several countries have implemented comprehensive green tax reforms. 'Green' taxes should preferably be implemented in the context of broader tax

reforms providing an opportunity to reduce or eliminate tax distortions and 'niches' and modernize taxation systems, hence achieving effective adjustments of economies and greater economic efficiency. In this context, the removal or reform of environmentally harmful subsidies is essential.

There is now ample evidence of the environmental effectiveness of environmentally related taxes. These taxes should be implemented in a long-term perspective, in particular because transport and energy demand elasticities are significantly larger in the long term than in the short term: structural adjustments and technological change can take a long time to be implemented.

A number of policy issues remain to be addressed; in particular, the implication for income distribution and, more so, the possible impact on sectoral competitiveness. This is why an internationally coordinated implementation of environmental taxes would strongly facilitate more widespread and more efficient environmental taxes and green tax reforms; this is a key challenge for the future. Clear objectives, transparent systems, stakeholders' involvement, gradual implementation, and well-designed compensation mechanisms are amongst the prominent aspects of a well-balanced 'political economy' of environmental taxes.

Despite the indispensable role of government, sustainable development cannot be achieved without the active participation of the business sector through which most natural resources are extracted, processed and distributed. In many respects, it is in this sector that the greatest challenges lie because of the fundamental distinction between private and social costs and benefits, for without appropriate economic signals and incentives, it is unrealistic to expect any business to adopt policies conducive to sustainable development. Just how difficult this challenge remains is described in Chapter 3 by Ray Anderson, Chairman and CEO of Interface Inc., the world's largest producer of commercial carpeting. Devoted to making his corporation a model of true sustainability, Anderson has attempted to move his company over the last decade off the path of unsustainability. His achievements to date have been exemplary, but much remains to be accomplished. As the author clearly articulates, this momentous undertaking requires more than changes in the values and actions of selected corporations – it requires a fundamental redesign of commerce as we know and practice it today; it requires a 'new industrial revolution'. The avatar of this revolution is the prototypical and sustainable corporation of the twenty-first century. As envisaged by Anderson, it is:

strongly service-oriented, resource-efficient, wasting nothing, solar-driven, cyclical (no longer take–make–waste linear), strongly connected to our constituencies – our communities (building social equity), our customers, and our suppliers – and to one other. Our communities are stronger and better-educated . . . . Furthermore, this 21st Century company is way ahead of the regulatory process, which has become irrelevant. The company's values have shifted, too, and it is successfully committed to taking nothing from Earth's lithosphere that's not renewable, and doing no harm to the biosphere. . . . Sustainable and just, giving social equity its appropriate priority, and creating sustainable prosperity, an example for all, this company is doing well by doing good. And it is growing, too; it is expanding its market share at the expense of inefficient adapters, those competitors that remain committed to the old, outdated paradigm and dependent on Earth's stored natural capital. . . . It makes such absolute business sense to win this way; not at Earth's expense nor at our descendants' expense, but at the expense of inefficient competitors. Most importantly, we will have proven the feasibility of . . . making technology part of the solution, and reducing environmental impact. If we can do that in a petro-intensive company such as Interface, anyone can do it. The next industrial revolution can be.

There are at least two notable, but potentially offsetting, observations about Interface's achievements to date. First, the company has successfully capitalized on an emerging reconceptualization of the products of a modern post-industrial economy. The traditional distinction between goods and services is fading, replaced with an economic model which considers durable and non-durable products not as goods per se, but rather as vehicles for delivering services. Through its Evergreen Lease © program, Interface sells the services of carpetry, such as 'color, design, texture, warmth, acoustics, comfort under foot, cleanliness and improved air quality, but not the carpet itself'.

The second tentative observation follows from a visual examination of the data presented for energy and water use in Anderson's chapter. Economic theory dictates that the most productive investments be undertaken first – in modern parlance, 'picking the low-hanging fruit'. The question arises as to whether there are thermodynamic limits to the reduction in material and energy throughput required to produce carpet or, indeed, many other essential modern industrial products. This is the essence of the challenge facing not only Interface, but also the entire manufacturing sector. A recent research report from the World Resources Institute (Matthews et al., 2000, p. xi) found mixed results:

> Industrial economies are becoming more efficient in their use of materials, but waste generation continues to increase. Despite strong economic growth in all countries studied, resource inputs and waste outputs between 1975 and 1996 rose relatively little, on a per capita basis, and fell dramatically when measured against units of economic output. Even as decoupling between economic growth and resource throughput occurred on a per capita and per unit GDP basis, however, overall resource use and waste flows into the environment continued to grow. We found no evidence of an absolute reduction in resource throughput. One half to three quarters of annual resource inputs to industrial economies are returned to the environment as wastes within a year. . . . When 'hidden flows' are included – flows which do not enter the economy, such as soil erosion, mining overburden, and earth moved during construction – total annual material outputs to the environment range from 21 metric tons per person in Japan to 86 metric tons per person in the United States. Outputs of some hazardous

materials have been regulated and successfully reduced or stabilized but outputs of many potentially harmful materials continue to increase. . . . Our estimates indicate that many potentially hazardous flows in the United States increased by 25 to 100 percent between 1975 and 1996.

Nevertheless, the pioneering approach adopted by Interface provides powerful evidence to support Michael Porter's seminal observation that the apparent dichotomy between environmental control and profitability is illusory, and that incorporation of environmental issues into corporate strategy is the key to long-term competitive advantage (Porter and van der Linde, 1995).

REFERENCES

Cass, Glen and Robert Hahn (1983), *Implementing Tradable Emissions Permits for Sulfur Oxide Emissions in the South Coast Basin*, (3 vols), Report to California Air Resources Board, Caltech Environmental Quality Laboratory, June.

Matthews, Emily et al. (2000), *The Weight of Nations. Material Outflows From Industrial Economies*, Washington, DC: World Resources Institute.

Porter, Michael and Claas van der Linde (1995), 'Green and competitive: ending the stalemate', *Harvard Business Review*, Sep/Oct, **73** (5), 120–34.

1. Emissions trading: US experience implementing multi-state cap and trade programs

Brian J. McLean

INTRODUCTION

In order to reduce the cost of compliance with air pollution reduction requirements, several flexibility mechanisms were introduced in the United States in the late 1970s. Referred to generally as emissions trading, they included emissions offsets, plant-specific 'bubbles', and emission reduction credits. The offset mechanism was introduced to permit economic growth in areas that were not meeting air quality goals. For example, a new source could locate (or an existing source could expand) in a non-attainment area by reducing emissions at another source (usually by more than the increment of new emissions). In this way, the economy could grow and the environment could improve.

Under the bubble concept, limitations on individual emissions points within a facility could be adjusted upward and downward to minimize compliance costs as long as the total emissions at the facility remained below the level that would have occurred under the original command and control regulations and there were no adverse impacts on air quality.

Emission reduction credits (ERCs) were the most flexible of the three because they allowed a facility to earn credits by reducing its emissions below the required level and to sell those credits to another facility, either directly or through an emissions credit broker. The use of the credits, however, needed to cover the same time period as that for which the reductions occurred; that is generation and use of credits needed to be contemporaneous.

A derivative of ERCs, called 'discrete emissions reductions' (DERs) allows credits earned during one period of time to be 'banked' and used by a source in lieu of a required emissions reduction during a future period. This further flexibility is a feature of 'open market' trading introduced in the late 1990s.

Although emissions offsets and emissions credit trading have been used for over 20 years to reduce the cost of complying with command and control regulations, the underlying regulatory infrastructure had not originally been designed with the intent of supporting emissions trading, and the marriage raised environmental concerns and incurred transaction costs that inhibited more extensive use of emissions trading.

CONCERNS WITH EMISSIONS TRADING

Traditional air pollution control regulations focus on source-specific requirements to reduce the rate at which pollutants are emitted (for example, pounds of pollutant per quantity of heat input) but generally do not limit the use of the facility. Therefore, neither mass emissions on a source-by-source basis, nor overall area-wide emissions are usually established as enforceable limits. Coupled with the tendency of sources to aim for slightly lower rates to ensure compliance, this has the desired effect of reducing air pollution, but it does not provide a very precise level from which to determine emissions reduction credits, nor does this system assure that emissions will not increase as facilities are utilized more (or expanded) or as new facilities are built in the future. In fact, regulators informally have relied on the extra control to provide a margin of safety for the environmental uncertainty of the command and control system.

Consequently, environmental concerns arose when facilities wanted to receive 'credit' for emitting below their required levels in order to sell those credits to another facility (so that it could emit more) or to permit new sources of pollution to locate in an area. First, were these credits (or portions of these credits) a result of the over-control inherent in the traditional program, and not 'real' or 'additional' reductions? Was the source simply commoditizing the safety margin and allowing other sources to use the credits to emit more, with the environment being worse off as a result?

Second, when a source sought credit for taking actions that actually reduced emissions, might those actions have happened 'anyway' (or eventually) as part of modernization efforts and, therefore, were they not already being relied upon to temper the growth in emissions allowed under the traditional emissions rate approach to regulation?

Third, a lack of rigor and consistency in emissions measurement and the uncertainties regarding projected emissions (the product of future emissions rates and future activity levels) contributed to the difficulty in establishing current and future baseline emission levels from which credits could be earned.

Fourth, since emissions trading per se did not reduce emissions (or reduce them significantly), was it simply moving emissions around, and perhaps making air quality in some areas worse? Assurance of no harm often required air quality modeling which introduced additional analyses and costs.

Addressing and resolving these concerns took time, added to the transaction costs of emissions trades, and consequently, limited the application of emissions trading.

CAP AND TRADE

During the 1980s, the United States was confronted with the problem of reducing acid rain – a regional air pollution problem caused not by a single source, but by the collective emissions of SO_2 and NO_x primarily from hundreds of electric power plants in the eastern half of the country. In 1989, a new program was proposed that would be separate from the combined command and control and trading approach to address the problems identified above. The new approach would:

- establish limitations on sources in terms of allowable mass emissions rather than emissions rates and express those allowable emissions in terms of tradable 'allowances' (each allowance being an authorization to emit one ton of a pollutant)
- require a significant reduction in emissions for an entire industrial sector
- place a 'cap' or limit on total emissions, requiring any emissions increases by new or existing sources to be offset
- require accurate and consistent measurement and reporting of all emissions from all sources
- establish automatic and significant penalties for exceeding allowable emissions
- allow sources total flexibility in selecting and revising control approaches, including using emissions trading; that is government approval would not be necessary
- retain source-specific emission limitations designed to protect local air quality; that is buying 'allowances' would not entitle a source to exceed limits established to protect public health.

This new approach, which became known as 'cap and trade', was the centerpiece of Title IV of the Clean Air Act Amendments of 1990. The goal of Title IV was to address the problem of acid rain by reducing annual SO_2

emissions in the contiguous 48 states and the District of Columbia by 10 million tons from the 25.9 million ton level that had been emitted in 1980. This would represent a 40 per cent reduction. Of the 10 million ton reduction, an 8.5 million ton reduction was to come from electric utility plants by using the new cap and trade approach. The cap, or permanent emissions limit, would be introduced in phases by first requiring the 263 largest and highest emitting electric utility boilers to reduce their collective emissions by 50 per cent beginning in 1995. From 2000 through 2009, emissions from all existing electric utility boilers and turbines serving generators larger than 25 megawatts (approximately 2000 units) and all new units would be limited to receiving no more than 9.48 million allowances per year. Finally, in 2010 and thereafter, emissions from all affected electric utility units (including new units) would be limited to receiving no more than 8.95 million allowances per year. This would result in a reduction of almost 50 per cent in annual utility SO_2 emissions from their 1980 level of 17.5 million tons.

Figure 1.1 shows the location of the affected sources and the geographic scope of the program along with the emission changes between 1990 to 2001–03. Figure 1.2 shows the emissions expected from utility sources with and without the Acid Rain Program as well as the emissions allowed each year. Because sources may save or 'bank' allowances not used in one year and use them to comply in a future year, the figure shows how such behavior is smoothing the actual reduction in emissions over time.

OPERATING RESPONSIBILITIES

Responsibilities for implementing the program are clear and somewhat different from existing command and control programs and previous trading programs. Sources are free to choose their compliance strategy (and to change it as circumstances require) without needing government approval. However, all sources must install, operate and quality assure emissions monitoring equipment and must report emissions data and test results periodically to the government. In addition, sources do not need government approval to transfer allowances, but they must hold sufficient allowances in their accounts at the end of each compliance period to cover their emissions. A fluid, active market is assisted by the government's issuance of allowances for 30 years into the future.

In contrast to traditional command and control programs, the government does not tell the source how to comply or even collaborate with the source in determining a compliance strategy. The government is responsible for ensuring that each source accurately accounts for all its emissions, for tracking allowance transfers and holdings, for enforcing penalties for

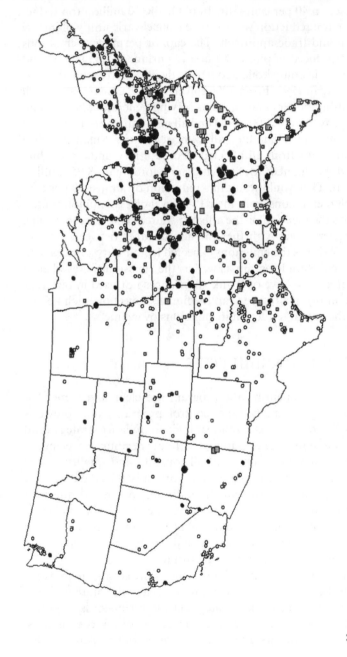

Notes:
Solid circles: sources that reduced emissions more than 1000 tons.
Squares: sources that increased emissions more than 1000 tons.
Hollow circles: emissions did not change more than 1000 tons.
Size of symbols proportional to magnitude of change in emissions.

Figure 1.1   Scope of SO₂ program (over 3000 sources affected) and SO₂ emissions changes between 1990 and 2001–03

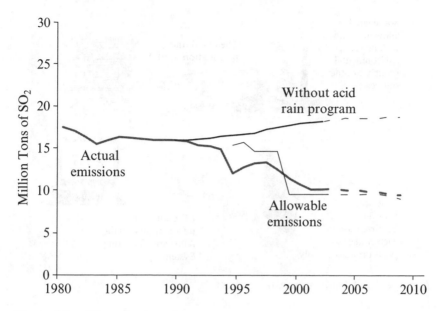

Figure 1.2   SO$_2$ reductions from power generation

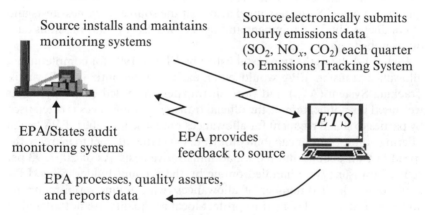

Figure 1.3   Emissions monitoring and reporting

non-compliance, and for making all emissions and trading information publicly available. This last function enhances accountability and public credibility of the program.

Figure 1.3 shows how the emissions monitoring and reporting process works under the Acid Rain Program. A source submits its SO$_2$, NO$_x$, and CO$_2$ emissions data via the Internet to the Emissions Tracking System

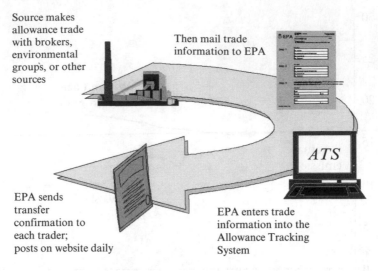

Source makes allowance trade with brokers, environmental groups, or other sources

Then mail trade information to EPA

ATS

EPA sends transfer confirmation to each trader; posts on website daily

EPA enters trade information into the Allowance Tracking System

Figure 1.4   Allowance transfer process

(ETS) operated by the US Environmental Protection Agency (EPA), and EPA provides electronic feedback so that the source can correct errors quickly. EPA and State personnel also visit the source to witness tests and to conduct audits of equipment and operations. EPA posts emissions data on its website quarterly.

Figure 1.4 shows the steps established by EPA in 1994 for completing an allowance transfer. EPA would enter each transfer into its Allowance Tracking System (ATS) and post all transfers recorded each day on its website. This notification of the official transfer of allowances is often used by parties to signal payment for allowances purchased. In 2001, EPA began offering online transfer capability for traders via the Internet to increase the speed of transactions and reduce administrative costs. As of 2004, 93 per cent of transfers were handled online by the account holder. Since EPA issues only a limited number of allowances (with unique serial numbers) and emission limits designed to protect local air quality are not altered, it is not necessary for EPA to approve trades as was the case with previous trading regimes.

PROGRAM RESULTS

In the first five years of the Acid Rain Program, SO_2 emissions from the 263 Phase I sources were reduced substantially and all sources were in

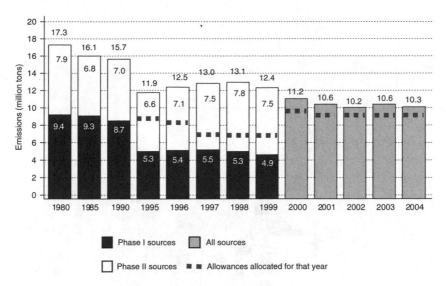

Figure 1.5   SO$_2$ emissions from Title IV sources

compliance with respect to their allowable emissions (see Figure 1.5). It was also apparent that Phase II sources, which were not subject to the emissions cap until 2000, did little to reduce emissions during this period. However, data for 1999 and beyond indicate that Phase II sources are reducing their emissions (US EPA, 2005b). Figure 1.6 shows the geographic distribution of the SO$_2$ emissions reductions under the Acid Rain Program with significant reductions taking place in the Midwest where emissions have historically been the highest and where the cost of reducing emissions is most economical.

Through a 200-station wet deposition monitoring network it is possible to assess the impact of these emissions reductions on the chemistry of rain and snow. Figure 1.7 shows the changes in wet sulfate deposition across the eastern United States from the 1989–1991 period to the period from 2001 through 2003. Reductions of up to 40 per cent in the concentrations of sulfate ions in wet deposition occurred throughout a large portion of the northeastern United States.

When the full SO$_2$ reductions are achieved in 2010, a significant benefit to public health is expected because of the reduction in airborne fine particulate matter, much of which is due to sulfates. Monetized benefits from the entire Acid Rain Program (both SO$_2$ and NO$_x$) are estimated at \$122 billion annually (Chestnut and Mills, 2005).

In stark contrast to the benefits of the emissions reductions is the cost of compliance shown in Figure 1.8. When the Acid Rain Program was being

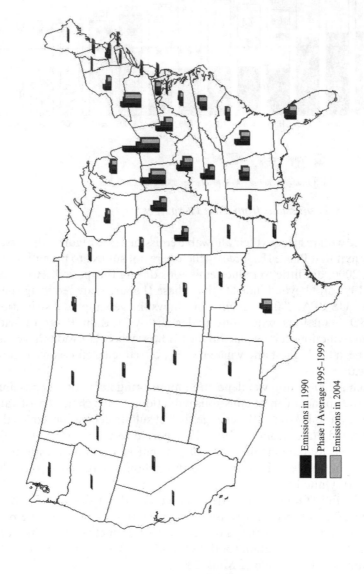

Emissions in 1990

Phase 1 Average 1995–1999

Emissions in 2004

Figure 1.6   Geographic distribution of utility SO₂ emissions reductions

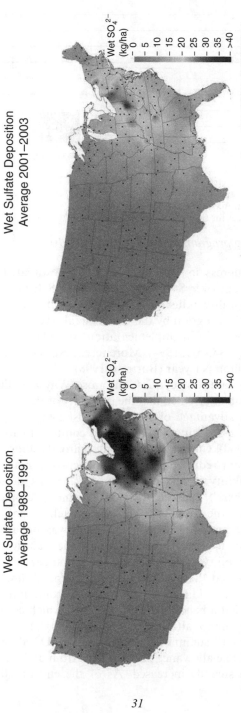

Figure 1.7   Wet sulfate deposition reduction (kg/ha) since start-up of acid rain program

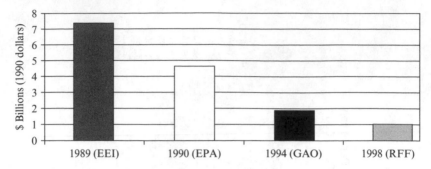

Notes: EEI = Edition Electric Institute (assumes no trading)
           EPA = Environmental Protection Agency
           GAO = General Accounting Office
           RFF = Resources for the Future.

Figure 1.8   Trading program: expected costs by 2010

considered by Congress in 1989 and 1990, the estimated cost of the
program ranged from over $4 billion per year (US EPA, 1990) to over
$7 billion per year (utility industry estimate). But four years after its enact-
ment, an audit of the program by the US General Accounting Office concluded that the cost of full implementation was likely to be closer to
$2 billion per year (US GAO, 1994). More recent estimates have placed the
cost closer to $1 billion per year (Burtraw, 1998).

As cost estimates came down, questions arose. Why were the earlier estimates so far off? Studies revealed that the flexibility of the program allowed
companies to take advantage of numerous cost saving opportunities as
multiple methods for reducing SO_2 emissions competed with one another
(Ellerman et al., 2000). Competition among railroads shipping low sulfur
coal led to significant reductions in transport costs, a major component
of coal cost; flexibility in the operation of flue gas desulphurization
equipment ('scrubbers') coupled with design and equipment advances
significantly reduced the cost of scrubbing high sulfur coal; and medium
sulfur coal became marketable now that there was no arbitrary sulfur
content for 'compliance coal' as existed under the traditional regulatory
program. Also, the ability of sources to bank allowances earned from extra
control actions allowed them to reduce future expenditures. Finally, the
allowance market, in addition to providing a compliance option for
sources, also provided a benchmark price against which companies could
better evaluate compliance alternatives.

Figures 1.9 and 1.10 summarize activity in the SO2 allowance market
from 1995–2003. While allowance prices ranged from under $100 to a little
over $200, volume steadily increased. As of the end of 2003, over 250

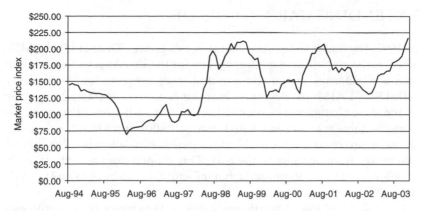

Figure 1.9   SO₂ allowance market

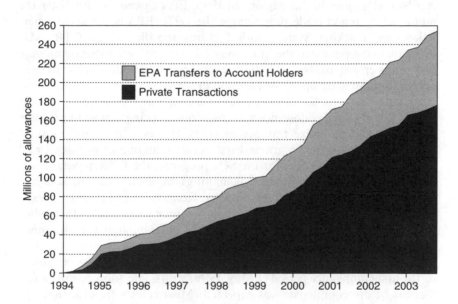

Figure 1.10   Cumulative SO₂ allowances transferred (through 2003)

million allowances had been transferred, through more than 50,000 official transactions. Although many of the transfers have occurred between units owned by the same companies, an increasing number took place between unrelated companies, reflecting an increasing acceptance and reliance on the trading mechanism.

EXTENDING CAP AND TRADE

In 1993, the South Coast Air Quality Management District (SCAQMD), which is the air pollution control agency for the Los Angeles metropolitan area of California, instituted a cap and trade program for SO_2 and NO_x called RECLAIM (the Regional Clean Air Incentives Market). It has many of the same characteristics outlined above, but with a few differences. For example, there are two zones with trading of allowances into the zone with the more severe air quality problem restricted. Also, there is no banking of allowances from one year to the next. This chapter does not report on the details or results of this program, but information can be obtained from the SCAQMD (www.aqmd.gov).

In 1994, 11 of the 12 Northeast States of the Ozone Transport Region (OTR) signed a Memorandum of Understanding agreeing to reduce and cap NO_x emissions in that region. In 1996, EPA agreed to administer the multi-state cap and trade program for the OTR. EPA constructed a new Allowance Tracking System with features specific to the OTR NO_x Program and augmented the Emissions Tracking System to accommodate NO_x mass emissions data as well as several hundred additional sources in preparation for start-up of the program in 1999.

As is the case with the SO_2 cap and trade program, the NO_x program for the OTR had a single allowance and emissions tracking system to promote fungibility and minimize transaction costs. However, there were several differences between the programs. First, rather than one set of rules for all participants, as is the case for the SO_2 program, the OTR program was implemented through separate rulemakings by each state. Although a model rule was developed, states deviated from the model in several ways. For example, some allocated allowances for four years while others allocated allowances one year at a time. This differentiated the allowance market and reduced fungibility.

Second, the rules were adopted less than one year before the beginning of the first compliance period (1 May, 1999) with some adopted only a few months before compliance was expected. Most rules were challenged in state courts with resolution extending into the compliance period. As rules were adopted and concern over the ability of sources to comply rose, so did allowance prices. Prices peaked in February and March after all rules had been adopted and then dropped after a Maryland court ruled in favor of industry petitions in that state to delay compliance. Emissions in Maryland were expected to be about 23 000 tons above available allowances, and sources had not taken actions to reduce their emissions, hoping for a favorable ruling. This contributed to a concern that demand for allowances would exceed supply.

Third, the OTR program allowed sources to earn allowances for taking actions in 1997 and 1998, prior to the first compliance period in 1999. However, the first of these early reduction credits was not given to EPA to put into the allowance market until May, 1999. By October, a total of 24 635 allowances were added to the market because of actions taken in 1997 and 1998. The withdrawal of Maryland sources' demand for 23 000 allowances coupled with the increase in supply of allowances throughout the compliance period and the knowledge of the actual emissions as the season progressed, helped to drive down allowance prices.

In addition to the variations in allowance allocation procedures across the various states, the OTR had a provision to limit the use of banked allowances. Known as 'progressive flow control' this provision required that after the current year's allowances were used to cover emissions, a portion of the previous years' unused (or banked) allowances (up to 10 per cent of the region's current year's allocation) could be used to cover emissions on a one-allowance-for-one-ton basis. However, after those banked allowances were used, two banked allowances for every ton would be required. This was intended to discourage the excessive use of banked allowances (and subsequently lessen the chance that emissions would rise significantly during the summer ozone season). However, this caused allowances of different year vintages to be valued differently, further segmenting the allowance market into smaller pools of similarly valued products and further reducing fungibility and liquidity.

From Figure 1.11 one can see that trading volume was lower than for the SO_2 market and prices spiked just prior to the first compliance period. To varying degrees these factors may help to explain the lower volume and higher volatility of the NO_x market compared to the SO_2 market. Nonetheless, the NO_x allowance market settled down as the first summer season progressed.

At the same time that the OTR NO_x Budget Program was beginning operation, efforts were underway to expand the NO_x Budget Program to 22 states in the eastern United States. In 1998, EPA took the lead in establishing the criteria for determining which states would be included and for setting the rules for this expanded cap and trade program (US Federal Register, 1998).

Although EPA would set the emissions 'budgets' for the region and each state as well as the monitoring, trading and reporting rules states would still retain the responsibility for allocating allowances to specific sources within their states. The program was very similar to the OTR program, including the provision for progressive flow control. Originally intended to start in 2003 (the same year as the second phase of the OTR program), litigation

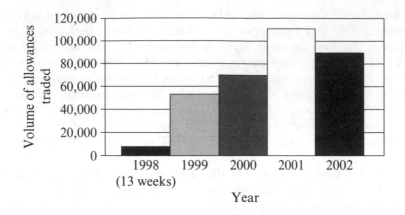

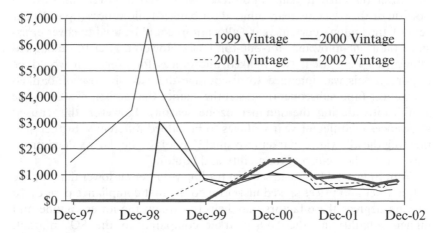

Figure 1.11 NO$_x$ allowance market

delayed the start until 2004. Figure 1.12 shows the significant emissions reductions achieved in 2003 and 2004.

One of the concerns with using a seasonal cap and trade program (with banking) was the possibility that daily emissions might 'spike' on the hottest days of the summer when electricity demand is highest and when ozone is often highest. Figure 1.13 shows that when seasonal NO$_x$ emissions declined from 2003 to 2004, emissions also declined on a daily basis (US EPA, 2005a).

Given the success of the SO$_2$ and NO$_x$ cap and trade programs, in 2005 EPA issued rules to further reduce annual emissions of SO$_2$ by more than 65 per cent, to keep the seasonal NO$_x$ Budget Program but add an annual NO$_x$ reduction program of over 60 per cent, and for the first time to reduce

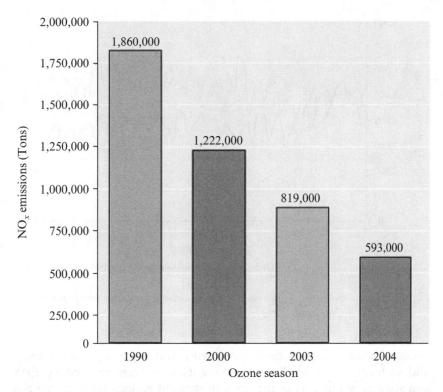

Figure 1.12　Total NBP ozone season NOx emissions

mercury emissions from coal-fired power plants by more than 65 per cent – all using the cap and trade mechanism (Clean Air Interstate Rule (CAIR): US Federal Register, 2005a; Clean Air Mercury Rule (CAMR): Federal Register, 2005b).

COMPLIANCE AND ENFORCEMENT

Since the beginning of the SO_2 Acid Rain Program in 1995 and the NO_x Budget Program in 1999, compliance has been over 99.9 per cent. It is important to note that all emissions from every source have been accounted for and that every time emissions exceed allowances, the exceedance has been offset by a removal of an equivalent or greater number of allowances from the source's allowance account. Also, there have been no exceptions, waivers or variances approved that could lead to higher emissions.

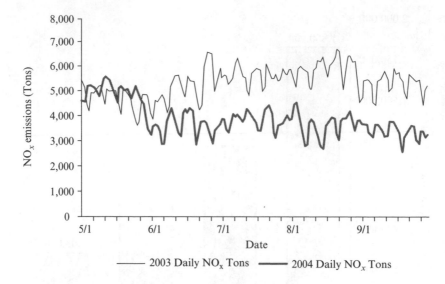

Figure 1.13   Daily emission trends for NOx budget trading program units in 2003 and 2004

Compliance with emissions monitoring and reporting requirements and with allowance holding requirements have been handled by EPA and state personnel. Also, the few enforcement actions taken have been handled by federal and state authorities. In neither compliance nor enforcement situations has it been deemed necessary or appropriate to employ third parties.

COMPARING POLICY OPTIONS

For many air pollution problems, command and control (or direct regulation) may be the best course. For example, where a specific facility can be identified as the source of a public health problem, limiting its emissions may be the simplest and most effective solution. Also, in the multi-industry transportation sector where fuel characteristics can have a direct impact on the effectiveness of engine technology, it may be best to directly specify fuel parameters, such as sulfur content, to permit engines to be designed in the most cost-effective way to reduce harmful emissions of NO_x, hydrocarbons and carbon monoxide.

However, specificity of requirements may also inhibit innovation, in which case economic instruments such as taxes or tradeable permits may be preferred to encourage new and more efficient solutions. If properly designed, economic incentives can harness market forces to work toward environmental improvement. By internalizing pollution control costs, they can make pollution reduction in the interest of the firm and promote innovation.

Whether such instruments should be tradable permits or taxes is a topic for other papers and research. However, setting the quantity of allowable emissions (and letting the price of allowances vary), as is the case with cap and trade programs, is more attractive to many environmental policy makers than setting the price (and letting emissions fluctuate), as is the case with environmental taxes. One may also want to consider the behavioral component of markets in choosing between these instruments. For those engaged in the competitive business world, the 'greed and fear' of the marketplace may be viewed as more conducive to creativity than the simple price signal offered by a tax. Some might argue that the prospect of making money (by freeing up allowances for sale) as well as saving money by avoiding the need to buy allowances is more motivating than simply saving money (by minimizing taxes).

The tradable permit instrument can be further subdivided into tradable credits and tradable allowances. Tradable credits are based on traditional emissions rate regulation where credits are created on a project-by-project basis when the emissions rate is reduced. This approach is preferred by some companies because it provides a predictable plant operating parameter and allows flexible utilization of the facility. However, as with the price-versus-quantity debate, the emissions rate (and tradable credit) approach provides less certainty regarding environmental impact than the emissions cap (and tradable allowance) approach. As a consequence, where emissions grow, the government needs to lower emissions rates periodically simply to maintain environmental quality; this, in turn, undermines the purported predictability of the rate approach.

On the other hand, an emissions cap with tradable allowances provides more environmental certainty and is consistent with the notion that natural resources – air, land and water – are finite and that impacts to them must be limited to protect them. An emissions cap, such as those established under the Acid Rain and NO_x Budget Programs, do not restrict economic growth as some have charged. It simply requires that sources consider the emission implications of their business plans, and if they plan to increase production (and emissions), they must either reduce their emissions rate commensurately or purchase allowances from other sources sufficient to offset their increased emissions. This internalization of environmental consequences can probably be achieved at lower cost to sources than the iterative (and less predictable) government-imposed requirements intended to achieve the same effect. Furthermore, should the economy contract, this approach automatically allows some relaxation of emissions rates without increasing overall emissions or worsening the environment.

CONCLUSIONS

The benefits of an emissions cap and trade approach compared to the traditional command and control approach (even coupled with credit trading) can be summarized as follows:

- more certainty that a specific level of emissions will be achieved and maintained over time
- more regulatory certainty for sources
- more compliance flexibility and lower transaction costs for sources
- fewer administrative resources needed by industry and government

Since cost is often an obstacle to pollution reduction, it should also be noted that by driving down the cost of compliance, the flexible cap and trade approach actually makes further environmental improvement feasible. Based on the experience of designing and implementing multi-state SO_2 and NO_x cap and trade programs, there appear to be three keys to a successful program:

1. **The Cap.** The allowance cap (which needs to cover all major existing and new sources of an industrial sector to avoid 'leakage') ensures achievement of the environmental goal and provides predictability for the tradeable permit market.
2. **Accountability.** To determine environmental compliance and to support the integrity of the tradable allowances, it is critical that emissions data be accurately and consistently measured and that all emissions be accounted for. It is also important that all emissions and allowance information be publicly accessible both to facilitate the market and to overcome public reservations regarding emissions trading. Finally, it is important that there be predictable and significant consequences for noncompliance.
3. **Simplicity.** To keep transaction and administrative costs low, facilitate active trading and innovation, and maximize cost savings, program rules must be simple and easily understood by all participants. Simplicity can best be achieved if the government focuses on setting goals and measuring results, and lets sources and the market figure out how to meet those goals. Command and control programs (even with

credit trading) are more complex because they try to address all three – often prescribing in great detail exactly how goals are to be met.

Although there is much rhetorical support for designing and implementing a successful emissions trading program, those involved (policy makers, legislators, regulators, affected sources, environmentalists, and would-be litigators) often find it difficult in practice to accept one or more of the above elements. However, as they are omitted or diminished, so too is the likelihood of success.

NOTE

The conclusions and opinions expressed are those of the author and do not necessarily reflect those of the US Environmental Protection Agency.

REFERENCES

Burtraw, Dallas, Alan J. Krupnick, Erin Mansur, David Austin and Deidre Farrell (1998), 'Costs and benefits of reducing air pollutants related to acid rain', *Contemporary Economic Policy*, **16**, 379–400.

Chestnut, L.G. and D.M. Mills (2005), 'A fresh look at the benefits and costs of the US acid rain program', *Journal of Environmental Management*, **77**(3), 252–66.

Ellerman, A. Denny, Paul L. Joskow, Richard Schmalensee, Juan-Pablo Montero and Elizabeth M. Bailey (2000), *Markets for Clean Air: The US Acid Rain Program*, Cambridge: Cambridge University Press.

US Environmental Protection Agency (EPA) (1990), 'Comparison of the economic impacts of the acid rain provisions of the Senate Bill (S.1630) and the House Bill (S.1630)', Draft report prepared by ICF Resources Inc, Washington, DC, July.

US Environmental Protection Agency (EPA) (2005a), 'Evaluating ozone control programs in the Eastern United States: focus on the NO_x budget trading program, 2004', August 2005.

US Environmental Protection Agency (EPA) (2005b), www.epa.gov/airmarkets.

US Federal Register (1998), 63 Fed. Reg. 57356.

US Federal Register (2005a), 70 Fed. Reg (FR) 25162.

US Federal Register (2005b), 70 Fed. Reg. (FR) 28606.

US General Accounting Office (GAO) (1994), *Allowance Trading Offers an Opportunity to Reduce Emissions at Less Cost*, GAO/RCED-95-30, Washington, DC.

2. Green tax reforms in OECD countries: an overview

Jean-Philippe Barde and Nils Axel Braathen*

The last 15 years have witnessed a large increase in the use of economic instruments to protect the environment in OECD countries, with a growing emphasis on tax instruments – often in the context of 'green tax reforms' – and on emission trading systems. This tendency is due to many factors such as the need to improve the effectiveness of policies based to a great extent on rigid and cumbersome regulations, the need to integrate environmental policies effectively with sectoral policies (such as energy, transport or agriculture), and, sometimes, the search for more tax revenues to finance the general government budget, as well as specific environmental funds or programmes (Barde, 1992; Barde and Smith, 1997; OECD, 2001a). In this context, fiscal instruments provide an ideal means of injecting appropriate signals into the market, of eliminating or reducing structural distortions (such as unsuitable energy and transport tariffs) and of internalizing externalities.

ENVIRONMENTAL TAXES AND GREEN TAX REFORM

Most countries need to introduce more flexibility and efficiency in their economic structures. This implies, *inter alia*, adjusting tax systems in order to reduce distortions, increasing market flexibility and making environmental policies more effective. Over the past 15 years, there has been a general trend in OECD countries to reduce both personal and corporate income tax rates, accompanied by base-broadening and an increasing use of consumption taxes such as VAT. The trend to reduce income tax rates has accelerated recently, with the OECD average of marginal tax rates on high-income earners falling by 2 percentage points from 2000 to 2003, while for average workers it fell by about 1 percentage point. Meanwhile, the average corporate tax rate fell by about 3 percentage points. These developments have contributed to reductions in the OECD average tax-to-GDP ratio of about 1 percentage point.

These tax reforms provide an excellent opportunity to introduce an environmental dimension in taxation; that is a 'greening' of tax systems. This greening of taxation may consist of three complementary policies: eliminating environmentally harmful tax exemptions, restructuring existing taxes, and introducing new environmental taxes.

BOX 2.1 DEFINING ENVIRONMENTALLY RELATED TAXES

Environmentally related *taxes* are defined as any compulsory, *unrequited* payment to general government levied on tax bases deemed to be of particular environmental relevance. Taxes are unrequited in the sense that benefits provided by government to taxpayers are not normally in proportion to their payments.

Requited compulsory payments to the government that are levied more or less in proportion to services provided (for example, the amount of wastes collected and treated) can be labelled as *fees* and *charges*. The term *levy* covers taxes, fees and charges.

Eliminating Environmentally Harmful Subsidies and Tax Provisions

Many fiscal measures can either directly or indirectly produce adverse effects for the environment. One such measure is *subsidies*.[1] Available data indicate that subsidies are pervasive throughout OECD countries (with wide variations between countries) and worldwide. Every year, OECD countries give about US$ 400 billion in subsidies to different economic and often environmentally sensitive sectors.[2] Due to the lack of data on energy subsidies and manufacturing, this figure is probably an underestimate. *Agricultural subsidies* are particularly high. In 2004, estimated total support to agriculture amounted to US$ 378 billion (OECD, 2005a), which represents 1.16 per cent of GDP in OECD countries and of which US$ 279 billion represented support to producers. These subsidies are one of the causes of over-farming of land, excessive use of fertilizers and pesticides, soil degradation and other problems (OECD, 2003a; 2003b). Similarly, irrigation water is often charged below marginal social cost, which leads to wastage.

Subsidies for energy production in OECD countries are intended mainly to protect domestic producers and maintain employment in given sectors. Data is lacking and estimates range between US$ 20 billion and 82 billion per year; coal subsidies amounted to US$ 5.4 billion in 2000.

Manufacturing is also subsidized, although it is difficult to obtain detailed data. When subsidies encourage the use of certain raw materials and greater energy consumption, there can be negative fallout in terms of recycling and waste and a lock-in of inefficient technologies.

Subsidies to *fisheries* are also important: US$ 5.8 billion in 2002, representing 20 per cent of the total value of landings (OECD, 2005b), contributing to over-capacity in fishing fleets and depletion of fish stocks.

BOX 2.2   DEFINING SUBSIDIES

The concept of subsidy is not straightforward. While the term 'subsidy' is used in this chapter, it is as common to use the terms transfers, payments, support, assistance or protection associated with governmental policies in OECD work. Sometimes these terms are used interchangeably, but often they are associated with different methods of measurement and thus different economic indicators. Subsidies have been defined to 'comprise all measures that keep prices for consumers below market level or keep prices for producers above market level or that reduce costs for consumers and producers by giving direct or indirect support' (see, for example, de Moor and Calamai, 1997). This definition is consistent with the OECD approach of defining environmentally harmful subsidies and tax concessions to include 'all kinds of financial support and regulations that are put in place to enhance the competitiveness of certain products, processes or regions, and that, together with the prevailing taxation jurisdiction, (unintentionally) discriminate against sound environmental practices' (OECD, 1998). It is not necessary to make a distinction between subsidies and tax expenditures as the latter can be regarded as implicit subsidies.

Subsidies take different forms: budgetary payments or support involving tax expenditures (various tax provisions that reduce the tax burden of particular groups, producers or products), market price support, subsidized input prices, preferential interest rates. This is why the more generic terminology of '*support measures*' is often used. There is, however, no international consensus: different definitions prevail for specific purposes, fields (for example, agriculture or transport) or contexts (for example, international trade).

There has been much controversy over whether the non-internalization of external costs should be construed as a subsidy, the argument being that, as external costs are not internalized, the environment is used 'freely' by the users: in a sense, a public good is freely supplied to users. Those who object to such an expanded definition observe that the notion of a subsidy has traditionally connoted an explicit government intervention, not an implicit lack of intervention. As well, for these and more practical purposes, namely the difficulty of quantifying external costs, non internalization is generally not regarded as a subsidy, except for the transport sector where this definition is currently used (Nash et al., 2002).

The *transport* sector, a major source of pollution and other harmful effects, is also affected by many direct and indirect subsidies. In nearly all countries, revenues from road transport cover the cost of providing and maintaining infrastructures and cover total social cost (Nash et al., 2002). However, comparing the marginal social cost of a given transport mode with the price paid gives a different picture, indicating that road transport is often charged much below marginal social cost. Calculations of the optimal transport pricing in urban areas for five EU countries are presented in ECMT (2003): for cars, this indicates, for example, that optimal prices would imply an increase in peak-period prices of about 70 per cent in the Paris suburban area (Ile de France), 95 per cent in Munich and over 150 per cent in London. This price increase would provide a significant fall in car passenger kilometres and significant welfare gains.

A second category of distortion arises from *specific tax provisions* (tax rate variations or exemptions). For instance, coal, the most polluting fuel, is taxed in only five OECD countries and is subject to many tax rebates. Another example is the widespread under-taxing of diesel oil in many countries. This contributes to a constant increase in the number of diesel-driven vehicles, which are more polluting and noisy than petrol-driven vehicles, and to a sharp increase of road freight transport (see also Figure 2.1). In OECD countries, the consumption of diesel fuel for road transport grew from 15 per cent of total motor fuel consumption in 1970 to 33 per cent in 2002 (OECD, 2005c). Other indirect subsidies in many countries include deductibility of commuting expenses from taxable income, company cars not being included in the taxable income, and tax exemptions for aviation fuels.

It is clear that the 'greening' of taxation should start with a systematic inventory and a correction of fiscal measures (subsidies and taxes) which are harmful for the environment.

Restructuring Existing Taxes

Many existing taxes can be changed so as to benefit the environment. It is a question of adjusting relative prices by increasing taxes on the most

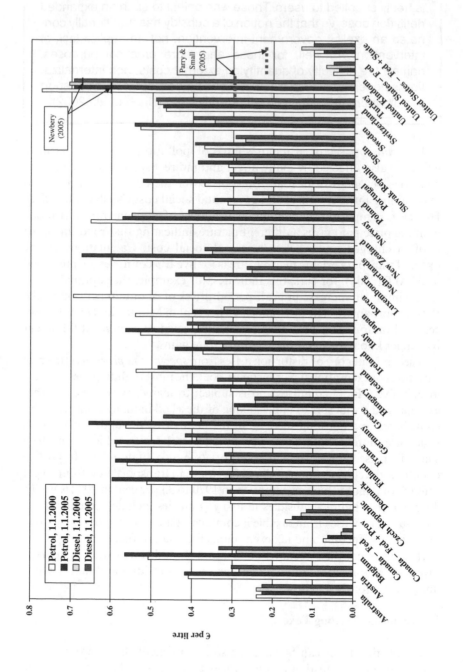

Notes: It is emphasised that developments in tax rates expressed in euro over time for countries outside the euro area can both be due to changes in tax rates in national currencies and to changes in the exchange rates.

There is no taxation of diesel fuel in Iceland and New Zealand. Separate taxes are instead levied on the use of diesel-driven vehicles. Information on tax rates as of 1.1.2005 is missing for Korea, while no information is available regarding the fuel tax rates in Turkey. For Canada and United States two sets of bars are shown; one that only includes the federal tax rates and one that also includes unweighted averages of the taxes levied at a provincial or state level, based on information from The International Fuel Tax Association, cf. www.iftach.org/index50.htm.

The dotted horizontal lines shown for the United Kingdom and United States are estimates of second-best optimal petrol tax rates made by Parry and Small (2005), made on the assumption that revenues from petrol taxes replaces revenues on distorting taxes on labour income. If instead revenues from petrol taxes financed additional public spending, the optimal tax rates would be higher than that calculated here (to the extent that the social value of additional public spending were greater than the social value of using extra revenue to cut distortionary income taxes). The continuous lines shown for the United Kingdom indicate 'optimal' tax rates for petrol and diesel respectively as estimated by Newbery (2005).

Source: The OECD/EEA database on instruments used for environmental policy.

Figure 2.1 Tax rates for petrol and diesel in OECD member countries

47

polluting products and activities in order to properly reflect the environmental harm they cause.

The tax category that dominates the revenues raised by environmentally related taxes is taxes on motor fuels. Such taxes were introduced many decades ago, primarily for fiscal reasons. Their level and design, however, nevertheless have important environmental implications, affecting the composition of the car fleet and the use of motor vehicles. Figure 2.1 illustrates the tax rates applied to petrol and diesel in OECD member countries as of 1.1.2000 and 1.1.2005 – expressed in euros per litre.[3] One of the most striking points that can be made is that the tax rate for diesel is much lower than the tax rate for petrol in most countries – with the notable exception of Australia, Switzerland, United Kingdom and United States. From an environmental point of view, this is regrettable, as diesel-driven vehicles cause more local air pollution and are noisier than petrol-driven vehicles.[4] Hence, there is significant scope for restructuring of existing motor fuel taxes to better reflect differences in environmental impacts of the various fuels. This could – obviously – also include lower tax rates for relatively benign fuels like Liquid Petroleum Gas.

Ideally, the tax rate on motor fuels should – as for other tax bases – reflect the size of the negative environmental externalities associated with each fuel (and account for the fact that any revenues raised can be used to lower other, more distorting, taxes, for example on labour incomes). It is always difficult to estimate exactly what an 'optimal' level for the different tax rates would be; in the right end of Figure 2.1, the estimates of optimal *petrol* tax rates made by Parry and Small (2005) are depicted. The difference in the estimates for the US and UK countries is to a large extent explained by higher assumed marginal congestion costs in the United Kingdom. According to their findings, one should increase the tax rates on petrol considerably in the United States, while the petrol tax rate in the United Kingdom could be considerably higher than 'optimal'.[5] Due to the larger negative environmental impacts of diesel use, the optimal tax rate on diesel could be significantly higher than the rates Parry and Small estimated for petrol.[6]

There is also much scope for restructuring existing taxes on the basis of (other) environmental parameters, such as the sulphur content of different fuels. As shown in Figure 2.2, 13 OECD member countries have introduced a differentiation in their taxes on petrol and/or diesel according to the sulphur content of these fuels. For diesel, some of the countries apply three steps in their taxes: one tax rate for diesel with a sulphur content above 50 mg per kg fuel (or 50 ppm), a lower tax rate for diesel where the sulphur content is between 10 and 50 mg per kg, and a still lower tax rate for diesel where the sulphur content is below 10 mg per kg (or 10 ppm). The large differences in the size of the 'premium' given to lower-sulphur fuels *among*

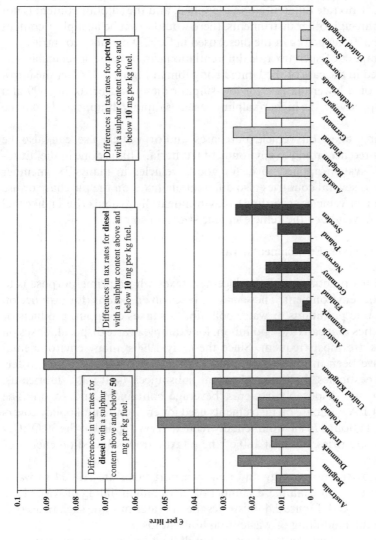

Figure 2.2 Differentiation in tax rates for petrol and diesel according to the sulphur content of the fuels in OECD member countries

different countries are remarkable – especially as concerns diesel with a relative high sulphur content.

The fact that the tax differentiation is larger *within* a given country above and below 50 mg per kg than above and below 10 mg per kg is not surprising, as this 'premium' triggers a larger *absolute* reduction in the sulphur content. If no rate differentiation is applied, and the sulphur content is not limited through other instruments, there would often be a sulphur content of some 350 mg per kg in the diesel used in OECD member countries.

The impact of such tax rate differentiation can be quite spectacular – as illustrated in the case of the United Kingdom in Figure 2.3. After the introduction of a lower tax rate for low-sulphur diesel and petrol in 1999 and 2001 respectively, the higher-sulphur varieties rapidly disappeared from the market.[7]

Existing taxes on vehicle purchases and/or vehicle use can also be restructured according to environmental criteria. This is done in the 'Eurovignette' system applied to heavy goods vehicles in many EU member states, and several countries also differentiate taxes on the purchase or use of passenger vehicles according to environmentally related criteria, like fuel efficiency, weight of the vehicle, engine size, and so on.

Introducing New Environmental Taxes

An obvious practice is to introduce new taxes whose prime purpose is to protect the environment. These may be taxes on emissions (for instance on atmospheric pollutants or water pollution) or taxes on input, products or on activities that can cause pollution, for example, waste disposal. Taxes on products are most frequent. Since the early 1990s, many environmental taxes have been introduced on products ranging from packaging to fertilizers, pesticides, batteries, chemical substances (solvents), lubricants, tyres, razors, disposable cameras, beverage containers, and so on. The OECD/EEA database on instruments used for environmental policy covers at present about 375 environmentally related *taxes* applied in the 30 OECD member countries.[8] Almost 100 of these taxes are *not* levied on energy or transport.

Many of the non-energy and non-transport taxes are related to waste management. For example, a number of taxes on landfilling of waste have been introduced. Figure 2.4 illustrates the tax rates in some such taxes that apply to the landfilling of waste from households.

It can seem that the tax rates for landfilling set in some countries are relatively high compared to the size of the environmental externalities involved – at least as far as regards landfills that respect new standards concerning, for example, leaching, landfill gas recuperation and energy

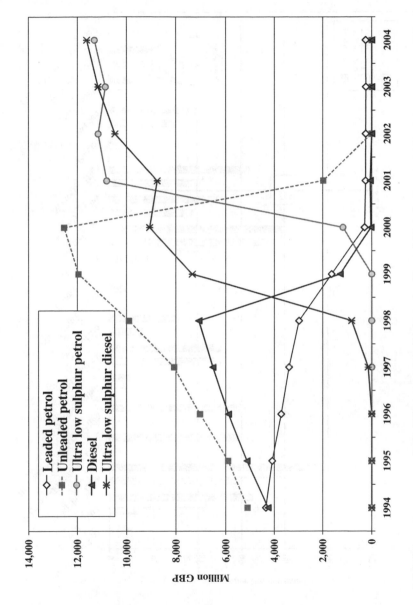

Figure 2.3   Tax revenues raised on different motor fuels in the United Kingdom

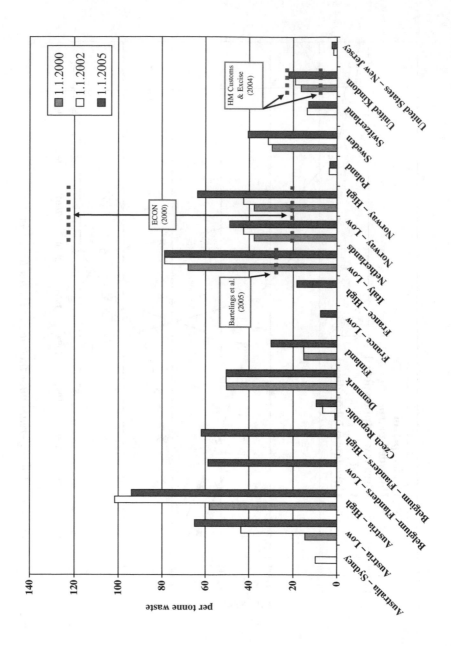

Notes: Several countries differentiate their tax rates depending on the quality of the environmental quality of the landfill site. This is represented in the figure with a low tax rate that apply to the deposits with the highest environmental quality, and a high tax rate, for deposits with the lowest standards that are authorised to receive household waste.

The dotted horizontal lines illustrate various recent estimates of the environmental externalities related to the landfilling of household (or municipal) waste. Bartelings *et al.* (2005) estimated these externalities related to a new landfill in the Netherlands. ECON (2000) presents estimates for both existing and new deposits in Norway – with the (very) high estimate related to old-fashioned existing sites. HM Customs & Excise (2004) presents a low and a high estimate for the externalities relating to landfilling in the United Kingdom, building on DEFRA (2004a, 2004b and 2004c), a scientific study of the health and environment impacts of different waste management options and a survey of recent valuation studies.

Source: The OECD/EEA database on instruments used for environmental policy.

Figure 2.4   Tax rates applicable to the landfilling of household waste in OECD countries

utilization. For landfills without such high standards, the tax rates currently applied could in some cases be too low. In any case, introduction of taxes that reflect the respective externalities related to both landfilling and incineration (and, for that matter, various composting methods) clearly is an option for the more than half of OECD member countries that have not yet done so.[9]

Recent Developments in Selected Countries

Any 'green' tax reform entails many aspects, ranging from the in-depth reform of existing taxation to the introduction of new taxes. This means that the objective pursued by the reforms may not only be environmental. In particular, broader use of economic instruments to achieve environmental targets – replacing or supplementing other policy instruments – can increase economic efficiency through a reduction in compliance costs.

Since the early 1990s, several countries have introduced comprehensive green tax reforms; in most cases, in a context of a constant tax burden, in the sense that new environmental taxes offset reductions in existing taxes. In fact, a constant tax burden can be a condition for the acceptability of the reform as a whole. Industry, in particular, is usually strongly opposed to environmental taxes on the grounds of a possible loss of competitiveness (see section entitled 'Environmental taxes and competitiveness' below). Similarly, consumers may fear that environmental taxes might lead to price increases; it can then be important to show clearly that other taxes are being reduced to ensure the political acceptability of green tax reforms. A few significant examples are presented below.

Finland was the first country to introduce a carbon tax in 1990, followed by a progressive greening of the tax system. While the carbon tax started in 1990 at a fairly modest level of FIM 24.5 per tonne of carbon, the rate increased to reach FIM 374 (approximately 63 euros) in 1998. However, industrial process use of fossil fuels is exempted from the tax, and there is a tax per kWh electricity, instead of a tax on fuels used to generate electricity.[10] The greening of the tax system also includes, for example, the implementation of a waste landfill tax in 1996. The increase in green taxes took place in parallel with a significantly larger reduction in the taxation of labour (decreased income tax and social insurance contributions), with the explicit objective to stimulate economic growth and reduce unemployment. Since 2005 – like in the other member states of the European Union – a tradable emission system for CO_2 emissions is in place.[11]

Norway implemented a CO_2 tax on mineral oils in 1991. The tax was later extended to cover the use of oil and natural gas in petroleum exploration activities on the continental shelf, while the use of natural gas on the mainland is exempted. At one stage the tax also covered coal and coke used for energy purposes, but this had very limited practical implications, and has since been stopped.[12] Interestingly, fuels used in domestic air transport and in coastal transport of goods are included in the CO_2 tax, with relatively low tax rates. All in all, about 68 per cent of all CO_2 emissions were somehow covered by the CO_2 tax in 2005. Even though Norway is not a member of the EU, a CO_2 emission trading system similar to the EU one was implemented in 2005. A tax on the sulphur content of fuels is also being applied, with tax rates corresponding to NOK 17 per kg of SO_2. As industrial use of fossil fuels is exempted, the tax covered about 45 per cent of all SO_2 emissions in 2003.[13] A number of other environmentally related taxes are also applied.

In *Sweden*, a major tax reform was introduced in 1991 in a revenue neutral context. It was based on a significant reduction in income tax, which *inter alia* was offset by a series of new environmental taxes and by a broadening of the VAT tax base. On the other hand, energy taxes on industry were significantly reduced. The environmental levies included taxes or charges on carbon, sulphur and nitrogen oxides. The sulphur tax (SEK 30 per kg sulphur content) is imposed on peat, coal, petroleum, coke and other gaseous products. In addition, the tax rates differ between different categories of diesel and petrol according to the sulphur content. The net effect of these reforms was a 6 per cent redistribution of GDP, including about 1 per cent related to environmental taxes. In 2001, a new round of environmental tax reforms was initiated, meant to result in a tax shift of some 1.3 per cent of GDP in the period up to 2010. Taxes on motor fuels and households' energy use have been increased further, compensated by increases in the basic allowances in the income tax.

The revenues of the Swedish NO_x charge levied on combustion plants are repaid to the firms affected according to the amount of energy they produce.[14] Seen as a group, the plants are, in other words, not much affected by the charge payments. As shown in Figure 2.5, there are, however, large differences between the production units in all of the sectors affected by the charge. The most energy efficient units in each sector receive a net payment from the charge-and-refund mechanism, while the least energy efficient units are net losers.

Denmark introduced a CO_2 tax on fuels in 1992, and has also introduced a large number of other environmentally related taxes in subsequent years. Many of the new taxes were introduced as part of a larger reform involving the reduction of marginal tax rates in all income brackets, the elimination of a series of loopholes in the tax law, and a gradual transfer of tax revenue from income and labour to pollution and scarce environmental resources. One key aspect of the Danish tax reform was the introduction in

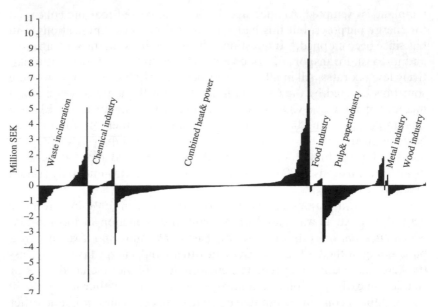

Note: Reproduced with the permission of the Swedish Environmental Protection Agency.

Figure 2.5   Net payers and receivers in relation to the refunded NO$_x$ charge in Sweden

1995 of the 'Energy Package' consisting mainly of an increase of the CO_2 tax and a tax on SO_2 emissions (DKK 10 per kg of SO_2). The revenue raised by these taxes was returned to industry in the form of investment aids for energy saving and reductions in employers' social security contributions. In the preparation of a new Action Plan for the Aquatic Environment in 2003, it was found that major savings probably could be made if most of the regulations addressing nitrogen applications at individual farms were replaced by a tax on the nitrogen surplus in the agriculture sector as a whole. However – in part because the existing regulations were found to produce the desired environmental improvements – such a policy change was not made.

The *Netherlands*, through the 1988 'General Environmental Provision Act', introduced a 'general fuel charge' which replaced five previous charges (on air pollution, traffic and industrial noise, chemical waste and lubricants). Between 1992 and 2000, a number of other taxes were introduced. The 'Regulatory tax on energy' (introduced in 1996) was levied on small, non-transport, energy consumers (households, small businesses, office blocks, and so on), with the revenue returned in the form of reduced social security contributions (Vermeend and Van der Vaart, 1998).

In *France*, a restructuring of environmental taxes and charges was initiated in 1999. Like the Netherlands, one objective was to streamline and simplify a set of existing earmarked emission charges. As from 1 January 2000, existing charges on air pollution, household waste, special industrial waste, lubricating oils and noise (hitherto levied by the ADEME, Agence de l'Environnement et de la Maîtrise de l'Energie), were merged into a single 'Taxe générale sur les activités polluantes' (General Tax on Polluting Activities – TGAP), levied by the Ministry of Finance. The revenue of the TGAP is paid back to ADEME as an annual budget allocation. Taxes on pesticides, granulates and detergents were also introduced. A progressive reduction of the tax differential between gasoline and diesel fuel for automobiles also started in 1999. However, an attempt to introduce new taxation of energy used by industry was rejected by the French Constitutional Court in late 2000. Similarly, in 2004, a proposal to differentiate taxes on car purchase according to environmental and energy features was rejected. Following a recent OECD review of French environmental policy (OECD, 2005d), it was decided to revisit the issue of green tax reform by setting up a 'green tax commission' in late 2005.

Germany initiated a green tax reform in April 1999. The main goals are to stimulate energy savings and to increase employment. The green tax reform comprises two main components: a new taxation on electricity and an increased taxation of mineral oil; both taxes were regularly increased over the period 1999–2003. The increased tax burden on energy is compensated by reduced social security contributions. As in most other countries, a number of special provisions and exemptions apply to different energy sources, in particular renewable energy sources, co-generation power plants, and to the production sector. Since 2005, a new electronically collected, distance-based motorway toll for all heavy commercial vehicles and vehicle combinations with a permissible total weight of 12 tonnes or more has been in operation.

Switzerland has introduced environmentally related taxes on heating oils, volatile organic compounds, and landfilling of waste, and a carbon tax of 35 CHF per tonne CO_2 is expected to be introduced from 2006. The revenue will be returned to households in the form of reduced compulsory sickness insurance premiums. In 2001, a distance-related user charge for all Swiss roads was introduced for heavy goods vehicles – in combination with an increase in the maximum weight limits on these vehicles.[15]

Over the last decade, the *United Kingdom* has developed a comprehensive set of environmentally related taxes and economic instruments. In 1993 a 'Fuel Duty Escalator' (FDE) was introduced, implying increases in the excise taxes on transport fuels 3 to 6 per cent per annum over and above the rate of inflation. The FDE, which by many was considered as a carbon tax on the transport sector, was discontinued in 1999 in anticipation of increases in the price of crude oil and fuel tax protests.[16]

A 'Landfill Tax' was introduced in 1996.[17] A 'Climate Change Levy' (CCL) on energy use by business (including agriculture) and public sectors was introduced in 2001; transport and households are exempted. The CCL is a key component of the UK programme of meeting the obligations of the Kyoto Protocol. Firms meeting the objectives of agreed energy efficiency targets are granted an 80 per cent rebate on the CCL. Firms can also 'opt in' to a domestic greenhouse gas trading scheme (launched in April 2002) as a means to achieve the negotiated agreement target.[18] In 2002, the Aggregates Tax, a tax on the extraction of, for example, rock, sand and gravel, was introduced. Most of the revenues of all these taxes are recycled back to industry through reductions in employers' social security contributions, but a minor share is allocated to related environmental purposes.

REVENUE FROM ENVIRONMENTAL TAXES

The Revenue of Environmentally Related Taxes

The revenue from environmentally related taxes on average represents some 2–2.5 per cent of GDP and 6–7 per cent of total tax revenues in OECD member countries. Despite clear differences from country to country, the revenues from these taxes are thus significant in all these countries (Figure 2.6).

Practically all the revenues (90 per cent) from environmentally related taxes arise from petrol, diesel fuel and motor vehicle taxes (Figure 2.7). Very few taxes are levied on fuels used by heavy industry. The proportion accounted for by other environmentally related taxes (such as waste management, pesticides, and so on) is negligible. Another feature is that industry is little affected, owing to numerous tax exemptions, so that the bulk of the tax burden of energy-related taxes falls on households. Note, however, that the revenue of taxes is not an indication of their environmental effectiveness (indeed it should be the contrary), but it is important information for the implementation of any tax reform with respect to competitiveness and distributive implications, scope for reform, overall structure of the tax system, and so on.

The Sustainability of Revenue

From a fiscal point of view, a 'good' tax is one that produces a given revenue with efficiency, stability and simplicity. In the case of environmentally related taxes, this configuration may turn out to be complex or even paradoxical.

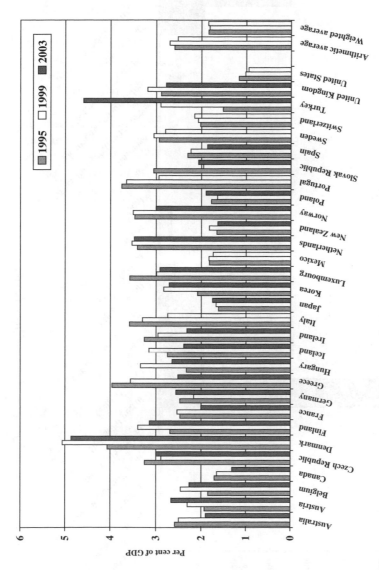

Note: For the Slovak Republic, 2002 figures are used for 2003. The averages are calculated only across the countries for which 2003 numbers are available.

Figure 2.6 Revenues raised through environmentally related taxes in per cent of GDP (1995, 1999 and 2003)

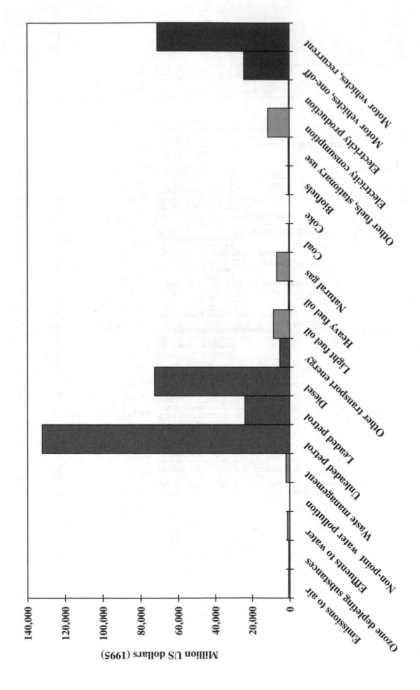

Figure 2.7   Revenue raised on different environmentally related tax bases

The tax rate must be sufficiently high to have an incentive effect.[19] However, the more the incentive works, the more pollution will diminish and therefore the less tax revenue will be collected. As illustrated above, the tax differentiation of petrol and diesel taxes according to sulphur content in the United Kingdom led to the virtual disappearance from the market of the high-sulphur varieties. In Sweden, the revenue obtained from the sulphur tax fell rapidly owing to the environmental success of the tax: before the tax was introduced, annual revenue was estimated at SEK 0.5–0.7 billion; between 1991, when the tax was introduced, and 2004, revenue fell from SEK 0.3 to under 0.1 billion. For similar reasons, leaded petrol has disappeared altogether in many OECD countries. In Denmark, the revenue from the tax on nickel-cadmium batteries decreased from DKK 35 million in 1996 to DKK 20 million in 2002 because of a reduction of the consumption of these batteries.

In other words, there is a contradiction, at least once rigidities and reaction times have been allowed for, between the environmental effectiveness of the tax and its fiscal effectiveness, leading to a potential conflict between the ministries of finance and the environment. In practice, however, the conflict between effectiveness and revenue is not so clear-cut. For some of the most relevant tax bases, like energy, the demand elasticities are relatively low (see below). Moreover, when environmentally related taxes produce long-term or gradual effects, the fall in revenue is deferred or gradual, which allows for appropriate tax adjustments and smoothing of revenue in good time. One last point is that the stability of the tax base is never guaranteed for any tax, as illustrated, for instance, by the fall in revenue from labour taxes and the difficulties affecting social security financing as a result of high rates of unemployment.

The Use of Revenue

How should environmentally related tax revenues be used? This is a key question which has not only fiscal, but also environmental implications. The revenue of environmentally related taxes can be used in two ways.

The first way such tax revenue can be used is by paying it into the general government budget, in accordance with fiscal orthodoxy. The revenue can then be used to reduce public sector deficits, to increase public expenditure or, the tax burden remaining equal, to reduce other distortionary taxes (for example, in search of a 'double dividend').

Secondly, the tax revenue can be *earmarked* for specific public expenditure or particular government agencies, a case in point being environmental expenditures. There are many examples in waste management and water management (through the financing of public equipment or the payment of de-pollution subsidies). In most cases, however, this category concerns charges rather than taxes, that is requited payments (see Box 2.1). The amounts involved are far from negligible: in France, water effluent and abstraction charges amounted to 1.64 billion euros in 2004, while the charges on water consumption and on municipal waste collection and treatment represented 9 and 4.1 billion euros respectively in the same year.

Taxes may also be earmarked, as in the case where fuel taxes are allocated to road building. Out of the approximately 375 taxes in OECD countries covered by the OECD/EEA database, about one-third are fully or partially earmarked.[20] About 75 of the earmarked taxes are levied on energy products, 15 are levied on motor vehicles, while 20 are waste-related taxes. Whereas the earmarked transport-related taxes (including taxes on motor fuels) tend to be allocated to the construction or maintenance of roads, and so on, earmarked waste-related taxes are normally used for environmental purposes, in particular for the operation of waste collection or recycling systems, for the clean-up of contaminated sites, and so on.

Earmarking entails serious drawbacks, however. Fixing the use of tax revenue in advance, without evaluating its economic or even environmental rationale beforehand, may lead to economic wastage. This may prevent a good prioritization of public expenditure. Spending becomes less governed by Government priorities than by the revenue from the earmarked tax, as the revenue cannot be used for other purposes. In the case, for instance, of the considerable revenue generated by energy and transport taxes, allocation may prove dangerous and may introduce rigidities. Allocating taxes to road infrastructures may lead to over-investment in that sector. Programmes may also last longer than their optimal period as a result of habits, administrative slowness, situation returns or other 'acquired rights'. If the allocation of a certain proportion of public revenue creates a precedent, the public authorities may over time find themselves unable to redefine priorities.

Nevertheless, allocating revenues to 'popular' purposes can be an attractive option. In particular, the political acceptability of taxes and charges might be enhanced thanks to transparency of use, clearly dedicated to the popular cause of environmental protection. Similarly, payers feel, rightly or wrongly, that the revenue from such taxes or charges is in some way returned to them in the form of subsidies or public investments. However, rather than making a legally binding link between the revenues raised through a particular tax (or tax increase) it could be better to announce simultaneously with the introduction of the tax that the spending for a given purpose will be increased by a certain amount during a specified time period.

Another option is 'revenue recycling', when environmentally related taxation, particularly those taxes that impact on industry, are fully or partially recycled back to industry by some mechanism. For example, the Swedish NO_x charge is refunded back to industry in proportion to the polluters' energy production. In several countries, parts of the revenues from energy-related taxes are recycled back to industry as financial assistance for energy savings. Another form of tax revenue use is a 'tax shift', where new environmentally related taxes are compensated by reduction in other existing taxes in a revenue neutral context (see below).

TAX SHIFTS IN PRACTICE: IS THERE A 'DOUBLE DIVIDEND'?

In most cases, green tax reforms are implemented within a context of *revenue neutrality*, usually by using the revenues raised through environmental taxes to reduce tax rates in existing distortionary taxes. According to Bovenberg and De Mooij (1994), this concept of a 'double dividend' may have three meanings: in one sense, the double dividend arises from greater economic efficiency due to the environmental tax, compared with direct controls (the static efficiency concept of taxes); in a second sense, the double dividend is related to the 'ancillary benefits' resulting from the supplementary environmental improvements obtained for example by a carbon-energy tax beyond the targeted gains and objectives (for example, through greater energy efficiency, less road transport congestion, fewer emissions of other air pollutants produced by fossil energy combustion); in the third sense, a double dividend relates to efficiency gains obtained with an environmental tax, which both internalizes external costs and replaces existing distortionary taxes. In this third case, the important question is whether this type of fiscal reform could help reduce unemployment by financing a reduction in labour taxes (including employers' social security contributions) with new environmental taxes, especially on energy (CO_2 tax).

This question of a double environment–employment dividend has generated a prolific literature and lively controversy, which is still not over,[21] in particular in the context of high structural unemployment prevailing in a number of EU countries in the early 2000s. There are many conditions for any employment 'double dividend' to occur.

- The initial structure of the tax system should be sub-optimal in order for a dividend to emerge from removing sub-optimal tax provisions. It should, however, be kept in mind that the price increases directly related to the introduction of environmentally related taxes will tend to increase the pre-existing distortions in the tax system, thus harming economic growth and employment.

- The tax incidence is a crucial issue. If the burden of pollution taxes finally falls upon households (that is on labour) through higher prices of the taxed commodities (which is a reasonable assumption), the reduction of the tax wedge on labour will be small and the employment effect reduced or cancelled. Since labour is a relative immobile factor of production, this ultimate tax incidence on labour is likely to occur.
- The degree of substitutability between factors of production is important: if there is a possibility to use more labour instead of energy and capital, increased employment is more likely to occur.
- Reduced unemployment can result in increased wages, hence offsetting, at least in part, the reduction of labour cost.
- The issue of the mobility of production factors is crucial. In the case of an energy tax, if labour is a better substitute for energy than capital, there will be a shift to more labour-intensive production techniques. If capital is relatively immobile internationally, the tax burden will be shifted to capital. If the capital is internationally mobile, it will move abroad to avoid the tax. In this case a high degree of international co-ordination is required.
- The more effective the environmental tax is, the more rapidly the tax base will erode. Therefore, to maintain the same revenue flow, governments will have to increase other taxes or increase existing environmental taxes with two possible consequences: a further incidence on employment (due to the increased tax burden) and a possible reduction of pollution beyond the optimal level. In this case, environmental taxes exacerbate tax distortions.

What happens in reality? A number of simulations have been done using economic models. The results of many models converge to indicate that a carbon energy tax could yield some, albeit small, double employment–environment dividend. Yet, despite the many restrictive hypotheses for the realization of an environment–employment double dividend, most countries that have implemented green tax reforms have in one way or another bet on a double dividend effect, or are considering doing so. How effective in terms of employment these mechanisms really are, still remains to be seen. Carrying out *ex post* evaluations to shed more light on this issue is a major challenge.

THE ENVIRONMENTAL EFFECTIVENESS OF ENVIRONMENTAL TAXES

While the theoretical advantages (especially the static and dynamic efficiency) of environmental taxes are well known, *ex post* data on environmental effectiveness is still relatively scarce – although price elasticity estimates are available for many energy products. There are several reasons for this. In the first place, experience is often too recent to allow for a meaningful evaluation. Secondly, there is a shortage of data and practice when it comes to policy evaluation. The problem of evaluating environmental taxes is particularly complex insofar as they are generally applied simultaneously with other instruments (such as regulations), which makes it difficult to isolate the impact of a tax. However, a growing body of data is available, albeit still dispersed.

Price Elasticities of Demand

Most environmentally related taxes apply to the energy and transport sectors. The magnitude of the responses to environment related taxes can be measured in terms of price elasticities. If, after the introduction of an environmentally related tax, the price of the taxed good increases by 10 per cent and, as a result of the higher price, its consumption falls by 2 per cent, the price elasticity in this particular case is −0.2. Therefore, in order to evaluate behavioural responses to environmentally related taxes, OECD has collected information on the own price elasticities of energy and transport related goods.[22]

Available estimates show that, in most cases, demand for energy in total is rather inelastic in the short term; estimates for short-run elasticities range between −0.13 to −0.26. However, long-run elasticities are significantly higher (−0.37 to −0.46). Nevertheless, a price elasticity significantly different from zero indicates that price increases *can* substantially reduce the demand for energy. Therefore, environmentally related taxes can have a significant impact on reducing energy demand, especially in the long run.

Studies on the price elasticities specifically for petrol show comparable, albeit less homogeneous results – as can be seen in Table 2.1.[23] While most estimates show relatively low elasticities in the short run (−0.15 to −0.28), some estimates indicate significantly higher values (−0.51 to −1.07). Long-term elasticities tend to be clearly higher (−0.23 to −1.05). There are differences between countries and variances are to some extent explained by the use of different estimation methods. This leaves policy makers with certainty about the fact that taxes will have a significant behavioural effect, but uncertainty about the exact magnitude of this effect. This again underlines the fact that 'green tax policies' should be implemented *in a long-term perspective*, avoiding steps back due to political pressure (for example, when world oil prices increase), and with advanced planning and warning of the introduction and/or gradual increase of the taxes.

As an example not related to energy use, available estimates indicate a price elasticity of pesticide use in the range of −0.2 to −1.1 (Hoevenagel

Table 2.1　Selected estimates of price elasticities of petrol

		Short run	Long run	Ambiguous
Pooled time series/cross section	Micro	−0.30 to −0.39 (USA)	−0.77 to −0.83 (USA)	
	Macro	−0.15 to −0.38 (OECD*) −0.15 (Europe) −0.6 (Mexico)	−1.05 to −1.4 (OECD*) −1.24 (Europe) −0.55 to −0.9 (OECD 18**) −1.13 to −1.25 (Mexico)	
Cross section	Micro	−0.51 (USA) 0 to −0.67 (USA)		
	Macro	Mean −1.07 (−0.77 to −1.34) (OECD*)		
Time series	Macro	−0.12 to −0.17 (USA)	−0.23 to −0.35 (USA)	
Meta-analyses and surveys		Average −0.26 (0 to −1.36) (international) Mean−0.27 (time series) Mean−0.28 (cross section)	Average −0.58 (0 to −2.72) (international) Mean−0.71 (time series) Mean−0.84 (cross section)	Average −0.53 (−0.02 to −1.59) (USA) Mean−0.53 (time series) Mean−0.18 (cross section) −0.53 (panel data) −0.1 to −0.3 (22 estimates)

Notes:
* OECD except Luxembourg, Iceland, and New Zealand.
** OECD 18 covers Canada, the USA, Japan, Austria, Belgium, Denmark, France, Germany, Greece, Ireland, Italy, the Netherlands, Norway, Spain, Sweden, Switzerland, Turkey, and the UK.

Source:　Barde and Braathen (2005).

et al., 1999, and Muños Piña, 2004). The estimates are in most cases below −1.0 in absolute value, meaning that the demand in economic terms is described as 'inelastic'. However, the available estimates are clearly different from 0, meaning that a tax on pesticides should contribute to lower pesticide use.

Cross-price elasticities (for example, between different fuels) should also be considered. This is to some extent shown by the rapid switch from high-sulphur to low-sulphur petrol and diesel in the United Kingdom illustrated in Figure 2.3 above – although that resulted more from changes in supply than from changes in demand. The more gradual, but still very significant, change in the composition of motor fuels used in Europe – from petrol to diesel – is probably a better case in point, reflecting *inter alia* the lower taxes on diesel than on petrol in these countries.

Examples of Available Estimates of Changes in Demand

As experience in environmental taxes grows, an increasing body, albeit still limited, of estimates of changes in demand becomes available. A few examples are presented below.

There are several estimates relating to the impacts of the CO_2 tax in *Denmark*.[24] According to the Nordic Council of Ministers (2002), CO_2 emissions in Denmark decreased by 6 per cent during the period 1988–1997 while the economy grew by 20 per cent. They also decreased by 5 per cent just between 1996 and 1997, when the tax rate was raised.

According to Schou (2005), the introduction of the pesticides tax in Denmark in 1996 contributed to a reduction in pesticides use by some 10–13 per cent from 1995 to 1996 (although other factors can also have influenced the development). A doubling of the tax rates in 1998 contributed to a reduction in the treatment frequency from 2.45 to 2.10 from 1999 to 2002.[25]

To reveal the driving forces behind the changes in *Norwegian* emissions of the three most important climate gases, CO_2, methane and N_2O in the period 1990–1999, Bruvoll and Larsen (2002) decomposed the actually observed emissions changes, and used an applied general equilibrium simulation to look into the specific effect of carbon taxes. Although total emissions did increase, they found a significant reduction in emissions per unit of GDP over the period due to reduced energy intensity, changes in the energy mix and reduced process emissions. Despite considerable taxes and price increases for some fuel types, the effect of the carbon tax was, however, modest. While the partial effect from lower energy intensity and energy mix changes was a reduction in CO_2 emissions of 14 per cent, the carbon taxes contributed to only a 2 per cent emission reduction. This relatively small effect can be explained by extensive tax exemptions and relatively inelastic demand in the sectors in which the tax is actually implemented.

The *Swedish* charge on NO_x emissions has been quite effective in reducing emissions from the combustion plants for energy production that it covers – in part because the rate is quite high, at 4.4 euros per kg NO_x emitted. When the charge was introduced, only plants producing more than

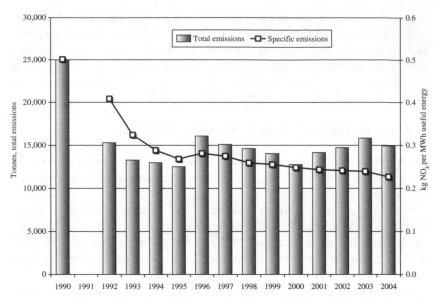

Note: Reproduced with the permission of the Swedish Environmental Protection Agency

*Figure 2.8   Total and specific NO$_x$ emissions from the energy-producing
plants covered by the NO$_x$ charge in Sweden*

50 GWh per year were included, but this limit was reduced to 40 GWh
in 1995, and further to 25 GWh in 1996. Figure 2.8 illustrates both total
emissions from the increasing number of plants covered, and the emissions
per MWh energy produced. The emissions per unit energy produced
are now less than a half of what they were in 1990, before the charge was
introduced.[26]

The Swedish sulphur tax (introduced in 1991) led to a fall in the sulphur
content of oil-based fuels of more than 50 per cent beyond the legal standards. The sulphur content of light oils has now fallen below 0.076 per cent
(that is, less than half the legal limit of 0.2 per cent). The tax is estimated
to have reduced emissions of sulphur dioxide by 80 per cent compared to
1980 (Nordic Council of Ministers, 1999).

Cambridge Econometrics (2005) presents an in-depth analysis of the
impacts of the Climate Change Levy in the *United Kingdom*, comparing
actual emission developments to a counterfactual reference case with no
levy in place and estimating developments up to 2010 under various
assumptions. The study found *inter alia* that total CO_2 emissions were
reduced by 3.1mtC (million tonnes carbon), or 2.0 per cent, in 2002 and by
3.6mtC in 2003 compared to the reference case. The reduction is estimated

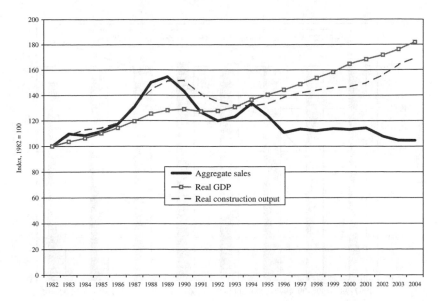

Note: Reproduced with the permission of the British Geological Survey

Figure 2.9 Sales of aggregates, real construction output and real GDP in the United Kingdom

to grow to 3.7mtC, or 2.3 per cent, in 2010. Most of the reduction (1.8mtC in 2010) was found to take place among 'other final users', that is in commerce and the public sector, but 'other industry', that is industry other than basic metals, mineral products and chemicals, was also found to reduce emissions around 0.8mtC in 2010. Emissions from power generation were also found to decrease, due to lower demand for electricity. When interpreting these results it should be kept in mind that households are exempted from the Climate Change Levy, and that energy-intensive industries can benefit from an 80 per cent tax rate reduction if they fulfil negotiated energy efficiency targets.

The aggregates tax in the United Kingdom, introduced in April 2002 on the extraction of rock, sand and gravel, has also been found to be effective. According to HM Treasury (2005), sales of primary aggregate in Great Britain fell by 8 per cent between 2001 and 2003, against a backdrop of buoyant construction activity and GDP growth, as can be seen in Figure 2.9.

HM Treasury (2005) also contains an evaluation of the Landfill Tax in the United Kingdom. The quantity of inactive or inert waste disposed to landfill fell by 60 per cent between 1997–98 and 2003–04. Allowing for the fact that some of this material may have been reclassified as exempt, there is still an

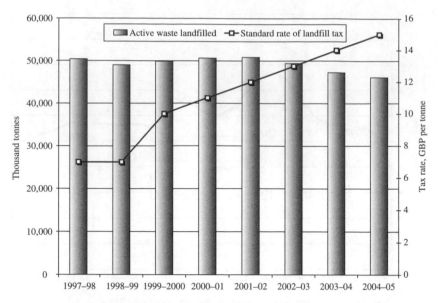

Source: HM Treasury (2005).

*Figure 2.10   Landfilling of active waste and the standard tax rate of the
            Landfill Tax in the United Kingdom*

overall reduction in inert or exempt material of 16 million tonnes (35 per
cent) over the period. The total amount of waste landfilled has decreased
less, as the reduction in the landfilling of active (biodegradable) waste has
been smaller than for inactive waste, but – as can be seen in Figure 2.10 – a
reduction is now occurring in the landfilling of active waste.[27]

In most countries, the tax differentiation between leaded and unleaded
petrol, combined with a series of measures such as regulations making it
compulsory for service stations to offer unleaded petrol and introducing
new emission standards for motor vehicles (based on such requirements as
catalytic converters), led to a heavy fall in consumption and in the share of
leaded petrol, which is now withdrawn from sale in almost all OECD countries. The fiscal incentive greatly speeded up the process, despite slow penetration of new vehicles equipped with catalytic converters.

Not all taxes have been successful, however. The effects of taxes in
Belgium on disposable razors, and other items, were hardly noticeable. The
rates of French tax on SO_2 emissions (38 euros per tonne) – only a fraction
of similar rates in the Nordic countries – are, according to Riedinger (2005)
well below the cheapest abatement measures industry could take. The tax
has, hence, minimal impact on firms' behaviour. Similarly, the rates of the

Swedish tax on pesticides were according to the Swedish Environmental Protection Agency (1997) too low to produce incentive effects.

DISTRIBUTIONAL IMPLICATIONS OF ENVIRONMENTAL TAXES

Potential Distributive Effects

Are environmental taxes socially regressive? This question is increasingly being asked by stakeholders, in particular, households and the business community. The distributional effects of environmental taxes, especially those on energy, may be observed in three ways (Smith, 1998):

1. There will be a direct distributional impact related to the structure of household energy expenditure (on heating and transport) for different income brackets. The bigger the proportion of low-income household expenditure devoted to energy, the more regressive will be the impact of the tax.
2. Indirect distributional effects will result from the taxation of production inputs. The more the processes are energy-intensive, the greater will be the incidence of a tax on the goods produced. Of course, the more the products fall into the prime necessity category, the more regressive the tax will be.
3. Lastly, the distributional impact will be related to the incidence of the tax. An energy tax may affect end consumers, but it may also affect energy producers or production factors (for example, through a fall in wages or lower return on capital). At the same time, part of the tax may be borne by energy-consuming countries, and another part by energy-exporting countries, according to the elasticities of supply and demand.

In so far as many environmental taxes apply to mass consumption products, such as motor-driven vehicles and energy, they can have a potentially substantial effect on lower-income households.[28] The level of the tax also matters; taxes on products that in any case form a low share of household expenditures, such as detergents, fertilizers, batteries and pesticides, are likely to have limited distribution impacts, while large-scale and fiscally heavier environmental taxes, such as those on energy, can have more profound implications.

Ekins and Dresner (2004) looked in detail at income distribution impacts of various possible environmentally related taxes and charges in the United Kingdom. In general they concluded that it is possible to solve any regressivity problems related to such taxes and charges either through the tariff/charging design or through a targeted compensation scheme. However, regarding a possible tax on domestic energy use, they found that there were such large variations in energy use *within* different income deciles that it would not be possible to construct a revenue-neutral tax and compensation scheme that would protect *all* households in the lowest income group.[29]

A complete assessment of the distributive impacts should include an assessment of the possible mitigation and compensation measures and the possible induced employment effects. Ideally, the distribution of the environ-onmental *benefits* of the tax should also be accounted for.

Available Evidence

Evidence on the distributive implications of environmental taxes remains scant. It indicates some, but limited regressivity, as can be expected from any indirect tax. But little systematic, in-depth *ex ante* or *ex post* analysis has been carried out.

In its 1997 report, the Swedish Green Tax Commission estimated that doubling the CO_2 tax (from a 1997 rate of 0.37 to 0.74 Kronor per kg of CO_2) would have a fairly marked regressive impact. In order to maintain the same consumption level, the lowest incomes would need to receive compensation of 1.24 per cent of their consumption expenditure, and the highest revenues only 0.78 per cent. In Denmark, the distributional impact of taxes on water, heating and electricity seems to be of particular concern. In the UK, the lowest income decile spend 5.6 per cent of net household income on road fuel duty, three times more than the richest decile and more than twice as much as the average. In Norway, environmental taxes are not seen to cause any significant regressivity; but one issue is an income distribution effect between regions where public transportation is available (hence a possibility to switch to public transports when fuel taxes increase), vs. regions where it is not the case.

Policy Options

Basically, three types of corrective measures can be envisaged: mitigation, compensation and tax shift.

(a)   Mitigation consists in a reduction of the rates of environmental taxes to alleviate the tax burden on specific segments of the population. This can take two forms: (1) definition of a consumption floor below which no tax is levied (for example, for heating fuels, water consumption); this option, however, also benefits the higher income segment of the population. (2) Establishment of a dual rate structure of the tax, targeting tax reductions to specific segments of the population (for example, zero rate for lower income households). There are a number of problems with this approach: administrative complexities, distortions in the income tax; also, taxable income does not reflect accurately the ability to pay of households (for example, those benefiting from non-taxable transfers). Generally speaking and most importantly, mitigation measures result in a weakening of the desired environmental impact of the tax. Nevertheless, a large number of special tax provisions are applied in OECD countries. The OECD/EEA database indicates hundreds of provisions such as tax exemptions and reduced rates. Note that these provisions are introduced both on distributive and competitiveness grounds, to the benefit both of households and the business sectors, which makes the assessment of the strictly 'social' benefit of these measures quite uncertain.

(b) Compensation measures are basically outside the realm of the taxes as such; that is they do not affect their rate or structure. These are corrective measures, such as lump sum compensation calculated on the basis of average tax payments per household. In this case, compensation will have a progressive incidence on the assumption that the poorest households on average pay less tax than the richest households. Tax refunds are a typical compensation measure; for instance, the Swiss taxes on VOCs and light heating oil are refunded to households through lump-sum payments. In several countries, energy taxes are partly repaid to household and/or business in the form of subsidies for energy saving investments/expenditures.

(c) Tax shifts; for example, the reduction of other taxes, such as labour and income taxes, is a widespread form of compensation. It is assumed that the regressive impact of the new environmental tax will be compensated by the reduction of other taxes. The net distributional implication of this approach is not clear, however, considering that the poorest households pay the least income tax, unlike wealthy households, who will benefit most from any lowering of income tax. According to Smith (1998), this form of compensation may even prove to be strongly regressive.

A number of approaches may be considered to provide relief from an environmental tax through a country's personal income tax system. These include:

- An increase in the basic personal allowance (or introduction of an environmental tax allowance);

- The introduction of a 'wastable tax credit';
- The introduction of a 'non-wastable tax credit'.

Unlike tax credits, the amount of tax relief from a tax allowance depends on the taxpayer's marginal personal income tax rate. This is because allowances are deductions from the tax base, whereas tax credits provide dollar-for-dollar reductions in tax payable. Where personal tax rates rise with the level of taxable income, a fixed personal tax allowance provides more tax relief to high-income individuals than to low-income individuals, tending to *aggravate rather than alleviate regressivity* in the tax system. Such a result may be avoided by denying a tax allowance to individuals with taxable income above the first positive income band in the rate schedule. However, this may conflict with the intended target group to obtain relief from environmental taxes. More generally, on account of interactions with the tax rate schedule, reliance on an environmental tax allowance may constrain policy choices (over the target group, and possibly over the personal income tax rate structure), leading one to consider alternative approaches.

'Wastable' tax credits (that is a tax credit that cannot exceed tax liability of the tax payer) are attractive, relative to tax allowances, because they avoid interactions with the tax rate structure. However, wastable tax credits do not deliver in full the intended amount of tax relief where an individual has insufficient income (and therefore insufficient tax payable) to fully absorb the tax credit.

'Non-wastable' tax credits provide cash transfers for credit amounts that cannot be used to offset personal income tax liabilities. Hence, there is no risk that relief directed at low-income taxpayers gets wasted: they will get a cash payment for the remainder if their original tax liabilities are lower than the intended relief. However, like the other tax-relieving measures, 'non-wastable' tax credits exclude from the net individuals who do not file tax returns. This may not present a major problem in countries where all residents are expected to file tax returns, and may indeed be a desirable feature in countries that aim to discourage non-filing. But where filing tax returns is not expected, other complementary approaches for low-income households may be required.

ENVIRONMENTAL TAXES AND COMPETITIVENESS

A Stumbling Block?

The key issue confronting countries which implement green tax reform is the possible loss of international competitiveness. Since the bulk of environmentally related taxes concern energy and transport taxes, there is an obvious risk that heavy industry's competitiveness be hurt. This is why some industry sectors (in particular energy-intensive industries) are strongly opposed to environmental taxes and tend to promote other instruments such as voluntary approaches. Furthermore, the greater the 'visibility' of environmental taxes compared with other environmental policy instruments, the more outright the opposition will be, insofar as taxes are payments in addition to the costs of other anti-pollution measures. Another problem, which may turn into an explicit threat, is the 'relocation' of activities to countries which are less fussy about environmental protection or to other 'pollution havens'.

It is important to note that the concept of 'competitiveness' can be interpreted in different ways. For instance, one should differentiate between the competitiveness of individual companies and sectors of the economy and of the economy of a country. Similarly, competitiveness may have a national or an international dimension.[30]

It should be underlined that *any* policy instrument used to achieve environmental targets *should* cause changes in consumption and/or production patterns. If a policy fails to create such changes, it simply cannot deliver any environmental improvements. Thus, the relevant issues are *who* should change their behaviour, by *how much* and within which *timeframe*.[31]

Competitiveness Impacts is a Genuine Issue

More ambitious environmental policies could indeed have negative impacts on the sectoral competitiveness of certain industrial sectors. OECD (2003d) analysed possible impacts of a 'carbon price' of US\$ 25 per tonne CO_2 for the steel sector, using a general equilibrium model that distinguishes between several technologies for producing steel.

The two dominating steel production routes are:

- The integrated steel plant, where iron ore and coke are used to produce iron, and where iron is transformed to steel in a Basic Oxygen Furnace (the BOF process).
- The mini-mills, where steel is produced from recycled scrap in an Electric Arc Furnace (the EAF process).

Environmental taxes would affect the costs of these processes quite differently due to the different input combinations and the resulting differences in emission profiles.

An OECD-wide carbon tax would reduce OECD steel production significantly, by an estimated 9 per cent. The estimated reduction is much greater for the heavily polluting integrated steel mills (-12 per cent) than for the scrap-based mini-mills (-2 per cent). Non-OECD production would increase by almost 5 per cent, implying a fall in world steel production of 2 per cent. OECD emissions of CO_2 from the steel industry were found to decrease by 19 per cent. Despite relatively high emission intensities in non-OECD countries, global emissions from the steel sector would decline by 4.6 per cent; that is more than twice the reduction in global steel production. This is due to substitution towards a cleaner input mix and cleaner processes in the OECD area.

It was found that unilateral carbon taxes by single regions or countries could lead to quite dramatic cutbacks in the production of BOF steel, because in these cases there are smaller opportunities to shift the tax burden over to suppliers or customers. For EAF steel producers, the net effect of unilateral policies would not differ much from an OECD-wide approach, because unilateral policies will lead to a smaller increase in scrap prices.

The study looked at some potential ways the burden on steel firms could be limited, while maintaining their abatement incentives. One option could be to recycle (a part of) the revenues raised back to the firms in question. If the tax revenues were recycled back to the steel industry as an output subsidy, the decline in OECD steel production was found to be quite small (<1 per cent). If a tax refund were uniform across processes, there would, however, be a significant restructuring in the OECD towards the relatively clean process (EAF steel making). Revenue recycling would *reduce* global emission *reductions* in the sector from 4.6 per cent to around 3 per cent, and hence make the policy as a whole less environmentally effective.

A first lesson that can be drawn from this case study is that different firms within a given sector will *not* be affected in the same way by any use of economic instruments due to the different input combinations and the resulting differences in emission profiles.

A second lesson is the importance of taking into account possible adjustments in *related markets* when considering the impacts of a given policy on a particular sector. A part of any initial burden placed on a sector is likely to be shifted backwards to input suppliers and forward to customers.[32] In the steel case, this is illustrated by the (somewhat crudely) estimated impacts on scrap metal prices, and the increase in steel prices.

A third lesson is that, in spite of *some* element of 'carbon leakage' also when policies to combat climate change are put in place on a relatively broad front, significant global reductions in carbon emissions – compared to a reference scenario – can be achieved.[33]

A fourth lesson is that, while the importance varies between different firms, the larger the group of countries that put similar policies in place, the more limited the impacts on sectoral competitiveness.

Another important point is that protecting the competitiveness of energy-intensive sectors in the OECD area through the recycling of tax revenues to the given sectors is likely to lower the environmental effectiveness of the policy as a whole.

From an environmental point of view there could in some cases be advantages related to the use of so-called 'border tax adjustments' instead of revenue recycling. However, both practical and legal issues related to their implementation would need to be solved.

Current Mitigation Practices

A review of current green tax policies in OECD countries shows clearly that a wide array of measures have been implemented to prevent any negative impact on sectoral competitiveness; at least six different measures are applied.

1. *Reduced tax rates for certain sectors, products or inputs.* Most countries apply reduced tax rates on the production sector. For instance, Sweden initially gave industry a 75 per cent rebate on the carbon tax (and total exemption in the case of the energy tax); this rebate was then reduced to 50 per cent in July 1997. In Denmark, a 50 per cent rebate on the CO_2 tax was granted to industry for the period 1993–1995. Both cases are interesting examples of 'front runners' who were amongst the first set of countries to introduce CO_2 taxes. Energy-intensive firms in Germany have obtained a 97 per cent reduction in the tax rates of the ecological tax reform there – without any new commitments to specific emission reductions.[34] A number of tax breaks are also granted on environmental grounds (for example, renewable energies or clean processes); this nevertheless is likely to affect positively the competitiveness of the beneficiaries.

2. *Tax exemptions for specific activities, sectors or products.* There are a large number of tax exemptions related to environment related taxes; the OECD/EEA database includes more than 1100 exemptions in the 375 or so taxes applied in OECD countries.[35] This information must be interpreted with caution: exemptions are introduced for a number of social, environmental and economic reasons, and only part of these exemptions can be construed as motivated by competitiveness concerns.

   The various sorts of information in the database have been linked to *one or more* ISIC production sectors.[36] In all, more than 1800 links have been made between a sector and an exemption – either because the sector produces a product that is exempted, or because it is a major user of an exempted product. Only for about 50 exemptions has it not been found meaningful to make a link to one or more ISIC sectors – but many of the exemptions to which one or more sectors have been linked have been introduced primarily for other concerns than the international competitiveness of these sectors.

3. *Tax refunds for certain sectors or activities.* The OECD/EEA database records about 175 refund mechanisms in the environmentally related taxes in all – not all for competitiveness reasons. The refunds have been linked to various ISIC sectors in a similar way to the exemptions described above. All in all, about 150 links have been made between sectors and refunds. Here again, it is difficult to ascertain whether refunds are specifically crafted to alleviate possible competitiveness effects: while a few refunds aim at 'rewarding' environment-friendly practices or processes (for example, taxes paid on LPG, natural gas, low-sulphur and sulphur-free diesel and electricity used in public transportation are reimbursed in Denmark), most other cases are designed to lighten the tax burden of industry and agriculture under specific conditions.

4. *Recycling tax revenue.* This is a specific form of tax refund. For example, in several countries revenues raised are fully or partially redistributed to industry in the form of lower employers' social security contributions.

5. *Ceilings on tax payments.* For example, in Sweden, if a manufacturing industry or a greenhouse cultivator has a remaining CO_2 tax, after the 50 per cent rate reduction, that exceeds 0.8 per cent of the turnover, the company only has to pay 12 per cent of the energy and CO_2 tax above the ceiling.

6. *Gradual phasing in of taxes.* This tool is used to soften the financial impact of the tax, and allow businesses time to adjust to changing relative prices.

Concluding Remarks

The rather reassuring view that environmental policies have negligible effects on international trade and competitiveness is only provisional: first, as mentioned earlier, heavy and export industries are generally totally or partially exempted from carbon and energy taxes. Furthermore, this view is based on fairly limited data and reflects a situation where these policies have perhaps not yet crossed a certain intensity threshold. It is likely that environmental taxes will grow in number (more taxes) and in intensity (higher levels). The competitiveness issue will thus become more and more acute.

Therefore, an international co-ordination of policies is needed. The European Commission has been striving to promote such co-ordination at the EU level for six years. Following a 'Communication on environmental taxes and charges in the single market' in 1997, it was only in 2003 that the Directive 2003/96/EC 'Restructuring the community framework for the taxation of energy products and electricity' was agreed upon. This Directive fixes minimum tax rates on energy products and introduces new taxes on coal, natural gas and electricity at the EU level. Whilst this directive amounts to a 'least common denominator' type of agreement for the then existing 15 member states, it has significant implications for some of the new EU member states.

Obviously, the question of competitiveness will remain central to the debate on environmental taxes and the most advanced countries in this area will continue to proceed very carefully, in particular through specific tax provisions designed to mitigate the competitiveness impact, at the expense of environmental effectiveness. Some kind of co-ordination between OECD countries would avoid the 'prisoner's dilemma' whereby countries hesitate to move forward in a significant way from fear of losing competitiveness.

ACCEPTANCE BUILDING

Environmental taxes face opposition from stakeholders for a variety of reasons, such as fear of competitiveness losses, reduced profits or possible income regressivity. For instance, the sharp increase in nominal oil prices in the year 2000 exacerbated the opposition to energy taxes in Europe; this is likely to occur again with the 2005 sharp increase in oil prices. Therefore acceptance building is a key component of the implementation strategy of environmental taxes. Three series of measures can contribute to a better acceptance.

First, the purpose of the tax must be clear from the outset; in particular, the fact that the objective is to reduce a specific pollution, rather than provide government revenue.

Second, the active involvement of stakeholders is crucial. Several countries have set up successfully 'green tax commissions', where public and private stakeholders can meet and work together. For example, these commissions may include different government departments (for example, finance and environment), representatives from the concerned economic sectors (agriculture, energy, transport, industry, and so on), environmental NGOs and technical experts. These green tax commissions provide public and technical legitimacy to the tax reform. They usually have a mandate of several years, enabling them to achieve solid work and progressively build confidence and dialogue. When the tax reform is decided, these commissions may also have to monitor and assess the implementation.

Third, green tax reforms must be implemented gradually. In particular, the initial introduction of environmental taxes is often followed by a gradual increase in tax rates, a widening of the application of the tax and the progressive introduction of new taxes. For instance, in Finland, the rate of the CO_2 tax was raised from FIM 24.5 per tonne of carbon in 1990 to FIM 374 per tonne in 1998; the tax was initially limited to heat and electricity production and later broadened to transport and heating fuels. In Norway, the CO_2 tax is now applied to hitherto exempted sectors like domestic air transport and coastal maritime transport. In Denmark, the CO_2 tax introduced in 1992 was followed by a multi-annual 'Energy Package' (1995–2002) comprising a progressive increase of the tax. The green tax reforms initiated in 1999 in Germany, and the UK are being gradually implemented over several years.

CONCLUSIONS

In the context of growing environmental challenges, both nationally and internationally, environmentally related taxes are now recognized as an environmentally effective and economically efficient policy instrument. As a matter of fact, virtually all OECD countries are using such taxes to a larger or lesser extent, while several countries have implemented comprehensive green tax reforms. 'Green' taxes should preferably be implemented in the context of broader tax reforms providing an opportunity to reduce or eliminate tax distortions and 'niches' and modernize taxation systems, hence achieving effective adjustments of economies and greater economic efficiency. In this context, the removal or reform of environmentally harmful subsidies is essential.

There is now ample evidence of the environmental effectiveness of environmentally related taxes. These taxes should be implemented in a long term perspective, in particular because transport and energy demand elasticities are significantly larger in the long term than in the short term: structural adjustments and technological change can take a long time to be implemented.

A number of policy issues remain to be addressed; in particular, the implication for income distribution and, more so, the possible impact on sectoral competitiveness. This is why an internationally coordinated implementation of environmental taxes would strongly facilitate more widespread and more efficient environmental taxes and green tax reforms; this is a key challenge for the future. Clear objectives, transparent systems, stakeholders' involvement, gradual implementation, and well-designed compensation mechanisms are amongst the prominent aspects of a well-balanced 'political economy' of environmental taxes.

NOTES

* The opinions in this chapter are those of the authors and they do not necessarily reflect those of the OECD or its member countries. A further discussion of many of the issues addressed in this chapter can be found in OECD (2006).

1. For a detailed assessment on subsidies, see OECD (1998, 2003b and 2005f, Barde and Honkatukia (2004).
2. Subsidies include a variety of support measures such as direct payments, price support, subsidized input prices, tax breaks and preferential interest rates.
3. One should be careful when interpreting changes in the tax rates between 2000 and 2005 for countries outside the euro area, as these can result both from changes in the tax rates expressed in national currencies (which is what would have an impact on relative prices in the country concerned) and from changes in the relevant exchange rates. In fact, the tax rates in national currency for neither petrol nor diesel changed between 2000 and 2005 in Japan and at the federal levels in Canada and United States.
4. It is emphasized that the comparisons made here concern the taxes on diesel for 'normal' uses. In addition many countries have special, even lower, tax rates for diesel used in professional activities (transport, fisheries, agriculture, and so on).
5. Recent work on optimal transport pricing places emphasis on variable road-user charges partly to replace taxes on fuels – in order better to reflect differences in the negative externalities over the day and depending on the location of the transport activity. See, for example, ECMT (2000, 2003), Newbery (2005) and Glaister and Graham (2004).
6. Ongoing efforts to reduce emissions of particles and NO_x from (in particular) diesel-driven vehicles will, of course, tend to reduce the differences in optimal tax rates. The fact that diesel-driven vehicles are more energy-efficient than petrol-driven vehicles, and thus cause lower CO_2 emissions, is *not* an argument in favour of a reduced tax rate for diesel, as this effect is already fully internalized in the user costs of the vehicles. In any case, according to Parry and Small (2002), CO_2 emissions represent only a small share of the externalities related to petrol use.
7. This obviously represented a *supply-side* response much more than a change in the demand from the individual vehicle users. In contrast to what earlier was the case regarding leaded and unleaded petrol, petrol stations generally do not offer customers a choice between high-sulphur and low-sulphur fuels.
8. It also covers more than 250 environmentally related fees and charges levied in OECD member countries, in addition to more than 60 taxes and more than 180 fees and charges levied in some Central and Eastern European countries that are not OECD member countries. The database further provides information on 44 tradable permits systems (all in OECD countries), 51 deposit-refund systems (38 in OECD countries), 214 environmentally motivated subsidy schemes (of which 194 are in OECD countries) and 101 voluntary approaches (thereof 97 in OECD countries). The database aims to cover instruments levied at both a national and a sub-national level (states, provinces, länder, and so on), but the coverage of the latter category is not complete. It is freely available at www.oecd.org/env/policies/database.
9. Like a few other countries, Norway has also introduced taxation of waste incineration. An interesting and useful new development is that the tax is levied according to measured or estimated emissions of a number of pollutants coming out of the incinerators rather than on the amount of waste delivered for incineration. This gives the operators of the incinerators an incentive to lower the emissions per tonne of waste burned. One

can, however, ask why similar taxes are not levied on the same type of emissions stemming from other (large) stationary sources. See Martinsen and Vassnes (2004) for further details on the incineration tax.

10. A tax on fuels used for electricity generation could in principle provide incentives for the plant operators to switch to low-carbon energy sources. However, international trade in electricity complicates the implementation of such taxes. The exemptions mentioned in the Finnish carbon tax are in accordance with EU rules on energy taxation.

11. See http://europa.eu.int/comm/environment/climat/emission.htm.

12. Almost all electricity generation in Norway is based on hydro power. Hardly any coal and coke is hence used for energy purposes. A much more significant use of fossil fuels in industrial processes has all the time been exempted.

13. Between 1999 and 2001, industrial process uses were covered by the tax on sulphur contents in fuels – with reduced tax rates corresponding to 3 NOK per kg of SO_2. From 1 January 2002 this taxation was replaced by a negotiated agreement, whereby the industrial firms affected committed to undertake significant emission reductions. The firms continue to pay a 'fee' of 3 NOK per kg of SO_2 to a fund managed by the industry, which is used to help finance abatement measures. See Braathen (2005) for further details.

14. For more information, see the Swedish Environmental Protection Agency (2000) and Naturvårdsverket (2003).

15. For more information on the heavy goods vehicle charge see OECD (2005e).

16. As could be seen in Figure 2.2, the taxes on petrol and diesel were still the highest among all OECD member countries as of both 1 January 2000 and 1 January 2005 – and the tax rates on petrol are possibly considerably higher than the related externalities.

17. See Davies and Doble (2004) for more information.

18. For a discussion of the 'political economy' surrounding the introduction of the Climate Change Levy, see OECD (2005g). For a discussion of the interactions between the CCL, the Climate Change Agreements and the domestic carbon trading scheme, see Braathen (2005).

19. Considering that we are in a 'second best' universe, below the ideal of a 'Pigovian' tax.

20. Half of the approximately 250 environmentally related fees and charges in OECD member countries covered by the database are also fully or partially earmarked. In the non-OECD member countries covered by the database, only 4 out of 60 taxes are earmarked, while 40 of the 180 fees and charges are earmarked. This information could, however, be incomplete.

21. See, for example, Fullerton and Metcalf (2001), Goulder et al. (1999) and OECD (2004b).

22. For more information see OECD (2000, 2001) and Barde and Braathen (2005).

23. Results of a survey of price elasticity estimates undertaken among ministries of finance and ministries of environment in OECD countries in the summer of 2005 are in line with what is shown in Table 2.1: estimates of short-term price elasticities for petrol (reflecting demand changes taking place within one year) are in the range -0.15 to -0.3, medium term estimates (up to 10 years) range between -0.35 and -0.52, while long-term estimates vary between -0.8 and -1.0.

24. See Nordic Council of Ministers (2001, 2002) for additional information.

25. Treatment frequency expresses the number of times the total area of arable land can be treated on average with the sold quantities of pesticides, when they are used at the normal dose rates.

26. A side effect of the NO_x charge is higher emissions of, among other things, carbon monoxide and N_2O, which are not regulated by charges.

27. While the tax rate for inactive waste (for example construction and demolition waste) has been kept at its original level of 2 GBP per tonne ever since the Landfill Tax was introduced in 1999, the tax rate for active waste (for example unsorted waste from households) has been steadily increasing – and is set to increase significantly further in the years to come.

28. In low-income countries, poor people will normally not have cars at all. In such cases, taxes on motor vehicles and motor vehicle fuels could be quite *progressive*.

29. Their finding could to some extent result from the fact that they looked at expenditures on energy use in per cent of total income – not in per cent of total expenditure. *Some* of the low-income households with particularly high energy expenditures could be relatively rich elderly persons living off earlier savings, for example, in large houses.
30. Ideally policy-makers should focus more on competitiveness impacts at a national level, rather than on impacts for individual firms or sectors. However, perceived negative impacts for certain firms or sectors tend to play an important role for practical policy formulation. See OECD (2003c) for a more in-depth discussion.
31. In addition, it is a relevant issue whether or not given environmental targets – or the lack of such targets – represent a reasonable balance between the benefits and costs of environmental improvements. The choice of policy instruments can, however, affect the efficiency at which a given target is reached – and affect the rate of new technology developments, which can be of importance for the cost to society of reaching given policy targets in the longer term. Economic instruments, like taxes or tradable permits, *can* help in achieving a given target at the lowest possible cost to society as a whole, both in the short term, as they can equalize marginal abatement costs between polluters (obtain *static efficiency*), and in the long term, as they provide a continuous incentive for further technology development.
32. It is very important to keep this point in mind these days, when many sectors in most OECD countries are asking for 'compensation' due to the high crude oil prices. The current crude price increase is an 'exogenous shock' that affects (almost) all firms in the relevant sectors across the world, and it seems very likely that they will *gradually* be able to shift a significant share of the cost increase on to their customers or their (non-energy) input suppliers.
33. The word 'significant' is of course relative. The emission reductions obtained in the simulations discussed here are small compared to what would be needed to fulfil the long-term objectives of the UN Framework Convention on Climate Change.
34. According to Heinrich Böll Stiftung (2004), the UK chemical industry pays 0.14 euro cents per kilowatt hour (kWh) tax on electricity and in return, agreed to reduce emissions by 18 per cent; the UK aluminium industry pays the same low rate and committed to reduce emissions by 32 per cent in return. In Germany, both sectors are required to pay 0.06 euro cents per kWh – without accompanying emission reduction agreements.
35. The database also details more than 200 exemptions in the 250 fees and charges included from OECD countries, plus more than 100 and about 50 exemptions respectively in the 60 taxes and the 180 fees and charges from non-OECD member countries. The fact that there are fewer exemptions per fee or charge on average than per tax could in part be because the information on fees and charges in general is less complete than it is for taxes.
36. See http://unstats.un.org/unsd/cr/registry/regcst.asp?Cl=17 for further information on ISIC.

REFERENCES

Andersen, M.S. (1998), 'Assessing the effectiveness of Denmark's waste tax', *Environment*, **40**(4).

Anderson, R.C., A.Q. Lohof and A. Carlin (1997), 'The United States experience with economic incentives in pollution control policy', Washington DC: Environmental Law Institute and US EPA.

Barde, Jean-Philippe (1992), *Économie et politique de l'environnement*, Paris: Presses Universitaires de France.

Barde, Jean-Philippe and Nils Axel Braathen (2005), 'Environmentally related levies', in Sijbren Cnossen (ed.), *Theory and Practice of Excise Taxation*, Oxford: Oxford University Press.

Barde, Jean-Philippe and Outi Honkatukia (2004), 'Environmentally harmful subsidies', in Tom Tietenberg and Henk Folmer (eds), *The International Yearbook of Environmental and Resources Economics 2004/2005, a Survey of Current Issues*, Cheltenham, UK and Northampton, MA, USA: Edward Elgar.

Barde, Jean-Philippe and St. Smith (1997), 'Do economic instruments help the environment?', *The OECD Observer*, No. 204, March.

Bartelings, Helen et al. (2005), *Effectiveness of Landfill Taxation*, report prepared for the Dutch Ministry of Housing, Spatial Planning and the Environment, Institute for Environmental Studies, Vrije Universiteit, Amsterdam, available at www.ivm.falw.vu.nl/Research_output/index.cfm/home_subsection.cfm/subsectionid/ FF91BCBD-EAFE-426A-ABB8184073A39BBF.

Bovenberg, L. and R. De Mooij (1994), 'Environmental levies and distortionary taxation', *American Economic Review*, **84**(4), September.

Braathen, Nils Axel (2005), 'Environmental agreements used in combination with other policy instruments', in Edoardo Croci (ed.), *The Handbook of Environmental Agreements*, Dordrecht, the Netherlands: Springer.

Bruvoll, Annegrete and Bodil Merete Larsen (2002), 'Greenhouse gas emissions in Norway: Do carbon taxes work?', Discussion Papers 337, Statistics Norway, Oslo, available at www.ssb.no/cgi-bin/publsoek?job=forside&id=dp-337&kode=dp&lang=en.

Cambridge Econometrics (2005), *Modelling the Initial Effects of the Climate Change Levy,* report submitted to HM Customs and Excise by Cambridge Econometrics, Department of Applied Economics, University of Cambridge and the Policy Studies Institute, available at http://customs.hmrc.gov.uk/channelsPortalWebApp/channelsPortalWebApp.portal?_nfpb=true&_pageLabel=pageLibrary_MiscellaneousReports&propertyType=document&columns=1&id=HMCE_PROD1_023971.

Cnossen, Sijbren (ed.) (2005), *Theory and Practice of Excise Taxation*, Oxford: Oxford University Press.

Davies, Bob and Michael Doble (2004), 'The development and implementation of a landfill tax in the UK', in *Addressing the Economics of Waste*, Paris: OECD.

De Moor, A. de and Calamai P. (1997), *Subsidizing Unsustainable Development: Undermining the Earth with Public Funds*, Institute for Research on Public Expenditure (IRPE), commissioned by the Earth Council, San José, Costa Rica.

DEFRA (2004a), 'Review of environmental and health effects of waste management: municipal solid waste and similar wastes', DEFRA, London, available at www.defra.gov.uk/environment/waste/research/health/pdf/health-report.pdf.

DEFRA (2004b), 'Review of environmental and health effects of waste management: municipal solid waste and similar wastes. Extended summary', DEFRA, London, available at www.defra.gov.uk/environment/waste/research/health/pdf/health-summary.pdf.

DEFRA (2004c), 'Economic valuation of the external costs and benefits to health and environment of waste management options', DEFRA, London, available at www.defra.gov.uk/environment/waste/research/health/pdf/costbenefit-valuation.pdf.

Dijkgraaf, Elbert and Herman R.J. Vollebergh (2004), 'Burn or bury? A social cost comparison of final waste disposal methods', *Ecological Economics*, **50**(3–4), 207–31.

ECMT (2000), *Efficient Transport Taxes & Charges*, Paris: OECD/ECMT.

ECMT (2003), *Reforming Transport Taxes* (chapter 2), Paris: ECMT.

ECON (2000), 'Miljøkostnader ved avfallsbehandling (Environmental costs of waste treatment)', Report 85/00, Oslo (in Norwegian).

Ekins, P. and S. Dresner (2004), *Green Taxes and Charges. Reducing their Impact on Low-income Households*, York: Joseph Rowntree Foundation.

Fullerton, Don and Gilbert E. Metcalf (2001), 'Environmental rents, scarcity rents, and pre-existing distortions', *Journal of Public Economics*, **80**(2), 249–67.

Glaister, Stephen and Daniel J. Graham (2004), 'Pricing our roads: vision or reality?', London: The Institute of Economic Affairs.

Goulder, L.H., I.W.H. Parry, R.C. Williams and D. Burtraw (1999), 'The cost-effectiveness of alternative instruments for environmental protection in a second-best setting', *Journal of Public Economics*, **72**(3), 329–60.

Heinrich Böll Stiftung (2004), 'Ecotaxes in Germany and the United Kingdom – a business view', Report on a Conference hosted by Green Budget Germany in cooperation with The Heinrich Böll Foundation and the Anglo-German Foundation, available at www.eco-tax.info/2newsmit/index.html.

HM Customs and Excise (2004), 'Combining the government's two health and environment studies to calculate estimates for the external costs of landfill and incineration', HM Customs and Excise, London, available at http://customs.hmrc.gov.uk/channelsPortalWebApp/channelsPortalWebApp.portal?_nfpb=true&_pageLabel=pageVAT_ShowContent&id=HMCE_PROD_011566&propertType=document.

HM Treasury (2005), 'Protecting the environment', in *Budget 2005*, London: HM Treasury, available at www.hm-treasury.gov.uk/media/AA7/59/bud05_chap07_171.pdf.

Hoevenagel, Ruud, Edwin van Noort and Rene de Kok (1999), 'Study on a European Union wide regulatory framework for levies on pesticides', report commissioned by the European Commission, DG XI, available at http://europa.eu.int/comm/environment/enveco/taxation/eimstudy.pdf.

Martinsen, Torhild H. and Erik Vassnes (2004), 'Waste tax in Norway', in *Addressing the Economics of Waste*, Paris: OECD.

Muños Piña, Carlos (2004), 'Effects of an environmental tax on pesticides in Mexico', *UNEP Industry and Environment*, April – September, available at www.uneptie.org/division/media/review/vol27no2-3/530904_UNEP_BD. pdf.

Nash, Chris, Peter Bickel, Rainer Friedrich, Heike Link and Louise Steward (2002), 'The environmental impact of transport subsidies', prepared for the OECD Workshop on Environmentally Harmful Subsidies, 7–8 November 2002, Paris, http://interprod.oecd.org/agr/ehsw/index.htm.

Naturvårdsverket (2003), *Kväveoxidavgiften – ett effektivt styrmedel. Utvärdering av NO_X-avgiften* (Reducing NO_X emissions. An evaluation of the Nitrogen Oxide charge), includes extended summary in English, Stockholm: Swedish Environment Protection Agency, available at www.naturvardsverket.se/bokhandeln/pdf/620-5335-3.pdf.

Newbery, David Michael (2005), 'Road user and congestion charges', in Sijbren Cnossen (ed.), *Theory and Practice of Excise Taxation*, Oxford: Oxford University Press.

Nordic Council of Ministers (1999), 'The scope for Nordic co-ordination of economic instruments in environmental policy', TemaNord, 1999:550, Copenhagen: Nordic Council of Ministers.

Nordic Council of Ministers (2001), 'An evaluation of the impact of green taxes in the Nordic countries', TemaNord 2000:561, Copenhagen: Nordic Council of Ministers, available at www.norden.org/pub/ebook/2001-566.pdf.

Nordic Council of Ministers (2002), 'The use of economic instruments in Nordic environmental policy 1999–2001', TemaNord 2002:581, Copenhagen: Nordic Council of Ministers, available at www.norden.org/pub/ebook/2002-581.pdf.

OECD (1998), *Improving the Environment through Reducing Subsidies*, in three volumes, Paris: OECD.

OECD (2000), 'Behavioural responses to environmentally-related taxes', Paris: OECD, available at www.olis.oecd.org/olis/1999doc.nsf/LinkTo/com-env-epoc-daffe-cfa(99)111-final.

OECD (2001), *Environmentally-Related Taxation in OECD Countries: Issues and Strategies*, Paris: OECD.

OECD (2003a), *Agricultural Policies in OECD Countries: Monitoring and Evaluation*, Paris: OECD.

OECD (2003b), *Environmentally Harmful Subsidies: Policy Issues and Challenges*, Paris: OECD.

OECD (2003c), *Environmental Taxes and Competitiveness: An Overview of Issues, Policy Options and Research Needs*, Paris: OECD.

OECD (2003d), *Environmental Policy in the Steel Sector: Using Economic Instruments*, Paris: OECD, available at www.oecd.org/env/taxes.

OECD (2004a), *Addressing the Economics of Waste*, Paris: OECD.

OECD (2004b), *Environment and Employment: An Assessment*, Paris: OECD, available at http://appli1.oecd.org/olis/2003doc.nsf/linkto/env-epoc-wpnep(2003)11-final.

OECD (2005a) *Agricultural Policies in OECD Countries: Monitoring and Evaluation*, Paris: OECD.

OECD (2005b), *Review of Fisheries in OECD Countries: Policies and Summary Statistics*, Paris: OECD.

OECD (2005c), *OECD Environmental Data Compendium 2004*, Paris: OECD, table 6A.

OECD (2005d), *Environmental Performance Reviews: France*, Paris: OECD.

OECD (2005e), *The Window of Opportunity: How the Obstacles to the Introduction of the Swiss Heavy Goods Vehicle Fee Have Been Overcome*, Paris: OECD, available at www.oecd.org/env/taxes.

OECD (2005f), *The United Kingdom Climate Change Levy: A Study in Political Economy*, Paris: OECD, available at www.oecd.org/env/taxes.

OECD (2005g), *Environmentally Harmful Subsidies: Challenges for Reform*, Paris: OECD.

OECD (2006), *The Political Economy of Environmentally Related Taxes*, Paris: OECD.

Parry, I. and K.A. Small (2005), *Does Britain or the United States Have the Right Gasoline Tax? American Economic Review*, **95**(4). A previous version is available as Discussion Paper 02-12, Washington, DC: Resources for the Future, available online at www.rff.org/Documents/RFF-DP-02-12.pdf.

Riedinger, Nicolas (2005), 'Challenges and obstacles in French environmental taxation: recent developments', presentation made at the Workshop for Practitioners of Environmental Taxes and Charges, Vancouver, Canada, 17–18 March 2005.

Schou (2005), 'The Danish pesticide tax', presentation made at the Workshop for Practitioners of Environmental Taxes and Charges, Vancouver, Canada, 17–18 March 2005.

Smith, S. (1998), 'Distributional incidence of environmental taxes on energy and carbon: a review of policy issues', presented at the colloquy of the Ministry of the Environment and Regional Planning, 'Green tax reform and economic instruments for international cooperation: the post-Kyoto context', Toulouse, 13 May.

Swedish Environmental Protection Agency (1997), 'Environmental taxes in Sweden', Stockholm: Swedish Environmental Protection Agency.

Swedish Environmental Protection Agency (2000), 'The Swedish charge on nitrogen oxides – cost-effective emission reduction', Stockholm: Swedish Environmental Protection Agency, available at www.internat.naturvardsverket.se/documents/pollutants/nox/nox.pdf.

Vermeend, Willem and Jacob Van der Vaart (1998), *Greening Taxes: The Dutch Model*, Deventer: Kluwer.

3. Mid-course correction: toward a sustainable enterprise

Ray Anderson

THE SHAPE OF THE NEXT INDUSTRIAL REVOLUTION

On a Thursday in April 1996, I was in Boston on a panel speaking to 500 people. The subject was 'Planning for tomorrow', and the panel was about technology's role and impact on the strategic decisions companies make. The discussion was sponsored by the International Interior Designers Association. The audience was about one-third interior designers and two-thirds business people, including some of Interface's competitors.

While the subject of the discussion was technology, I think that the audience's understanding of the term probably had to do with the technology in the offices where most of them worked: information technology such as office automation, computers, email, radio mail, laptops, word processors, CADs, telephones, voice mail, video conferencing, faxes, Internet, intranets, websites, and so on. There is an infinite variety of gadgets, networks and servers that helps us do arithmetic faster and store, manipulate, retrieve, transmit, receive and examine information – in written, spoken, picture and virtual reality form. Technology gives us faster, surer information when, where and in whatever form we want it. Understanding the information and using it wisely, of course, is then up to you and me. Technology does not do that for us. We're on our own in developing the wisdom, knowledge and understanding to make the information useful.

That's my mental map of what most people – especially people who work in offices – think and mean when they talk about technology. But the definition of 'technology' in The American College Dictionary states:

1a. The application of science, especially to industrial or commercial objectives.
1b. The entire body of methods and materials used to achieve such industrial or commercial objectives.
2. The body of knowledge available to a civilization that is of use in fashioning implements, practicing manual arts and skills, and *extracting* [emphasis added] or collecting materials.

There's quite a lot there that we don't find if we just look in the office: technology that's not electronic, and not about storing, manipulating, sending, receiving and examining information. There's chemical, mechanical, electrical, civil, aeronautical and space technologies, construction, metallurgical, textile, nuclear, agricultural, automotive technologies, and now even biotechnology.

I illustrated the point for my Boston audience with an example: I told them that I run a manufacturing company that produced and sold $802 million worth of carpets, textiles, chemicals and architectural flooring in 1995 for commercial and institutional interiors. We have offices chock full of technology: mainframes, PCs, networks, you name it. And people who are hotelling and teaming, working anywhere, any time. Information technology makes it all possible, hooking us up around the world.

But we also operate factories that process raw materials into finished, manufactured products, and our raw material suppliers also operate factories. When we first examined the entire supply chain comprehensively, we found that in 1995 the technologies of our factories and our suppliers, together, extracted from the earth and processed 1.224 billion pounds of material so we could produce those $802 million worth of products – 1.224 billion pounds of materials from earth's stored natural capital. I asked for that calculation and when the answer came back, I was staggered.

Of the roughly 1.2 billion pounds, about 400 million pounds was relatively abundant inorganic materials, mostly mined from the earth's lithosphere (its crust), and 800 million pounds was petrobased, coming from either oil, coal, or natural gas. Roughly two-thirds of that 800 million pounds of irreplaceable, non-renewable, exhaustible, precious natural resource was burned up to produce the energy to convert the other one-third, along with the 400 million pounds of inorganic material, into products. That fossil fuel, with its complex, organic molecular structure, is gone forever – changed into carbon dioxide and other substances, many toxic, that were produced during combustion. These substances were dumped into the atmosphere to accumulate, and to contribute to global warming, to melting polar ice caps, and someday in the not-too-distant future to flooding coastal plains, such as much of Florida and, in the longer term, maybe even the streets of Boston, New York, London, New Orleans and other coastal cities. Meanwhile, we breathe what we burn to make our products and our livings.

Don't get me wrong. I let that Boston audience know that I appreciated their business! And that my company was committed to producing the best possible products to meet their specifications as efficiently as possible. But my company's technologies and those of every other company I know of anywhere, in their present forms, are plundering the earth. This cannot continue indefinitely.

However, is anyone accusing me? No! I stand convicted by myself, alone, and not by anyone else, as a plunderer of the earth. But no, not by our civilization's definition. By our civilization's definition, I am a captain of industry. In the eyes of many people, I'm a kind of modern day hero, an entrepreneur who founded a company that provides over 5000 people with jobs that support them, many of their spouses, and more than 10 000 children – altogether some 20 000 people. Those people depend on those factories that consumed those materials. Anyway, hasn't Interface paid fair market prices for every pound of material it has bought and processed? Doesn't the market govern?

Yes, but does the market's price cover the cost? Well, let's see. Who has paid for the military power that has been projected into the Middle East to protect the oil at its source? Why, you have, in your taxes. And who is paying for the damage done by storms, tornadoes, and hurricanes that result from global warming? Why you are, of course, in your insurance premiums. And who will pay for the losses in Florida and the cost of the flooded, abandoned streets of Boston, New York, New Orleans and London someday in the distant future? Future generations, your progeny, that's who. (Bill McDonough, former Dean of the School of Architecture at the University of Virginia, and a leading proponent of 'green' architectural design for many years, calls this 'intergenerational tyranny', the worst form of remote tyranny, a kind of taxation without representation across the generations, levied by us on those yet unborn.) And who pays for the diseases caused by the toxic emissions all around us? Guess! Do you see how the revered market system of the first industrial revolution allows companies like mine to shift those costs to others, to externalize those costs, even to future generations?

In other words, the market, in its pricing of exchange value without regard to cost or use value, is, at the very least, opportunistic and permissive, if not dishonest. It will allow the externalization of any cost that an unwary, uncaring, or gullible public will permit to be externalized – *caveat emptor* in a perverse kind of way.

Business writer Paul Hawken and architect Bill McDonough have called for 'the next industrial revolution', an idea that, as you can see, I have latched onto, because I agree with them that the first one is just not working out very well, even though I am as great a beneficiary of it as anyone.

To my mind, and I think many agree, Rachel Carson, with her landmark book, *Silent Spring*, started the next industrial revolution in 1962, by beginning the process of revealing that the first industrial revolution was ethically and intellectually heading for bankruptcy. Her exposure of the dangers of pesticides began to reveal the abuses of the modern industrial system.

So, by my own definition, I am a plunderer of the earth and a thief –
today, a legal thief. The perverse tax laws, by failing to correct the errant
market to internalize those externalities such as the costs of global
warming and pollution, are my accomplices in crime. I am part of the
endemic process that is going on at a frightening, accelerating rate worldwide to rob our children and all their descendents of their futures.

There is not an industrial company on earth, and – I feel pretty safe in
saying – not a company or institution of any kind that is sustainable, in the
sense of meeting its current needs without, in some measure, depriving
future generations of the means of meeting their needs. When the earth
runs out of finite, exhaustible resources and ecosystems collapse, our
descendants will be left holding the empty bag. Someday, people like me
may be put in jail. But maybe, just maybe, the changes that accompany the
next industrial revolution can keep my kind out of jail.

I have challenged the people of Interface to make our company the first
industrial company in the world to attain environmental sustainability, and
then to become restorative. To be restorative means to put back more than
we take, and to do good to the earth, not just no harm. The way to become
restorative, we think, is first to become sustainable ourselves and then to
help or influence others toward sustainability.

When we think of the technologies of the future, sustainability – this
issue of absolute, overriding importance for humankind – will depend on
and require what I believe are the really and truly vital technologies,
whether developed by us, our suppliers, or others like us; the technologies
of the next industrial revolution. I don't believe we can go back to pre-
industrial days; we must go on to a better industrial revolution than the last
one, and get it right this time.

But what does that mean? I have read Lester Thurow's view that we are
already in the third industrial revolution. He holds that the first was steam-
powered; the second, electricity-powered; making possible the third, which
is the information revolution, ushering in the information age. Clearly, all
three stages have emerged with vastly different characteristics, and it can be
argued that each was revolutionary in scope.

However, I take the view that they all share some fundamental characteristics that lump them together with an overarching, common theme.
They were and remain an unsustainable phase in civilization's development.
For example, someone still has to manufacture your 10-pound laptop computer, that icon of the information age. On an 'all-in' basis, counting everything processed and distilled into those 10 pounds, it weighs as much as
40 000 pounds, and its manufacturers, going all the way back to the mines
(for materials) and wellheads (for energy), created huge abuse to the earth
through extractive and polluting processes to make it. Not much has

changed over the years except the sophistication of the finished product. So I refer to all three of those stages collectively as the first industrial revolution, and I am calling for the next truly revolutionary industrial revolution. This time, to get it right, we must be certain it attains sustainability. We may not, as a species, have another chance. Time is short.

At Interface, we have undertaken a quest, first to become sustainable and then to become restorative. And we know, broadly, what it means for us. It's daunting. It means creating and adopting the technologies of the future – kinder, gentler technologies that emulate nature. That's where I think we will find the model.

Someone has said, 'A computer, now that's mundane; but a tree, that's technology!'. A tree operates on solar energy and lifts water in ways that seem to defy the laws of physics. When we understand how a whole forest works, and apply its myriad symbiotic relationships analogously to the design of industrial systems, we'll be on the right track. That track will lead us to technologies that will enable us, for example, to operate our factories on solar energy. A halfway house for us may be fuel cell or gas turbine technologies. But ultimately, I believe we have to learn to operate off current income the way a forest does and, for that matter, the way we do in our businesses and households; not off capital – stored natural capital – but off current energy income. Solar energy is current energy income, arriving daily at the speed of light and in inexhaustible abundance from that enormous fusion reactor just eight minutes away.

Those technologies of the future will enable us to feed our factories with recycled raw materials – closed loop, recycled raw materials that come from harvesting the billions of square yards of carpets and textiles that have already been made: nylon face pile recycled into new nylon yarn to be made into new carpet; backing material recycled into new backing material for new carpet; and, in our textile business, polyester fabrics recycled into polyester fiber, to be made into new fabrics, closing the loop. We will be able to use those precious organic molecules over and over in cyclical fashion, rather than sending them to landfills, or incinerating them, or down-cycling them into lower value forms by the linear processes of the first industrial revolution. Linear must go; cyclical must replace it. Cyclical is nature's way.

In nature, there is no waste; one organism's waste is another's food. For our industrial process, so dependent on petrochemical, man-made raw materials, this means 'technical food' to be reincarnated by recycling into the product's next life cycle, and the next. Of course, the recycling operations will have to be driven by renewable energy, too. Otherwise, we will consume more fossil fuel for the energy to recycle than we will save in virgin petrochemical raw materials by recycling in the first place. We want a gain, not a net loss.

But if we get it right during the next industrial revolution, we will never have to take another drop of oil from the earth for our products or industrial processes. That epitomizes my vision for Interface.

Those technologies of the future will enable us to send zero waste and scrap to the landfill. We're already well down this track at Interface. We have become disciplined and focused on what is sometimes called the 'low-hanging fruit', the easiest savings to realize. We named this effort QUEST, an acronym for Quality Utilizing Employees' Suggestions and Teamwork. In the first three-and-a-half years of this effort, we reduced total waste in our worldwide business by 40 per cent, which saved $67 million, and those savings are paying the bills for the rest of this revolution in our company. We are on our way to saving $80 million or more per year when we reach our goals. [Editor's note: By the end of 2005, waste savings had grown to $300 million, cumulatively.]

We're redesigning our products for greater resource efficiency, too; for example, we are producing carpets with lighter face weights (less pile) and better durability. It sounds paradoxical, but it's actually working, in a measurable way. We're making carpets with lower pile heights and higher densities, utilizing carpet face constructions that wear better in high traffic, but use fewer materials – a tiny, but important, step in 'de-materializing' business and industry, an intriguing aspect of the next industrial revolution. The embodied energy not used to produce the nylon not consumed is enough to power the entire factory making the redesigned products – ten times!

Those technologies of the future will enable us to operate without emitting anything into the air or water that hurts the ecosystem. We're just beginning to understand how incredibly difficult this will be, because the materials coming into our factories from our suppliers are replete with substances that never should have been taken from the earth's crust in the first place. But just imagine factories with no outlet pipes for effluent and no smokestacks because they don't need them! Paul Hawken and Bill McDonough were the first people I heard articulate this concept.

Those technologies of the future must enable us to get our people and products from Point A to Point B in resource-efficient fashion. In our company alone, at any hour of the day, we have more than 1000 people on the move, while trucks and ships (and sometimes planes) deliver our products all over the world. Part of the solution will be Rocky Mountain Institute physicist Amory Lovins' Hypercar. When this super lightweight, super aerodynamic Hypercar is using solar energy for electrolysis of water to extract hydrogen to power its fuel cells, and a flywheel, magnetically levitating at 100 000 rpm, in lieu of a battery, or an ultracapacitor with nothing moving and nothing to wear out, to store energy, including recapturing the energy generated in braking the car, with this energy going to power electric motors on each wheel without any drive train to waste energy, we'll be getting there with an important technology of the next industrial revolution.

To complement and reinforce these new technologies, we will continue to sensitize and engage all 5000 of our people in a common purpose, right down to the factory floor and right out there face to face with our customers, to do the thousands and thousands of little things – the environmentally sensitive things, energy saved here, pollution avoided there – that collectively are just as important as the five big technologies of the future: solar energy, closed loop recycling, zero waste, harmless emissions, and resource-efficient transportation.

Finally, I believe we must redesign commerce in the next industrial revolution, and redesign our role as manufacturers and suppliers of products and services. Already, we are forming alliances with the dealers and contractors that install and maintain our products. With these moves downstream into cooperative distribution, we are preparing to provide cyclical, 'cradle-to-cradle' (another term borrowed from Bill McDonough) service to our customers, to be involved with them beyond the life of our products, into the next product reincarnation, and the next. The distribution system will, through reverse logistics, become, as well, a collection and recycling system, keeping those precious molecules moving through successive product life cycles.

In our re-invented commercial system, carpet need not be bought or sold at all. Leasing carpet, rather than selling it, and being responsible for it cradle-to-cradle, is the future and the better way. Toward this end, we've created and offered to the market the Evergreen Service Agreement™, the first ever perpetual lease for carpet. We sell the services of the carpet: color, design, texture, warmth, acoustics, comfort under foot, cleanliness, and improved indoor air quality, but not the carpet itself. The customer pays by the month for these services. In this way we make carpet into what Michael Braungart, a German chemist and associate of Bill McDonough in McDonough Braungart Design Chemistry, terms a 'product of service', what Paul Hawken (1994) described as 'licensing' in *The Ecology of Commerce*, and what the President's Council on Sustainable Development (1996) calls 'extended product responsibility'. Walter Stahel (1982), Swiss engineer and economist, was perhaps the first person to conceptualize such a notion – the true 'service economy'.

Environmental sustainability, redefined for our purpose as taking nothing from the earth that is not naturally and rapidly renewable and doing no harm to the biosphere, is ambitious; it is a mountain to climb, but we've begun the climb. Each of the seven broad initiatives we've undertaken – the five areas of new technologies, plus sensitized people (the culture shift) and re-invented commerce – is a face of that mountain. Teams all through our company in manufacturing locations on four continents are working together on hundreds of projects and technologies that are taking us up those seven faces toward the summit–sustainability. We know we are on just the lowest slopes of that mountain, but we believe we have found the direction that leads upward.

As a compass to guide our people, we've embraced The Natural Step, the frame of reference conceived by Dr Karl-Henrik Robert (1991) of Sweden to define the system conditions of ecological sustainability. In the thousands and thousands of little things, The Natural Step is helping provide what we have termed the 'sensitivity hook-up' among our people, communities, customers and suppliers. We want to sensitize all our constituencies to the earth's needs and to what sustainability truly means to all of us. We want to engage all of them in an ecosystem of cooperation.

We started this whole effort in our company on two fronts: the first was focused on waste reduction. That's the revolution we call QUEST. It's our total quality management program, and more; the emphasis is broad. We define waste as any cost that goes into our product that does not produce value for our customers. Value, of course, embraces product quality, and more – aesthetics, utility, durability and resource-efficiency. Since in pursuit of maximum value any waste is bad, we're measuring progress against a zero-based waste goal. A revolutionary notion itself, our definition of waste includes not just off-quality and scrap (the traditional notion of waste); it also means anything else we don't do right the first time – a misdirected shipment, a mispriced invoice, a bad debt, and so forth. In QUEST there is no such thing as 'standard' waste or 'allowable' off-quality. QUEST is measured in hard dollars and, as I said, we took 40 per cent, or $67 million, out of our costs in three-and-a-half years. [Editor's reminder: through 2005, $300 million, cumulatively.] One quick result: scrap to the landfills from our factories is down 80 per cent since the beginning of QUEST in 1995; in some factories, more. Net greenhouse gas production for 2005 has declined 56 per cent in absolute tons of CO_2 equivalents, compared with the baseline year 1994.

We've also begun to realize that conceptually it might even be possible to take waste, by its current definition, below zero as measured against our 1994 benchmark. If we substitute one form of energy (solar) for another (fossil), or one form of material (recycled) for another (virgin), we are making systemic changes that create, in effect, negative waste when measured against the old norms. If successful, we will have replaced the old system, now obsolete and shown in comparison to have been wasteful all along, with the new, non-wasteful system. So, to give this new meaning to everyday activities, we have further changed our definition of waste in one category and declared all energy that is derived from fossil fuels to be waste, to be eliminated systematically, first through efficiency improvement and, eventually, to be replaced by renewable energy. Even the irreducible minimum of energy needed to drive our processes is waste by this definition, if it comes from non-renewable sources. QUEST is a revolution in operational philosophy.

The second parallel effort we've called EcoSense®. It focuses on those other four major categories, the technologies of the future, together with the thousands of little things and the redesign of commerce. Measurement is more difficult for EcoSense. We're dealing here with 'God's currency', not dollars, guilders, or pounds sterling – the field called EcoMetrics®. Here's an example of EcoMetrics: How do you evaluate the following hypothetical trade-off? One product consumes 10 pounds (per unit) of petrochemically-derived material, a non-renewable resource. Another, functionally and aesthetically identical to the first, consumes only six pounds, substituting four pounds of abundant, benign, inorganic material, but through the addition of a chlorinated paraffin. That chlorine could be the precursor of a deadly dioxin. How does one judge the true cost or value (which is it?) of that chlorinated paraffin – in God's currency? That's EcoMetrics. It's perplexing – a scale that weighs such diverse factors as toxic waste, dioxin potential, aquifer depletion, carbon dioxide emissions, habitat destruction, non-renewable resource depletion, and embodied energy. EcoMetrics: we need God's own yardstick, and wisdom, to help us measure where we are, which direction we're headed, and to tell us when we reach sustainability. Dollars and cents alone won't tell us.

In February 1996, we brought these two revolutionary efforts, QUEST and EcoSense, together. We merged the two task forces into one, and formed 18 teams with representatives from all of our businesses worldwide, each team with an assigned scope of investigation. This merger is integrating these closely related efforts and positively changing our corporate culture because it is making us think differently about who we are and what we do. As my associate, Dr Mike Bertolucci, says, 'It is as if you enter every room through a different door from the usual one, so different is the perspective from which you view every opportunity.' I call it 'piercing the veil' and finding on the other side a whole new world of opportunity and challenges. Today there are more than 400 projects, from persuading our landlord to install compact florescent light bulbs in our corporate headquarters office, to creating new, sustainable businesses within our company.

Other companies, different from ours, will have to pursue different technologies. I believe they must if they expect to survive in the next industrial revolution. In the twenty-first century, as the revolution gathers speed, the winners will be the resource-efficient. At whose expense will they win? At the expense of the resource-inefficient. Technology at its best, emulating nature, will eliminate the inefficient adapters.

Meanwhile, the argument goes on between technophiles and techno-phobes; one saying technology will save us, the other saying technology is the enemy. I believe the next industrial revolution will reconcile these opposing points of view, because there is another way to express the differences between the first industrial revolution and the next. The well-known environmental impact equation, popularized by Paul and Anne Ehrlich in their writings, declares that:

$$I = (P) \times (A) \times (T)$$

where I is negative environmental impact, P is population, A is affluence, and T is technology. An increase in P, A or T results in a greater environmental impact. Technology is part of the problem; this is the technophobes' position. But that is the technology of the first industrial revolution, call it T_1. Now the equation reads:

$$I = (P) \times (A) \times (T_1)$$

What a dilemma! T is not the answer. T will not lead us out of the environmental mess, no matter how vigorously the technophiles assert it will. The more technology we have, the greater the impact. Remember that '10-pound' laptop computer and the extractive, abusive processes that produced it?

But just what are the characteristics of T_1, the technologies of the first industrial revolution? For the most part, they are extractive, linear, fossil fuel-driven, focused on labor productivity, abusive and wasteful – the destructive, voracious, consuming technologies of the first industrial revolution. And they are unsustainable. They are consuming the earth.

But what if the characteristics of T were changed? Call it T_2 now, the technologies of the next industrial revolution. Let's say they were renewable, rather than extractive; cyclical (cradle to cradle), rather than linear; solar- or hydrogen-driven, rather than fossil fuel-driven; focused on resource productivity, rather than labor productivity; and benign in their effects on the biosphere, rather than abusive. And what if they emulated nature, where there is no waste?

Mightn't it then be possible to restate the environmental impact equation as:

$$I = (P \times A)/(T_2)$$

Then the technophiles, technophobes, industrialists and environmentalists could be aligned and allied in their efforts to reinvent industry and civilization. Move T from the numerator to the denominator and we change the world as we have known it. Now, the more technology the better (that is, less impact). Furthermore, it begins to put the billion unemployed people of the earth to work – working on increasing resource productivity, using an abundant resource – labor – to conserve diminishing natural resources. Technology becomes the friend of labor, not its enemy. Technology becomes part of the solution rather than part of the problem. Again, I credit Bill McDonough for this insight: T must move to the denominator.

What will drive technology from the numerator to the denominator? I believe getting the prices right is the biggest part of the answer; that means tax shifts and, perhaps, new financial instruments such as tradable emission credits, to make pollution cost the polluter – in effect, a carbon tax. In any event, it means eliminating the perverse incentives and getting the incentives right for innovation, correcting and redressing the market's fundamental dishonesty in externalizing societal costs, and harnessing honest, free market forces. If we can get the incentives right, entrepreneurs everywhere will thank Rachel Carson for starting it all. There are new fortunes to be made in the next industrial revolution.

But what in turn will drive the creation of tax shifts and other politically-derived financial instruments? It seems to me that those will ultimately be driven by a public with a high sense of ethics, morality, a deep-seated love of the earth, and a longing for harmony with nature. When the marketplace, the people, show their appreciation for these qualities and vote with their pocketbooks for the early adopters, the people will be leading; the 'good guys' will be winning in the marketplace and the polling booth; the rest of the political and business leaders will have to follow. As a politician once said, 'Show me a parade and I'll gladly get in front of it.' So will business and industry respond to the demands of this new marketplace, and the earth will gain a reprieve.

THE PROTOTYPICAL COMPANY OF THE TWENTY-FIRST CENTURY

What will the prototypical company of the twenty-first century look like? The company that I want Interface to become is the model for the sustainable enterprise of the next industrial revolution.

Figure 3.1 depicts a typical company of the twentieth century (and the early twenty-first century), such as Interface. The innermost circle, representing what exists within a company, contains people, capital and

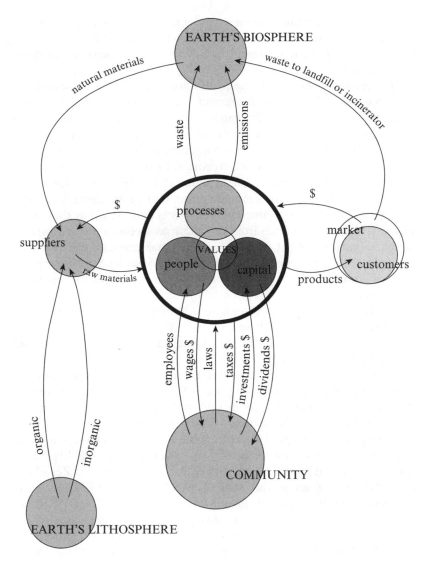

Figure 3.1   Typical company of the twentieth century

processes. Economists often put 'technology' where I have put 'processes'. To my mind, 'processes' is the broader word and the better choice. At the core are the company's values. The four elements vary specifically from company to company, but the general pattern holds for all.

But, of course, no company stands alone. Any company is connected to some important constituencies. In our case, Interface is part of a supply chain, with suppliers and customers and a market. Products flow through that supply chain in one direction; money flows in the other. But the supply chain doesn't stand alone either. It is connected to some other important constituencies.

Suppliers are dependent on the earth's lithosphere for organic and inorganic materials. A very small amount of our raw material is natural, coming from the biosphere. Our processes are, unfortunately, connected to the earth's biosphere by the waste streams and emissions we produce. And the products we make end up too often, at the ends of their useful lives, in landfills, or worse, in incinerators, creating a further pollution load for the earth's biosphere to digest. Carpet in a landfill will last 20 000 years.

We are connected to our community, too. Our people come from there, and their wages return to the community's economy; often they are its lifeblood. Our capital comes from the financial sector; if we are fortunate enough to earn sufficient profits, dividends and capital appreciation are returned to those investors, along with interest to our lenders. Government is part of community, too. We are connected to it through laws, regulations and the taxes we pay.

With these linkages in place, we have a description of almost every manufacturing company on earth and, by analogy, many other businesses and organizations. I have called this the Typical Company of the twentieth century. Interface, too, is just typical.

However, we are trying to transform Interface into something different, a sustainable industrial enterprise. I call that enterprise the Prototypical Company of the twenty-first century. How do we get there from here, and, in the process, pioneer the next industrial revolution?

We are pursuing the goal of creating the Prototypical Company of the twenty-first century simultaneously on seven fronts (see Figure 3.2) though we are at different stages with each. The first front is Zero Waste (Link #1). In pursuit of this goal to attack unwanted linkages to the biosphere, we have launched the effort we call QUEST. In QUEST, any waste is bad, and anything we don't do right the first time is waste. Against ideal operational standards – zero waste – we identified $70 million in waste, based on 1994 operations, representing 10 per cent of sales! We set out in 1995 on a mission to cut that in half by the end of 1997, then in half again and again with hundreds of active projects, until we approach zero waste.

When we get to zero waste, the savings will be much greater because our company will have continued to grow, and the opportunity will also have grown. Further, as we redesign our products to use less and less material and to last longer and longer, we are de-materializing the business and reducing the load on the biosphere at the end of the supply chain.

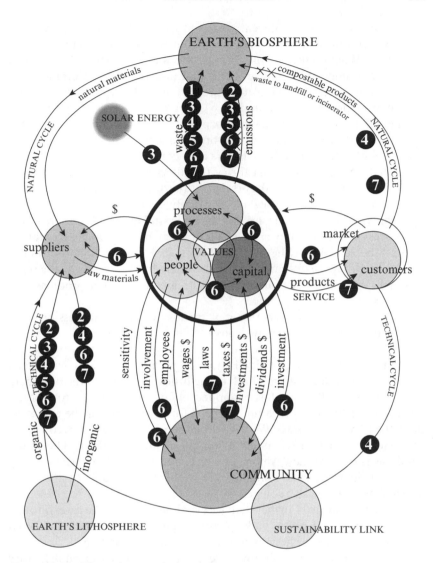

Figure 3.2   The redesign of commerce

The second front (see Link #2) is Benign Emissions, to attack another unwanted linkage to the biosphere. We have inventoried every stack and outlet pipe in our company, to see what is going out and how much of it there is, and we are reducing emissions daily. We have identified the world's most stringent regulatory standards anywhere and adopted them everywhere we operate.

But we know that to prevent toxic emissions altogether we must go upstream and prevent toxic substances from entering our factories in the first place. What comes in will go out, one way or another. We are just beginning to understand how difficult that undertaking is. Commercially available raw materials are replete with substances that violate the first and second principles of The Natural Step (Robert, 1991). Screening them out and remaining in business is a monumentally complicated undertaking. Yet we must. End-of-pipe solutions are unsustainable; they don't satisfy the principles of The Natural Step. Filters only concentrate the pollution, and then what do we do? We can't throw the filters away. There is no 'away'. Nothing is destroyed, under the first law of thermodynamics. It will just disperse, under the second law of thermodynamics. Stopping pollution upstream is what we must do, leaving the toxic stuff in the lithosphere where the process of evolution, over 3.85 billion years, put it to make way for us. It must be left there (the Natural Step's first system condition). Bill McDonough says that we must move the filters from the ends of the pipes to our brains, and focus our brains upstream to redesign products and processes.

The third front, Renewable Energy, means eventually harnessing solar energy. In the short term, maybe gas turbines will run our processes, but eventually we believe it must be photovoltaic (pv) or wind (a form of solar) or biomass-generated electricity. Harnessing renewable energy will attack numerous unwanted linkages, both to the lithosphere and to the biosphere (Link #3), and will allow closed loop recycling, the next front, to produce a net resource gain by obviating the need for fossil fuels for the energy to drive the recycling process. We have declared all fossil fuel-derived energy to be waste and targeted it for elimination under QUEST. The initial emphasis is on efficiency. Amory Lovins is our mentor. Only when energy usage is at its irreducible minimum are we likely to be able to afford the investments in renewable sources.

How far can we go? Further than we ever imagined! In one case, through resizing pumps and pipes, under Amory's guidance, we made a 12-fold reduction in connected horsepower for a key production line.

Our first application of photovoltaic (pv) power was in our Intek factory in Aberdeen, North Carolina. It was a nine kWp (kilowatt peak) unit that ran one 10 hp motor at a cost of 32 cents per kWh. (The cost was primarily depreciation on the capital investment.) A better use of the pv power was to peak shave electrical demand during the hottest part of the day when the air conditioning load was greatest, and realize an effective cost of 15 cents per kWh, still four times the cost of fossil fuel electricity. Because it's not cost-effective, the pv array is a symbolic token. Greater savings are coming from natural daylight reflectors that track the sun from horizon to horizon to light the plant with daylight; the tracking is driven by a fraction of the pv-generated power.

Yet, we are pressing on. The next pv project was a 127 kWp unit in southern California to produce the world's first Solar-made™ carpet. Solar-made™ sells; our specifier customers love the idea. Who cares if the energy costs a little more, if the product sells and helps the earth even a tiny bit? We're doing well and doing (a little bit of) good.

In Canada we contracted with Ontario Hydro for 'green power' (solar and wind). Even though it costs more, it's the right thing to do. Solar-made carpet sells in Canada, too.

The next front is Closing the Loop (Link #4), to introduce closed loop recycling. Look at the impact this has on unwanted linkages and see the new linkages that come into being. Two cycles are introduced: a natural, organic cycle, emphasizing natural raw materials and compostable products ('dust to dust') and a technical cycle, giving man-made materials and precious organic molecules life after life, through closed loop recycling. The 'sustainability link', the part of the technical cycle where closed loop recycling will happen, must be invented and developed. It will be difficult and expensive to do, and we cannot do it alone. We need our suppliers' help here most of all.

But look at the power of it! The supply of recycled rather than virgin molecules in the technical loop, analogous to the supply of money in an economic system, will affect directly the resource-efficient 'prosperity' of the enterprise. What if everybody did it? It would provide that rising tide that would lift the lowest on the economic scale, because recycling is labor-intensive. Labor for natural resources is a good trade-off that will get better as the prices of petro-resources get right.

This front goes hand in glove with the previous front, renewable energy. What's the gain if it takes more petro-stuff to create the process energy than is saved in virgin raw materials by recycling? If we can get both right, we'll never have to take another drop of oil from the earth. That's the goal. It epitomizes our vision, along with factories with no outlet pipes; except, unavoidably, the next front stands in the way.

Resource-Efficient Transportation, the fifth front (Link #5), is the front that is least within our control and the hardest for us to crack, especially with 100 per cent sustainability as the ultimate goal. We can video conference to avoid the unnecessary trip for a meeting, and we can drive the most efficient automobiles available. We can site our factories near the markets they serve, and plan logistics for maximum efficiency. But unless we choose to shut down contact with our customers and go out of business, we are dependent, as are most businesses, on the transportation industry.

The good news is, progress is being made – with hybrid gas/electric cars, jet engines powered by hydrogen (coming from biomass or, someday, water), and hydrogen fuel cells that are advancing in efficiency and cost reduction. Peter Russell's 'global brain' (Russell, 1995) is waking up, and the transportation industry is part of it. We need to speed the process. We need Amory Lovins' Hypercar. At the end of the day, we will have to resort to carbon offsets to completely resolve this one. We have already signed up with Trees for Travel, an organization planting trees in the rainforests and ecological 'hot spots' to close the gap. One tree over its life will sequester the carbon emitted in 4000 passenger miles of commercial air travel, but 2.6 trees must be planted for one to live to full growth. We expect to plant a lot of trees, one for every 1500 miles flown.

The Sensitivity Hookup, our sixth front (Link #6), spawns numerous desirable connections: service to the community through involvement and investment in the community (especially in education), closer relations among ourselves (inside the circle) to get all of us in alignment, and with suppliers and customers. (I use 'sensitivity' as Brian Swimme (1988) uses it in his book, *The Universe is a Green Dragon*, meaning heightened awareness brought about by absorbing a stimulus – an influence – and being changed in the process into a new person.)

This front leads to increases among all, including our communities by way of our people, in the awareness of and sensitivity to the thousands of little things each of us can do to inch toward sustainability, breaking unwanted linkages to the earth. Ties to the community, our suppliers and customers, and within our organization are all strengthened. We hope our customers will see their role and become engaged in helping us increase our leverage with our suppliers to bring them along.

Community is redefined to include all of the community of life; our people are becoming sensitized to their stewardship responsibility for the treasure of life in all its forms, as well as the earth's life support systems. So we've adopted streams and sponsored a television program to expose the plight of our own Chattahoochee River, one of Georgia's most polluted rivers. We're planting flower and vegetable gardens on our factory grounds and creating bird sanctuaries, too.

The Natural Step becomes our shared framework, our compass pointing the way, and a magnet, drawing us toward the summit of that mountain that is higher than Everest, called Sustainability: the ISO 14001 environmental management system is only a threshold – a given for all our factories. It will help us track our progress.

The seventh and final front (Link #7) calls for the redesign of commerce itself. Redesigning commerce probably hinges, more than anything else, on the acceptance of entirely new notions of economics, especially prices that reflect full costs. To us, it means shifting emphasis from simply selling products to providing services; thus, our commitment to downstream distribution, installation, maintenance and recycling. These are all aimed at forming cradle-to-cradle relationships with customers and suppliers, relationships based on delivering, via the Evergreen Service Agreement™, the services our products provide, in lieu of the products themselves. As a result, we further break the undesirable linkages to the lithosphere and the biosphere, those that deplete or damage. Another highly desired result is increasing market share at the expense of inefficient competitors. But full cost pricing is necessary if those salvaged molecules are to be, financially, worth salvaging to replace virgin petrochemicals.

Enlightened legislation might eventually shift taxes from good things we want to encourage, such as income and capital, to bad things we want to discourage such as pollution, waste and carbon dioxide emissions. What if perversity could once and for all be purged from the tax code? It must, for the next industrial revolution to put T (Technology) in the denominator. When the price of oil reflects its true cost, we intend to be ready. That would truly change the world as we have known it, especially the world of commerce.

Figure 3.3 portrays a simplified schematic of the Prototypical Company of the twenty-first century. What are its characteristics? It is strongly service-oriented, resource-efficient, wasting nothing, solar-driven, cyclical (no longer take–make–waste linear), strongly connected to our constituencies – our communities (building social equity), our customers, and our suppliers – and to one other. Our communities are stronger and better-educated, and the most qualified people are lining up to work for Interface. Customers prefer to deal with us, and suppliers embrace our vision.

Furthermore, this twenty-first century company is way ahead of the regulatory process, which has been made irrelevant. The company's values have shifted, too, and it is successfully committed to taking nothing from earth's lithosphere that's not rapidly and naturally renewable, and doing no harm to the biosphere. The undesirable linkages are gone!

Sustainable and just, giving social equity its appropriate priority, and creating sustainable prosperity; an example for all, this company is doing well by doing good. And it is growing, too; it is expanding its market share at the expense of inefficient adapters, those competitors that remain committed to the old, outdated paradigm and dependent on earth's stored natural capital, even when oil's price finally reflects its cost ($100–$200 per barrel, or more?). The growth is occurring while extracted throughput (materials from the mine and wellhead) is always declining, eventually to reach zero. Only zero extracted throughput is sustainable over evolutionary time.

It makes such absolute business sense to win this way; not at earth's expense, nor at our descendants' expense, but at the expense of inefficient competitors. Most importantly, we will have proven the feasibility of moving

T (Technology) from the numerator to the denominator, making technology part of the solution, and reducing environmental impact. If we can do that in a petro-intensive company such as Interface, anyone can do it. The next industrial revolution can be.

In that new era, the technophobes and technophiles, the interests of labor and capital, and the interests of nature and business will be reconciled. The

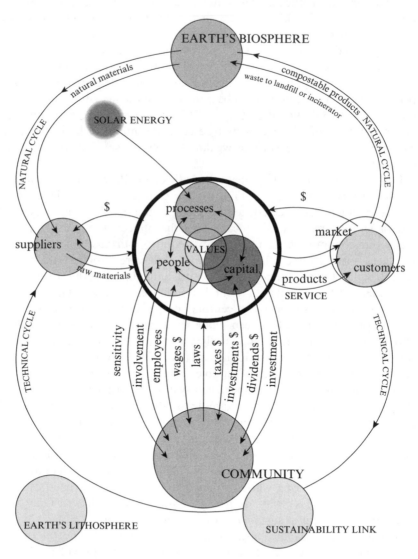

Figure 3.3   Prototypical company of the twenty-first century

Hegelian process of history – thesis, antithesis, synthesis – will lead to a sustainable society and world. The mindset behind the industrial system will have been transformed.

The tangible results of this seven-front assault at Interface are shown in Figures 3.4–3.11. It's a start, but the top of the mountain is a long way away.

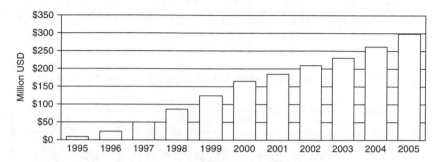

Figure 3.4   Cumulative avoided cost from waste elimination activities

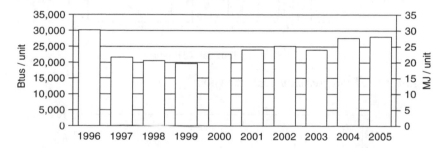

Figure 3.5   Total energy use: fabric manufacturing facilities (per linear yard)

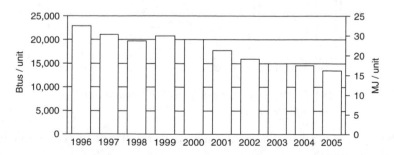

Figure 3.6   Total energy use: carpet manufacturing facilities (per square meter)

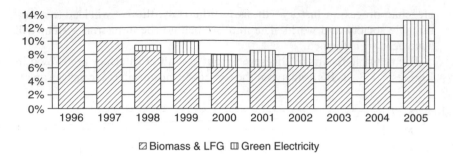

Figure 3.7   Energy from renewable sources (percentage of total energy)

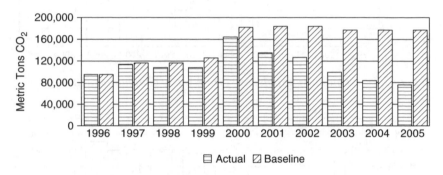

Figure 3.8   Total greenhouse gas emissions

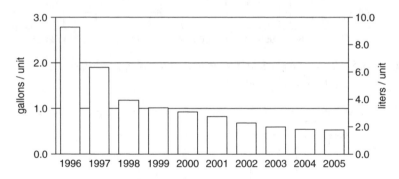

*Figure 3.9   Total water intake: modular carpet manufacturing
            (per square meter)*

The top means zero extracted throughput per dollar of sales and no harm to the biosphere.

Meanwhile, the new thinking and mindset is beginning to permeate everything we do, especially product design and development. In our textile

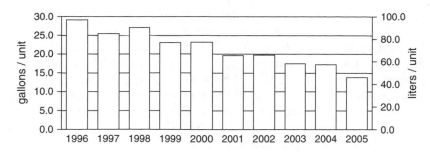

Figure 3.10   Total water intake: broadloom carpet manufacturing (per square meter)

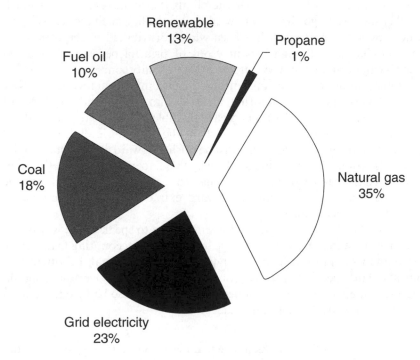

Figure 3.11   Total energy consumption by source in 2005

business, we've introduced fabrics produced from 100 per cent recycled polyester and shifted entire product lines from virgin to recycled fiber. This has been accomplished, but not without painstaking and excruciating effort on the part of ourselves and our suppliers. Further, we've initiated ReSku®, closing the materials flow loop for fabrics that are removed from furniture at the end of its first useful life. Fibers are seeing life after life. In our carpet tile business, a recent product introduction was inspired by Janine Benyus' book, *Biomimicry* (nature as inspiration, mentor and measure). How would nature design a floor covering? The result was a product we named 'Entropy'® It became the best seller faster than any other product ever has. We've also begun the transition to carbohydrate polymers from hydrocarbon polymers. Carbohydrate polymer, derived from corn, is beginning to replace hydrocarbon polymers, derived from fossil fuels, in both carpets and textiles.

Interface, Inc. made its first published progress report about sustainability to the public in November 1997, the *Interface Sustainability Report*. It described the problems of industrialism as we see them, the solutions we are pursuing, and where we are in our climb. It also makes clear how much farther we have to go. To our knowledge, it is the first such report ever produced by a corporation. It has been widely distributed to the company's stakeholders and, though it is now out of print, a perpetually updated report can be viewed at www.interfacesustainability.com.

Other things need to change during the next industrial revolution. New technologies and manufacturing methods, tax shifts and products of service are not enough. By every means possible, extractive throughput per unit of sales (gross domestic product on the national level, gross global product on the worldwide level) must be pushed toward zero. Sustainability depends ultimately on getting all the way there, to zero extractive throughput, given the perspective of evolutionary or geologic time and all the time yet to be. Again, we must remove the word 'extracting' from the dictionary's definition of technology.

In October 1996, I was invited to Amsterdam to speak to the worldwide partners' meeting of one of the large international accounting firms. Since accountants tend to be highly analytical and unemotional, I thought that my standard speech, which has considerable emotional overtones, should be augmented if I wanted to connect with this group. So I added these comments just for the Amsterdam audience:

> Now, what does this discussion have to do with you, your profession, and this meeting? I want to suggest that you and your profession are the scorekeepers in the game of business, but the rules of the game will change during the next industrial revolution; therefore, the method of scorekeeping will have to change, too, as business and commerce, and civilization, are re-invented. You could, with an early understanding of what might be, lead this change and help turn humankind from its course of self-destruction, unless, of course, you would rather just keep score as the world collapses around you. You could, for example, help to develop the field of EcoMetrics and help us understand God's currency, which certainly is not dollars or guilders, nor even pounds sterling.

I know that already you are faced with assessing environmental liabilities, but let's go further. For example, let us consider how we value assets today. Take a forest, a stand of trees. What is its value? I think most would say: x boardfeet of lumber at $y per boardfoot equals $z, less the cost of harvesting; that is the value.

But let me tell you a story about a small city on the banks of the Chattahoochee River in west-central Georgia in the United States, which in the first 100 years of its existence – through years of heavy rain and drought alike – never once experienced a flood. Then one year the banks of the river overflowed and $5 million of damage occurred. So the city fathers commissioned a dike to be built at a cost of $3 million, and that dike was sufficient to prevent flooding for five years. But then there was a season of especially hard rains, and the dike was breached, and the damage was $10 million this time. Therefore, the dike was rebuilt, higher this time, at a cost of $8 million, and the city was saved from flood for another seven years. And then the floods came higher still and the dike was breached again and someone finally said, 'What is going on here?'. So a team of experts was engaged to analyze the problem and one of the experts was an ecologist. And he, with brilliant insight, looked not at rainfall records, nor at dike construction, nor at laminar or turbulent flows of a river. He looked *upstream* and found that the forests for 50 miles upstream had been clear-cut over a period of 20 years and the clear-cutting had changed the hydrology of the area. Root systems no longer existed to hold the rainfall, so the rain ran off into the streams and rivers, eroding the land in the process and filling the river with silt and killing fish, too, depriving the poor people of the area of one source of sustenance, while flooding the plains downstream, including the unfortunate small city.

So, the question arises, 'What is the value of a forest?' The short-sightedness of conventional economics lies exposed. And I have not mentioned the value of a tree in removing carbon dioxide, a greenhouse gas, from the atmosphere, sequestering carbon, and producing oxygen for us to breathe, nor the songs of birds that are heard no more where the forests used to be. Neither have I mentioned the disease-spreading insects that now proliferate unchecked because the birds, their predators, are gone, resulting in an increase of encephalitis in the children in the region. So you see, there are serious questions to be raised about the traditional calculation of profit on the sale of the timber harvested from that clear-cut forest.

The ultimate solution to the flooding, pursued by our federal government in its dubious wisdom, was to build a dam at a cost of $100 million, which took 28 000 acres of prime agricultural land out of use and destroyed the habitat of uncounted creatures. Today the lake, thus created, is a polluted cesspool, collecting Atlanta's sewage. The value of a forest? Think again.

[*Though based on actual facts, the story is largely apocryphal and exaggerated, but I tell it for effect. I do know this river, though. As a boy I caught 20-pound channel catfish there that our family would eat for a week. Channel catfish no longer exist in the river.*]

Or, staying with assets, what is the value of a mine – say a uranium mine – that at first blush would seem to be highly treasured? But on second thought, when we consider the cost of the nuclear clean-up that earth faces, somewhere between $300 billion and $900 billion, depending on just how bad the Russian and Ukrainian situations turn out to be, uranium somehow seems not to be so valuable any more. Think of the liability we have transferred to future generations! Enlightened accounting would figure out how to incorporate that liability into the evaluation of that mining asset today.

Let's look at Gross Domestic Product (GDP) for another exercise in new vs. old economics. Consider, for example, that the Exxon Valdez disaster in Prince William Sound *added* to GDP. Reflect also on the absurdity of the fact that the medical expenses for a child dying of environmentally-related cancer *add* to GDP. And that the costs to clean up and rebuild after a hurricane exacerbated by global warming also *add* to GDP. Clearly, as a measure of standard of living, much less as a measure of progress or well-being, GDP is sorely lacking.

I spoke earlier about the cost of a barrel of oil, compared with its price, and how the market is oblivious to the notion of external costs, both those passed on to our neighbors and those passed on to our grandchildren, what I've called intergenerational tyranny. We must think more about discount rates. Perhaps they should be negative, increasing the present value of future liabilities, rather than decreasing them. The earth cries out for a carbon tax to increase the price of fossil fuels to internalize the societal costs of military power in the Middle East and global warming, and thus hasten the development of alternative energy sources.

Herman Daly, an economist at the University of Maryland, has been considered a heretic by mainstream economists for years. Daly criticizes conventional economics as 'empty world' economics and the economics of 'unlimited resources' in what's clearly an emerging era of a 'full world' with physical constraints and finite resources. Daly thinks that economics must recognize reality and acknowledge that earth's capacity to provide and endure is, in fact, limited and not infinite. People are now listening to him, even those who once derided him.

I think you should rethink economics and accounting. I urge you to think about EcoMetrics, to join the search for God's currency. Talk with Herman Daly. Change is coming. Change creates opportunity. A growing number of companies are beginning to think differently about their scorekeeping. It's just a matter of time until all will have to. You could lead the way in this, and you should – for earth's sake and for our grandchildren's sakes.

I could not tell from the immediate feedback whether I did, in fact, connect with that audience. There were a lot of stony faces; it would be unkind to describe them as blank. Afterward, there was just one request for a copy of my speech. I suppose time will tell; one never knows when a seed has taken root. The head of the firm did write to me to say that my thoughts would not be ignored. I took great heart from that.

BIBLIOGRAPHY

Anderson, Ray, Charlie Eitel and J. Zink (1996), *Face It: A Spiritual Journey of Leadership*, Peregrinzilla Press.
Bailey, Ronald (ed.) (1995), *The True State of the Planet*, Free Press.
Bast, Joseph L., Peter J. Hill and Richard C. Rue (1994), *Eco-Sanity: A Common-Sense Guide to Environmentalism*, Madison Books.
Brower, David (1995), *Let the Mountains Talk, Let the Rivers Run: A Call to Those Who Would Save the Earth*, San Francisco: Harper.

Brown, Lester R. (1998), *State of the World 1998: A Worldwatch Institute Report on Progress Toward a Sustainable Society*, W.W. Norton & Company.

Brown, Lester R. (various years) *Vital Signs; The Trends That are Shaping Our Future*, World Watch Institute, W.W. Norton & Company.

Capra, Fritjof (1988), *The Turning Point: Science, Society, and the Rising Culture*, Bantam Doubleday Dell Publishers.

Carson, Rachel (1962; 1993 reissue), *Silent Spring*, Houghton Mifflin Company.

Daly, Herman and John Cobb (1994), *For the Common Good*, Beacon Publishers.

Ehrlich, Paul (1997), *The Population Bomb*, Buccaneer Books.

Eitel, Charlie (1995), *Eitel Time: Turnaround Secrets*, The Peregrinzilla Press.

Eitel, Charlie (1998), *Mapping Your Legacy, A Hook-It-Up Journey*, The Peregrinzilla Press.

Goleman, Daniel P. (1997), *Emotional Intelligence*, Bantam Books.

Gore, Al (1993), *Earth in the Balance: Ecology and the Human Spirit*, Plume.

Hartmann, William K. and Ron Miller (1991), *The History of Earth: An Illustrated Chronicle of an Evolving Planet*, Workman Publishing Company.

Hawken, Paul (1983), *The Next Economy*, Holt, Reinhart, and Winston.

Hawken, Paul (1994), *The Ecology of Commerce: A Declaration of Sustainability*, Harper Business.

Hawken, Paul, Amory Lovins and Hunter Lovins (1999), *Natural Capitalism*, Little Brown & Company.

Kant, Immanuel (1788), *The Critique of Practical Reason*,

Maslow, Abraham (1987), *Motivation and Personality*, Addison-Wesley Publishing Company.

McDonough, William (1993), 'A centennial sermon, design, ecology, ethics and the making of things', The Cathedral of St. John the Divine, New York, 7 February.

McDonough, William (1995), *The William McDonough Collection*, DesignTex Environmentally Intelligent Textiles.

McDonough, William, Architects (1992), *The Hannover Principles Design for Sustainability*, Papercraft.

Meadows, Donella H. (1997), 'Places to intervene in a system (in increasing order of effectiveness)', *Whole Earth*, Fall, p. 78.

Meadows, Donella H., Dennis L. Meadows and Jorgen Randers (1993), *Beyond the Limits: Confronting Global Collapse, Envisioning a Sustainable Future*, Chelsea Green Publishing Co.

The President's Council on Sustainable Development (1996), *Sustainable America, A New Consensus*.

Quinn, Daniel (1993), *Ishmael*, Bantam Books.

Quinn, Daniel (1997a), *My Ishmael: A Sequel*, Bantam Books.

Quinn, Daniel (1997b), *The Story of B*, Bantam Books.

Robert, Karl-Henrik (1991), 'Educating a nation: the natural step', in *Context*, No. 28, Spring, p. 10.

Robert, Karl-Henrik, Herman Daly, Paul Hawken and John Holmburg (1996), 'A compass for sustainable development', *The Natural Step News*, No. 1, Winter, p. 3.

Romm, Joseph J. (1994), *Lean and Clean Management: How to Boost Profits and Productivity by Reducing Pollution*, Kodansha.

Russell, Peter (1995), *The Global Brain Awakens: Our Next Evolutionary Leap*, Global Brain.

Stahel, Walter R. (1982), *The Product Life Factor*, The Houston Area Research Center.

Swimme, Brian (1988), *The Universe is a Green Dragon: A Cosmic Creation Story*, Bear & Co.

Thomas, Glenn C. (1996), 'Tomorrow's Child', all rights reserved, reprinted with permission.

Thurow, Lester C. (1997), 'Brains power business growth', *USA Today*, 18 August, p. 13A.

PART III

Challenges within specific resource domains

PART II

Introduction

This section focuses on six critical challenges to sustainable development: the energy–environment nexus, most particularly the impact of energy production and consumption on global climate; the preservation of human health in a rapidly industrializing world; and emerging threats to global fisheries, agriculture, biodiversity and forestry. In many respects, how we use energy may pose both the greatest threat to, yet greatest promise of, sustainable development. Energy utilization is fundamentally a double-edged sword. The advent of the era of non-renewable fossil fuels has permitted the rapid acceleration of industrial activity in the developed world, and has facilitated the attainment of unprecedented levels of human affluence. Yet, energy production and consumption represents the most significant anthropogenic impact on the integrity of the global environment – including, *inter alia*, acid rain, photochemical smog, stratospheric ozone depletion, and the greenhouse effect.

While much has been made of the geopolitical implications of possible oil and natural gas depletion, the issue of medium-term energy supply and security may not be critical, as global supplies of coal are sufficient to meet rising industrial demand for several generations. The decisive issue is one of achieving a rate of energy utilization that does not make the earth increasingly uninhabitable through global climate change.

It is the position of Burton Richter, Nobel Laureate in physics, that there is no short-term solution to this problem (Chapter 4). In his view, a mixed strategy must be adopted which encompasses increased energy conservation and efficiency, emission trading, reforestation and intensified R&D on renewables, fuel cells and hydrogen systems. To Richter, a fundamental component of this transition strategy must be nuclear power, despite the widespread concern over the safety of reactor operation and storage of radiological waste. The author concludes that a hybrid technological–economic approach is the most desirable:

> Action is required. Surely the economists and politicians can design an incentive system that would encourage entrepreneurial innovation. To a physicist it is easy; a carbon tax would do the job quite effectively, discouraging the most polluting fuels and encouraging the least polluting. A waste disposal charge, like that imposed on nuclear power, would do well also and could raise considerable money.

Unfortunately, the 'Faustian bargain' first articulated by Alvin Weinberg (1972) when commercial nuclear power first became established in the 1950s remains with us today: our inability to devise a successful technology to isolate atomic wastes from humanity for periods in excess of 25 000 to 100 000 years. Weinberg mentioned the necessity of creating a 'nuclear priesthood' of experts devoted to sheltering humanity from exposure to nuclear wastes over time periods far in excess of the historical lifetimes of stable governments and civilizations.

While the implications of increasing energy use and consequent global warming have been extensively studied in many resource sectors, one area which has only recently been addressed is that of human health. The linkages which define the global warming–human health nexus are numerous, indirect and complex. Clyde Hertzman, an epidemiologist, poses the specific question in Chapter 5 concerning whether 'wealthy societies [can] maintain their health status while consuming less of the world's "photosynthetic resources".' Drawing on his extensive research for the World Bank on environment–health–economy linkages throughout the world, the author concludes that:

> Wealthy societies consume too much of the world's resources, and need to cut back. In principal, this can be done without sacrificing human health. There are examples of societies that consume at globally sustainable levels and maintain a health status that is similar to ours. We know that the principal determinants of health in wealthy societies reside, broadly speaking, in the social environment. But do we know how to reduce our levels of consumption without sacrificing those aspects of our society that are health-giving? At present, the answer is a qualified 'yes', but we are steadily gaining insights that are changing the answer to an unqualified 'yes'.

The logical corollary of this conclusion is that it is ultimately in the best interests of the developed world to transfer sufficient resources to developing nations in order to achieve acceptable levels of health in the Third World, irrespective of the obvious issues of ethics and equity. Global warming and globalization threaten to facilitate the transfer of dangerous pathogens to the developed nations (Garrett, 1994) from what has been called a vast biotic sea of 'human Petri dishes' (*New York Times*, 1994).

The historical forces which have facilitated the spawning and spread of epidemic and pandemic diseases since the time of the Agricultural Revolution – population density, human–animal interactions, large groups of vulnerable individuals, the international movement of goods and people – are even more relevant today than ever (see, for example, Garrett, 2000).

While the maintenance of standards of human health will be extremely challenging in a dynamically changing global environment, the outlook for the maintenance of food supplies from global fisheries resources is even less sanguine. In many respects, fisheries is an archetypal example of the failure of sustainable management of a resource critical to human survival. Ironically, the magnitude of this failure has only become apparent in the last decade due, in no small part, to the pioneering research of Daniel Pauly (Pauly and Maclean, 2003; Pauly et al., 1998) who has shaken the foundations of much of current fisheries theory and management. Through a series of scientific publications detailing a phenomenon he has termed 'fishing down the food web', Pauly has exposed the ongoing loss of global fisheries resources in a time when others had considered these resources to be stabilized or growing. In Chapter 6, with co-author Ratana Chuenpagdee, Pauly outlines the nature and magnitude of the problem and concludes with five policy prescriptions aimed at rescuing global fisheries resources from extinction. The authors observe that:

> Despite encouraging noises. . . . we cannot at present conceive of the societal framework within which these issues would be seriously addressed and some of the mitigating approaches mentioned above implemented. As is the case for the issue of global warming . . . , these issues will not go away, and the underlying trends, notably a declining fisheries catch, will worsen until they are effectively addressed. Capacity building at the local level, particularly for alternative employment, and an education and public awareness program for marine conservation and stewardship are two initiatives that need active promotion and firm support from all government levels and governance institutes as they are promising means that can help alleviate the current fisheries crises.

In contrast to the momentous difficulties facing fisheries management, land-based food production, in the form of the North American agricultural system, has been considered the model of efficiency, providing bountiful harvests not only for its own citizens but also for many less well endowed nations of the world. Yet, this system, referred to as 'industrial agriculture', represents in many respects the antithesis of sustainable development. The illusion of efficiency rests upon an exceptionally narrow concept of system boundaries. The paradox of industrial agriculture is the result of a pervasive market failure which has failed to internalize both temporal and spatial externalities. In toto, the social costs contained within the total boundary which encompasses the industrial agricultural system and all its offsite and temporal effects suggest that this model of 'efficiency' with its harvest of 'inexpensive' food is fundamentally unsustainable (see Figures III.1 and III.2).

In Chapter 7, Miguel Altieri details the 'ecological tragedy of modern agriculture' by focusing in particular on the impacts of monoculture, transgenic

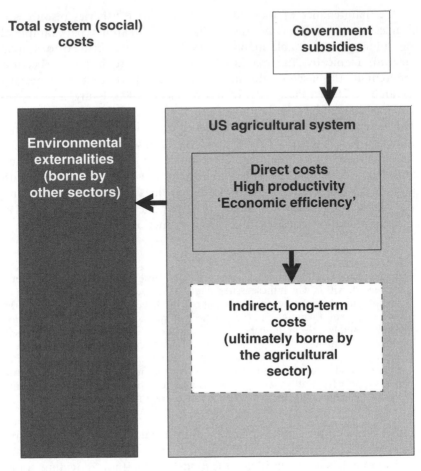

Figure III.1   Agricultural systems boundaries

crops and genetic homogenization on ecological vulnerability and social structures. He advances the cause of *agroecology*, an alternative strategy, in both the developed and developing world:

> In general, data show that over time agroecological systems exhibit more stable levels of total production per unit area than high-input systems; produce economically favorable rates of return; provide a return to labor and other inputs sufficient for a livelihood acceptable to small farmers and their families; and ensure soil protection and conservation as well as enhanced biodiversity. In North America and Europe, researchers have demonstrated in commercial systems that it is possible to provide a balanced environment, sustained yields, biologically-mediated soil fertility and natural pest regulation

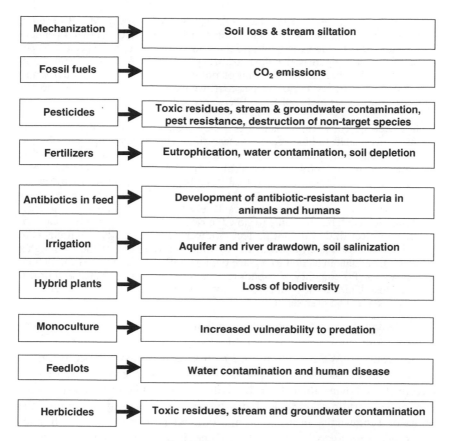

Figure III.2 Agricultural spatial and temporal externalities

through the design of diversified agroecosystems and the use of low-input technologies. Many alternative cropping systems have been tested, such as double cropping, strip cropping, cover cropping and intercropping. More importantly, concrete examples from real farmers show that such systems lead to optimal recycling of nutrients and organic matter turnover, closed energy flows, water and soil conservation and balanced pest-natural enemy populations.

The concept of biodiversity encompasses numerous resource domains, and it is in this area that some of the most flagrant examples of the counterproductive effects of conventional wisdom with respect to sustainability are most apparent. As Anthony Sinclair observes in Chapter 8,

In 1984 Jeff McNeely and colleagues at the International Union for the Conservation of Nature reported that 4 per cent of the world habitats had been put aside in reserves. In 1987 the Prime Minister of Norway, Mrs Bruntlund, wrote a report for the United Nations in which she commented that 4 per cent was not enough, and we should save three times that amount, hence the 12 per cent figure. This figure is, therefore, arbitrary and has no biological justification. Yet, it has now become the set point of politics, written in stone. In addition to the biological irrelevance of 12 per cent, we have the problem that we do not know what 12 per cent applies to. Twelve per cent of what?

. . .

In reviewing conservation activities I have considered a number of simple questions related to biodiversity preservation. The answers appeared obvious until we started to think about them and then we realized that there are some extremely thorny problems to deal with. Indeed some problems seem intractable. . . . Conservation has traditionally protected biodiversity by setting up reserves. There is ample evidence to show that all reserves in the world are presently in a state of decline as a result of attrition from human interference. Reserves, therefore, serve only to slow the rate of decay compared to areas that are unprotected; they do not protect biodiversity forever as is commonly conceived. Reserves merely allow us to buy time to reverse the attrition through a policy of adding in habitat to replace the lost portions – a process I call habitat renewal. So far no policy of habitat renewal has been contemplated and time is being lost. Unless such a policy is instituted we will lose as much biodiversity as if no reserves had been set up.

Biodiversity presents a complex challenge to operationalizing sustainable development because of the difficulty of assigning an economic value to this concept (WRI, 2005, p. 6). From a reductionist perspective, marginal losses of biodiversity appear to have almost zero costs, thereby effectively removing them from the calculus of public and private sector economic decision-making. Perhaps the most effective way of framing the value of biodiversity in an economic context is to borrow from finance theory where a diversified portfolio reduces investment risk. This parallels ecological research which has demonstrated that diverse ecosystems are more resilient (Peterson et al., 1998).

The last natural resource considered in this part – forestry – is arguably the keystone species of many ecological systems. It is in this domain that the extraordinary complexity of sustainable resource management is most evident. Figure III.3 portrays a simplified representation of the potential impact of loss of forest cover on a diverse range of other tightly linked ecological resources. In essence, the decimation of forest cover can represent a 'tipping point' where its cascading effects can have a devastating impact on a region's or country's economic, political and social stability, or even viability. It is clear that the preservation of sufficient global forest cover is the absolute *sine qua non* of global sustainable development.

The recent history of sustainable forest management is one of remarkable contrasts. At one end of the spectrum is the continuing destruction of

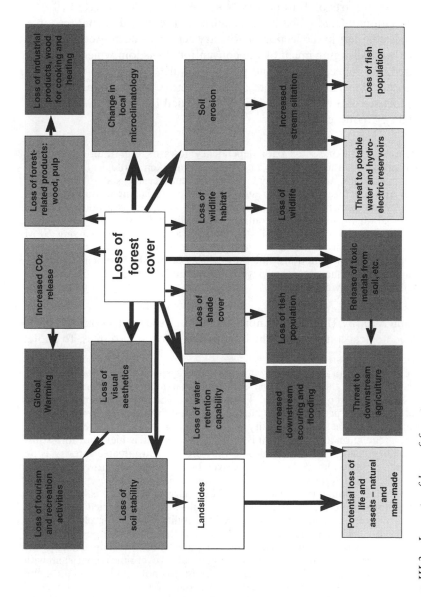

Figure III.3   Impacts of loss of forest cover

vast tracts of tropical forests in South America and Southeast Asia threatening biological diversity, water quality and global climate stability. At the other end is the relatively successful efforts to achieve sustainable forest production in parts of Europe and North America. A concerted effort – locally, nationally and globally – is required to preserve this vital resource. The three chapters in the section on forestry demonstrate how complex this goal is, by challenging much of the conventional wisdom which has characterized our conceptions of and policies towards forest resources in the last century. Jane Lister provides an introductory overview in Chapter 9 which focuses on five myths which have impeded the achievement of sustainability. To quote:

> There is a 'stickiness' or path dependency towards the traditional timber management paradigm that is anchored in mistaken ecological, social and economic assumptions and re-enforcing, rigid market and state-based institutions and organizations. As a result, assumptions inherent in the traditional timber management paradigm, while generally accepted as invalid under the SFM paradigm, nevertheless continue to misdirect forest management decisions. Five of these 'mythical' assumptions and the accompanying SFM reality are . . . discussed in . . . [this] chapter. A hope is that by explicitly revealing these assumptions, not only will a set of SFM principles become clear, but also the accompanying challenge and necessity for institutional change will be evident.

Chapter 10, by Hamish Kimmins, examines in greater depth the often subtle ecological complexities which characterize forest resources. To quote:

> The assessment of sustainability of biophysical systems is both time and space dependent. Whether or not one concludes that a forest is being sustained depends as much or more on the spatial scale at which the assessment is made and on the time period that is included as it does on the actual trends in forest values. Unless the full complexity of the question is explicitly recognized in policy, regulation and practice, it is unlikely that we will achieve our forest sustainability goals; whatever we decide they are. . . . Sustainable forestry is an imperative, not a choice. The need is driven by the inexorable growth in human numbers and deterioration of the global environment. However, it is much easier to talk about it than to achieve it. This is largely because it is such a multi-dimensional concept. There are so many values to be sustained at so many different temporal and spatial scales. Sustainability does not imply constancy over time . . . The challenge is to decide at what spatial and temporal scales we will evaluate sustainability, what balance of values is to be sustained in any particular forest, and what pattern of variation in values over time is consistent with the concept of sustainability. Sustainable forestry is not simply a technical and scientific issue; although to be sustainable, forestry must be well founded in science and use appropriate technologies. Sustainable forestry is also a political, social, cultural and economic issue. Only if all the dimensions of sustainability

are considered will we be able to develop land-use plans and management methods that achieve this laudable but often elusive goal.

In many respects, the most pressing issues in forestry today find their sharpest focus in the Third World where tropical and semi-tropical forests are under increasing pressure from both international commercial interests and local populations struggling to survive at subsistence levels. With expected growth in population, industrialization and accompanying pressure on the land base, forests of Africa, Asia and Latin America increasingly bear the ultimate burden of feeding the population, assisting in the creation of national wealth, and safeguarding the global climate. The third chapter on forestry issues (Chapter 11) challenges the conventional wisdom among foresters and many development economists that plantation forestry in developing nations is economically preferable to natural forest management. Using a case study from Indonesia, Roger Sedjo finds that 'the financial returns to natural forest management systems can be much more favorable than is commonly believed, and . . . financial returns to natural forest management are comparable to those likely to accrue to plantation forests in many situations that are common in the Asia-Pacific region.' In light of these findings, Sedjo asks the central question, 'why isn't natural forestry practiced more often?', and offers three answers:

> governments frequently undertake inappropriate policies related to their natural resources, often, in effect, promoting economically and ecologically inferior projects. These policies fail to value properly the timber resource as well as the environmental and other non-timber benefits provided by the forest. . . . Furthermore . . . concession agreements typically are provided for too short a period of time to provide the firms with incentives to take a long-term view toward the management and sustainability of the resource. . . . A final speculation as to the apparent preference of non-economic plantation forestry over natural tropical forest management is consistent with the well-known preference of the large international development banks for large over smaller projects.

REFERENCES

Garrett, Laurie (1994), *The Coming Plague. Newly Emerging Diseases in a World Out of Balance*, New York: Farrar, Straus and Giroux.

Garrett, Laurie (2000), *Betrayal of Trust. The Collapse of Global Public Health*, New York: Hyperion.

New York Times (1994), 'Panic everywhere', book review of *The Coming Plague. Newly Emerging Diseases in a World Out of Balance*, by Laurie Garrett, 30 October.

Pauly, Daniel and Jay Maclean (2003), *In a Perfect Ocean. The State of Fisheries and Ecosystems in the North Atlantic Ocean*, Washington, DC: Island Press.

Pauly, D., V. Christensen, J. Dalsgaard, R. Froese and F.C. Torres Jr (1998), 'Fishing down marine food webs', *Science*, 279, 860–63.
Peterson, Garry, Craig R. Allen and C.S. Holling (1998), 'Ecological resilience, biodiversity, and scale', *Ecosystems*, 1, 6–18.
Weinberg, Alvin M. (1972), 'Social institutions and nuclear energy', *Science*, 7 January, pp. 27–34.
World Resources Institute (WRI) (2005), *Ecosystems and Human Well-Being. Biodiversity Synthesis*, Millennium Ecosystem Assessment, published for the United Nations.

SECTION A

Energy and global climate

4. Reconciling global warming and increasing energy demand

Burton Richter

INTRODUCTION

Economic activity and energy use are closely coupled. Today the yearly increase in economic activity is larger than the totality of world economic activity of 200 years ago; the population is huge compared to then and will continue to increase; and the energy we now use affects the world's entire environment in many ways. This is the source of the global warming problem.

Large-scale, anthropogenic environment problems have happened before and governments have responded collectively to the dangers. More than 30 years ago Rachel Carlson's famous book, 'Silent Spring', awoke us to the dangers of DDT, and DDT was phased out. More recently, scientific evidence showing depletion of ozone over the Antarctic (the ozone hole) resulted in the Montreal Treaty phasing out chlorofluorocarbons. The response to these two environmental problems was relatively easy because the economic impact of the required response was limited.

We now face a more complex problem, global climate change. Response to this problem will be much more difficult because its source is the carbon-based energy systems (oil, gas and coal) that drive our economy. This issue first leaped into the consciousness of governments at the 1992 World Summit in Rio de Janeiro, although it had been worrying the scientific community for 40 years. We know that energy use is coupled to economic development. A growing population in the developing world aspires to a standard of living approaching that of the rich nations, and this requires that energy use increase.

The greenhouse gases emitted in energy production drive global warming, and limiting global warming requires that the use of carbon-based fuels decrease at the same time that energy use increases. This can be done, in principle, by using a combination of conservation and efficiency and carbon-free energy sources; renewables (hydropower, wind, geothermal, biomass, solar), fusion and nuclear. However, the nations of the world have yet to make a real start on the necessary changes. The not yet ratified Kyoto Protocol is only the barest of beginnings. Here I want to discuss the problem, the numbers, the options and conclude with some recommendations.

THE PROBLEM

The picture of the earth taken by the Apollo astronauts on their way to the moon has, I believe, had a profound effect on thinking about global ecology. This picture shows our world hanging in a black void, our nearest neighbor a dead moon 240 000 miles away, and no signs of life anywhere else in our solar system. We live on a thin skin on our world about 13 miles thick from the top of the highest mountain to the depths of the deepest ocean, tiny compared to our world's 8000-mile diameter. It is what we put into this thin skin that is responsible for global climate change.

The scientific evidence for climate change is clear. The last 100 years has seen a rapid increase in temperature (Figure 4.1) that is unprecedented and which tracks the increase in greenhouse gases that we have put into our atmosphere mainly from carbon-based fuels. The evidence comes from actual temperature data, growth rings in trees, gas bubbles trapped in glaciers, coral reefs, and so on. The 1990s were the warmest decade in recorded history, and there is more carbon dioxide in the atmosphere now than has been there in the last 400 000 years.

After the Rio de Janeiro World Summit, governments set up the Intergovernmental Panel on Climate Change (IPCC) to analyze the problem. The scientific community, led by the IPCC, has been working to predict the consequences of the increasing level of greenhouse gases. Modeling the world climate system is complex because of the interaction of the atmosphere, landmasses, and the oceans, but the models continue to improve and now give a quite reasonable agreement with what has happened in the past (Figure 4.2). Using the newest models to predict the future (Figure 4.3) gives a 'business as usual' expectation that by the year 2100 the world average temperature will have increased by something between 3.5°C and 6°C, and that this increase will be smaller near the equator and higher near the poles.

Such a large temperature increase would be very bad. The oceans will rise from one to two meters, driven simply by thermal expansion of the water. The increase will be more if there is a significant amount of melting of the icecaps. All the mid-latitude glaciers will disappear. Rainfall patterns will change. There will be more extreme weather events. Most dangerous of all is the potential for large-scale climate instabilities driven by things that we do not yet fully understand.

Will we see that large temperature change? It is very unlikely because business will almost certainly not go on as usual. Already there are signs

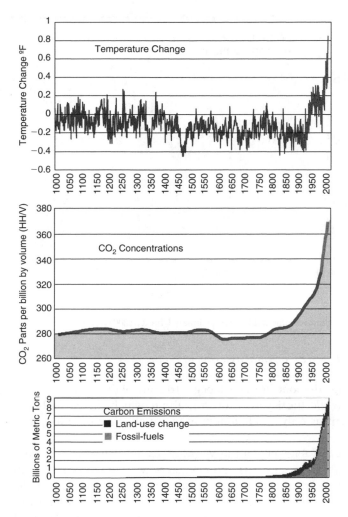

Note: Records of northern hemisphere surface temperatures, CO_2 concentrations, and carbon emissions show a close correlation. Temperature Change: reconstruction of annual-average northern-hemisphere surface air temperatures derived from historical records, tree rings and corals, and air temperatures directly measured. CO_2 concentrations: record of global CO_2 concentration for the last 1000 years, derived from measurements of CO_2 concentration in air bubbles in the layered ice cores drilled in Antarctica and from atmospheric measurements since 1957. Carbon Emissions: reconstruction of past emissions of CO_2 as a result of land clearing and fossil fuel combustion since about 1750 (in billions of metric tons of carbon per year).

Source: National Assessment Synthesis Team; Climate Change Impacts on the United States; US Global Change Research Program (2000).

Figure 4.1   1000 years of global CO_2 and temperature change

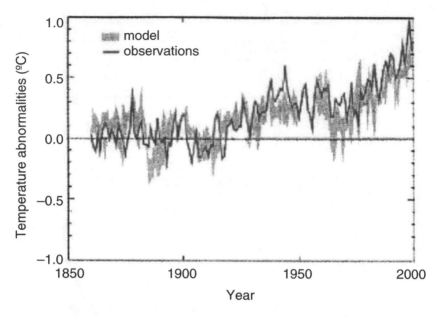

Source: Intergovernmental Panel on Climate Change (2001), p. 11. Reproduced with the permission of the IPCC.

Figure 4.2   IPCC: third assessment report

of change that one hopes will begin to control the emission of greenhouse gases. While the Kyoto Protocol, about which there has been so much argument, is only a pale imitation of an effective program, it is a beginning.

There is a tendency in this world of technology-driven rapid change to believe that the scientists and engineers will come up with technological quick fixes for almost anything that will solve whatever problem comes along. However, in this case, nature prevents such a quick fix because greenhouse gases have a long residence time in the atmosphere (Table 4.1). It will, in fact, take hundreds of years to undo what we can do in a few decades. Björn Lomborg (2001), in his most interesting book, *The Skeptical Economist*, agrees that there is a problem, but thinks we can wait before trying to solve it. Once the effects are manifest, it is too late.

THE NUMBERS

If a physicist is to preserve his scientific credentials he has to include at least one equation. I will use only one, which I call the energy identity. It relates population (P), per capita income (I/R), and energy intensity (E/I) (the amount of energy required to produce a given amount of GDP) to energy.

$$E = P \times I/P \times E/I$$

Where: E = energy; P = population; I = world income; I/P per capita income; E/I energy intensity.

Put in these terms, the energy required by a country, a region, or the entire world is easy to predict. Simply multiply the expected population, the desired per capita income, and the expected energy intensity and you have the answer. Note that when I talk about energy, I will mean what is called primary energy. This is different from the energy each of us uses directly. For example, if you plug an appliance into an electrical supply, you use a certain amount of electrical energy; but the primary energy required is larger than that by a factor of about 1.5 to 3, depending on the efficiency of the power plant.

Look first at the population term. The United Nations' population projection (Figure 4.4) in their medium-growth scenario predicts that the world population will grow from its present 6 billion to about 10 billion in the year 2050, and to about 11.5 billion in the year 2100. Almost all the growth is predicted to occur in the developing countries. This growth may slow down with the empowerment of women as well as with an increase in per capita income. Be that as it may, the first term in our equation is predicted to nearly double in this century.

Next, look at the predictions of GDP and per capita GDP (Table 4.2). The uncertainties here are clearly large and depend strongly on assumptions about economic growth. They are from the International Institute of Applied Systems Analysis (IIASA) middle-growth projection (their Scenario B). World GDP is projected to grow nearly eight-fold, again with most of the growth occurring in the developing world. The numbers are reasonable and assume that the amount of growth is 1.3 per cent per year in the industrialized world and 3.2 per cent in the developing world.

Per capita GDP in the year 2000 in the industrialized world is twenty times that in the developing world, and the ratio is expected to fall to six to one by the year 2100. The ratio would be even smaller if the developing world's population increase were smaller than projected, and there are signs that this may come to pass. Whether the consumption level indicated by the industrialized nations' year 2100 per capita GDP is appropriate is not a question for here.

Next I turn to the third term in the equation. Energy intensity has been declining by about 1 per cent a year for decades. The decline is related to increased efficiency in primary energy use, and to economic changes that

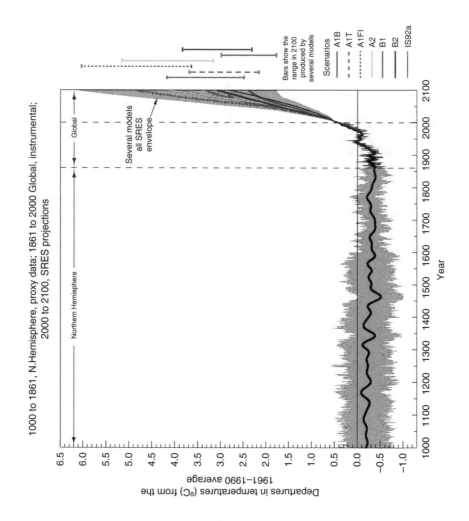

1000 to 1861, N.Hemisphere, proxy data; 1861 to 2000 Global, instrumental; 2000 to 2100, SRES projections

Note: From year 1000 to year 1860 variations in average surface temperature of the Northern Hemisphere are shown (corresponding data from the Southern Hemisphere not available) reconstructed from proxy data (tree rings, corals, ice cores and historical records). The line shows the 50-year average, the grey region the 95% confidence limit in the annual data. From years 1860 to 2000 are shown variations in observations of globally and annually averaged surface temperature from the instrumental record; the line shows the decadal average. From years 2000 to 2100 projections of globally averaged surface temperature are shown for the six illustrative SRES scenarios and IS92a using a model with average climate sensitivity. The grey region marked 'several models all SRES envelope' shows the range of results from the full range of 35 SRES scenarios in addition to those from a range of models with different climate sensitivities. The temperature scale is a departure from the 1990 value; the scale is different from that used in Figure SPM-2. Q9 Figure 9-1b.

Source: Intergovernmental Panel on Climate Change (2001). Reproduced with the permission of the IPCC.

Figure 4.3 Climate change 2001: synthesis report

135

Table 4.1   Removal time and percentage contribution to climate forcing

Agent	Rough removal time	Approximate contribution in 2006
Carbon Dioxide	>100 years	60%
Methane	10 years	25%
Tropospheric Ozone	50 days	20%
Nitrous Oxide	100 years	5%
Fluorocarbons	>1000 years	<1%
Sulfate Aerosols	10 days	−25%
Black Carbon	10 days	15%

Source: National Research Council (2003, p. 3).

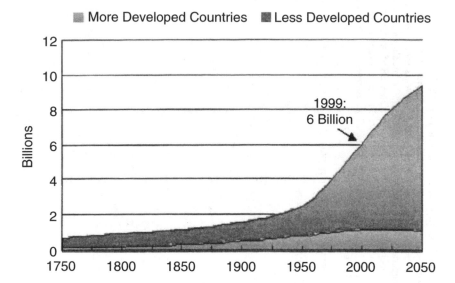

Sources: Before 1950: PRB estimates, 1950–2050; UN *World Population Projections to 2150*, 1998 (medium scenario). United Nations, Department of Economic and Social Affairs, Population Division (1998). World Population Projections to 2150 (United Nations Publication, Sales No. E. 98. XIII. 14).

Figure 4.4   World population growth

increase the amount of services compared to the amount of heavy industry. The IIASA projections (Table 4.3) assume a continuation of this trend throughout the century. By the year 2100, the developing world is projected to achieve an energy intensity that is the same as the industrialized world has today, while the industrialized world will have improved by a factor of three.

*Table 4.2   Comparison of GDP and per capita GDP in years 2000
and 2100*

	2000		2100	
	GDP	GDP/Person	GDP	GDP/Person
Industrialized	20.3	22.2	71	70.5
Reforming	0.8	1.8	16	27.4
Developing	5.1	1.1	116	11.5
World	26.2	4.2	202	17.3

Source: International Institute of Applied Systems Analysis, Vienna, Austria, 2001
(Scenario B).

Table 4.3   Energy intensity: IIASA scenario B

Watt-year/dollar	2000	2050	2100
Industrialized	0.3	0.18	0.11
Reforming	2.26	0.78	0.29
Developing	1.08	0.59	0.3
World	0.52	0.36	0.23

Source: International Institute of Applied Systems Analysis, Vienna, Austria, 2001.

We can now put all of these terms together to get the world projected primary energy use (Figure 4.5). Under these assumptions, primary energy use will go from 14 TW-years now to 27 TW-years in the year 2050, to 40 TW-years in the year 2100 (a terawatt (TW) is one million megawatts). Almost all the increase occurs in the developing world as its standard of living improves. By the year 2020, the developing world is projected to be using as much primary energy as all of the rest of the world combined. The summary table (Table 4.4) shows the relations among the numbers.

There remains one missing piece that is necessary to complete the puzzle. What is the goal? Do we wish to return to the level of greenhouse gases in the atmosphere in the pre-industrial era (280 parts per million or ppm), or will we accept some higher level? Personally, I regard a 50 per cent increase over the pre-industrial level to about 450 ppm as probably acceptable, twice the pre-industrial level as risky, and anything more as unacceptably dangerous.

In what follows I will use 450 ppm as the target and focus on what we need to do by the year 2050 to be on track to stabilize the greenhouse

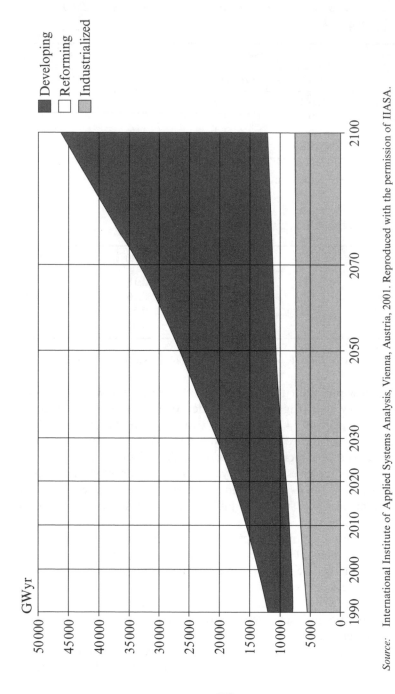

Source: International Institute of Applied Systems Analysis, Vienna, Austria, 2001. Reproduced with the permission of IIASA.

Figure 4.5 Three regions, scenario B (primary energy consumption: total)

Table 4.4   Summary table of world power projections

Item	2000	2050	2100
Primary power (Terawatts)	14	27	40
Population (billions)	6.2	10	11.6
Energy intensity (watt-year/$)	0.52	0.36	0.23

Table 4.5   Primary power requirements for 2050

Source of primary power	2000	2050
Carbon-based	11 TW	7 TW
Carbon-free	3 TW	20 TW

Note: For this and other scenarios, see, for example, Hoffert et al. (1998).

gases in the atmosphere at that level (not then, but later). We now, worldwide, use 11 TW of carbon-based and 3 TW of carbon-free primary power (Table 4.5). By 2050, of the predicted 27 TW we should be using only 7 TW of carbon-based and 20 TW of carbon-free power. This is a daunting challenge; to produce more carbon-free power in the next 50 years than exist now in totality, and to do it at the same time that carbon-based power is being reduced, which will make powerful economic interests very unhappy. Carbon emissions will have to go down further as time goes on, but I will stay with requirements for 2050 because anything that can have a major impact has to begin to be deployed soon.

This is the context in which I said earlier that the Kyoto Protocol was an insignificant baby step. If carried out successfully, the industrialized world will decrease its use of carbon-based energy by 0.5 to 1 TW-year per year, while the developing world will increase its use by 2 to 3 TW-years per year. This is not much of an advance toward a goal that requires the reduction of worldwide use of carbon-based energy.

THE OPTIONS

There are only two large-scale options available now that can make a major impact on greenhouse gas emissions in the next 30 to 40 years. They are conservation and efficiency, and nuclear power. The renewables on which so many in the environment movement pin so much hope are in their infancy. What has to be done to begin to bring greenhouse gases under control has to be done on a very large scale and soon. But, while development of the renewables should be strongly supported, the problem cannot wait on their maturity. The world economy will be using an additional 13 TW in the next 50 years, and to make an impact on this requires large-scale action. Remember that 1 TW of primary power represents the power going into 400 to 500 GW electric power plants. Only mature technologies can have a real impact in the next several decades.

Hydropower

It is currently widely deployed but it is near its limits. Hydropower might expand by a factor of two but it generates its own environmental problems as, for example, with the Three Gorges dams in China.

Biomass

In theory, plants get all of their structural material from the carbon dioxide in the atmosphere, so if you grow plants and then burn them to produce energy, you put back into the atmosphere only the same carbon dioxide that you took out in the first place. In practice it is not quite so simple. It takes energy to produce the required fertilizer, to dry the crops, and to transport them. Biomass is a net carbon dioxide generator and no one has done a really thorough analysis on just how much it will generate. In addition, food crops are already feeling pressure from water limits and it may be hard to find the necessary water to grow energy crops. Growing forests is a different matter; that takes carbon dioxide out of the atmosphere and keeps it in the trees.

Wind

It is useful where steady winds exist as, for example, in western Denmark and California. There are about 16 GW of wind power installed now but, because of the intermittency of winds, they only produce about 4 GW-years per year of energy, an average efficiency of 25 per cent. They are cost effective and should be deployed widely, but cannot be used for base-load power.

Geothermal

This is useful in volcanic areas like northern California or Hawaii. However, sites are limited.

Solar Photo Voltaic

Unfortunately the sun does not shine for 24 hours, even when the days are clear. A solar plant that produces an average power of 1 GW with low-cost 15 per cent efficient solar cells (not yet available) produces 3 GW of power at noon and zero at midnight, and it occupies 20 million square meters of land. Such power can be very useful in supplying peak daytime loads in regions without extended heavy cloud cover (not in India during the monsoon, for example). Costs are high now, but will come down by 2020 to a predicted $1.50 per peak watt.

Fuel Cells

These are the hope of the future for transport. They can efficiently convert chemical energy to electricity. I believe we will first see them in trucks and buses around 2010 using hydrocarbon fuels, improving efficiency by a factor of roughly three. Hydrogen cells that produce nothing but water as a byproduct will come later, perhaps by 2020. However, hydrogen does not exist freely in nature and has to be produced by using some other form of energy. The emissions from that energy have to be factored into the environmental equation. Hydrogen may be the perfect energy storage medium for solar voltaic systems.

Conservation and Efficiency

The rationale for emphasizing conservation and efficiency is simple – if you don't use it, it produces no greenhouse gases. The potential for huge savings is there. Built into the forecast that energy use will double by the year 2050 is the assumption that energy intensity will continue its historic rate of decline of 1 per cent per year (Figure 4.6). If we don't do that well, while assuming the same population and per capita GDP, we will use more energy; if we do better, we will use less. If the decline in energy intensity could be improved to 2 per cent per year, the same population and GDP assumptions would require 7 TW-years less than that which is required under the standard projections. To be on our track to stabilize CO_2 in the atmosphere at 450 ppm, the world would then need only 13 TW of carbon-free power compared to the 20 TW required under the standard assumption. The practical minded might note that avoiding the cost of 7 TW-yrs per year of primary energy would save the world economy more than $1 trillion per year.

Making energy intensity decline by 2 per cent per year will not be easy, but it can be done. China has set an example where carbon dioxide

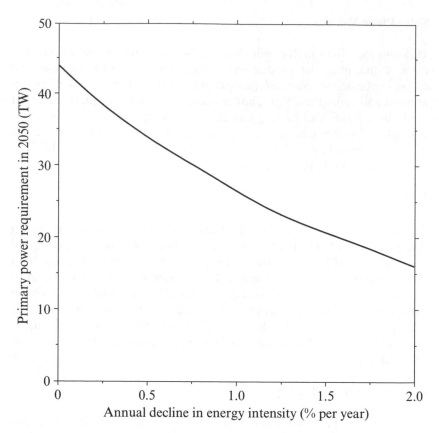

*Figure 4.6   Power (TW) required in 2050 versus rate of decline in energy
             intensity*

emissions have actually declined by 8 per cent while their economy has
grown (Figure 4.7). They have accomplished this by closing some of their
least efficient power plants, shutting down some of their inefficient heavy
industry, and beginning the switch of households to cleaner fuels for
heating and cooking. It is also worth noting that China's reforestation
program is removing significant amounts of carbon dioxide from the
atmosphere.

The best opportunities are in the developing world where energy use is
expanding fastest. The industrialized world should assist the developing
countries in installing the most efficient energy systems as those countries'
energy needs grow. The best natural gas-fired power plants are nearly twice
as efficient as old coal plants in producing output energy from primary
energy and, in addition, for the same amount of primary energy, natural

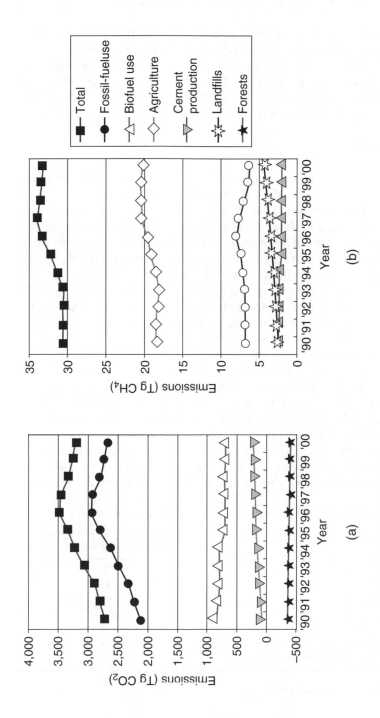

Source: Data provided by Dr David G. Streets (2001).

Figure 4.7 Recent reductions in China's greenhouse gas emissions

143

gas produces one half of the carbon dioxide of coal. It is, thus, possible to get the same energy output with a quarter of the CO_2 emissions.

Conservation and efficiency should be the centerpiece of the early programs to improve energy intensity. There are also huge opportunities in transportation, lighting, heating, insulation and appliances. This is the most economically efficient way to attack the greenhouse gas problem.

Nuclear Power

This is the most controversial option. There are about 400 nuclear power plants operating in the world today using about 1 TW of primary power to produce 400 GW of electrical output. All of this is carbon-free. With a coordinated effort to design the next generation of improved reactors, nuclear power could be expanded by about a factor of three to five over the next 50 years. However, if such an expansion is to occur, public concerns about radiation, accidents and radioactive waste disposal must be addressed.

Radiation exposure from operating plants is not something to worry about (Table 4.6). Natural radioactivity from cosmic rays bombarding the earth from space, and from radioactive materials that exist all around us, deliver an annual radiation dose to each person of about 240 millirem (mr) per year. Of this amount, 40 mr comes from materials in our own bodies, such as potassium-40 and carbon-13. Medical x-rays give an average annual dose to each individual of 60 mr. A nuclear power plant gives a negligible amount of radiation in comparison, about four one-thousandths of a mr. Incidentally, a typical coal-fired power plant gives about the same radiation from natural impurities of coal.

The Chernobyl accident, a truly horrific incident, occurred in a type of reactor that has never been allowed to be built outside of the old Soviet Bloc. This type of reactor can become unstable under certain conditions.

Table 4.6   Radiation exposures

Source	Radiation dose (millirem/year)
Natural radioactivity	240
Natural in body (75kg)*	40
Medical (average)	60
Nuclear plant (1GW electric)	0.004
Coal plant (1GW electric)	0.003
Chernobyl Accident (Austria: 1988)	24
Chernobyl Accident (Austria: 1996)	7

Note: * Included in the natural total.

At Chernobyl, the operators systematically disconnected all of the reactor's safety systems as part of a misguided test and brought the reactor into the unstable region with the consequences that we all know. Even so, radiation levels outside Chernobyl's immediate vicinity were not significant compared to natural radiation.

The Three-Mile Island accident in the US is the worst to have occurred in the water-moderated reactors that produce most of the world's nuclear power. The operators of Three-Mile Island made almost every error that could be made in operating the reactor and thereby melted the reactor core. However, because of the reactor's design and the reactor's containment, the largest dose that anyone outside of the plant itself received was a few mr.

Safety is extremely important in nuclear power. It must be incorporated in the design from the beginning and plant operations must be overseen by tough regulators. Given that, the public health impacts of nuclear power (Table 4.7) are less than those of any other energy source except wind power. Even the solar cells used in photovoltaic systems have much more

Table 4.7   Public health impacts of alternative energy sources per TW

	Coal	Lignite	Oil	Gas	**Nuclear**	PV	Wind
Years of life lost: Non-radiological effects	138	167	359	42	**9.1**	58	2.7
Radiological effects: Normal operation Accidents					**16** **0.015**		
Respiratory hospital admissions	0.69	0.72	1.8	0.21	**0.05**	0.29	0.01
Cerebrovascular hospital admissions	1.7	1.8	4.4	0.51	**0.11**	0.7	0.03
Congestive heart failure	0.8	0.84	2.1	0.24	**0.05**	0.33	0.02
Restricted activity days	4751	4976	12248	1446	**314**	1977	90
Days with bronchodilator usage	1303	1365	3361	397	**86**	543	25
Cough days in asthmatics	1492	1562	3846	454	**98**	621	28
Respiratory symptoms in asthmatics	693	726	1786	211	**45**	288	13
Chronic bronchitis in children	115	135	333	39	**11**	54	2.4
Chronic cough in children	148	174	428	51	**14**	69	3.2
Non-fatal cancer					**2.4**		

Source: Krewitt et al. (1998).

Table 4.8　The spent fuel problem

Component	Fission fragments	Uranium	Long-live component
Per cent of total	4	95	1
Radio-activity	Intense	Negligible	Medium
Untreated required isolation time (years)	200	0	300,000

severe public health consequences than does nuclear power, because of the toxic chemicals used in their manufacture.

Safe disposal of spent fuel from nuclear power plants is appropriately a major concern of the public. This spent fuel is intensely radioactive when it comes out of a reactor and must be handled with great care. It has three main components that could be handled separately in principle, but are now lumped together. The three are uranium (95 per cent), fission fragments (4 per cent), and the long-lived components (1.5 per cent). The uranium is no more of a hazard than the ore that was mined to make the fuel. The fission fragments need to be stored for only a few hundred years until their radioactivity falls below the level of concern. The long-lived component, if left untreated, must be isolated for hundreds of thousands of years (Table 4.8).

At present, the favorite method of protecting the public from this material is called geological disposition, which keeps all of the components together and stores them in special mines such as Yucca Mountain in the United States. This method will work, but, if that is to be the solution, it will have to be in an international context because not all nations have appropriate geological formations.

People who are concerned about geological storage should consider the case of the OKLO natural reactor in Gabon, Africa. This natural formation began operating as a nuclear reactor about two billion years ago when the ratio of the fissionable uranium-235 to uranium-238 was larger, because of the different lifetimes of these isotopes, and when climatic conditions were correct. OKLO produced about 100 MW of power for many millions of years, and no trace of its existence can be found a few tens of kilometers away.

The scientific community is looking at an alternative to handling the long-lived component called transmutation. The long-lived component can be recycled in reactors where it will be fissioned into shorter-lived elements. If this works out, it appears possible to shorten the required period of isolation to a few thousand years, less than the lifetime of the pyramids, man-made structures that have lasted a very long time. It is too early to say if this will work out or to say what impact it might have on the cost of nuclear power.

It is worth noting that at least in the United States nuclear power cost includes an allowance for disposition of the spent fuel. A charge of 0.1 cents per kilowatt-hour is added to the price of nuclear electricity and that money goes to the government for the eventual disposition of waste. The fund is now $20 billion. It is not clear if that is the correct charge, but it is interesting to note that no such charge is imposed on any of the carbon-based power sources. If one were imposed, there would be a great deal of money to use for conservation, efficiency and carbon-free alternatives.

It is also worth noting that there is no equivalent charge on energy for disposal of the CO_2 from hydrocarbon power systems. There has been talk of CO_2 sequestration; pumping it deep underground for long-term storage. There is some experience with this technique from the use of CO_2 injection for enhanced oil recovery from wells. Based on this, there are estimates that range from one to four cents per kilowatt-hour to sequester the CO_2 from a coal-fired power plant.

CONCLUSIONS AND RECOMMENDATIONS

It has been said by some anthropologists that our behavior today is conditioned by our experiences hundreds of thousands of years ago when human ancestors were primitive, few in number, and scattered. Then one worried about the tiger behind the next tree, not about the one miles away. If so, I want you to know that the climate change tiger is behind the next tree.

Energy use is going to increase inexorably, driven by the needs of the developing world. These countries will not and should not live in energy poverty while the industrialized nations live in energy plenty.

It must be recognized that scientists and engineers have no quick fix for the problem of global warming because of the long residence time of greenhouse gases in the atmosphere.

A goal has to be set for the allowable increase in carbon dioxide and other greenhouse gases, for without a goal there can be no coherent program. Politicians will want the problem to go away. Economists will want the goal set as high as possible so that the cost of mitigation is minimized. Scientists will want the goal set as low as possible to minimize the consequences. A consensus has to be reached to define a long-term program and, whatever plan is decided upon, it should be designed to minimize the cost of achieving the desired results.

A concerted effort to drive down energy intensity through conservation and efficiency should be the first element of any such plan. Conservation and efficiency may even save money in the long run, and it is obvious that energy not used is carbon-free and non-polluting. Emissions trading and reforestation should be practiced to the maximum possible extent. It is much more economical to introduce new efficient power plants, for example, in places where demand increases, than to shut down and replace a less efficient plant that still has considerable useful life left.

Nuclear power should be expanded. Concerns about radiation and waste storage have been blown out of all proportion. Environmentalists in countries like Belgium, Germany and Sweden, where nuclear power is to be phased out, should be prepared to tell their neighbors why more years of their lives should be lost by being non-nuclear. Some people consider nuclear power to be the devil himself; but I would ask them which devil would they prefer to live with, nuclear power or climate change?

Research and development on renewables, fuel cells, hydrogen systems, and so forth, should be expanded. They do have a role to play and, while they are not ready now for large-scale deployment, they should be readied with all deliberate speed.

Effective action in a market-based world can only be accomplished with aware governments that will put in place sensible policies involving both incentives and penalties. It is time to stop posturing. The United States government does not seem to have any awareness of the problem, and too many nations in Europe, through their positions on emissions trading and reforestation, seem more interested in making sinners suffer than in solving the problem.

Action is required. Surely the economists and politicians can design an incentive system that would encourage entrepreneurial innovation. To a physicist it is easy; a carbon tax would do the job quite effectively, discouraging the most polluting fuels and encouraging the least polluting. A waste disposal charge, like that imposed on nuclear power, would do well also and could raise considerable money.

In conclusion, please remember this: global warming will be our grandchildren's problem, but they are too young to do anything about it.

REFERENCES

Hoffert, Martin I. et al. (1998), 'Energy implications of future stabilization of atmospheric CO_2 content', *Nature*, **395**, 881–4.
Intergovernmental Panel on Climate Change (2001), *Third Assessment Report – Climate Change 2001: The Scientific Basis. Summary for Policy Makers.*
IPCC (2001), *Climate Change 2001: Synthesis Report. A Contribution of Working Groups I, II and III to the Third Assessment Report of the Intergovernmental Panel on Climate Change* [Watson, R.T. and the Core Writing Team (eds)], Cambridge, UK and New York, USA: Cambridge University Press.

Krewitt, Wolfram et al. (1998), 'Health risks of energy systems', *Risk Analysis*, **18** (4), 377–84.

Lomborg, Björn (2001), *The Skeptical Environmentalist*, Cambridge: Cambridge University Press.

National Research Council (2001), *Climate Change Science, An Analysis of Some Key Questions*, Washington, DC: National Academy Press.

Streets, David G. et al. (2001), 'Recent reductions in China's greenhouse gas emissions', *Science*, 294, 1835–7, 30 November.

US Global Change Research Program, National Assessment Synthesis Team (2000), *Climate Change Impacts on the United States: The Potential Consequences of Climate Variability and Change*, Cambridge: Cambridge University Press.

SECTION B

Human health

5. Global consumption from the perspective of population health

Clyde Hertzman

Can wealthy societies maintain their health status while consuming less of the world's 'photosynthetic resources'? This may seem like an esoteric question, yet Canada has recently ratified the Kyoto Accord. In order to meet its commitments under the Accord, Canada will need to reduce emissions of carbon dioxide by approximately 20 per cent over the next decade. Since carbon dioxide is the end product of consumption of 'photosynthetic resources' the question is de facto irresistible.

In the modern world, health, wealth and consumption tend to occur together. Increasing per capita income among countries tends to be associated with increasing longevity. Early in this century the relationship was simple: life expectancy was longer in countries with higher per capita incomes. However, in recent decades the relationship between health and wealth has become more complex as rich nations have grown richer. The specific character of this complexity forms a basis for a more encouraging answer to the question posed above.

When longevity and national income curves are plotted together on a single graph, the cause for optimism can be seen in the changing character of the curves throughout the twentieth century. Figure 5.1 shows that, in 1900, the relationship between increasing national health and wealth was nearly linear. Wealthier meant healthier. But throughout the twentieth century the strength of this association increasingly broke down. By 1960, the slope of the health–wealth curve had flattened at the 'rich end', such that variations in national income per capita were no longer strongly associated with further increases in life expectancy. By 1990 all the world's wealthiest nations (those belonging to the Organization for Economic Co-operation and Development) found themselves on this 'flat of the curve' (World Bank, 1993). At the same time, the traditional monotonic relationship between health and wealth persisted among the world's poorer countries; a pattern referred to here as the 'steep incline', to distinguish it from the 'flat of the curve'.

There are several ways to interpret these trends. One of the simplest is to assert that the material factors that limit health status in poor societies,

153

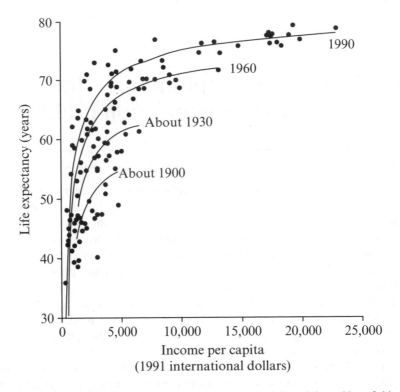

Figure 5.1   *Life expectancy and income per capita for selected countries and periods*

such as food, clothing, shelter and clean water, become relatively unimportant determinants of health when national income reaches a certain level. This is intuitively appealing because there is such a thing as a sufficient amount of food, clothing, shelter, and clean water, beyond which further consumption should not lead to further health benefit. It may be pleasant to have better food, clothing and shelter, but they would not necessarily confer additional health benefits.

One simple conclusion, from the standpoint of economic development and health, is that poorer countries' attempting to match the rich, and reach the flat of the curve, is an essentially benign objective. In other words, the relationship between healthy and wealthy countries and poor and unhealthy countries ought to be one of imitation of the former by the latter.

This interpretation assumes that economic growth, traditionally defined, is a laudable objective regardless of the forms that it takes. But this view is challenged by evidence that shows how differently rich and poor nations appropriate global photosynthetic resources. This is best represented in the calculation of the 'ecological footprint', which is a measure of the area of the earth's surface appropriated for its use by a given population in a given year (Wackernagel and Rees, 1995).

Consumption of ecologically productive land (that is, land appropriated for energy, agriculture and forest products as well as the area of the built environment per se) has grown rapidly across the globe in recent decades. Between 1950 and 1990, the appropriation of ecologically productive land by the world's richest countries increased from approximately 2 hectares to between 4 and 6 hectares per capita. Over the same time period, the global supply of ecoproductive land declined from approximately 3.6 hectares to 1.7 hectares per capita, primarily as a result of population growth. In other words, during the last half of the twentieth century the fraction of the world's ecoproductive resources appropriated by the world's richest countries has exceeded a level of global sustainability. The world's poorest nations have little room to increase consumption of those goods and services derived from ecologically productive land. To achieve equivalent levels of consumption, the planet earth would need to appropriate at least two more planets' worth of ecoproductive land for the use of the developing world (Wackernagel and Rees, 1995). This is clearly an impossible dream.

This perspective sheds new light on the relationship between the health and wealth of nations. To begin with, the seemingly benign construct of per capita income should be replaced in international comparisons with more stringent measures of ecologically productive land appropriation. Calculations of the size of various countries' ecological footprints have been carried out for the year 1993 (Wackernagel, 1997). Figure 5.2 shows the relationship between life expectancy for 1993, or nearest year, by country, in relation to its ecological footprint. As ecological footprints rise from zero, life expectancy increases rapidly. Once again, however, there is a flattening of the curve wherein the vast differences in the size of the world's richest countries' ecological footprints do not correlate with further increases in life expectancy. Indeed, there are no improvements in life expectancy, on average, above an ecological footprint of 4 hectares per capita. Indeed, average life expectancies in excess of 75 years are compatible with ecological footprints of less than 3 hectares per capita.

When this observation is combined with the fact of limited global resources, the relationship between countries on the steep incline and those on the flat of the health–wealth curve is transformed. The flat of the curve

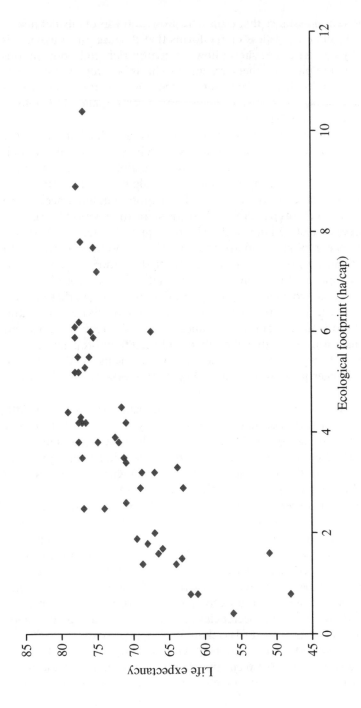

Sources: World Bank (1993) and Wackernagel (1997).

Figure 5.2 Life expectancy and ecological footprint, 1993

no longer seems benign, but begins to look as though it exists at the expense of the steep incline. This, in turn, transforms the definition of success in national development and health. The most successful group of countries are those that maximize their health status while limiting their consumption. From the standpoint of global citizenship, these are the countries found at the left end of the flat of the curve, where the world's best health status coexists with the minimum appropriation of photosynthetic resources. Those countries found further to the right are increasingly inefficient producers of health that, through competition for global resources, may well be limiting the health chances of countries on the steep incline.

The prospect of richer countries playing the role of a global consumer to the poorer countries' global supplier raises obvious ethical issues, but a realist might suppose that these will not be decisive in determining the behaviour of nations in the future.

If success were measured by the ratio of life years produced to ecoproductive land consumed, the world's healthiest country would not be found on the flat of the curve. It would be Costa Rica. By 1991 it delivered a life expectancy of 76 years to its citizens, compared with an average of 77 years for the world's 22 richest countries. This was accomplished with a national income of US \$1850 per capita, and an ecological footprint of 2.5 hectares per capita compared with an average of US \$21 050, and an average ecological footprint of greater than 6 hectares per capita (Wackernagel and Rees, 1995), for the 22 richest nations. In other words, Costa Rica would be found up, and to the left hand corner, of both Figures 5.1 and 5.2.

Costa Rica is not the only poor, low-consuming society with world-class longevity, and recognition of this group of societies is not new. These countries are characterized by high levels of literacy, independence among the female population, and high levels of spending on education and welfare (Caldwell, 1986), as well as strong civic cultures, compared with other countries in their income bracket (Heller, 2000).

The characteristics of poor but healthy societies may be useful to other developing countries striving to make the best use of scarce resources, but this knowledge provides little help to wealthy societies that, over time, must reduce their current appropriation of global ecoproductive resources to make room for others. The fact that health and low appropriation of ecoproductive resources are compatible states does not mean that we know how to get there from where we currently are. What will happen if the developing world decides that the products of ecoproductive land that are currently being exported to the developed world for cash ought to stay where they are? This circumstance raises an important question: can wealthy societies maintain their health status while making a transition to lower consumers of the world's ecologically productive resources?

This question forces us to envision the developmental pathway from how we live now to how it might look under conditions of globally sustainable consumption. The flat of the curve, and the existence of countries like Costa Rica, demonstrate that lower levels of consumption are compatible with high levels of health status. What is at issue is the following: can the highest consuming societies successfully become more like a Costa Rica in terms of consumption patterns without undermining social stability and sharply increasing inequality in the socioeconomic domain? To answer this question, we need to consider much more carefully the determinants of health in human societies.

UNDERSTANDING THE DETERMINANTS OF HEALTH IN HUMAN SOCIETIES

Thomas McKeown (1979) showed that the precipitous decline in mortality from infectious diseases such as tuberculosis during the past century was *not* due to clinically effective vaccinations and antibiotic treatments. These diseases had been the major causes of mortality for centuries, yet effective clinical prevention and treatment interventions were developed and implemented *after* approximately 90 per cent of the historical decline in mortality had already occurred. Thus, in direct contradiction to received wisdom, the vaccine and antibiotic revolution played a rather minor role in lengthening human life expectancies in Western Europe, North America, Japan and other wealthy countries.

Historically, the principal factors responsible for increasing life expectancy from less than 50 years to more than 70 years were found outside the health care system as traditionally defined, in the broader social/ economic environment: improvements in housing, water supply, pollution control, nutrition, child spacing, working conditions, education, and a wide range of psychosocial factors which are thought to improve as societies become more prosperous, tolerant, democratic and inclusive. Some of these improvements were part of conscious efforts to improve the health of the population, and others not.

We now understand that factors that influence health are found at three levels of aggregation in society. At the broadest level of aggregation are those related to the state and the socioeconomic environment, in particular, national wealth, income distribution and social transfers, degree of industrialization and urbanization, level of unemployment, and the structure of opportunity created by history, geography and fortune. At the intermediate level, there is the quality of civil society; that is, those features of social organization, such as institutional responsiveness, social trust and social cohesion, which facilitate or impede coordination and cooperation

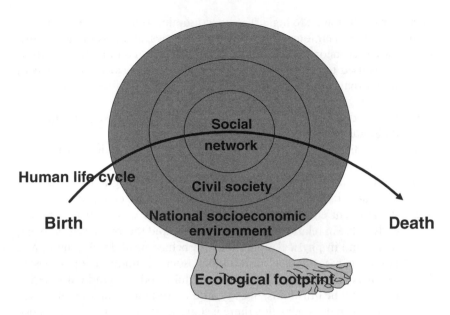

Figure 5.3   Determinants of health

for mutual benefit (Putnam, 1993) and, in so doing, exaggerate or buffer the stresses of daily existence. Finally, at the 'micro' level, there is the intimate realm of the family and the personal support network.

This conception is illustrated in Figure 5.3, wherein society is represented by three concentric circles, forming a bull's eye, that stand for the clusters of determinants of health and well-being at the three levels of social aggregation described above. An arrow is piercing the bull's eye, which represents the individual life course. Health in human societies is 'determined' by the interplay between the cognitive, social–emotional–behavioural, and physical development of each member of society, at each stage in the life course, and the day-to-day conditions of life that they encounter at the intimate, civic and state level, as they go through life. The healthfulness of human society is the sum of these interactions across all members of society. Herein, this conjunction is referred to as 'lived experience'.

GRADIENTS: THE LINK BETWEEN LIVED EXPERIENCE, CONSUMPTION AND HEALTH

Lived experience expresses itself in health status through a phenomenon known as the 'gradient effect', wherein health status increases *in a stepwise fashion* from the lowest to highest socioeconomic strata of society. This gradient effect has been found in all wealthy societies, and it is found regardless of whether income, education, occupation or a combination of these measures is used to define socioeconomic status. There are four aspects of the gradient that point to lived experience as the basis of causation:

- the gradient cannot be explained away by reverse causation or differential mobility.
- the gradient effect is evident for virtually all of the major diseases that affect health and well-being in our society.
- as the major diseases have changed over time, the gradient effect has replicated itself on the new diseases as they have emerged.
- the gradient effect exists across the entire life course. It is apparent early in life in relation to infant mortality and low birth weight. Next, it is found in physical, cognitive and behavioural development, and has been measured as (modifiable) socioeconomic inequalities in readiness for school. During early adulthood the gradient emerges for mental health status, obesity, and limiting longstanding illnesses. By the fifth decade of life, there is a gradient in relation to the major causes of morbidity and mortality.

In other words, the gradient represents a 'causal' relationship between lived experience and health over the life course. The characteristics of the gradient point to the existence of fundamental biological processes connecting social circumstances to human resilience and vulnerability to disease, and strongly suggest a role for early child development in the process (Hertzman, 2000).

The principal significance of the gradient for this discussion is that gradients appear to 'flatten up'. Those societies that produce the least inequality in health and human development across the socioeconomic spectrum have the highest average levels of health and development (see Figure 5.4). 'Raising the bottom' of the socioeconomic spectrum does not 'lower the top', a fundamental challenge to the folk wisdom surrounding economic models currently in vogue. These would predict that reductions in societal inequalities for those at the low end of the socioeconomic spectrum could only occur at the expense of those at the upper end. In other words, population health reminds us, first and foremost, that we are a social species, and our health and development depend upon the quality of the social environments where we grow up, live and work.

An optimist might see these findings as evidence supporting the view that wealthy societies can maintain or improve their health status irrespective of income level and presumably, their level of consumption, by addressing

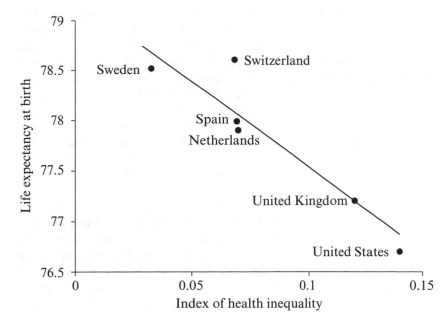

Source: Hertzman (2001), p. 543.

Figure 5.4   Longevity and health inequality

Table 5.1   Life expectancy, health inequality and ecological footprint

	Health inequality (rank order)	Life expectancy (rank order)	Ecological footprint (ha/cap)
Sweden	lowest	2	5.9
Spain	2	3	3.8
Netherlands	3	4	5.3
Switzerland	4	1	5
United Kingdom	5	5	5.2
United States	highest	6	10.3

equity issues. In that claim the optimists would be supported by the data in Table 5.1. It builds upon Figure 5.4 and suggests that, in wealthy societies, health equality is not purchased with a large ecological footprint. If anything, the reverse may better characterize the pattern.

The optimist would conclude that a healthy and sustainable society is achievable in any society committed to simultaneously reducing health inequalities and the consumption of photosynthetic resources. This would be a case of premature optimism. Consider, for example, some rough calculations that have been made about the size of the ecological footprint of different classes of Canadian citizens. The rich leave a much larger footprint than the poor. Professional couples with two cars and no children leave a footprint that is approximately three times as large as an average-income Canadian family, and four times as large as a family living on social assistance. Indeed, consumption among those on social assistance approaches a level that is globally sustainable (Wackernagel, 1993). Unfortunately, the health status of such families is not as good as those who consume more. Those families in the lower one-fifth of the Canadian income spectrum have life expectancies approximately six years shorter for men and two years shorter for women than those with the highest one-fifth of income (Wilkins and Adams, 1992). When one considers healthy life expectancy, by removing from consideration those periods of life in which individuals are disabled, the differences across the income spectrum increase. In both sexes, healthy life expectancy is approximately 10 years lower among those in the lowest one-fifth of the income spectrum compared with those in the highest one-fifth (Wilkins, 1992).

Canadians who are consuming at a globally sustainable level appear to pay a price in terms of their health; a price not paid by those in places like Costa Rica who consume at the same or lower levels. It is unlikely that these international differences are tied to the material advantages of consumption. The most likely explanation is that individuals consuming at a globally sustainable level in a country like Costa Rica have, on average, higher social status within that country than their counterparts consuming at the same level in Canada. In the absence of further evidence, consideration should be given to the prospect that trying to drive down the consumption of the wealthy to the level of those whose consumption is globally sustainable would disrupt society in ways that could well drive down the health status of the whole population.

CENTRAL AND EASTERN EUROPE: A CAUTIONARY TALE

Are there natural experiments available that might be informative about the pitfalls of reductions in consumption across societies as a whole? It is true that acute reductions in consumption during famine are a threat to life and limb, but no one would suggest that episodes of starvation share important characteristics with the problem at hand. More relevant are the experiences of middle-income societies where purchasing power has been sharply curtailed, but where outright starvation has not resulted.

The best documented of these is the experience of Central and Eastern Europe since 1989. Within three years of the sudden political and economic changes, real wages in every country of the former Warsaw Pact fell between 15 and 35 per cent (UNICEF, 1993). These changes were accompanied by increases in the proportion of household income being spent on food in some countries in the region. Average per capita consumption of meat, fish and dairy products declined in these countries, with an accompanying decline in the size of the ecological footprint. At the same time there was marked disruption of the social environment, as demonstrated by declines between 19 and 35 per cent in crude marriage rates and more modest reductions in pre-primary school enrolment. In all cases, life expectancy showed an immediate decline, driven by increased mortality among adults (especially men) of working age.

After an initial period of shock, however, the countries of Central and Eastern Europe divided into three groups. The successful societies (Czech, Poland, Slovakia and Slovenia) re-established trajectories of health gain such that, by the end of the 1990s, they had improved over their position over 1989 (Table 5.2). The second group of societies 'broke even' in health status terms within a decade of the beginning of transition (Table 5.3). Finally, there were the failures (Table 5.4). In these societies, mostly former Soviet Republics, the initial decline in health status was followed by a continuing decline throughout the 1990s, leading to truly remarkable excess mortality. For instance, in Russia the excess mortality over the decade 1989–1999 has been estimated at greater than 4 million (Cornia and Paniccia, 2000). It is vital to understand why some societies handled the disruption with relative ease while others collapsed, because the transformation of Central and Eastern Europe is the world's natural experiment that comes closest to the scenario of a forced reduction in the ecological footprint.

Table 5.2   Change in life expectancy, 1989–1999, successful societies

	Male	Female
Czech Republic	3.3	2.7
Slovenia	2.6	2.1
Slovakia	2.2	1.8
Poland	2.1	2.0

Source: Cornia and Paniccia (2000).

Table 5.3   Change in life expectancy, 1989–1999, in-betweeners

	Male	Female
Hungary	0.9	1.3
Bulgaria	−0.7	−0.3
Romania	−0.4	1.3
Latvia	−0.4	1.0
Estonia	−0.3	1.4
Lithuania	0.2	1.4

Source: Cornia and Paniccia (2000).

Table 5.4   Change in life expectancy, 1989–1999, failed societies

	Male	Female
Belarus	−4.6	−2.5
Russia	−4.3	−2.1
Ukraine	−3.0	−1.3
Kazakhstan	−3.6	−2.1

Source: Cornia and Paniccia (2000).

Table 5.5   Success versus failure, 1: 1989–1997

		Czech Republic	Russia
% of births to women < 20		−43%	32%
Infant mortality		−41%	−3.50%
< 5 mortality		−36%	−5%
Mortality 20–39	women	−13%	43%
	men	−13%	45%
Mortality 60+		−14%	15%

Source: UNICEF (1999).

Tables 5.5–5.8 present a case study comparing one society that succeeded in the transition (Czech Republic) to another that failed (Russia). Table 5.5 shows the dramatic differences in age-specific patterns of mortality between the two countries, emphasizing the particular importance of the working age population as being most sensitive to the transition. This is an unusual pattern, suggesting that the stresses of transition fell mostly on those participating in the workforce and supporting dependants but not on

Table 5.6   Success versus failure, 2: 1989–1997

	Czech Republic	Russia
Kindergarten enrolments	−7.50%	−19%
Children in infant homes (per 000, 0–3)	no change	64%
Sentencing rate	4%	132%
Change in GDP	−3%	−44.3%
Real wages	2.30%	−55.4%
GINI coefficient (1989–1996/7)	0.20–0.26	0.27–0.48

Source: UNICEF (1999).

Table 5.7   Success versus failure, 3: 1989–1997

	Czech Republic	Russia
Privatization	slow, equitable	fast, inequitable
Wage arrears	very rare	common
Minimum wage/average wage 1995	26.9%	8.8%
Migration rate (1989–94)	0.98%	5.5%

Source: Cornia and Paniccia (2000).

those typically at greatest biological risk at the beginning and end of the life course. Table 5.5 also shows a remarkable difference in fertility patterns between the two societies. Whereas in the Czech Republic childbirth was delayed and teenage childbirth rates declined during the transition, quite the opposite happened in Russia. The Russian pattern, in particular, suggests a breakdown in social discipline not apparent in the Czech Republic.

Table 5.6 continues the theme of social disruption, showing steep declines in kindergarten enrolment, and huge rises in orphans and in sentencing rates in Russia not seen in the Czech Republic. At the same time, the economic recovery in the Czech Republic was not matched in Russia. Table 5.6 shows that, in Russia, the 1990s brought a precipitous decline in real wages and GDP. Perhaps of greatest significance, the Gini coefficient of income inequality rose in both countries, as one would expect in a transition to a capitalist style economy. Yet, the differences between the countries are much more impressive than the similarities. By the late 1990s the level of income inequality in the Czech Republic was still at the level of the most egalitarian members of the OECD. In contrast, the rise in Russia took it from one of the most egalitarian societies in the world from the standpoint of income distribution, to one of the least, in less than ten years.

Table 5.8   Institutional trust (mid-1990s)

	Czech Republic	Russia
Political parties	15%	11%
Courts	25%	20%
Police	29%	16%
Civil servants	27%	16%
Military	31%	47%
Parliament	15%	22%
Churches	29%	29%
Trade unions	28%	17%
President	60%	25%
Private	34%	16%
Ratio: non-military trust/ military trust	0.94	0.41

Source: New Democracy/New Russia Barometers.

Table 5.7 emphasizes how different the management of economic transition and the experience of labour market participation has been in the two societies. In Russia, privatization was carried out as a fire sale; wages frequently went unpaid, and a huge gap opened up between minimum and average wages. Moreover, vast numbers of workers began drifting around the country in search of the means of economic survival. In the Czech Republic, privatization was conducted in a slow, deliberate manner and produced none of the other stresses and disruptions found in Russia. Finally, Table 5.8 shows the differences in trust for key institutions of society. Most significant is the ratio of trust for civil institutions versus the military. These differences contrast a functioning civil society (Czech) from one in which civil institutions have either been discredited or have not been creditable from the outset.

Thus, the resource rich, land rich society failed in its transition while the landlocked, land poor, resource poor society succeeded. Although this may seem like a startling outcome, it shows the same patterns as Cornell and Kalt's studies (Cornell and Kalt, 2000) of economically successful versus failed Aboriginal communities in the United States, and Chandler and Lalonde work on the determinants of high and low suicide rates in British Columbia Aboriginal communities (Chandler and Lalonde, 1998). In each of these cases, the success factors were not related to land, resources and consumption. Instead, some combination of cultural continuity, strong civic community, high levels of formal and informal social trust, and high levels of affiliation to social institutions differentiated success from failure.

SUMMING UP

Wealthy societies consume too much of the world's resources, and need to cut back. In principal, this can be done without sacrificing human health. There are examples of societies that consume at globally sustainable levels and maintain a health status that is similar to ours. We know that the principal determinants of health in wealthy societies reside, broadly speaking, in the social environment. But do we know how to reduce our levels of consumption without sacrificing those aspects of our society that are health-giving? At present, the answer is a qualified 'yes', but we are steadily gaining insights that are changing the answer to an unqualified 'yes'.

REFERENCES

Caldwell, J.C. (1986), 'Routes to low mortality in poor countries', *Population and Development Review*, **12**, 171–220.

Chandler, M.J. and C. Lalonde (1998), 'Cultural continuity as a hedge against suicide in Canada's First Nations', *Transcultural Psychiatry*, **35**(2), 191–219.

Cornell, S. and J.P. Kalt (2000), 'Where's the glue? Institutional and cultural foundations of American Indian economic development', *Journal of Socio-Economics*, **29**, 443–70.

Cornia, G.A. and R. Paniccia (2000), 'The transition mortality crisis: evidence, interpretation and policy responses', in G.A. Cornia and R. Paniccia (eds), *The Mortality Crisis in Transitional Economies*, New York: Oxford University Press, pp. 3–37.

Heller, P. (2000), 'Social capital and the developmental state: industrial workers', in G. Parayi (ed.), *Kerala: The Development Experience*, London: Zed Books.

Hertzman, C. (2000), 'Early child development in the context of population health', in A. Tarlov and R.F. St. Peter (eds), *The Society and Population Health Reader Volume II. A State and Community Perspective*, New York: The New Press.

Hertzman, C. (2001), 'Health and human society', *American Scientist*, November–December.

McKeown, T. (1979), *The Role of Medicine: Dream, Mirage, or Nemesis?*, Princeton, NJ: Princeton University Press.

Putnam, R.D. (1993), 'The prosperous community: social capital and public life', *The American Prospect*, **13** (Spring), 35–42.

Putnam, R.D., R. Leonardi and R.Y. Nanetti (1993), *Making Democracy Work. Civic Traditions in Modern Italy*, Princeton: Princeton University Press.

Smeeding, T.M. and P. Gottschalk (1996), 'The international evidence on income distribution in modern economies: where do we stand?', for the *Population Association of America*, 1996 Annual meeting, New Orleans.

Statistics Canada (1996), *Income after Tax, Distributions by Size in Canada 1994*, Ottawa: Minister of Industry.

Suomi, S.J. (1987), 'Genetic and maternal contributions to individual differences in rhesus monkey biobehavioral development', in N. Krasnegor et al. (eds), *Perinatal Development: a Psychobiological Perspective*, New York: Academic Press.

UNICEF (1993), *Central and Eastern Europe in Transition. Public Policy and Social Conditions* (Regional Monitoring Report No. 1. United Nations Children's Fund), Florence: International Child Development Centre.

UNICEF (1999), *After the Fall: the Human Impact of Ten Years of Transition* (The MONEE Project, CEE/CIS/Baltics) Florence: International Child Development Centre.

Vagero, D. and O. Lundberg (1989), 'Health inequalities in Britain and Sweden', *Lancet*, ii: 35–6.

Wackernagel, M. (1993), *How Big is our Ecological Footprint?*, The Task Force on Planning Healthy and Sustainable Communities, University of British Columbia.

Wackernagel, M. (1997), *Ecological Footprints 1993*, Mexico: Centro de Estudios para la Sustentabilidad.

Wackernagel, M. and W. Rees (1995), *Our Ecological Footprint: Reducing Human Impact on the Earth*, Gabriola Island, BC: New Society Publishers.

Wackernagel, M., N.B. Schulz, D. Deumling, A.C. Linares, M. Jenkins, V. Kapos, C. Monfreda, J. Loh, N. Myers, R. Norgaard and J. Randers (2002), 'Tracking the ecological overshoot of the human economy', *PNAS*, **99**(14), 9266–71.

Wilkins, R. and O. Adams (1992), 'Health expectancy trends in Canada, 1951–1986', in J.M. Robine, M. Blanchet and J.E. Dowd (eds), *Health Expectancy. First Workshop of the International Healthy Life Expectancy Network*, Office of Population Censuses and Surveys, London: DMSO: pp. 109–12.

World Bank (1993), *World Development Report. Investing in health. World development indicators*, New York: Oxford University Press.

World Health Organization MONICA Project (1994), 'Ecological analysis of the association between mortality and major risk factors of cardiovascular disease', *International Journal of Epidemiology*, **23**(3), 505–16.

SECTION C

Fisheries

6. Fisheries and coastal ecosystems: the need for integrated management

Daniel Pauly and Ratana Chuenpagdee

INTRODUCTION

How can it be that fisheries appear in trouble every time newspapers report on them? Coastal and marine fisheries have existed for a long time. Initially, people waded along the shore gathering shells and harpooned whatever marine mammal or large fish ventured inshore. Only those fish and other animal species that were large and had very narrow coastal distribution were then in danger of being over-fished. The invention and increased sophistication of crafts gradually extended our reach offshore but, for millennia, the elements and the very vastness of the ocean protected most fish populations from being over-fished; hence the notion that earlier, pre-industrial fisheries were 'sustainable' (Pauly et al., 2002). The gradual expansion of European fishing fleets in the seventeenth and eighteenth centuries, and their impact on the cod and other fish populations they exploited in European waters and off New England and Eastern Canada did not appear to change this, though signs of localized, fisheries-induced depletion were already then beginning to occur.

Things really changed when, as a result of the Industrial Revolution, steam trawlers began to expand into the North Sea, gradually mowing down one coastal stock after the other, then moving on to do the same offshore, inducing the first 'serial depletions' on record (Pitcher, 2001). Further technical developments – the invention of hydraulic winches, inboard refrigeration, acoustic fish finders, and so on – increased the ability of these boats effectively to locate and catch large quantities of fish and to bring them back from longer distances, thus opening up the entire North Atlantic to fishing operations (Cushing, 1988).

Similar development occurred in other industrialized parts of the world, for example in North America, North Asia and Australia. There as well, this occurred in waves following on the two World Wars, both of which accelerated the development of technologies that were later transferred to fishing operations.

Thus, in the early 1950s, the industrial fleets of the world were poised for global expansion. Their effects became intensified by another great wave of fisheries industrialization, this time in newly independent and other countries of Southeast Asia, Africa and South America. As a result, global catches strongly increased in the 1950s and 1960s, grew more slowly in the 1970s, and peaked in the late 1980s, as for the first time, catches from newly exploited stocks failed to compensate for depleted ones. Global catches have been declining since, despite the ever-increasing capacity of the world's fishing fleets (Watson and Pauly, 2001) (Figure 6.1). This implies a massive decrease in the inherent profitability of these fleets now maintained in most parts of the world by massive government-sponsored subsidization schemes (Munro and Sumaila, 2001).

Growing populations in developing countries, and a growing taste for fish in many developed countries led at the same time to a great increase in demand which, being increasingly hard to meet, is causing fish prices to increase more rapidly than that of most other foodstuff (Sumaila, 1999). This has also led to an increasing export of fish from developing to developed countries, thus reducing access to the poor of many developing countries of a previously cheap source of animal protein.

While it is usually possible for the agricultural sector to intensify its productivity in response to increase in demand and thus to preserve food security, yields from fully developed fisheries can, at best, be maintained (Ricker, 1975; Hilborn and Walters, 1992). It is more common, however, for yields to decline due to excessive levels of fishing effort, and for over-expansion of fishing and coastal developments (including mariculture – the farming of marine fish and shellfish) to destroy the structural integrity of coastal and other marine food webs, as is presently occurring in most parts of the world (Pauly et al., 1998; 2002).

Clearly, we must try to prevent the situation from worsening by searching for proactive and integrative measures for managing our fisheries and other coastal activities, and for minimizing negative environmental impacts on our coastal ecosystems (Costanza et al., 1998). The task for scientists and others engaged in coastal and marine resource management is thus to find ways to accommodate the need of coastal populations for sources of food and gainful employment with practices that are compatible with the continued productivity of natural coastal and marine resources. Or, in other words, we must show that fisheries exploitation and resource conservation are mutually compatible.

This contribution discusses related fisheries research and coastal area governance issues based mainly on (a) insights gained during the first years of the 'Sea Around Us' project devoted to studying global fisheries impacts on coastal and marine ecosystems, initially focused on the North

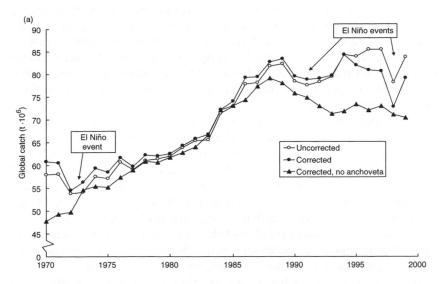

Note: Excluding freshwater catches and aquaculture production, displaying – since the late 1980s – a downward trend that is visible once the over-reporting of catches from China is corrected for, and the widely fluctuating Peruvian anchoveta is disconsidered.

Source: Modified from Watson and Pauly (2001).

Figure 6.1 Trends in world global marine fisheries catches

Atlantic, led by the first author (see www.seaaroundus.org), and on (b) research by the second author on innovative methods for involving stake-holders in decision-making processes for ecosystem-based management.

These issues are presented under three headings, dealing with:

1.   Downstream implications of fisheries impacts on marine ecosystems;
2.   Fisheries and other human impacts on coastal systems; and
3.   Alleviation of fisheries and other impacts at local and regional levels.

DOWNSTREAM IMPLICATIONS OF FISHERIES IMPACTS ON MARINE ECOSYSTEMS

Marine fisheries systems comprise the productive shelves surrounding continents down to a depth of 200 m, and the deeper, oceanic waters of tropical, temperate and polar areas. In these systems, fisheries activity is the dominant force behind environmental change. Though extremely variable in term of their physical features, these systems are all strongly and similarly impacted by fisheries. Those biomass withdrawals modify ecosystem biodiversity and functioning, the latter also through habitat modification resulting from bottom trawling (Watling and Norse, 1998). The polar components of these systems are also beginning to show direct effects of global warming.

As mentioned above, reported global marine fisheries catches (or more precisely: landings), now of the order of 80 million tonnes per year (including 30 million tonnes(t) used for fish meal and oil), which had increased rapidly following World War II, have peaked in the late 1980s. This is in spite of continued massive private investments and government subsidies which have increased fishing capacity several times beyond that required, given the size of global marine fisheries resources (Mace, 1997). Continuation of present trends will thus lead to a significant decrease in global fish supply. This potential shortfall is particularly worrisome given an increasing demand unlikely to be met by fish farming (especially not the farming of carnivorous fishes such as salmon, which requires meal and oil derived from small fishes also suited for human consumption; Naylor et al., 2000).

Considering other components of fisheries catches, that is discarded by-catch (10 million t), and illegal/unreported catches, including 'ghost fishing', that is fishing by lost gear (20–30 million t; Pauly et al., 2002) results in a global marine catch largely exceeding previous estimates of potential yields (Pauly, 1996). Available ecosystem indicators suggest present catches (and especially fishing effort) levels to be unsustainable, despite institutionalized systems for 'single-species' assessments and management of fleet operations (Ludwig et al., 1993). Fisheries impacts have caused shifts in species composition, notably toward species with lower sizes and trophic levels (Pauly et al., 1998; Pauly and Watson, 2005), (Figure 6.2), and decline in biomass (often by one order of magnitude; Christensen et al., 2003).

Also, with onboard high technology (fish finding and navigation) having enabled access to previously inaccessible natural refugia (great depths and distances offshore, rough bottoms, and so on), fisheries have caused numerous local extinctions of marine fish and higher vertebrate populations and caused widespread habitat alteration and loss. As some of these are still reversible, this has led to increasing calls for the (re-)establishment of marine refugia and other forms of ecosystem-based management (National Research Council, 1999; Pauly et al., 2002) that would encourage resource conservation.

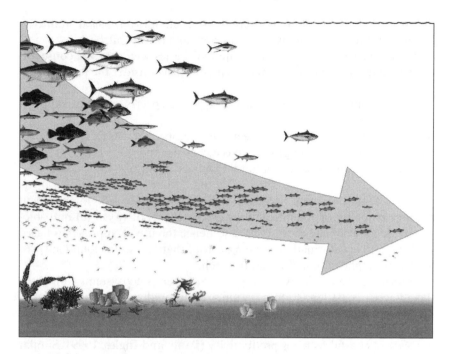

Note: A fishery starts by catching abundant large fish high in the food web (upper left corner), then gradually shifts to smaller fish, lower in the food web, as the former resource becomes less abundant. This process, which occurs in virtually all fisheries of the world, usually goes along with habitat destruction, as illustrated here by the gradual disappearance of the bottom structure created by bottom organisms.

Figure 6.2   Schematic representation of 'fishing down the the food web'

FISHERIES AND OTHER HUMAN IMPACTS ON COASTAL SYSTEMS

A large fraction of the global human population lives on coastal lands, and the building of cities and their resulting effluents have always had a strong impact on coastal ecosystems. These impacts have much increased in the last decades, especially in tropical developing countries which saw, besides the expansion of cities, a massive expansion of brackish water shrimp culture in areas previously covered by mangrove (Pauly and Ingles, 1999; Chuenpagdee et al., 2001a), direct exploitation of coral reef for lime and building materials, dredging of seagrass areas, and so on.

This makes ecosystem-based management even more important in coastal waters (down to 30–50 m), whose previously abundant fisheries resources have traditionally been managed based on single-species, sectoral approaches.

Given the downstream impacts of land-based activities on coastal productivity, these approaches were even less justified than further offshore.

A consensus is slowly emerging among fisheries scientists and conservationists that ecosystem-based management must consider the following:

a. The trophic relationship between exploited species and their supportive forage base;
b. The competition between fleets or sectors that express themselves through trophic linkages within ecosystems; and
c. The direct and indirect habitat impacts of fishing.

It is also becoming evident that ecosystem-based management requires mapping of the interactions of the effects of (a) to (c) onto biogeographically defined ecosystems, and hence the use of approaches based on Geographic Information Systems, a tool that has so far found surprisingly little application in fisheries research.

In terms of research, extending coastal fisheries ecosystems to include the adjacent coast lands zones requires, additionally, the identification of land-based activities impacting on the relationships in (a), (b) and (c), and quantifying, as opposed to only assuming, relationships between mangroves and coastal fisheries productivity (Pauly and Ingles, 1999). Similar research is required for seagrasses, estuaries, coral reefs and other sensitive coastal features in order to allow consideration in coastal project developments of the benefits forgone by the loss of such features (Costanza et al., 1998). Valuation of the importance of these ecosystems can be undertaken using the damage schedule approach, a non-monetary valuation method developed by Chuenpagdee et al. (2001a) (see also Appendix 6.1).

ALLEVIATION OF FISHERIES' AND OTHER IMPACTS AT LOCAL AND REGIONAL LEVELS

How could the dire and worsening situation of fisheries develop as it did? One answer clearly lies in the 'open-access' nature of marine resources which encourages the much decried 'race for fish'. Studying the actors involved provides another useful perspective. Who are the actors in fisheries? Are they being included in or excluded from the governance of fisheries? We shall elaborate on these two questions, as they provide a foundation for discussion of structure and power related to the principles of fisheries governance.

Actors are normally seen as those who are 'directly' or 'indirectly' related to the fisheries' resources or those with 'in-vested' interests. The general public, although frequently mentioned in the fisheries management literature, is generally not well represented in such discussions, as the government agencies tasked with managing fisheries on behalf of the citizenry at large (the true owner of the resources) have been 'captured', in most countries by the very industry they are supposed to regulate.

It is obvious, however, that unless all major actors who take part in fisheries are being effectively represented in the governance process, fisheries' resource sustainability and the related food security issues will continue to worsen. In addition, the inclusion of all concerned by the state and management of the coastal and marine resources must be coherent with the ecosystem-based management introduced above.

Fishers and other persons who rely on fisheries as the major sources of income (for example, processors and suppliers) are the main, and often the only, group of actors considered in discussion about fisheries governance. Here, a gradual consensus has emerged in many parts of the world that a transition is required from a top-down, government-based, centralized approach to management to bottom-up, community-based, decentralized 'co-management' approaches (Pinkerton, 1989; Jentoft and McCay, 1995), which imply recognition of fishers and fishing community as quasi-owners of the resources. This movement also requires new institutional arrangements and strategies to deal with issues such as heterogeneity of user groups (Felt, 1990), community representation (Jentoft et al., 1998), community support (Noble, 2000), and genuine devolution of state power (Sandersen and Koester, 2000).

A variant of this approach, the community-based management (CBM) model, suggests that fishers, other resource users and the community at large should become increasingly engaged in decision-making, and ultimately taking leadership in management. In this model, power is shared between 'authorized' (that is government) managers and the community, with increasing responsibility for management and decision-making authority for the latter.

One of the most important issues associated with this model is the 'inclusiveness' of the actors in the community, and their interactions, which can be either positive or negative. Positive interaction involves open dialogue, communication, negotiation and transparency, which are expected to result in conflict resolutions and collaboration. Negative effects, on the other hand, are partly caused by marginalization (Pauly, 1997), when interaction is not considered fair or just by all involved parties. This may consequently result in rejection of the interactions or at least the growth of mistrust.

While the CBM model acknowledges the need to involve a wider range of actors than the naïve versions of co-management models, it fails to recognize that the fishers themselves may have short-term interests, such as repaying the loan used to purchase a new fishing vessel, that are incompatible with the continued existence of sensitive coastal or marine resources, and hence at variance with the non-extractive interests of other actors. This problem becomes even more acute (for example, in Southeast Asia) where growing numbers of impoverished coastal fishers are forced by circumstances to eke a living from finite coastal resources, that is from resources which, in the process, they may effectively annihilate.

Management models structured around fishers' (quasi)-ownership of coastal fishing grounds fail in such cases, as they lead to impoverished fishers being the owner of a non-existent resource.

Put differently: while some authors claim that small-scale fishers' ownership of the resources would lead to good stewardship practices and sustainable fisheries, the field evidence shows that in the absence of formal property rights, these fishers overwhelmingly compete for the resources, with the short-term objective of maximizing their individual benefits with no consideration of the costs to society, as do the owners of large industrial fleets (see contributions in Coward et al., 2000). While the CBM model appears a useful component of our response to the crisis in fisheries around the world, it is by no means sufficient. A 'proactive' governance model is urgently needed that would help us quickly halt further destruction, and to foster ecosystem-based management principles. Moreover, resources will have to be extended to motivating small-scale fishers (and especially their young sons) out of fishing, through training and livelihood schemes. This is in contrast to most field-based fisheries projects run so far, which seek to improve the conditions of existing fishers and thus contribute to attracting more landless farmers and other rural poor into fishing (Pauly, 1997). This is particularly true in the wake of the December 2004 tsunami which devastated fishing communities throughout South and Southeast Asia (Pauly, 2005). Appendix 6.1 presents an approach through which the views of communities regarding perceived impacts or merits of various interventions can be elicited without undue bias due to the subjective perceptions of individual benefits alluded to above. As illustrated in Appendix 6.1, scientists, fishers and representatives of the public at large agreed that human influence of fish habitats, fishing impacts on the ecosystem, and inclusion of fishers in fishery management were the most important considerations in the design of fishery policies (Figure 6.3). Incorporating the community's perspectives into ecosystem-based management framework, such as shown in Appendix 6.1, is one important step toward proactive governance.

At levels above that of fishing communities, dealing with overfishing will require abolishing the government subsidies that have so far kept the industrial fleets of the world's fishing nations afloat (Munro and Sumaila, 2001; Pauly and Maclean, 2003). It is hard to conceive that such economic

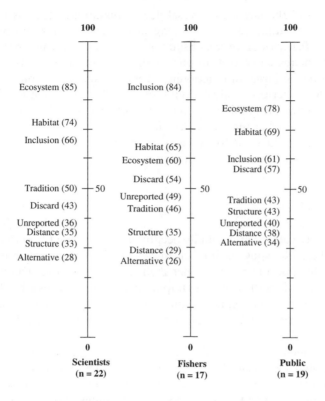

Code	Management considerations
Ecosystem	Fishing impacts on fisheries ecosystem
Habitat	Human influences on fish habitats
Inclusion	Inclusion of fishers in fishery management
Discard	Level of utilization of fish which are caught in a fishery
Tradition	Existence of traditional or historical fishing access
Unreported	Existence of fishing practices beyond regulations
Distance	Distance to and the reliance on the fishery
Structure	Existence of social/political structures influencing fishers' values
Alternative	Existence of alternative sources of livelihood

Note: Based on three respondent groups (see text in Appendix 6.1).

Figure 6.3 Damage schedule of fishery management decisions

intervention, and the large-scale vessel decommissioning schemes that it implies, could be implemented by the agencies presently responsible for managing the fisheries of various fishing nations. Rather, it will probably be necessary to create new institutions for the purpose, in which the interest of the public at large (in functioning ecosystems, and in economically viable, smaller fisheries) would be represented. This approach would be guided by a restorative ethic (see contributions in Coward et al., 2000), structured around what may be called 'fisheries conservation biology', a discipline that would need to be created around concepts drawn from fisheries biology and conservation biology.

CONCLUSIONS

Marine fisheries catches are globally declining, mainly due to overfishing, although other anthropogenic impacts in coastal areas have contributed to reducing the high productivity of inner shelf waters. The strong increase in small-scale fishers in the last decades implies decreasing catches for millions of small-scale fishers as well as declining incomes, as the increase of fish prices in the marketplace is not sufficient to compensate for the declining catches per fisher.

There is no techno-fix that will allow meeting, in the next decades, an increasing global demand for fish driven by increased population, increased incomes, increased taste for fish, and increased requirements for fish meal and oils for use in fish culture such as salmon farming. Indeed, maintaining present catch levels will not be possible if the present trend toward increasing fishing pressure continues (Pauly et al., 2003).

Present government arrangements, though they usually do not formalize property rights over marine resources, imply their quasi-ownership by the fishing industry. This can be inferred by the deferential treatment given to that industry by the government agencies tasked with regulating fishing fleets and gear deployment. It is clear that the public interest will have to be considered more explicitly in the governance and management of fisheries. This will involve the following:

1. The maintenance of marine ecosystems and their biodiversity as a public resource to be bequeathed to future generations;
2. A steady reliable supply of marine food stuffs, rather than the boom and bust operations resulting from serial depletions of marine resources;
3. An equitable use of the tax money presently wasted as subsidies whose major result is to maintain destructive fisheries that would otherwise have gone bankrupt;

4. Addressing the issue of poverty represented by millions of desperately poor Southeast Asian and other developing country fishers locked into a mode of resource exploitation that cannot support their activities in the long term, nor indeed meet their needs or those of their families; and

5. A transparent and inclusive process for incorporating communities' perspectives into an ecosystem-based management framework for fisheries and marine resources.

Despite encouraging noises (for example, at the recent World Conference on Sustainable Development in Johannesburg) we cannot at present conceive of the societal framework within which these issues would be seriously addressed and some of the mitigating approaches mentioned above implemented. As is the case for the issue of global warming (which, incidentally, also impinges on fisheries, by threatening the coral reefs sustaining many tropical fisheries, for example), these issues will not go away, and the underlying trends, notably a declining fisheries catch, will worsen until they are effectively addressed. Capacity-building at the local level, particularly for alternative employment, and an education and public awareness program for marine conservation and stewardship are two initiatives that need active promotion and firm support from all government levels and governance institutes, as they are promising means that can help alleviate the current fisheries crises.

Overall, we must conclude with an observation by Professor Katherine Richardson, Chair of the International Council for the Exploration of the Sea's Advisory Committee for the Marine Environment, that 'Sustainable management of fisheries cannot be achieved without an acceptance that the goals of fisheries management are the same as those of environmental conservation.'

ACKNOWLEDGEMENTS

We thank Professor Peter Nemetz for inviting this contribution, which updates a Vancouver Institute Lecture given by the first author, and entitled 'Global fisheries and marine conservation: is co-existence possible?' (documentation in www.library.ubc.ca/archives/ vaninsti.html). Our final quote is from a keynote presentation at the ICES/SCOR Conference on Ecosystem Effects of Fishing, Montpellier, France, March 1999.

APPENDIX 6.1   THE DAMAGE SCHEDULE
APPROACH AND ITS
APPLICATIONS TO COASTAL
AND MARINE ECOSYSTEMS

One promising valuation method to elicit preferences of stakeholders concerning the perceived impacts or merits of various interventions is called the 'damage schedule' approach. This methodology is based on the observation that it is usually far easier for individuals to compare pairs of choices, or objects, when asked to make a decision about them. By combining a number of decisions by a group of respondents, an investigator can then obtain a list ranked by preference, from least to most desirable (or important). Empirical research in various coastal and marine systems has established that such ranked lists will tend to reflect a consensus among respondents, even when they differ strongly in their perceived interests or even compete for the same natural resources (as do, for example, coastal fishers, shrimp farmers and tourist operators; see Chuenpagdee et al., 2001b).

Research by Power and Chuenpagdee (2003) has shown that this 'consensus-eliciting' aspect of the damage schedule approach can be used to identify important variables to consider when formulating fisheries policies. As the damage schedule relies on paired comparisons, it is constructed in this case from individuals' responses to a questionnaire containing a series of management considerations presented one pair at a time. The respondents, including scientists, fishers and general public, are then asked to select, for each pair, the management consideration that they consider more important. As shown in Figure 6.3, the ranking of important considerations varied slightly between the three respondent groups. These rankings were nonetheless significantly correlated at alpha level 0.05.

The detailed description of the approach is presented in Chuenpagdee et al. (2001a), and examples of application to coastal resources in Thailand and the Eastern Bering Sea Ecosystem are described in Chuenpagdee et al. (2001b), and in Chuenpagdee and Vasconcellos (2000), respectively. The damage schedule approach may also be used to help identify the optimal or most acceptable location of 'no-take' marine reserves and their surrounding marine protected areas (MPAs). The establishment of ecosystem-based fisheries management tools, increasingly required to restore damaged coastal and marine ecosystems, will be able to fulfill that role only with the acquiescence of the impacted communities in the context of new governance arrangements (Chuenpagdee et al., 2002).

REFERENCES

Christensen, V., S. Guénette, J.J. Heymans, C.J. Walters, R. Watson, D. Zeller and D. Pauly (2003), 'Hundred year decline of North Atlantic predatory fishes', *Fish and Fisheries*, **4**(1), 1–24.

Chuenpagdee, R. and M. Vasconcellos (2000), 'Application of the damage schedule approach on the Ecopath ecosystem modelling', in: U.R. Sumaila, R. Chuenpagdee and M. Vasconcellos (eds), *Proceedings of the INCO-DC International Workshop on Markets, Global Fisheries and Local Development*, Bergen, Norway, 22–23 March 1999, Brussels, ACP-EU Fisheries Research Report (7).

Chuenpagdee, R., J. Fraga and J. Euan (2002), 'Community's perspectives toward marine reserve: A case study of San Felipe, Yucatán, México', Coastal Management, **30**(2), 183–91.

Chuenpagdee, R., J.L Knetsch and T.C. Brown (2001a), 'Environmental damage schedules: community judgments of importance and assessments of losses', *Land Economics*, **77**(1), 1–11.

Chuenpagdee, R., J.L Knetsch and T.C. Brown (2001b), 'Coastal management using public judgments, importance scales, and predetermined schedule', *Coastal Management*, **29**(4), 253–70.

Costanza R., F. Andrade, P. Antunes, M. van den Belt, D. Boersma, D. Boesch, F. Catarino, S. Hanna, K. Limberg, B. Low, M. Molitor, J. Pereira, S. Rayner, R. Santos, J. Wilson and M. Young (1998), 'Principles for sustainable governance of the oceans,' Science, **281**, 198–99.

Coward, H., R. Omner and T.J. Pitcher (eds) (2000), *Just Fish: Ethics and Canadian Marine Fisheries*, Institute of Social and Economic Research, Memorial University of Newfoundland, St John's.

Cushing, D.H. (1988), *The Provident Sea*, Cambridge: Cambridge University Press.

Felt, L. (1990), 'Barriers to user participation in the management of the Canadian Atlantic salmon fishery: if wishes were fishes', Marine Policy, July, pp. 345–60.

Hilborn, R. and C.J. Walters (1992), *Quantitative Fisheries Stock Assessments: Choice, Dynamics and Uncertainty*, New York and London: Chapman and Hall.

Jentoft, S. and B. McCay (1995), 'User participation in fisheries management: Lessons drawn from international experiences', *Marine Policy*, **19**(3), 227–46.

Jentoft, S., B.J. McCay and D.C. Wilson (1998), 'Social theory and fisheries co-management', *Marine Policy*, **22**(4–5), 423–36.

Ludwig, D., R. Hilborn and C. Walters (1993), 'Uncertainty, resource exploitation and conservation: lessons from history', Science, **260**, pp. 17 and 36.

Mace, P.M. (1997), 'Developing and sustaining world fisheries resources: the state of fisheries and management', in: D.H. Hancock, D.C. Smith, A. Grant and J.P. Beumer (eds), *Proceedings of the 2nd World Fisheries Congress*, Collingwood, Australia: CSIRO Publishing, pp. 1–20.

Munro, G.R. and U.R. Sumaila (2001), 'Subsidies and their potential impact on the management of the ecosystems of the North Atlantic', in: T.J. Pitcher, R. Sumaila and D. Pauly (eds), *Fisheries Impacts on North Atlantic Ecosystems: Evaluation and Policy Exploration*, Fisheries Centre Research Reports, **9**(5), pp. 10–27, (Available online at www.seaaroundus.org/report/impactpolicyF.htm).

National Research Council (1999), *Sustaining Marine Fisheries*, Washington, DC: National Academy Press.

Naylor, R.L., J. Goldberg, J.H. Primavera, N. Kautsky, M.C.M. Beveridge, J. Clay,

C. Folke, J. Lubchenco, H. Mooney and M. Troell (2000), 'Effect of aquaculture on world fish supplies', *Nature*, **405**, 1017–24.
Noble, B.F. (2000), 'Institutional criteria for co-management', *Marine Policy*, **24**, 69–77.
Pauly, D. (1996), 'One hundred million tonnes of fish, and fisheries research', Fisheries Research, **25**(1), 25–38.
Pauly, D. (1997), 'Small-scale fisheries in the tropics: marginality, marginalization and some implication for fisheries management', in: E.K. Pikitch, D.D. Huppert and M.P. Sissenwine (eds), *Global trends: Fisheries Management*, American Fisheries Society Symposium 20, Bethesda, Maryland, pp. 40–49.
Pauly, D. (2005), 'Rebuilding fisheries will add to Asia's problems', Correspondence to *Nature*, **433**, 457.
Pauly, D. and J. Ingles (1999), 'The relationship between shrimp yields and inter-tidal vegetation (mangrove) areas: a reassessment', in: A. Yañez-Arancibia and A.L. Lara-Dominguez (eds), *Mangrove Ecosystems in Tropical America*, Instituto de Ecologia, A.C. Mexico, IUCN/ORMA, Costa Rica, NOAA/NMFS, Silver Spring, MD, USA, pp. 311–16.
Pauly, D. and J. Maclean (2003), *In a Perfect Ocean: The State of Fisheries and Ecosystems in the North Atlantic Ocean*, Washington, DC: Island Press.
Pauly, D. and R. Watson (2005), 'Background and interpretation of the "Marine Trophic Index" as a measure of biodiversity', *Philosophical Transactions of the Royal Society*, (B), **360**, 415–23.
Pauly, D., V. Christensen, J. Dalsgaard, R. Froese and F.C. Torres Jr (1998), 'Fishing down marine food webs', Science, **279**, 860–63.
Pauly, D., J. Alder, E. Bennett, V. Christensen, P. Tyedmers and R. Watson (2003), 'The future for fisheries', *Science*, **302**, 1359–61.
Pauly, D., V. Christensen, S. Guénette, T. Pitcher, U.R. Sumaila, C. Walters, R. Watson and D. Zeller (2002), 'Toward sustainability in world fisheries', *Nature*, **418**, 689–95.
Pinkerton, E. (1989), *Cooperative Management of Local Fisheries: New Directions for Improved Management and Community Development*, Vancouver: University of British Columbia Press.
Pitcher, T.J. (2001), 'Fisheries managed to rebuild ecosystem? Reconstructing the past to salvage the future', *Ecological Applications*, **11**, 601–17.
Pitcher, T.J., P.J.B. Hart and D. Pauly (eds) (2001), *Reinventing Fisheries Management*, Fish and Fisheries Series 23, Dordrecht: Kluwer Academic Publishers.
Power, D. and R. Chuenpagdee (2003), 'Fishers and scientists: no longer foe, but not yet friend', in: N. Haggan, C. Brignall and L. Wood (eds), *Putting Fishers' Knowledge to Work*, pp. 259–66, proceedings of a conference held at the Fisheries Centre, University of British Columbia, 27–30 August, 2001, Fisheries Centre Research Report 11(1). (Available on-line at www.fisheries.ubc.ca/publications/reports/11-1/28_power_chuenpagdee.pdf)
Ricker, W.E. (1975), 'Computation and interpretation of biological statistics of fish populations', *Bulletin of the Fisheries Research Board of Canada* (191).
Sandersen, H.T. and Koester, S. (2000), 'Co-management of tropical coastal zones: the case of the Soufrière marine management area, St. Lucia, WI', *Coastal Management*, **28**, 87–97.
Sumaila, U.R. (1999), 'Pricing down marine food webs', in: D. Pauly, V. Christensen

and L. Coelho (eds), *Proceedings of the '98 EXPO Conference on Ocean Food Webs and Economic Productivity*, pp. 13–15, Lisbon, Portugal, 1–3 July 1998, ACP-EU Fisheries Research Report, 5.

Watling, L. and E.A. Norse (1998), 'Disturbance of the seabed by mobile fishing gear: a comparison to forest clearcutting', *Conservation Biology*, **12**(6), 1180–97.

Watson, R. and D. Pauly (2001), 'Systematic distortion in world fisheries catch trends', *Nature*, **424**, 534–6.

SECTION D

Agriculture

7. Fatal harvest: old and new dimensions of the ecological tragedy of modern agriculture

Miguel A. Altieri

INDUSTRIAL AGRICULTURE AND BIODIVERSITY

Agriculture implies the simplification of nature's biodiversity and reaches an extreme form in crop monoculture. The end result is the production of an artificial ecosystem requiring constant human intervention. In most cases, this intervention is in the form of agrochemical inputs which, in addition to boosting yields, result in a number of undesirable environmental and social costs (Altieri, 1995).

Global threats to biodiversity should not be foreign to agriculturalists, since agriculture, which covers about 25–30 per cent of the world land area, is perhaps one of the main activities affecting biological diversity. It is estimated that the global extent of cropland increased from around 265 million hectares in 1700 to around 1.5 billion hectares today, predominantly at the expense of forest habitats (Clay, 2003). Very limited areas remain totally unaffected by agriculture-induced land use changes (McNeely and Scherr, 2003).

Clearly, agriculture implies the simplification of the structure of the environment over vast areas, replacing nature's diversity with a small number of cultivated plants and domesticated animals. In fact, the world's agricultural landscapes are planted with only some 12 species of grain crops, 23 vegetable crop species, and about 35 fruit and nut crop species; that is no more than 70 plant species spread over approximately 1440 million ha of presently cultivated land in the world. This is in sharp contrast with the diversity of plant species found within one hectare of a tropical rainforest which typically contains over 100 species of trees. Of the 7000 crop species used in agriculture, only 120 are important at a national level. An estimated 90 per cent of the world's calorie intake comes from just 30 crops, a small sample of the vast crop diversity available (Jackson and Jackson, 2002).

The process of ecological simplification associated with industrial agriculture can affect biodiversity in various ways:

- Expansion of agricultural land with loss of natural habitats
- Conversion into homogenous agricultural landscapes with low habitat value for wildlife
- Loss of wild species and beneficial agrobiodiversity as a direct consequence of agrochemical inputs and other practices
- Erosion of valuable genetic resources through increased use of uniform high-yielding varieties

As the industrial model was introduced into the developing world, agricultural diversity has been eroded as monoculture has started to dominate. For example, in Bangladesh the promotion of Green Revolution rice led to a loss of diversity including nearly 7000 traditional rice varieties and many fish species. Similarly in the Philippines, the introduction of HYV rice displaced more than 300 traditional rice varieties. In the North similar losses in crop diversity are occurring. Eighty-six per cent of the 7000 apple varieties used in the US between 1804 and 1904 are no longer in cultivation; of 2683 pear varieties, 88 per cent are no longer available. In Europe thousands of varieties of flax and wheat vanished following the take-over by modern variants (Thrupp, 1998; Lipton and Longhurst, 1989).

MODERN AGRICULTURE, GENETIC HOMOGENIZATION AND ECOLOGICAL VULNERABILITY

Modern agriculture is shockingly dependent on a handful of varieties for its major crops. For example, in the US two decades ago, 60 to 70 per cent of the total bean acreage was planted with two to three bean varieties, 72 per cent of the potato acreage with four varieties, and 53 per cent with three cotton varieties (National Academy of Sciences, 1972). Researchers have repeatedly warned about the extreme vulnerability associated with this genetic uniformity. Perhaps the most striking example of vulnerability associated with homogenous uniform agriculture was the collapse of Irish potato production in 1845, where the uniform stock of potatoes was highly susceptible to the blight *Phytophthora infestans infestans*. During the nineteenth century in France, wine grape production was wiped out by a virulent pest, *Phylloxera vitifoliae*, which eliminated 4 million hectares of uniform grape varieties. Banana monocultural plantations in Costa Rica have been repeatedly seriously jeopardized by diseases such as *Fusarium oxysporum* and yellow sigatoka. In the USA, in the early 1970s, uniform high-yielding maize hybrids comprised about 70 per cent of all the maize varieties; a 15 per cent loss of the entire crop by leaf blight occurred in that decade (Thrupp, 1998). Uniform commercial potato crops in western industrial nations are currently threatened by late potato blight, the same fungus that caused the potato famine in Ireland. Late blight is jeopardizing the $160 billion potato industry in the USA, and is causing losses of up to 30 per cent in Third World potato areas, and especially in those where potato diversity has been lost. A worrisome trend is the recent expansion of transgenic maize and soybean monocultures with a narrow genetic base and which reached about 70 million hectares worldwide in 2004.

Modern agroecosystems are unstable, and breakdowns manifest themselves as recurrent pest outbreaks in most cropping systems. The worsening of most pest problems has been experimentally linked to the expansion of crop monoculture at the expense of vegetation diversity. This diversity is a key landscape component providing crucial ecological services to ensure crop protection through provision of habitat and resources to natural pest enemies (Altieri, 1994). Ninety-one per cent of the 1.5 billion hectares of cropland worldwide are under annual crops and planted with mostly monocultures of wheat, rice, maize, cotton and soybeans. One of the main problems arising from the homogenization of agricultural systems is an increased vulnerability of crops to insect pests and diseases, which can be devastating if they infest a uniform crop, especially in large plantations. To protect these crops, copious amounts of increasingly less effective and selective pesticides are injected into the biosphere at considerable environmental and human costs. These are clear signs that the pesticide-based approach to pest control has reached its limits. An alternative approach is needed; one based on the use of ecological principles in order to design more sustainable farming systems that take full advantage of the benefits of biodiversity in agriculture.

THE EXPANSION OF MONOCULTURE IN NORTH AMERICA

Today, monoculture has increased dramatically worldwide, mainly through the geographical expansion of land devoted to single crops and year-to-year production of the same crop species on the same land. Available data indicate that the amount of crop diversity per unit of arable land has decreased and that croplands have shown a tendency toward concentration. There are political and economic forces influencing the trend to devote large areas to monoculture and, in fact, such systems are rewarded by economies of scale and contribute significantly to the ability of national agricultures to serve international markets.

The technologies which have facilitated the shift toward monoculture are mechanization, the improvement of crop varieties, and the development of agrochemicals to fertilize crops and control weeds and pests. Government commodity policies these past several decades have also encouraged the acceptance and utilization of these technologies. As a result, farms today are fewer, larger, more specialized and more capital-intensive. At the regional level, the increase in monoculture farming has meant that the entire agricultural support infrastructure (that is research, extension, suppliers, storage, transport, markets, and so on) has become more specialized.

From an ecological perspective, the regional consequences of monoculture specialization are manifold:

a. Most large-scale agricultural systems exhibit a poorly structured assemblage of farm components, with almost no linkages or complementary relationships between crop enterprises and among soils, crops and animals.

b. Cycles of nutrients, energy, water and wastes have become more open, rather than closed as in a natural ecosystem. Despite the substantial amount of crop residues and manure produced in farms, it is becoming increasingly difficult to recycle nutrients, even within agricultural systems. Animal wastes cannot economically be returned to the land in a nutrient-recycling process because production is geographically remote from other systems which would complete the cycle. In many areas, agricultural waste has become a liability rather than a resource. Recycling of nutrients from urban centers back to the fields is similarly difficult.

c. Part of the instability and susceptibility to pests of agroecosystems can be linked to the adoption of vast crop monocultures, which have concentrated resources for specialist crop herbivores and have increased the areas available for immigration of pests. This simplification has also reduced environmental opportunities for natural enemies. Consequently, pest outbreaks often occur with the simultaneous occurrence of large numbers of immigrant pests, inhibited populations of beneficial insects, favorable weather and vulnerable crop stages.

d. As specific crops are expanded beyond their 'natural' ranges or favorable regions to areas of high pest potential, or with limited water or low-fertility soils, intensified chemical controls are required to overcome such limiting factors. The assumption is that human intervention and the level of energy inputs that allow these expansions can be sustained indefinitely.

e. Commercial farmers witness a constant parade of new crop varieties as varietal replacement due to biotic stresses and market changes have accelerated to unprecedented levels. A cultivar with improved disease or insect resistance makes a debut, performs well for a few years (typically 5–9 years) and is then succeeded by another variety when yields begin to slip, productivity is threatened, or a more promising cultivar becomes available. A variety's trajectory is characterized by a take-off phase when it is adopted by farmers, a middle stage when the planted area stabilizes, and finally a retraction of its acreage. Thus, stability in modern agriculture hinges on a continuous supply of new cultivars rather than a patchwork quilt of many different varieties planted on the same farm.

f. The need to subsidize monoculture requires increases in the use of pesticides and fertilizers, but the efficiency of use of applied inputs is decreasing and crop yields in most key crops are leveling off. In some places, yields are actually in decline. There are different opinions as to the underlying causes of this phenomenon. Some believe that yields are leveling off because the maximum yield potential of current varieties is being approached, and therefore genetic engineering must be applied to the task of redesigning crops. Agroecologists, on the other hand, believe that the leveling off is because of the steady erosion of the productive base of agriculture through unsustainable practices.

MODERN SCIENCE, THE GREEN REVOLUTION AND PEASANT CROP DIVERSITY

Perhaps the greatest challenge to understanding how traditional farmers maintain, preserve and manage biodiversity is to acknowledge the complexity of their production systems. Part of this complexity involves the recognition that crop genetic resources are more than just a collection of alleles and genotypes of native crops and wild relatives. They also include ecological interactions such as gene flow via cross-pollination among crop populations and species, as well as human selection and management guided by systems of knowledge and practice associated with genetic diversity, especially complex folk taxonomies and selection about adaptation to heterogeneous environments. Today it is widely accepted that indigenous knowledge is a powerful resource in its own right and is complementary to knowledge available from Western scientific sources. Agronomists, other scientists and development consultants have struggled to understand the complexities of local farming methods and their underlying assumptions. Unfortunately, more often than not, they have ignored traditional farmers' rationales and imposed conditions and technologies that have disrupted the integrity of native agriculture (Shiva, 1991). This was prophetically stated by Berkeley geographer Carl Sauer after visiting Mexico at the invitation of the Rockefeller Foundation in the wake of the Green Revolution:

> A good aggressive bunch of American agronomists and plant breeders could ruin native resources for good and all by pushing their American commercial stocks. . . . And Mexican agriculture cannot be pointed toward standardization on a few commercial types without upsetting native economy and culture hopelessly. The example of Iowa is about the most dangerous of all for Mexico. Unless the Americans understand that, they'd better keep out of this country entirely. This must be approached from an appreciation of native economies as being basically sound. (Jennings, 1988)

Part of the problem arises from the fact that the association of genetic diversity with traditional agriculture is perceived in development and scientific circles as negative, and thus linked to underdevelopment, low production and poverty. Many people involved in international agriculture view on-farm conservation of native crop diversity as the opposite of agricultural development (Brush, 2000). The proponents of the Green Revolution assumed that progress and development in traditional agroecosystems inevitably required the replacement of local crop varieties by improved ones. They also assumed that the economic and technological integration of traditional farming systems into the global system is a positive step that enables increased production, income and social well-being (Wilkes and Wilkes, 1972). But, as evinced by the Green Revolution, integration also created several negative impacts (Tripp, 1996; Lappe et al., 1998):

- The Green Revolution involved the promotion of a package that included modern varieties (MVs), fertilizer and irrigation, marginalizing a great number of resource-poor farmers who could not afford the technology.
- In areas where farmers adopted the package stimulated by government extension and credit programs, the spread of MVs greatly increased the use of pesticides, often with serious health and environmental consequences.
- Enhanced uniformity caused by sowing large areas to a few MVs increased risk for farmers. Genetically uniform crops proved more susceptible to pests and diseases; and improved varieties did not perform well in marginal environments where the poor live.
- Diversity is an important nutritional resource of poor communities, but the spread of MVs was accompanied by a simplification of traditional agroecosystems and a trend toward monoculture which

affected dietary diversity, thus raising considerable nutritional concerns.

• The replacement of folk varieties also represents a loss of cultural diversity, as many varieties are integral to religious or community ceremonies. Given this, several authors have argued that the conservation and management of agrobiodiversity may not be possible without the preservation of cultural diversity.

It is important to point out that indigenous/traditional farmers are not totally isolated from industrial agriculture and many appear to be more than willing to experiment with MVs, adopting them when they fulfill complex criteria that include not only higher yield, but also local adaptation and cultural value. Once tested, farmers may integrate some MVs into the group of local landraces as done by farmers in Cuzalapa, in the state of Jalisco, Mexico. In this case, rather than displacing local cultivars, exotic varieties occupy a small proportion of the area planted to maize, but local landraces continue to dominate the agroecosystem. Introduced varieties more often have uses and modes of management that are complementary, rather than substitutable for those of the dominant local cultivars (Brush, 2000).

THE FIRST WAVE OF ENVIRONMENTAL PROBLEMS

The specialization of production units has led to the image that agriculture is a modern miracle of food production. Evidence indicates, however, that excessive reliance on monoculture farming and agroindustrial inputs, such as capital-intensive technology, pesticides and chemical fertilizers, has negatively impacted the environment and rural society. Most agriculturalists had assumed that the agroecosystem/natural ecosystem dichotomy need not lead to undesirable consequences, yet, unfortunately, a number of 'ecological diseases' have been associated with the intensification of food production. They may be grouped into two categories: (1) diseases of the ecotope, which include erosion, loss of soil fertility, depletion of nutrient reserves, salinization and alkalinization, pollution of water systems, loss of fertile croplands to urban development; and (2) diseases of the biocoenosis, which include loss of crop, wild plant and animal genetic resources, elimination of natural enemies, pest resurgence and genetic resistance to pesticides, chemical contamination, and destruction of natural control mechanisms. Under conditions of intensive management, treatment of such 'diseases' requires an increase in the external costs to the extent that, in some agricultural systems, the amount of energy invested to produce a desired yield surpasses the energy harvested (Altieri, 1995).

The loss of yields due to pests (reaching about 20–30 per cent in most crops), despite the substantial increase in the use of pesticides (about 500 million kg of active ingredient worldwide) is a symptom of the environmental crisis affecting agriculture. It is well known that cultivated plants grown in genetically homogenous monocultures do not possess the necessary ecological defense mechanisms to tolerate the impact of outbreaking pest populations. Modern agriculturists have selected crops for high yields and high palatability, making them more susceptible to pests by sacrificing natural resistance for productivity. On the other hand, modern agricultural practices negatively affect pests' natural enemies, which in turn do not find the necessary environmental resources and opportunities in monocultures to effectively suppress pests by natural biological means.

The lack of natural pest control mechanisms in monocultures makes modern agroecosystems heavily dependent on pesticides. In the past 50 years the use of pesticides in agriculture has increased dramatically worldwide and now amounts to some 2,56 million tons of pesticides per year. In the early twenty-first century the annual value of the global market was US$ 25 billion (Pretty, 2005). In the US approximately 324 million kg of 600 different types of pesticides are used annually at a cost of no less than $4.1 billion (Pimentel and Lehman, 1993; Pretty, 2005). The indirect costs of pesticide use to the environment and public health have to be balanced against their benefits. Based on the available data, the environmental costs (impacts on wildlife, pollinators, natural enemies, fisheries, water and development of resistance) and social costs (human poisonings and illnesses) of pesticide use reach about $8 billion each year (Pimentel et al., 1980). What is worrisome is that pesticide use is on the rise. Data from California shows that from 1991 to 1995, pesticide use increased from 161 to 212 million pounds of active ingredient. These increases were not due to expansion in planted acreage, as statewide crop acreage remained constant during this period. Crops such as strawberries and grapes account for much of this increased use, which includes toxic pesticides, many of which are linked to cancers. On top of this, 540 species of arthropods have developed resistance against more than 1000 different types of pesticides which have been rendered useless to control such pests chemically (Bills et al., 2003). During the 1990s there was a 38 per cent increase in products to which one or more arthropod species is now resistant and a 7 per cent increase in arthropod species that are resistant to one or more pesticides.

Pesticides in groundwater, surface waters and drinking water have become a serious and increasingly environmental side-effect of pesticide use. In the US, some 9900 wells out of 68 800 tested between 1971 and 1991 had pesticide residues exceeding EPA standards for drinking water (Pretty,

2005). Among the residues found are DDT, chlordane, dieldrin and PCBs – all persistent pesticides.

Fertilizers, on the other hand, have been praised as being closely associated with the increase in food production observed in many countries. National average rates of nitrate applied to most arable lands fluctuate between 120–550 kg N/ha. But the bountiful harvests created at least in part through the use of chemical fertilizers, have associated, and often hidden, costs. A primary reason why chemical fertilizers pollute the environment is due to wasteful application and the fact that crops use them inefficiently. The fertilizer that is not recovered by the crop ends up in the environment, mostly in surface water or in groundwater. Nitrate contamination of aquifers is widespread and at dangerously high levels in many rural regions of the world. In the US, it is estimated that more than 25 per cent of the drinking water wells contain nitrate levels above the 45 parts per million safety standard (Conway and Pretty, 1991). Such nitrate levels are hazardous to human health, and studies have linked nitrate uptake to methaemoglobinemia in children and to gastric, bladder and oesophageal cancers in adults (Conway and Pretty, 1991).

Fertilizer nutrients that enter surface waters (rivers, lakes, bays, and so on) can promote eutrophication, characterized initially by a population explosion of photosynthetic algae. Algal blooms turn the water bright green, prevent light from penetrating beneath surface layers, and therefore kill plants living on the bottom. Such dead vegetation serves as food for other aquatic micro-organisms which soon deplete water of its oxygen, inhibiting the decomposition of organic residues, which accumulate on the bottom. Eventually, such nutrient enrichment of freshwater ecosystems leads to the destruction of all animal life in the water systems. In the US it is estimated that about 50–70 per cent of all nutrients that reach surface waters are derived from fertilizers. Chemical fertilizers can also become air pollutants, and have recently been implicated in the destruction of the ozone layer and in global warming. Their excessive use has also been linked to the acidification/salinization of soils and to a higher incidence of insect pests and diseases through mediation of negative nutritional changes in crop plants.

It is clear then that the first wave of environmental problems is deeply rooted in the prevalent socioeconomic system which promotes monoculture and the use of high input technologies and agricultural practices that lead to natural resource degradation. Such degradation is not only ecological in nature, but also a social and political-economic process. This is why the problem of agricultural production cannot be regarded as only purely technological. While agreeing that productivity issues represent part of the problem, attention to social, cultural and economic issues that account for the crisis is crucial. This is particularly true today where the economic and political domination of the rural development agenda by agribusiness has thrived at the expense of the interests of consumers, farm workers, small family farms, wildlife, the environment and rural communities.

THE SECOND WAVE OF ENVIRONMENTAL PROBLEMS

Despite the fact that awareness of the impacts of modern technologies on the environment has increased, as we have traced pesticides in food chains and crop nutrients in streams and aquifers, there are those who still argue for further intensification to meet the requirements of agricultural production. It is in this context that supporters of 'status-quo agriculture' celebrate the emergence of biotechnology as the latest magic bullet that will revolutionize agriculture with products based on nature's own methods, making farming more environmentally friendly and more profitable for the farmer. Clearly, certain forms of non-transformational biotechnology hold promise for an improved agriculture. However, given its present orientation and control by multinational corporations, it holds more promise for environmental harm, for the further industrialization of agriculture, and for the intrusion of private interests too far into public interest sector research.

What is ironic is the fact that the biorevolution is being brought forward by the same interests (such as Monsanto, Novartis, DuPont, and so on) that promoted the first wave of agrochemically-based agriculture. By equipping each crop with new 'insecticidal genes', they are now promising the world safer pesticides, reduction of chemically-intensive farming and a more sustainable agriculture. As long as transgenic crops follow closely the pesticide paradigm, however, such biotechnological products will do nothing but reinforce the pesticide treadmill in agroecosystems, thus legitimizing the concerns that many scientists have expressed regarding the possible environmental risks of genetically engineered organisms.

So far, field research as well as predictions based on ecological theory indicate that the major environmental risks associated with the release of genetically engineered crops can be summarized as follows (Rissler and Mellon, 1996; Marvier, 2001):

- The intent of agrocorporations is to create broad international markets for a single product, thus creating the conditions for genetic uniformity in rural landscapes. History has repeatedly shown that a huge area planted to a single cultivar is extremely vulnerable to a new matching strain of a pathogen or pest;

- The spread of transgenic crops threatens crop genetic diversity by simplifying cropping systems and promoting genetic erosion;
- There is potential for the unintended transfer to plant relatives of the 'transgenes' and unpredictable ecological effects. The transfer of genes from herbicide resistant crops (HRCs) to wild or semi-domesticated relatives can lead to the creation of super weeds;
- It is likely that insect pests will quickly develop resistance to crops with *Bacillus thuringiensis* (Bt) toxin. Several Lepidoptera species have been reported to develop resistance to Bt toxin in both field and laboratory tests. Major resistance problems are likely to develop in Bt crops where the continuous expression of the toxin create a strong selection pressure;
- Massive use of Bt toxin in crops can unleash potential negative interactions affecting ecological processes and non-target organisms. Studies conducted in Scotland suggest that aphids are capable of sequestering the toxin from Bt crops and transferring it to its coccinellid predators, in turn affecting reproduction and longevity of the beneficial beetles (Hilbeck et al., 1998);
- Bt toxins can also be incorporated into the soil through leaf materials and litter, where they may persist for 2–3 months, resisting degradation by binding to soil clay particles while maintaining toxic activity. This negatively affects invertebrates and nutrient cycling;
- A potential risk of transgenic plants expressing viral sequences derives from the possibility of new viral genotypes being generated by recombination between the genomic RNA of infecting viruses and RNA transcribed from the transgene;
- Another important environmental concern associated with the large scale cultivation of virus-resistant transgenic crops relates to the possible transfer of virus-derived transgenes into wild relatives through pollen flow.

Although there are many unanswered questions regarding the impact of the release of transgenic plants and micro-organisms into the environment, it is expected that biotechnology will exacerbate the problems of conventional agriculture and, by promoting monoculture, will also undermine ecological methods of farming such as crop rotations and polyculture. Transgenic crops developed for pest control emphasize the use of a single control mechanism which has proven to fail over and over again with insects, pathogens and weeds. Thus transgenic crops are likely to increase the use of pesticides and to accelerate the evolution of 'super weeds' and resistant insect pest strains (Altieri, 2000). These possibilities are worrisome, especially when considering that during the period 1986–1997, approximately 25 000 transgenic crop field trials were conducted worldwide on more than 60 crops with 10 traits in 45 countries. The biotech industry and their research allies celebrated in 2004 the continual expansion of biotech crops for the ninth consecutive year at a sustained double-digit growth rate of 20 per cent, compared with 15 per cent in 2003. The estimated global area of approved biotech crops for 2004 was 81.0 million hectares in 22 countries, although most are concentrated in the USA, Canada and Argentina.

In most countries, biosafety standards to monitor such releases are absent or are inadequate to predict ecological risks. In the industrialized countries from 1986–1992, 57 per cent of all field trials to test transgenic crops involved herbicide tolerance pioneered by 27 corporations including the world's eight largest pesticide companies. As Roundup and other broad spectrum herbicides are increasingly deployed on croplands, the options for farmers for a diversified agriculture will be even more limited.

THE POTENTIAL IMPACTS OF TRANSGENIC CROPS ON SMALL-SCALE AGRICULTURE IN THE DEVELOPING WORLD

Concerns have been raised about whether the introduction of transgenic crops may replicate or further aggravate the effects of MVs on the genetic diversity of landraces and wild relatives in areas of crop origin and diversification and therefore affect the cultural thread of communities. The debate was prompted by a controversial article in *Nature* reporting the presence of introgressed transgenic DNA constructs in native maize landraces grown in remote mountains in Oaxaca, Mexico (Quist and Chapela, 2001). Although there is a high probability that the introduction of transgenic crops will further accelerate the loss of genetic diversity and indigenous knowledge and culture through mechanisms similar to those of the Green Revolution, there are some fundamental differences in the magnitude of the impacts. The Green Revolution increased the rate at which modern varieties replaced folk varieties without necessarily changing the genetic integrity of local varieties. Genetic erosion involves a loss of local varieties, but it can be slowed and even reversed through *in situ* efforts which conserve not only landraces and wild-weedy relatives, but also agroecological and cultural relationships of crop evolution and management in specific localities. Examples of successful *in situ* conservation have been widely documented.

The problem with the introduction of transgenic crops into regions characterized by diversity is that the spread of characteristics of genetically altered grain to local varieties favored by small farmers could dilute the natural sustainability of these races. Many proponents of biotechnology believe that unwanted gene flow from GM maize may not compromise maize biodiversity (and therefore the associated systems of agricultural knowledge and practice along with the ecological and evolutionary processes involved) and may pose no worse a threat than cross-pollination from conventional (non-GM) seed. In fact, some industry researchers believe that DNA from engineered maize is unlikely to have an evolutionary advantage, but if transgenes do persist, they may actually prove advantageous to Mexican farmers and crop diversity. But here a key question arises: can genetically engineered plants actually increase crop production and, at the same time repel pests, resist herbicides, and confer adaptation to stressful factors commonly faced by small farmers? Thermodynamic considerations suggest they cannot; traits important to indigenous farmers (resistance to drought, food or fodder quality, maturity, competitive ability, performance on intercrops, storage quality, taste or cooking properties, compatibility with household labor conditions, and so on) could be traded for transgenic qualities which may not be important to farmers (Jordan, 2001). Under this scenario, risk will increase and farmers will lose their ability to adapt to changing biophysical environments and their ability to produce relatively stable yields with a minimum of external inputs while supporting their communities' food security.

Most scientists agree that teosinte and maize interbreed. One problematic result from a transgenic maize-teosinte cross would be if the crop-wild relative hybrids become more successful by acquiring tolerance to pests (Ellstrand, 2001). Such hybrids could become problem weed upsetting farmers' management but also out-competing wild relatives. Another potential problem derived from transgenic crop-to-wild gene flow is that it can lead to extinction of wild plants via swamping and outbreeding depression (Stabinski and Sarno, 2001).

The impacts of transgenic contamination of landraces may not be limited to introgression mediated changes in the fitness of native crops or wild relatives. Introduction of transgenic crops could also affect the biological balance of insect communities within traditional agroecosystems. In the case of Bt maize, it is known that natural enemies of insect pests could be directly affected through inter-trophic level effects of the Bt toxin. The potential of Bt toxins to move through insect food chains has serious implications for natural biocontrol in agricultural fields. Recent evidence shows that the Bt toxin can affect beneficial insect predators that feed on insect pests present on Bt crops. Studies in Switzerland show that mean total mortality of predaceous lacewing larvae (*Chrysopidae*) raised on Bt-fed prey was 62 per cent compared to 37 per cent when raised on Bt-free prey. These

Bt prey fed *Chrysopidae* also exhibited prolonged development time throughout their immature life stage (Hilbeck et al., 1998).

These findings are of concern to small farmers who rely on the rich complex of predators and parasites associated with their mixed cropping systems for insect pest control (Altieri, 1994). Inter-trophic level effects of the Bt toxin raise serious concerns about the potential for the disruption of natural pest control. Polyphagous predators that move throughout the crop season within and between mixed crops cultivars subjected to transgenic pollution will surely encounter Bt-containing, non-target prey. Disrupted biocontrol mechanisms may result in increased crop losses due to pests or to increased use of pesticide by farmers, with potential consequent health and environmental hazards.

Still, the negative environmental effects are not limited to crops and insects. Bt toxins can be incorporated into the soil through leaf materials when farmers plow under transgenic crop residues after harvest. Toxins may persist for two to three months, resisting degradation by binding to clay and humic acid soil particles while maintaining toxin activity. Such active Bt toxins that end up and accumulate in the soil and water from transgenic leaf litter may have negative impacts on soil and aquatic invertebrates and nutrient cycling processes. The fact that Bt retains its insecticidal properties and is protected against microbial degradation by being bound to soil particles, persisting in various soils for at least 234 days, is of serious concern for poor farmers who cannot purchase expensive chemical fertilizers. These farmers rely instead on local residues, organic matter, and soil microorganisms for soil fertility (key invertebrate, fungal or bacterial species), which can be negatively affected by the soil-bound toxin. By losing such ecological services, poor farmers can become dependent on fertilizers, with serious economic implications (Altieri, 2000).

CREATING SAFEGUARDS AGAINST TRANSGENIC HOMOGENIZATION

In today's globalized world, technological modernization of small farmers, through monoculture, new crop varieties and agrochemicals is perceived as a critical prerequisite for increasing yields, labor efficiency and farm income. As conversion from subsistence to a cash agricultural economy occurs, the loss of biodiversity in many rural societies is progressing at an alarming rate. As peasants directly link to the market economy, economic forces increasingly favor a mode of production characterized by genetically uniform crops and mechanized and/or agrochemical packages. As adoption of modern varieties occurs, landraces and wild relatives are progressively abandoned, becoming relics or extinct. The greatest loss of traditional varieties is occurring more in lowland valleys close to urban centers and markets than in more remote areas (Brush, 2000). In some areas, land scarcity (resulting mostly from uneven land distribution) has forced changes in land use and agricultural practices. The result has been the disappearance of habitats that formerly maintained useful non-crop vegetation including wild progenitors and weedy forms of crops (Altieri et al., 1987).

This situation is expected to be aggravated by the evolution of agriculture based on emerging biotechnologies whose development and commercialization has been characterized by concentration of ownership, control by a small number of corporations, and the decreased presence of the public sector as major provider of research and extension services to rural communities (Jordan, 2001). The social impacts of local crop shortfalls, resulting from genetic uniformity or changes in the genetic integrity of local varieties due to genetic pollution, can be considerable in the margins of the developing world. In the extreme periphery, crop losses mean ongoing ecological degradation, poverty, hunger and even famine. It is under these conditions of systemic market failure and lack of public external assistance that local skills and resources associated with biological and cultural diversity should be available to rural populations to maintain or recover their production processes.

Diverse agricultural systems and genetic materials that confer high levels of tolerance to changing socioeconomic and environmental conditions are extremely valuable to poor farmers, as diverse systems buffer against natural or human-induced variations in production conditions (Altieri, 1995). Impoverished rural populations must maintain low-risk agroecosystems that are primarily structured to ensure local food security. Farmers at the margins must continue to produce food for their local communities in the absence of modern inputs, and this can be achieved by preserving *in situ*, ecologically-intact, locally-adapted agrobiodiversity. For this, it will be necessary to maintain pools of genetic diverse material, geographically isolated from any possibility of cross fertilization or genetic pollution from uniform transgenic crops. These islands of traditional germplasm within specific agroecological landscapes will act as safeguards against the ecological failure derived from the second green revolution imposed at the margins.

One way to isolate traditional varieties from exposure to transgenic crops is to declare a country-level moratorium on the field experimentation and commercial release of biotech crops. But this may not provide sufficient safeguards, as many developing countries receive food aid which is a major entry point for transgenic seeds. In 2001, the United States donated 500 000 tons of corn and corn products for international aid programs, and former president Clinton assigned US$ 300 million for a program called 'Global food for education', through which 680 000 metric tons of soybean, corn, wheat and rice surplus would be exported to Latin America, Africa, Asia and Oriental Europe.

THE IMPACTS OF ROUND-UP-READY SOYBEAN IN BRAZIL AND ARGENTINA

In Argentina and Brazil the expansion of soybean is driven by prices, government and agroindustrial support and importing countries' demand. China, the world's largest importer of soybean and soybean products, has a market that encourages rapid proliferation of soybean production. Soybean expansion is accompanied by massive transportation infrastructure projects that unleash a chain of events leading to destruction of natural habitats over wide areas and deforestation directly caused by soybean cultivation. In Brazil soybean profits justified improvement or construction of 8 industrial waterways, 3 railway lines and an extensive network of roads to bring inputs and take away produce. These have attracted private investment in logging, mining, ranching and other practices with severe impacts on biodiversity not accounted for by any impact assessment study (Fearnside, 2001). In Argentina, the agroindustrial cluster area for transformation of soybean into oils and pellets is concentrated in the Rosario region on the Parana River, turning it into the largest soy transformation area of the world, with all the associated infrastructure and environmental impacts that this entails (Pengue, 2005).

Deforestation

In Brazil, the area of land in soybean production has grown at an annual rate of 3.2 per cent, and soybean today occupies the largest area of any crop in Brazil with 21 per cent of the total cultivated land. The area planted to soybean has increased by 2.3 million hectares since 1995 for an average increase of 320 000 hectares per year. Since 1961, soybean acreage has increased 57 times and production volume has increased 138 times (Fearnside, 2001). In Paraguay soybeans are planted on more than 25 per cent of all agricultural land in the country, and in Argentina soybean acreage reached almost 15 million hectares in 2000, producing 38.3 million metric tons. All this expansion is occurring dramatically at the expense of forests and other habitats. In Paraguay much of the Atlantic forest is being cut (Clay, 2003). In Argentina 118 000 hectares of forests have been cleared to grow soybean: in Salta about 160 000 hectares and in Santiago del Estero a record of 223 000 hectares. In Brazil, the Cerrado and the savannas are falling victim to the plow at a rapid pace (Pengue, 2005).

Soil Degradation

Soybean cultivation has always led to soil erosion, especially in areas where soybeans are not part of a long rotation. Soil loss reaches an average of 16 t/ha in the US Midwest, a rate that is still greater than is sustainable, and it is estimated that in Brazil and Argentina soil losses average between 19–30 t/ha depending on management, slope and climate. No-till agriculture can reduce soil loss, but with the advent of herbicide-resistant soybeans, many farmers now cultivate in highly erodible lands. Farmers wrongly believe that with no-till systems there is no erosion, but research shows that despite improved soil cover, erosion and negative changes in soil structure can still be substantial in highly erodible lands if weed cover is reduced (Pengue, 2005).

Large scale soybean monocultures have rendered Amazonian soils unusable. In areas of poor soils, within two years of cultivation, fertilizers and lime have to be applied heavily. In Bolivia, soybean production is expanding toward the east and many such soybean growing areas are already compacted and soil degradation is severe; 100 000 hectares of land with soils exhausted due to soybean were abandoned for cattle grazing, which in turn further degrades the land. As soils are abandoned, farmers move to other areas to once again plant soybeans and thus repeat the vicious cycle of soil degradation (Clay, 2003).

AGROECOLOGY: AN ALTERNATIVE STRATEGY

Third World Agroecological Initiatives

Since the early 1980s, hundreds of agroecologically-based projects have been promoted by NGOs throughout the developing world, incorporating elements of both traditional knowledge and modern agricultural science. A variety of projects feature resource-conserving yet highly productive systems, such as polycultures, agroforestry, the integration of crops and livestock, and so on. Such alternative approaches can be described as low-input technologies, but this designation refers to the external inputs required. The amount of labor, skills and management that are required as inputs to make land and other factors of production most productive is quite substantial. So rather than focus on what is not being utilized, it is better to focus on what is most important to increase food output: labor, knowledge and management (Uphoff and Altieri, 1999).

Agroecological alternative approaches are based on using locally available resources as much as possible, though they do not totally reject the use of external inputs. However, farmers cannot benefit from technologies that are not available, affordable or appropriate to their conditions. Purchased inputs present special problems and risks for less-secure farmers, particularly where supplies and the credit to facilitate purchases are inadequate.

The analysis of dozens of NGO-led agroecological projects shows convincingly that agroecological systems are not limited to producing low outputs, as some critics have asserted. Increases in production of 50 to 100 per cent are fairly common with most alternative production methods. In some of these systems, yields for crops that the poor rely on most (such as rice, beans, maize, cassava, potatoes and barley) have been increased by several times. This process relies on labor and know-how more than on expensive purchased inputs, and capitalizes on processes of intensification and synergy.

In a recent study of 208 agroecologically-based projects and/or initiatives, Pretty and Hine (2000) documented clear increases in food production over some 29 million hectares, with nearly 9 million households benefiting from increased food diversity and security. Promoted sustainable agriculture practices led to 50–100 per cent increases in per hectare food production (about 1.71 tonnes per year per household) in rain-fed areas typical of small farmers living in marginal environments; that is, an area of about 3.58 million hectares cultivated by about 4.42 million farmers. Such yield enhancements are a true breakthrough for achieving food security among farmers isolated from mainstream agricultural institutions.

More important than just yields, agroecological interventions raise total production significantly through diversification of farming systems, such as raising fish in rice paddies, growing crops with trees, or adding goats or poultry to household operations. Agroecological approaches increased the stability of production as seen in lower coefficients of variance in crop yield with better soil and water management (Francis, 1986). Data from agroecological field projects shows that traditional crop and animal combinations can often be adapted to increase productivity when the biological structuring of the farm is improved and labor and local resources are efficiently used (Altieri, 1999). In general, data shows that over time agroecological systems exhibit more stable levels of total production per unit area than high-input systems; produce economically favorable rates of return; provide a return to labor and other inputs sufficient for a livelihood acceptable to small farmers and their families; and ensure soil protection and conservation as well as enhanced biodiversity.

Organic Farming

Organic agriculture is practiced in almost all countries of the world, and its share of agricultural land and farms is growing. The total organically managed area is more than 24 million hectares worldwide. Australia/ Oceania holds 42 per cent of the world's organic land, followed by Latin America (24.2 per cent) and Europe (23 per cent). Oceania and Latin America concentrate much of the land under organic management, but this is due to the fact that extensive organic livestock systems dominate in Australia (about 10 million hectares) and in Argentina (almost 3 million hectares). Europe and Latin America have the highest numbers of organic farms, and in Asia and Africa organic farming is growing and both regions are characterized by small farms.

In Europe organic agriculture is increasing rapidly. In Italy there are about 56 000 organic farms occupying 1.2 million hectares. In Germany alone, there are about 8000 organic farms occupying about 2 per cent of the total arable land, and in Austria about 20 000 organic farms account for 10 per cent of total agricultural output. In the UK the organic market is displaying growth rates of 30–50 per cent per annum.

Although in the USA organic farms occupy 0.25 per cent of the total agricultural land, organic acreage doubled between 1992 and 1997, and in 1999 the retail organic produce industry generated $6 billion in sales. In California, organic foods are one of the fastest-growing segments of the agricultural economy, with retail sales growing at 20–25 per cent per year for the past six years.

Research has shown that organic farms can be as productive as conventional ones, but without using agrochemicals. They also consume less energy and save soil and water. A strong body of evidence suggests that organic methods can produce enough food for all – and do it from one generation to the next without depleting natural resources or harming the environment. In 1984 the National Research Council wrote up case studies of eight organic farms that ranged from a 400-acre grain/livestock farm in Ohio to 1400 acres of grapes in California and Arizona. The organic farms' average yields were generally equal to or better than the average yields of the conventional high-intensity farms surrounding them – once again showing they could be sustained year after year without costly synthetic inputs (NRC, 1984).

Several recent long-term studies have been conducted, such as the Farming Systems Trial at the Rodale Institute, a non-profit research facility near Kutztown, Pennsylvania. Three kinds of experimental plots have been tested side by side for nearly two decades. One is a standard high-intensity rotation of corn and soybeans in which commercial fertilizers and pesticides have been used. Another is an organic system in which a rotation of grass/legume forage has been added and fed to cows, whose manure is then returned to the land. The third is an organic rotation in which soil fertility has been maintained solely with legume cover crops that have been plowed under. All three kinds of plots have been equally profitable in market terms. Corn yields have differed by less than 1 per cent. The rotation with manure has far surpassed the other two in building soil organic matter and nitrogen, and it has leached fewer nutrients into groundwater. The 10-year period from 1988–1998 included five years in which the total rainfall from April to August was less than 350mm (compared with 500mm in average years). Average corn yields in those dry years were significantly higher (28 per cent to 34 per cent) in the two organic systems: 6938 and 7235kg per ha in organic-animal and organic-legume systems compared with 5333kg per ha in the conventional system. During the extreme drought of 1999 (total rainfall between April and August only 224mm), the organic animals system had significantly higher corn yields (1511kg per ha) than either the organic legume (421kg per ha) or the conventional (1100kg per ha). Crop yield in the organic legume was much lower in 1999 because the high biomass of the hairy vetch winter cover crop used up a large amount of the soil water. During the 1999 drought soybean yields were 1400, 1800 and 900kg per ha for organic animal, organic legume and conventional. Economic comparison of the organic corn–soybean rotation with conventional corn–soybean systems from 1991–2000 showed that without price premiums for the organic rotation, the annual net returns for both were similar: $184 per ha for conventional, $176 per ha for organic legume (Pimentel et al., 2005).

In what must be the longest-running organic trial in the world – 150 years – England's Rothamsted Experimental Station (also known as the Institute of Arable Crops Research) reports that its organic manured plots have delivered wheat yields of 1.58 tons per acre, compared to synthetically fertilized plots that have yielded 1.55 tons per acre. That may not seem like much, but the manured plots contain six times the organic matter found in the chemically treated plots (Stanhill, 1990). FIBL scientists in Central Europe conducted a 21-year study of the agronomic and ecological performance of biodynamic, organic and conventional farming systems. They found crop yields to be 20 per cent lower in the organic systems, although input of fertilizer and energy was reduced by 31 to 53 per cent and pesticide input by 98 per cent. Enhanced soil fertility and higher biodiversity found in organic plots rendered these systems less dependent on external inputs (Mader et al., 2002).

In North America and Europe, researchers have convincingly demonstrated that it is possible to provide a balanced environment, sustained yields, biologically-mediated soil fertility and natural pest regulation through the design of commercial diversified agroecosystems and the use of low-input technologies (Altieri and Rosset, 1996). Many alternative cropping systems have been tested, such as double cropping, strip cropping, cover cropping and intercropping. More importantly, concrete examples from real farmers show that such systems lead to optimal recycling of nutrients and organic matter turnover, closed energy flows, water and soil conservation and balanced pest–natural enemy populations. Such diversified-organic farming exploits the complementarities that result from the various combinations of crops, trees and animals in spatial and temporal arrangements. In orchards and vineyards, the use of cover crops improves soil fertility, soil structure and water penetration, prevents soil erosion, modifies the microclimate and reduces weed competition. Entomological studies conducted in orchards with ground cover vegetation indicate that these systems exhibit lower incidence of insect pests than clean cultivated orchards. This is due to a higher abundance and efficiency of predators and parasitoids enhanced by the rich floral undergrowth. The challenge consists in assembling a functional biodiversity in each farm in order to initiate synergies which subsidize agroecosystem processes through the provision of ecological services such as activation of soil biology, recycling of nutrients, enhancement of beneficial arthropods and antagonists, and so on. Today there is a diverse selection of practices to achieve this purpose readily available to small, medium and large-scale farmers.

SCALING UP ALTERNATIVE AGRICULTURAL APPROACHES

Throughout the developing and industrialized world there are thousands of agroecological initiatives that have demonstrated a positive impact on the livelihoods of small farming communities (Pretty, 1995). Success is dependent on the use of a variety of agroecological improvements. In addition to farm diversification favoring a better use of local resources, they also emphasize human capital enhancement and community empowerment through training and participatory methods as well as greater access to markets, credit and income-generating activities. In most cases, farmers adopting agroecological models achieved significant levels of food security and natural resource conservation. Given the benefits and advantages of such initiatives, a key question that emerges is how to scale up these initiatives to enable wider impact and diffusion of benefits to more farmers.

Scaling up strategies must capitalize on mechanisms conducive to the spread of knowledge and techniques, such as:

- Strengthening producers' organizations through alternative marketing channels. The main idea is to evaluate whether the promotion of alternative farmer-led markets constitutes a mechanism to enhance the economic viability of the agroecological approach and thus provides the basis for the scaling-up process.
- Developing methods for rescuing/collecting/evaluating promising agroecological technologies generated by experimenting farmers and making them known to other farmers for wide adoption in various areas. Mechanisms to disseminate technologies with high potential may involve farmer exchange visits, regional–national farmer conferences, and publication of manuals that explain the technologies for use by technicians involved in agroecological development programs.
- Training government research and extension agencies in agroecology so they can include agroecological principles in their extension programs.
- Developing working linkages between NGOs and farmers' organizations. Such alliance between technicians and farmers is critical for the dissemination of successful agroecological production systems emphasizing biodiversity management and rational use of natural resources.

Other important requirements for the scaling up of agroecological innovations include more effective farmers' organizations, research-extension institutional partnerships, exchanges, training, technology transfer and validation in the context of farmer-to-farmer activities, enhanced participation of small farmers in niche markets, and so on. From their worldwide survey of sustainable agriculture initiatives, Pretty and Hine (2000) concluded that if sustainable agriculture is to spread to larger numbers of farmers and communities, then future attention needs to be focused on:

1. ensuring the policy environment is enabling rather than disabling;
2. investing in infrastructure for markets, transport and communications;
3. ensuring the support of government agencies, in particular, for local sustainable agricultural initiatives; and
4. developing social capital within rural communities and between external agencies.

The main expectation of a scaling-up process is that it should expand the geographical coverage of participating institutions and their target agroecological projects while allowing an evaluation of the impact of the strategies employed. A key research goal should be that the methodology allows for a comparative analysis of the experiences learned, extracting principles that can be applied in the scaling up of other existing local initiatives, thus illuminating other development processes.

REFERENCES

Altieri, M.A. and L.C. Merrick (1987), 'In situ conservation of crop genetic resources through maintenance of traditional farming systems', *Economic Botany*, **41**, 86–96.

Altieri, M.A. (1994), *Biodiversity and Pest Management in Agroecosystems*, New York: Harworth Press.

Altieri, M.A. (1995), *Agroecology: the Science of Sustainable Agriculture*, Boulder: Westview Press.

Altieri, M.A. (1999), 'Applying agroecology to enhance productivity of peasant farming systems in Latin America', *Environment, Development and Sustainability*, **1**, 197–217.

Altieri, M.A. (2000), 'The ecological impacts of transgenic crops on agroecosystem health', *Ecosystem Health*, **6**, 19–31.

Altieri, M.A. (2004), *Genetic Engineering in Agriculture: the Myths, Environmental Risks and Alternatives*, Oakland: Food First Books.

Altieri, M.A. and P. Rosset (1996), 'Agroecology and the conversion of large-scale conventional systems to sustainable management', *International Journal of Environmental Studies*, **50**, 165–85.

Bills, P.S., D. Mota-Sanchez and M. Whalon (2003), *Background to the Resistance Data base*, Michigan State University, at www.cips.msu.edu/resistance.

Brush, S.B. (2000), *Genes in the field: on-farm conservation of crop diversity*, Boca Raton, FL: Lewis Publishers.

Clay, Jason (2003), *World Agriculture and the Environment: A Commodity-by-commodity Guide to Impacts and Practices*, Washington: Island Press.

Cleaveland, D.A. and S.C. Murray (1997), 'The world's crop genetic resources and the rights of indigenous farmers', *Current Anthropology*, **38**, 477–92.

Conway, G.R. (1997), *The Doubly Green Revolution*, London: Penguin Books.

Conway, G.R. and J.N. Pretty (1991), *Unwelcome Harvest: Agriculture and Pollution*, London: Earthscan Publications.

Denevan, W.M. (1995), 'Prehistoric agricultural methods as models for sustainability', *Advanced Plant Pathology*, **11**, 21–43.

Donald, P.F. (2004), 'Biodiversity impacts of some agricultural commodity production systems', *Conservation Biology*, **18**, 17–37.

Ellstrand, N.C. (2001), 'When transgenes wander, should we worry?', *Plant Physiology*, **125**, 1543–5.

Fearnside, P.M. (2001), 'Soybean cultivation as a threat to the environment in Brazil', *Environmental Conservation*, **28**, 23–8.

Francis, C.A. (1986), *Multiple Cropping Systems*, New York: MacMillan.

Gliessman, S.R. (1998), *Agroecology: Ecological Process in Sustainable Agriculture*, Michigan: Ann Arbor Press.

Hilbeck, A., M. Baumgartner, P.M. Fried and F. Bigler (1998), 'Effects of transgenic *Bacillus thuringiensis* corn fed prey on mortality and development time of immature *Chrysoperla carnea* (*Neuroptera: Chrysopidae*)', *Environmental Entomology*, **27**, 460–87.

Holt-Gimenez, E. (2001), 'Measuring farms' agroecological resistance to Hurricane Mitch', *LEISA*, **17**, 18–20.

Jackson, D. and L. Jackson (2002), *The Farm as Natural Habitat: Reconnecting Food Systems and Ecosystems*, Washington, DC: Island Press.

James, C. (2004), *Global Review of Commercialized Transgenic Crops: 2004*, International Service for the Acquisition of Agri-Biotech Application Briefs No 23-2002, Ithaca, New York.

Jennings, B.H. (1988), *Foundations of International Agricultural Research*, Boulder: Westview Press.

Jordan, C.F. (2001), 'Genetic engineering, the farm crisis and world hunger', *BioScience*, **52**, 523–9.

Lappe, F.M., J. Collins and P. Rosset (1998), *World Hunger: Twelve Myths*, New York: Grove Press.

Lipton, M. and R. Longhurst (1989), *New Seeds and Poor People*, Baltimore: Johns Hopkins University Press.

Obrycki, J.J., J.E. Losey, O.R. Taylor and L.C.H. Jessie (2001), 'Transgenic insecticidal maize: beyond insecticidal toxicity to ecological complexity', *BioScience*, **51**, 353–61.

Mader, P. et al. (2002), 'Soil fertility and biodiversity in organic farming', *Science*, **296**, 1694–7.

Marvier, M. (2001), 'Ecology of transgenic crops', *American Scientist*, **89**, 160–67.

McNeely, J.A. and S.J. Scherr (2003), *Ecoagriculture: Strategies to Feed the World and Save Wild Biodiversity*, Washington: Island Press.

National Academy of Sciences (1972), *Genetic Vulnerability of Major Crops*, Washington, DC: NAS.

National Research Council (NRC) (1984), *Alternative Agriculture*, Washington, DC: National Academy Press.

Netting, R. McC. (1993), *Smallholders, Householders*, Stanford, CA: Stanford University Press.

Pengue, W. (2005), 'Transgenic crops in Argentina: the ecological and social debt', *Bulletin of Science, Technology and Society*, **25**, 314–22.

Pimentel, D. and H. Lehman (1993), *The Pesticide Question*, New York: Chapman and Hall.

Pimentel, D., P. Hepperly, J. Hunson, D. Douds and R. Seidel (2005), 'Environmental, energetic and economic comparisons of organic and conventional farming systems', *Bioscience*, **56**, 573–82.

Pimentel, D., D. Andow, R. Dyson-Hudson, D. Gallahan, S. Jacobson, M. Irish and M. Shepard (1980), 'Environmental and social costs of pesticides: a preliminary assessment', *Oikos*, **34**, 126–40.

Pingali, P.L., M. Hossain and R.V. Gerpacio (1997), *Asian Rice Bowls: the Returning Crisis*, Wallingford, UK: CAB International.

Pinstrup-Andersen, P. and M.J. Cohen (2000), 'The present situation and coming trends in world food protection and consumption', in: T.T. Chang (ed.), *Food Needs of the Developing World in the early 21st Century*, pp. 27–56, Proc. Studyweek of the Pontifical Academy of Science, Vatican City.

Pretty, J. (1995), *Regenerating Agriculture: Policies and Practices for Sustainability and Self-reliance*, Washington, DC: World Resources Institute.

Pretty, J. (2005), *The Pesticide Detox: Towards a More Sustainable Agriculture*, London: Earthscan.

Pretty, J. and R. Hine (2000), 'Feeding the world with sustainable agriculture: a summary of new evidence', final report from 'SAFE-World' Research Project, University of Essex, Colchester, England.

Quist, D. and I.H. Chapela (2001), 'Transgenic DNA introgressed into traditional maize landraces in Oaxaca, Mexico', *Nature*, **414**, 541–3.

Reganold, J.P., J.D. Glover, P.K. Andrews and H.R. Hinman (2001), 'Sustainability of three apple production systems', *Nature*, **410**, 926–30.

Reinjtes, C., B. Haverkort and Ann Waters-Bayer (1992), *Farming for the Future*, London: MacMillan.

Rissler, J. and M. Mellon (1996), *The Ecological Risks of Engineered Crops*, Cambridge: MIT Press.

Shiva, V. (1991), *The Violence of the Green Revolution: Third World Agriculture, Ecology and Politics*, Pengany, Malaysia: Third World Network.

Stabinski, D. and N. Sarno (2001), 'Mexico, centre of diversity for maize, has been contaminated', *LEISA magazine*, **17**, 25–6.

Stanhill, G. (1990), 'The comparative productivity of organic agriculture', *Agriculture, Ecosystems and Environment*, **30**, 1–26.

Thrupp, L.A. (1996), *New Partnerships for Sustainable Agriculture*, Washington, DC: World Resources Institute.

Thrupp, L.A. (1998), *Cultivating Diversity: Agrobiodiversity and Food Security*, Washington, DC: World Resources Institute.

Tripp, R. (1996), 'Biodiversity and modern crop varieties: sharpening the debate', *Agriculture and Human Values*, **13**, 48–62.

Uphoff, N. and M.A. Altieri (1999), *Alternatives to Conventional Modern Agriculture for Meeting World Food Needs in the Next Century*, Ithaca, NY: Cornell International Institute for Food, Agriculture and Development.

Wilkes, H.G. and K.K. Wilkes (1972), 'The green revolution', *Environment*, **14**, 32–9.

SECTION E

Biodiversity

8.   Is conservation a lost cause?

Anthony R.E. Sinclair

SERENGETI: A WORLD HERITAGE

The single most important problem facing the world *today* for the *future* survival of mankind is the loss of biodiversity (Schneider, 1997). Historically, conservation has protected biodiversity by setting up protected areas. UNESCO established the first list of protected World Heritage sites in 1972 at the Stockholm conference. The attending countries at that meeting listed the areas they would like to see protected in perpetuity. Canada has put forward a number of such places and some of those are now on the list. However, the site that was agreed upon as being number one in the world is Serengeti – a unique area, with open plains, active volcanoes, ironstone hills, limitless parklands of umbrella acacias and a vast array of wildlife. The large mammal fauna is the last holdout of the pleistocene, two million years old. Of the 28 species of large grazing mammals, the wildebeest is the dominant. The size of a small cow, it moves in great herds in an annual migration. When the plains are green, the wildebeest can be seen in long lines following the little paths that have obviously been made over the centuries. They congregate on the plains, sometimes in one herd of a million animals or more.

BIODIVERSITY: THE SIXTH GREAT EXTINCTION

The term biodiversity is becoming more familiar since the 1992 Biodiversity Convention in Rio. It is really a code word for a set of problems. What we really mean by this is the *loss* of biodiversity. We are concerned with changes in the ecosystem – the decline of populations, extinctions and how to prevent them. We are concerned with whether we preserve species, or sub-species and races, or even genotypes – different genetic groupings. Of course, because everything has to live in a place (which we call habitats) ultimately we have to talk about preserving habitats. The reason why we are so concerned about these questions is that we are this century losing species at about 100 times the rate that has occurred over the past one million years

(Pimm et al., 1995; Pimm, 1998). Indeed, this rate is similar to that in the five major extinction events in the history of life on our planet, including the extinction of the dinosaurs (Raup and Sepkoski, 1984). We are now in the sixth great extinction in world history. These are the problems that we as scientists are particularly concerned with. I start this chapter with the question: 'is conservation achieving its role?' You will answer that question for yourselves by the end. The answer will not be self-evident; it will depend on your own values and priorities for what you would like to do. I intend to pose some questions, examine some scenarios, as examples of the types of problems the world faces.

A HISTORY OF HUMAN EXTERMINATIONS

First, let us consider the history of human populations as they spread around the world. Modern humans came from Africa and spread across Eurasia some 200 000 years ago. Our evidence for human invasions starts after that, the earliest occurring in Australia somewhere around 50 000 years ago. North America was invaded over the Bering Straits about 15 000 years ago. From Indonesia, humans spread over the Polynesian Islands some 3000 years ago, reaching Hawaii 1500 years ago. Other invasions occurred in Madagascar about 1500 years ago, and finally in New Zealand about a thousand years ago (MacArthur, 1972).

The extinction of the large marsupials in Australia coincided with the arrival of man. These were species such as the elephant-like marsupial *Palorchestes* feeding on trees, the diprotodonts, the size of rhinos and possibly feeding on the spiny *Spinafex* grass of central Australia, and the giant kangaroos. In Europe, with the arrival of modern humans displacing Neanderthal man during the ice ages, species such as the Irish elk, mammoths and woolly rhinos disappeared. The arrival of humans in North America coincided with a spectacular increase in the frequency of extinctions beginning some twelve thousand years ago (Figure 8.1). Large mammals that disappeared from North and South America included the giant ground sloth, mastodons and glyptodonts (two-meter long, giant armadillos). Very large species such as mastodons, living in the slow-growing, low productivity conifer forests, would have had both low populations (a few thousand) and very low reproductive rates. If humans had simply killed some of the babies, this would have caused their extinction. Furthermore, humans may well have altered habitats through fire and so indirectly caused extinctions. Thus, evidence suggests these extinctions were human-related. It is strange to think that it was only a little while ago – in geological time, it was just a second ago – that we had those remarkable

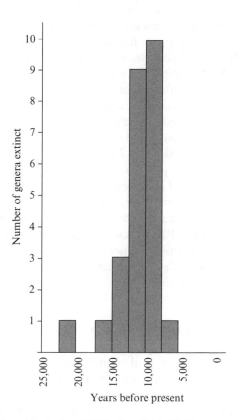

Source: Adapted from MacArthur (1972), after Webb, (1969).

Figure 8.1 Timing of extinctions of North American mammal genera

creatures roaming around here. We have no concept of what it was like to have those mammals – the woolly rhinos, the giant ground sloths – we have lost the memory.

In New Caledonia a meter-and-a-half long turkey-like bird disappeared 1700 years ago, at the same time as a primitive crocodile, as a result of hunting. Their remains are found in the aboriginal food middens. In Madagascar, elephant birds, like giant lumbering ostriches – the biggest birds in the world – disappeared along with giant lemurs a few hundred years ago as a result of hunting. The invasion of New Zealand by the Moa hunters (predecessors of the Maoris) about a thousand years ago killed these huge flightless birds similar to those on Madagascar – some dozen species.

In modern times, during the 1600s, we see the disappearance of the aurochs, the progenitor of the domestic cattle, despite efforts by the kings of central Europe to save that species. The Stellar's sea cow, a manatee, discovered by the Russians on our British Columbian coast in 1714, was extinct by 1740. The whalers and sealers killed off the great auk, a flightless seabird living off the Atlantic coast of Canada last century, the last one being recorded in 1844. The process of extermination continues today with the local common murre, a seabird related to the great auk on the coasts of Greenland and Canada, rapidly facing extinction because the local people who hunt them have been given modern weapons.

In general, therefore, we find that humans have systematically exterminated species as far back as paleohistory allows us to look (Webb, 1969; Day, 1989; Balouet, 1990). I focus on the large species because they are easily found in the fossil record. There are many other species, about which we have much less knowledge, that have also become extinct. Humans, in their expansion across the Pacific, exterminated fully 20 per cent of the world's bird species. In Hawaii, we know that some 40 species of birds went extinct after the arrival of the Polynesians a thousand years ago, and we should expect similar extermination elsewhere (Steadman, 1995).

SOCIETY'S LACK OF MEMORY FOR NATURE

There is another aspect to historical extinctions that we need to appreciate. Scotland is known for its beautiful rolling hills covered in heather. They are a tourist attraction, much loved. Poetry is written about the highlands. What people do not realize is that the heather moorlands are largely an artefact of human destruction (Smout, 2003). Two thousand years ago Scotland was covered in pine forest and even two hundred years ago it still had extensive areas of forest. It should look naturally much like Norway or Sweden today with pine, birch and aspen forests (Yalden, 1999). The remaining Scottish forest was cleared in the 1700s to graze sheep and evict people during the famous 'clearances'. Apart from a few small patches, virtually all of the forest has gone (Figure 8.2). People like Scotland as it is now; they do not appreciate that the highlands are no more natural than is a modern city park. The main point is that people have long forgotten what the highlands in their original state were really like.

In general, two important points emerge from a review of history. First, we have been exterminating species for as far back as we can see. Every time we make an advance in technology, a new round of killing takes place. Modern extinctions are merely the continuation of extinctions caused by the first peoples to visit our lands. Second, society has little or no 'memory' for what is lost or even for what is natural. It was just a blink of an eye ago that we had the mammoths and ground sloths in Europe and North

Original distribution of native pinewoods

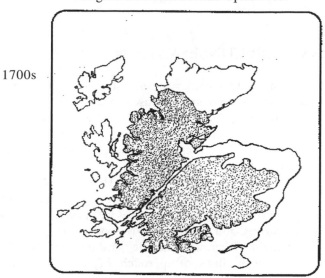

1700s

Surviving remnants

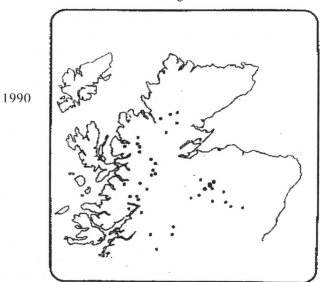

1990

Source: Adapted from Watson (1992).

Figure 8.2 Disappearance of Scottish pine forests

America, but we know nothing about that time; we have no appreciation for times past.

THE TASK FOR CONSERVATION

What are we trying to do in conservation? I start with the premise that we are trying to preserve species, and because species live in habitats, we have to preserve their habitats. There are about 10 to 30 million species of organisms in the world, give or take a few million (May, 1990; 1995). At the current rate at which we have been losing species, a million of them will be lost every ten years. Clearly, we cannot save them all, so that presents us with the problem of which to save or let go. How is society making such choices? In short, we make 'seat-of-the-pants' decisions, arbitrary and whimsical. We use rules such as 'save the ones we know about' – such as the large ones, pretty ones, and cuddly ones; we notice them, and we become aware of their plight. Other rules include 'save the areas which have the most species' – this is the 'hot spot' approach (Myers et al., 2000), to which I return below.

On the surface, these rules sound reasonable through the logic that if you 'save the large species, you 'save lots of little species' that go along with them. These large species are called 'umbrella' species, and examples include the giant panda in China, the tiger in India, elephants in Africa and other big and beautiful animals. They attract public attention. Conservation organizations, both government and non-government, such as the World Wildlife Fund, the International Union for Conservation of Nature, and many others use these large, charismatic species to raise funds for their preservation and hope the smaller species will be saved along with them. Most of their work is 'emergency room' crisis. Every time the phone rings, there is another species that somebody has discovered about to go extinct. Decisions as to where to put the funds and effort are short-term and local. Decisions are opportunistic: we do what we can at the time in terms of funds, people and politics, and we hope for the best. Often decisions end in confrontation. The confrontations so prevalent in the 1990s on the west coast of Canada and south-east Australia involve valley-by-valley fights between logging companies and environmentalists.

I call this technique of conservation the First World War approach of trench-by-trench warfare. Neither side is going to do well out of this. The companies understand that quite well. There are no natural 'stopping rules' to the fight, for once one valley dispute is settled, the next is in contention. Given this, it is logical for a company to put up a stand at the first valley, not the last. From the environmentalists' point of view such confrontation is enormously expensive in terms of time, money and people, with no assurance that such valleys are the ones that ought to be saved. They are the 'feel-good' valleys, but they could be the wrong ones because they have not been chosen on an objective basis. As a result many present day conservation actions are inappropriate or out of context.

Let us remind ourselves what the problem is – we do not have enough resources to save everything and so we must make a list of priorities for habitats and species. This will enable us to optimize the distribution of those resources to save the most species. What sort of resources? Time is one; every year passing means more is lost. The amount of land that we can put aside to save habitats is another, because there is a finite amount available. The more land set aside in one place means the less set aside in another because there is a limit to what society is willing to pay. Given this opportunity cost to land, we must be sure that the areas we spend time and money on are the ones we absolutely need above all others. Making decisions, though, on where we should spend our resources of time, area and money has to be done on a global and not a local basis. Decisions made on a local basis will result in more species becoming extinct.

CHOOSING SITES FOR CONSERVATION

Let us consider the 'hot-spots' approach to conservation. Figure 8.3 is a map showing the areas of highest Amazonian bio-diversity. The black areas represent the highest number of species, the shaded the next highest. By this rule, those areas with the highest biodiversity – the 'hotspots' – should be set aside first and, if there are resources left over, then areas of lower species richness are included next. It sounds reasonable at first sight. Unfortunately, it is inefficient and misses rare species. We can see this using Britain as an example (Prendergast et al., 1993). Britain is one of the best documented areas in the world for different types of organisms because the British love collecting, bird watching, and so on. The highest diversity areas for birds are on the south coast. For butterflies, high diversity areas are scattered all over the centre and east coast of England, whereas those for dragonflies are on the south coast. Liverworts, which are primitive plants, are largely in Scotland. I have considered only four groups, but there are many others. This group-by-group approach does not work because 'hotspots' do not overlap each other. To put reserves in hotspots for all biological groups would set aside a large part of Great Britain.

Consider British Columbia as another example. For bryophytes (mosses), the 'hotspots' are mainly on the Queen Charlotte Islands, whereas those for vascular plants (the more advanced plants), are largely on Vancouver

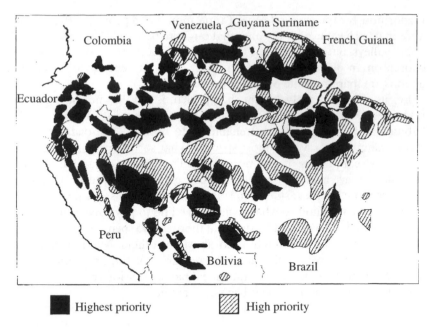

Highest priority   High priority

Source: Based on Figure 1 in Rylands, (1991).

Figure 8.3 *Priority areas for conservation in the Amazon region*

Island. The highest diversity of endemic insects, and other invertebrates, is in the Okanagan valley of southern British Columbia. Again, 'hotspots' do not overlap each other. Thus, setting priorities for conservation areas on the basis of 'hotspots' does not narrow our options sufficiently. In addition, this approach is uneconomical because it over-represents common species while often completely missing rare species. It does not give us the best distribution of land to represent as much as possible (Pressey and Tully, 1994).

An alternative approach is called 'complementarity'. It starts by taking the areas with the rarest species first, and then adding in, with more resources, the next areas with the next rarest species. If there is a choice, it adds in the areas with the most species. This proceeds stepwise until all species are included or one runs out of resources. Each area added to the set of reserves (the priority set) complements what is already saved, so duplication is held to a minimum, and all species are represented. It has now been tried in many countries (Nicholls and Margules, 1993; Pressey et al., 1993; 1994; Margules and Pressey, 2000). In each case, complementarity was more efficient than hotspots by as much as five times; that is five times as much can be saved for the same cost.

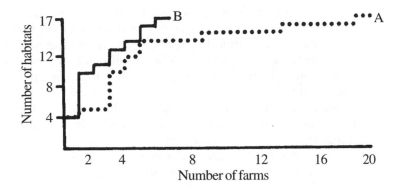

Note: The 'Hotspot' approach (Line A) requires 20 farms to represent 17 habitats whereas the 'Complementary' Approach (Line B) requires only 7.

Source: Based on Pressey and Tully (1994). Reproduced with the permission of the authors.

Figure 8.4   The 'hotspot' approach

For example, there were 17 different habitats on a group of farms in New South Wales, Australia. The task was to identify which farms had to have special protection to save a representative portion of each of those 17 habitats. The 'hotspot' approach starts with protecting the farm supporting the greatest number of habitats. In total, this approach required 20 farms to represent all 17 habitats (Figure 8.4, line A). The complementarity approach, by contrast, required only 7 farms (line B). The complementarity approach is a better way of doing things because, first, we get 'the most for the least' and, second, we obtain an objective estimate of the conservation value of each area. The farms chosen first have habitats with only one representative; if these are lost, they are gone forever – they are irreplaceable. Thus we can assign an irreplaceability index on the basis of how many alternative sites are available. With only one site, the irreplaceability index is 100, with two sites the index is 50, four sites it is 25, and so on. This is an objective score which we can apply to habitats containing rare species, based on the number of alternative sites to choose from.

In our example there were three farms that had the only representative of a habitat. We say those are completely irreplaceable (an index of 100). There were two pairs of farms with the same habitat, and one each had to be chosen. These had an irreplaceability value of 50. The important point for the management of conservation is that the index provides an objective method of conservation evaluation. This conservation index can then be compared with economic and social scores in negotiations. One could say:

'There are two areas here, we need to save one, but there is room to negoti-
ate on which one to set aside.' Decisions can then be made on the basis of
lost economic value, social, cultural or aesthetic values. With an objective
assessment, conflicts are better avoided. The cut-off point for how much
land, and hence how many species can be preserved, is of course a political
decision, but now we have a way of evaluating it.

The Australian farms are merely an example of this approach. It needs
to be used on a global scale, as Dick Vane-Wright and colleagues from the
British Natural History Museum have done for owls (Vane-Wright et al.,
1991). Owls are appropriate because of the spotted owl controversy in our
western forests. Figure 8.5 documents the priority areas of the world, which
combined represent all species of owl. The most important area for owls is
somewhere in Central America. The first site in North America is number
11, which represents the burrowing owl. The spotted owl is represented in
Central America. We do not have to worry, on this basis, about spotted owls
anywhere along this coast. We are not off the hook, of course, because
profits from logging the west coast must go to purchasing and maintaining
forests in Central America. Indeed, the tropical forests must be secured for
owls before the temperate forests are logged, not afterwards. In fact, the
majority of owl species are in Southeast Asia, and we should be spending our profits from logging there, not here in British Columbia, for
conservation.

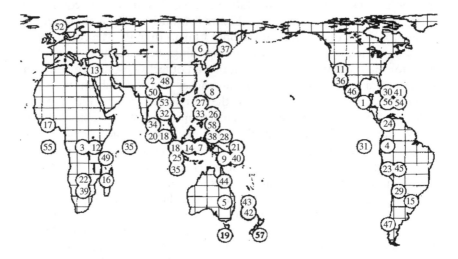

Source: Based on Pressey and Tully 1994. Reproduced with the permission of the authors.

Figure 8.5   Fifty-eight Priority regions for all world owl species

The same analysis for milkweed butterflies (family danaidae) shows that Southeast Asia is also the most important area for this group. A similar global assessment for bumblebees shows that an area in China has highest priority, followed by an area on the Canadian Shield. Perhaps we should consider a National Park for bumblebees. So far, no one has considered that aspect, but in principle there is no reason why we do not have a National Park for bumblebees, we merely need to think more broadly.

PROTECTING CONSERVATION SITES

The next question asks, how do we protect habitat? At first sight the answer is obvious. We set up reserves and then protect them in order to prevent losses of habitat and species taking place outside the reserves. For example, tropical forests are declining rapidly in all countries (Figure 8.6). Vancouver Island shows the same rate of loss for its temperate forest. Forest is disappearing because of human population pressure, and the proportion of tropical forest remaining in Southeast Asia declines as human population density increases (Figure 8.7) (Sinclair et al., 1995).

If reserves are the solution to preventing loss, we should expect habitats and species to be safe within them. Consider Strathcona Provincial Park on

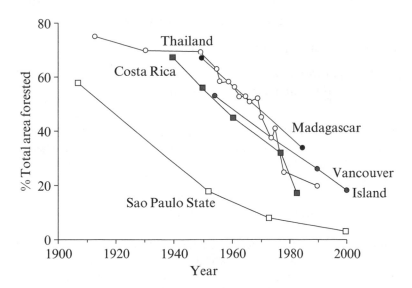

Source: From Sinclair et al. (1995). Reproduced with permission.

Figure 8.6   Loss of forested area: world examples

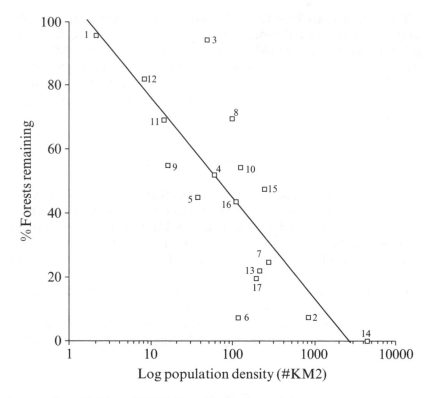

Source: From Sinclair et al. (1995). Reproduced with permission.

Figure 8.7   *Population density vs. percentage of tropical forests remaining
in different Southeast Asia countries*

Vancouver Island, to take an example close to home. Figure 8.8 compares
the Park boundary in 1954 with that in 1990. Mice seem to have been nib-
bling at it – there are little indentations in the south, we have lost the corner
in the south-east, and another big bite up in the north-west. It has been
chipped away at; much of the lowland temperate rainforest has been taken
out. As if in compensation, the government has added a bit on the eastern
side, but that bit is comprised of mountain peaks, snow, ice and rocks,
which can hardly compensate for the loss of forest. The point is that all
Parks and Reserves around the world suffer a gradual attrition. We are
losing our protected areas bit by bit. If we have lost this much in about forty
years, how much will be left after the next 200 or 500 years? That is the time
span we must think about, and at the present rate we will have lost it all by
the end of that time. Remember from our earlier discussion that society

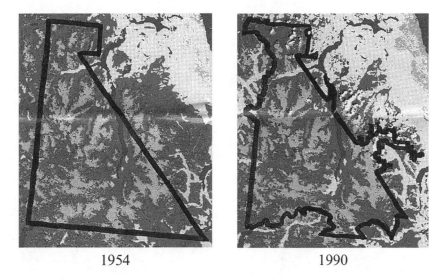

1954   1990

Source: Adapted from maps by The Sierra Club of Western Canada (1993).

Figure 8.8   Strathcona Park, Vancouver Island boundaries, 1954 and 1990

does not notice gradual change; it has no memory. We get used to what we have lost and so there is nothing to stop this loss.

Perhaps Strathcona Park is not important enough to protest its decay. If not, then Serengeti certainly is. If we cannot prevent attrition in Serengeti, we cannot prevent it anywhere. Serious poaching for rhino horn in Serengeti started in 1977 and by 1980 all rhinos had been exterminated from the Park. Between 1977 and 1988 some 80 per cent of elephants were killed and the rest were saved only with the ban in ivory trading in 1988. Wild dogs, some of the rarest carnivores in Africa, numbered over 100 in the 1960s in Serengeti but all are now gone. Some 40 per cent of the lions died in 1993 as a result of canine distemper contracted from domestic dogs. Canine distemper has spread as a result of the exploding human populations with their infected domestic dogs around the periphery of Serengeti; it appears that domestic dogs first made contact with wild dogs, then hyenas, and most recently lions. Such population declines are forms of attrition because they compromise the natural workings of the ecosystem. The natural area left in the Serengeti region this century (Figure 8.9) has been decreasing steadily. The legally protected area started in the 1920s and built up to the 1960s and 1970s. It levelled out and then declined somewhat as portions were removed, as in Strathcona Park. More significantly, the natural area is now less than the legally protected area. There are areas

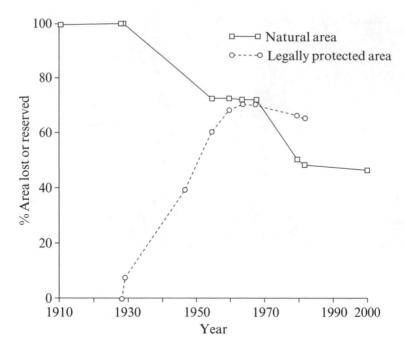

Source: From Sinclair et al. (1995). Reproduced with permission.

Figure 8.9   Natural area remaining and legally protected area in the Serengiti ecosystem

inside the Serengeti Park with no large mammals left; they have been removed by poaching. Thus, we must recognize that we cannot protect even the most important conservation areas in the world.

RENEWAL: REPLACING LOST HABITAT

It is, therefore, a delusion to think that a reserve will prevent the eventual loss of habitats and species. Within a reserve we lose as much as if no reserve had been present. The only advantage of a reserve is that it takes a little longer to lose everything. The solid curve (Figure 8.10) shows the rate of loss of area as a result of attrition over time. If we set up a reserve at a certain point (t_0), the rate of loss is not so fast but we still lose it all eventually. The reserve allows us to buy time to do something about the attrition. Are we using this extra time to do something about this attrition? To counteract the loss of this habitat requires an addition to the reserve to

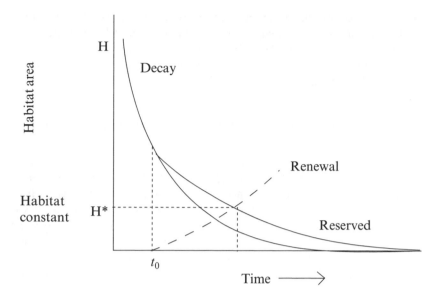

Notes: Loss of natural area (solid curve) results in none remaining. At time t_0, a reserve is established, and its area also declines to zero, but at a slower rate. If new habitat is added to the reserve (renewal, broken line), then we can maintain a constant area (H*) where the two lines cross.

Source: From Sinclair et al. (1995). Reproduced with permission.

Figure 8.10 Loss of natural area results in none remaining

balance the loss. We have to put in new habitat and new area. If we replace lost area with new area at the same rate, we can end up with some constant amount which we would call the 'habitat constant'. Thus, we must conclude that the only reason for having a reserve is to buy us time so that we can replace what is lost.

Are we replacing lost area, renewing lost habitat? Not only is there no renewal, but the policy has not even been considered. Therefore, unless we change policy, reserves will not achieve their ends and our descendants will have nothing left. At the present time we are so desperately responding to crises of extinction that we have not had time to examine our current long-term conservation strategies.

This is not good news for either side. Obviously, it is not good news to the conservationists to be told that merely setting up a reserve is not going to save anything. Neither is it good news to the logging companies because if they want to cut down 100 hectares of old growth forest within a reserve, they must first grow 100 hectares of old growth forest, not replace it after-wards – and that takes 200 years. If governments or companies are not prepared to do this, then reserves will not save anything. We did have some short-term successes in Serengeti. Both wildebeest and buffalo increased over the period 1963–1977. Wildebeest went up from a quarter of a million to 1.5 million animals. However, human hunting has counteracted these increases; buffalo numbers are now only a quarter of what they were.

HOW MUCH HABITAT? THE 12 PER CENT MYTH

Returning to problems in conservation, the next question I want to ask is: how much habitat should we save? British Columbia has assigned a maximum of 12 per cent of the land area for conservation. However, where does the 12 per cent figure come from? In 1984 Jeff McNeely and colleagues at the International Union for the Conservation of Nature reported that 4 per cent of the world habitats had been put aside in reserves (McNeely and Miller, 1984). In 1987 the Prime Minister of Norway, Mrs Bruntlund, wrote a report for the United Nations in which she commented that 4 per cent was not enough, and we should save three times that amount, hence the 12 per cent figure (Brundtlund, 1987). This figure is, therefore, arbitrary and has no biological justification. Yet, it has now become the set point of politics, written in stone. In addition to the biological irrelevance of 12 per cent, we have the problem that we do not know what 12 per cent applies to. Twelve per cent of what? It cannot simply be 12 per cent of what we have presently remaining because that is a nonsensical amount. Secondly, what habitats do we apply this 12 per cent to? Some habitats are very small – do we save 12 per cent of these also?

To understand the problem I return to our declining tropical Asian forests that I referred to earlier. The only logical and sensible way of applying the 12 per cent figure is to start with the original untouched amount of forest and take 12 per cent of that (Figure 8.11). What that means, of course, is that if there is only half of the forest left, then one must reserve 24 per cent, not 12 per cent of the remaining amount. If there is only 12 per cent of forest remaining, then all of it must be reserved; that is, 100 per cent. Figure 8.11 shows a curve of the proportion of remaining habitat that has to be reserved starting with 12 per cent of original habitat and ending with 100 per cent. Comparing the amount of forest reserved in these countries relative to this curve, we see there are only two countries doing better than 12 per cent. Almost all of the countries are far below the 12 per cent point. Thus, to achieve 12 per cent, they need to implement the concept of habitat renewal already.

How have we been succeeding with reserving 12 per cent in British Columbia? The areas of high diversity for invertebrates are in the south Okanagan, which includes habitats of antelope brush (*Purshia*), blue bunch

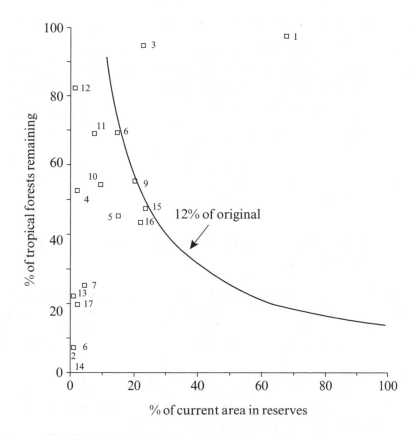

Source: From Sinclair et al. (1995). Reproduced with permission.

Figure 8.11 *The proportion of tropical forests remaining in 17 Southeast*
Asian countries relative to what should be reserved if 12% of
the original forest was protected

grassland and sagebrush. The area supports a number of important birds such as the sage thrasher and burrowing owl, and the tiger salamander. However, far more importantly, there are some 300 species of arthropods, insects, spiders, and so on. The way the British Columbia province is dealing with the 12 per cent is simply to take 12 per cent of the whole area. Since there are large tracts of conifer forests, almost all of the 12 per cent can be found by reserving that habitat. Indeed, well over 12 per cent of conifer forests have been reserved, but this habitat does not represent the habitat of endangered birds, salamanders and insects. Thus, nowhere close to 12 per cent of the bunch grass and antelope brush habitats, where these rare species occur, is reserved. British Columbia is failing to live up to its own arbitrary legislation.

We must ask whether 12 per cent of a habitat is sufficient to ensure long-term survival of species. Analysis of the minimum amount needed to ensure survival, using the complementarity approach, shows some 40 to 80 per cent of the habitat must be protected for rare and endangered species (Warman et al., 2004). For some of the rare habitats, such as the remaining bunch grass in the Okanagan, all of it must be protected. Unless society recognizes that far larger proportions of habitat than 12 per cent must be protected, most of our endemic species in Okanagan will become extinct. The debate over whether 8 per cent rather than 12 per cent should be reserved is merely splitting hairs in this context.

WHERE TO PLACE PROTECTED AREAS: GLOBAL CLIMATE CHANGE

The next question to ask is: where do we place reserves? As in every question I have asked so far, the answer is superficially obvious: we place them where the animals or plants occur. However, the world is changing from global climate change. Whether the climate gets colder or warmer is the subject of debate, but change is going on. The problem, however, is that when the climate changes, the species making up our communities change their geographic locations at different rates. We know this from changes in species distributions that have taken place after the last ice age 12 000 years ago (Davis, 1986). Following the ice age, forest communities in the southeast US moved northwards with the warmer climate. However, the various tree species moved at different rates so that species living together 12 000 years ago had different ranges by 6000 years ago. Thus, a reserve placed at present times to protect a community could easily lie outside the new range of the community under a warmer climate. We have to place our reserves *now* for future requirements to protect species because by the time they are needed, the areas will no longer be available. Furthermore, several such areas will be required because the species making up the community will be moving into different areas. So far, no efforts have been made to place reserves for future conservation.

LOSS OF BIODIVERSITY AND ECOSYSTEM FUNCTION

In 1994 members of a conference in the southern United States asked this question: given that we are going to lose species, how much can we afford to lose without impairing agriculture, forestry and other ecosystems? In general, the question is unanswerable because systems have an enormous number of species – in the soil, in the vegetation, and in the animals supported by them – and this complexity prevents us predicting what will happen from loss of species. One might be able to predict what would happen when A eats B; but one cannot predict what would happen two or three links down a longer line of species. One can understand each link individually, but not the outcome of a sequence of links. The technical term for this outcome is 'chaos'. What it says is that one can predict short-term consequences of change but not long-term consequences.

A better approach to the above question is the one medicine uses in pathology, namely to compare systems that have gone wrong with those that still work. There are no better experimental comparisons than the true ecological disaster areas of Australia, New Zealand and the Pacific islands. Several plant species of the group called *Hibiscadelphus* in Hawaii have become extinct because the birds that pollinated them, a group of endemic honeyeaters, themselves went extinct. Another example is that of *Calvaria*, a plant on the island of Mauritius in the Indian Ocean. It had not been known to germinate for at least 200 years until Stan Temple from the University of Wisconsin worked out the reason. The seeds of *Calvaria* had probably been eaten by the dodo, a giant flightless pigeon, the size of a turkey. It became extinct in the 1700s as a result of human hunting. To test this idea, Temple fed the seeds to turkeys, with a bit of help, because turkeys are smaller than the dodo. When the seeds came out the other end they germinated for the first time in 200 years (Temple, 1977). Thus, with the loss of the dodo, the link between the species was broken, and indirectly other species were endangered. These examples illustrate how species are co-evolved, one species depending on another; if you lose one, you lose the other. We cannot, therefore, allow any species to suffer extinction because we do not know the long-term effects on other species and on ecosystem function. The problem is that for most systems we do not know what those links are because they are so complicated.

The presence or absence of single species can upset even very complex habitats. Take the house mouse as an example. In North America, mice are a nuisance but they are not a serious problem. In Australia, however, house mouse populations expand into plagues; such events do not occur in North America or Europe. Why? We do not know the answer to that yet, but that problem is the one that should be attracting our attention. As another example, Asian water buffalo were imported to Australia in the early 1800s. Since then the population expanded and completely re-landscaped the habitats in the northern part of the country. Pathways created by the water buffalo drained fresh water from large areas and let in brackish water from the sea. Such major changes in hydrology have changed the habitats of northern Australia. Similar changes do not occur in Asia where water buffaloes occur naturally. Thus, we need to compare altered systems as in Australia or Hawaii with unaltered ones to understand how biodiversity loss will affect our planet.

IS CONSERVATION ACHIEVING ITS ENDS?

I started this chapter by asking whether conservationists are achieving their goals of saving the maximum amount of biodiversity. In reviewing conservation activities I have considered a number of simple questions related to biodiversity preservation. The answers appeared obvious until we started to think about them and then we realized that there are some extremely thorny problems to deal with. Indeed some problems seem intractable.

At the present time, conservationists have been confronted with an accelerating rate of loss of species. Their response has been to do what is possible for each extinction crisis. Areas for protection are currently decided by what is left out of reserves (gap analysis) or by which area contains the greatest number of species (hotspots). These approaches could well result in an inefficient use of valuable resources, with money and land area being allocated to species that do not warrant them while others are left with little help (Pressey and Tully, 1994). Other protocols such as complementarity or newer optimization procedures can represent more species with greater evenness of resources and for less cost.

Conservation has traditionally protected biodiversity by setting up reserves. There is ample evidence to show that all reserves in the world are presently in a state of decline as a result of attrition from human interference. Reserves, therefore, serve only to slow the rate of decay compared to areas that are unprotected; they do not protect biodiversity forever as is commonly conceived. Reserves merely allow us to buy time to reverse the attrition through a policy of adding in habitat to replace the lost portions – a process I call habitat renewal. So far no policy of habitat renewal has been contemplated and time is being lost. Unless such a policy is instituted we will lose as much biodiversity as if no reserves had been set up.

The amount of area assigned to conservation has been arbitrarily set at around 12 per cent of land area in British Columbia. This proportion has little biological relevance and is likely to be insufficient for most endangered and threatened species. Over 50 per cent of special habitats may be required to prevent extinction. Where habitats such as the Okanagan grasslands or tropical forests have already been reduced to less than 12 per cent of the original area, new grassland or forests must be grown or we will lose the species in those habitats.

The location of reserves has been decided entirely on present distributions of species. There has been no consideration for future range changes due to global climate change. Consequently, many of our current protected areas will be inappropriate in about 50 years' time. We should assign protected area status to future range *now* because such areas will not be available in the future.

In general, conservationists have not paid sufficient attention to these problems. Most conservationists work in the field and not enough have stood back to ask the question: are we doing the right thing? Some conservation biologists are now doing more to explore these issues and advising government field staff on the priorities of conservation (Sutherland, 1998). These priorities must be made on a global basis and not on a country-by-country basis. To achieve this role, an intergovernmental committee, similar to that advising on Global Climate Change (the Intergovernmental Program on Climate Change) should be set up.

REFERENCES

Balouet, J.C. (1990), *Extinct Species of the World*, New York: Barron's Educational Series, Inc.

Brundtland, H. (1987), *Our Common Future*, Oxford: Oxford University Press, for the World Commission on the Environment and Development.

Davis, M.B. (1986), 'Climatic instability, time lags, and community disequilibrium', in J. Diamond and T.J. Case (eds), *Community Ecology*, New York: Harper and Row, pp. 269–84.

Day, D. (1989), *The Encyclopedia of Vanished Species*, Hong Kong: McLaren Publishing, Ltd.

MacArthur, R.H. (1972), *Geographical Ecology*, New York: Harper & Row.

Margules, C.R. and R.L. Pressey (2000), 'Systematic conservation planning', *Nature*, **405**, 243–53.

May, R.M. (1990), 'How many species are there?', *Philosophical Transactions of the Royal Society of London, Series B*, **330**, 293–304.

May, R.M. (1995), 'Conceptual aspects of the quantification of the extent of biological diversity', in D.L. Hawksworth (ed.), *Biodiversity Measurement and Estimation*, London: Chapman & Hall, pp. 13–20.

McNeely, J.A. and K.R. Miller (1984), *National Parks, Conservation and Development: the Role of Protected Areas in Sustaining Society*, Washington, DC: Smithsonian Institute Press.

Myers, N., R.A. Mittermeir, C.G. Mittermeir, G.A.B. de Fonseca and J. Kent (2000), 'Biodiversity hotspots for conservation priorities', *Nature*, **403**, 853–58.

Nicholls, A.O. and C.R. Margules (1993), 'An upgraded reserve selection algorithm', *Biological Conservation*, **64**, 165–9.

Pimm, S.L. (1998), 'Extinction', in W.J. Sutherland (ed.), *Conservation Science and Action*, Oxford: Blackwell Publishing, pp. 20–39.

Pimm, S.L., G.J. Russell, J.L. Gittleman and T.M. Brooks (1995), 'The future of biodiversity', *Science*, **269**, 347–50.
Prendergast, J.R., R.M. Quinn, J.H. Lawton, B.C. Eversham and D.W. Gibbons (1993), 'Rare species, the coincidence of diversity hotspots and conservation strategies', *Nature*, **365**, 335–7.
Pressey, R.L. and S.L. Tully (1994), 'The cost of *ad hoc* reservation: a case study in western New South Wales', *Australian Journal of Ecology*, **19**, 375–84.
Pressey, R.L., I.R. Johnson and P.D. Wilson (1994), 'Shades of irreplaceability: towards a measure of the contribution of sites to a reservation goal', *Biodiversity and Conservation*, **3**, 242–62.
Pressey, R.L., C.J. Humphries, C.R. Margules, R.I. Vane-Wright and P.H. Williams (1993), 'Beyond opportunism: Key principles for systematic reserve selection', *Trends in Ecology and Evolution*, **8**, 124–8.
Raup, D.M. and J.J. Sepkoski (1984), 'Periodicity of extinctions in the geological past', *Proceedings of the National Academy of Science*, USA 81, pp. 801–5.
Rylands, A.B. (1991), 'Priority areas for conservation in the Amazon', *Trends in Ecology and Evolution*, **5**, 240–41.
Schneider, S.H. (1997), *Laboratory Earth: The Planetary Gamble we can't Afford to Lose*, New York: BasicBooks, HarperCollins Publishers Inc.
Sierra Club of Western Canada (1993), 'Ancient forests at risk' (Map), Victoria, BC, Canada.
Sinclair, A.R.E., D.S. Hik, O.J. Schmitz, G.G.E. Scudder, D.H. Turpin and N.C. Larter (1995), 'Biodiversity and the need for habitat renewal', *Ecological Applications*, **5**, 579–87.
Smout, T.C. (ed.) (2003), *People and Woods in Scotland, a History*, Edinburgh: Edinburgh University Press.
Steadman, D.W. (1995), 'Prehistoric extinctions of Pacific Island birds: biodiversity meets zooarchaeology', *Science*, **267**, 1123–31.
Sutherland, W.J. (ed.) (1998), *Conservation Science and Action*, Oxford: Blackwell Publishing.
Temple, S.A. (1977), 'Plant-animal mutualism: coevolution with dodo leads to near extinction of plant', *Science*, **197**, 885–6.
Vane-Wright, R.I., C.J. Humphries and P.H. Williams (1991), 'What to protect? Systematics and the agony of choice', *Biological Conservation*, **55**, 235–54.
Warman, L.D., A.R.E. Sinclair, G.G.E. Scudder, B. Klinkenberg and R.L. Pressey (2004), 'Sensitivity of systematic reserve selection to decisions about scale, biological data and targets – a case study from southern British Columbia', *Conservation Biology*, **18**, 655–66.
Watson, A. (1992), 'Regenerating the Caledonian forest', in: *Wild Earth* (Special Issue), the Cenozoic Society, Box 492, Canton, NY.
Webb, S.D. (1969), 'Extinction-origination equilibria in late cenozoic land mammals of North America', *Evolution*, **23**, 688–702.
Yalden, D. (1999), *The History of British Mammals*, London: Academic Press.

SECTION F

Forestry

9. The myth, reality and social process of sustainable forest management

Jane Lister

INTRODUCTION

The management of forests is not only contentious, but also complex. Forest ecology is dynamic and dependent on patterns of unpredictable natural disturbance. Market valuation of forest benefits is only partial, and the values that societies assign to forests are variable within and between communities. Sustainable forest management (SFM) is about integrating each of these uncertainties into multi-criteria decision-making processes in order to generate forest plans that will provide optimum economic and social benefits to present and future generations while maintaining the long-term ecological integrity of the forest ecosystem. The challenge is enormous. There is no single unit of measure that can capture the competing spectrum of forest interests. Criteria for determining the weighting of forest values and management trade-offs are inherently subjective, and institutional assumptions and organizational structures introduce rigidities and biases into decision-making paths.

The bottom line is that to be sustainable, forest management must be adaptive. It must evolve in response to changing social preferences, advances in scientific understanding, fluctuating market conditions and unpredictable ecological disturbance. There is no generic formula for achieving sustainable forest management. Rather, the effective management of the forest resource and ecosystem requires a consistently flexible and responsive process that is based on open social dialogue, ongoing forest research and education, and integrated consideration of ecological, economic and social criteria.

The purpose of this chapter is to highlight several principles of sustainable forest management that arise from an examination of certain myths of the traditional timber management paradigm. Rather than focusing on one 'patch' of forest management (for example, the economics or the ecology of forest management), the chapter provides an integrated examination of several key intertwined ecological, economic and social considerations that together form the landscape of an SFM approach. The nature of the shift from a traditional single-criterion focus on maximizing commercial timber production to the new sustainable forest management paradigm of managing the forest to optimize multiple values is described. The chapter begins with a brief discussion of the evolving paradigm and then turns to address five specific myths of traditional forest management and the associated ecological, financial and social reality. The chapter concludes with a summary of the SFM principles emergent from several institutionalized assumptions of the traditional forest management paradigm.

THE 'STICKY' PARADIGM

Forest management has traditionally focused on the goal of maximizing commercial timber production (Kimmins, 1992; 2006; Adamowicz and Veeman, 1998; Dellert, 1998). Private interests have typically sought to maximize the net present value of their capital investment through timber harvest, and governments have supported this approach by traditionally pursuing 'maximum sustained yield' policies[1] (Toman and Ashton, 1996; Kant, 2003). Maximizing timber volume and market value were assumed to maximize forest value to society. As Pearse (1967) described, 'as long as the value of the forest resource lies in the economic value of wood production, a forest policy that aims at maximizing any magnitude other than wood values will tend to prejudice the real contribution of forests to society, as well as to the forest owner.'

In recent years, increasing evidence of the deterioration of forest health and ecological functioning (for example, riparian damage, soil erosion, forest fragmentation and species extinction) has been accompanied by growing public interest and concern for the protection and maintenance of the forest for values other than timber (for example, recreation, scenic beauty, potential medicinal products, flood protection, carbon sequestration, biodiversity). These trends have created higher expectations of forest operators and managers, forcing a shift from a singular focus on timber towards sustainable management for multiple forest values (Toman and Ashton, 1996; Adamowicz and Veeman, 1998).

Sustainable forest management (SFM) is defined as 'management to maintain and enhance the long-term health of forest ecosystems, while providing ecological, economic, social and cultural opportunities for the benefit of present and future generations' (CCFM, 1995). If successful, SFM is ultimately ecologically appropriate, socially acceptable and economically viable. Within the paradigm of sustainable forest management, as with other areas of sustainable development, there are those with 'weak' and those with 'strong' sustainability interests (Adamowicz and Veeman, 1998). 'Weak' SFM is a resource management approach focused on maximizing sustained commercial timber production through technological innovation and potential substitution of manufactured capital for natural forest capital (for example, replacing non-timber ecological services with man-made services). 'Strong' SFM is an ecosystem management approach that emphasizes the optimization of multiple forest value objectives subject to the precautionary principle of maintaining the ecological integrity ('natural capital') of the forest.

In practice, sustainable forest management criteria and decisions can be found along the full spectrum between the 'weak' resource development sustainability approach and the 'strong' ecological sustainability perspective (Kant, 2003; Adamowicz and Veeman, 1998; Booth, 1994, p. 241). For example, public forest land in British Columbia has been classified into management zones emphasizing different sustainability criteria, including enhanced (timber production), general (multiple resource use) and special management zones (multiple resource and conservation values). A key SFM challenge is to determine the optimum position along the 'weak' to 'strong' sustainability spectrum within each unique forest community.

Although the concept of SFM is largely accepted by industry, government and society, an actual shift away from the traditional forestry paradigm is not yet fully realized (Lavoie, 2005; Kant, 2003). The underpinnings of traditional timber management continue to persist. For example, forest companies still must compete for maximum return in global commodity markets that only recognize the timber value of the forest. Governments continue to encourage and rely on a steady annual harvest to provide revenue and economic opportunity. As well, single-industry, forestry-based communities struggle to maintain an uncertain future dependent upon sustained commercial timber production.

There is a 'stickiness' or path dependency towards the traditional timber management paradigm that is anchored in mistaken ecological, social and economic assumptions and re-enforcing, rigid market and state-based institutions and organizations (Kant, 2003). As a result, assumptions inherent in the traditional timber management paradigm, while generally accepted as invalid under the SFM paradigm, nevertheless continue to misdirect forest management decisions.

Five of these 'mythical' assumptions and the accompanying SFM reality are listed in Table 9.1 and discussed in the remaining sections of the chapter. A hope is that by explicitly revealing these assumptions, not only will a set of SFM principles become clear, but also the accompanying challenge and necessity for institutional change will be evident.

Table 9.1　Myths and reality of forest management

Myth	Reality
1 Forests can be stable if managed correctly.	Healthy, productive forests are dynamic and dependent upon natural disturbance, not controlled management.
2 A non-declining, even flow harvest ensures forest industry jobs and local economic prosperity.	Local employment and prosperity are determined by technological change, global markets and regional economic diversity and not by a constant timber supply.
3 Timber companies operating on private land will have a financial incentive to consider long-term forest sustainability.	Financial decisions concern the present value maximization of the forest land investment through rapid timber growth and harvest and/or land conversion and not necessarily the maximization of long-term forest sustainability.
4 Price captures forest value.	Forests provide a multitude of values beyond market exchange value.
5 Individual preferences are consistent, and aggregate to a societal forest value preference.	Shared SFM preference is emergent through social dialogue guided by research and education.

1. Forest Dynamics

A focus of the traditional timber management paradigm is to convert the forest to a 'regulated' or 'normalized' managed landscape with an equal distribution of age classes in order to establish a stabilized, regular, non-declining, even flow of timber production (Kimmins, 2006; Dellert, 1998; Booth, 1994, p. 227). Silviculture techniques of pruning, thinning, spacing, fertilizing, pesticide and herbicide spraying, and planting with genetically superior individual species are utilized to control the natural disturbance and increase the growth and yield of commercial timber (Kimmins, 1992, p. 49).

The reality is that a forest is not the same thing as a homogeneous crop that can be controlled and regulated to maximize the production of a single product. Rather, a forest is a biologically diverse, dynamic, autogenic, successional community that provides a multitude of ecological and social benefits beyond timber. Instead of having a single, stable equilibrium, a forest is characterized by multiple equilibria, non-linearities and critical thresholds that vary by spatial and temporal scale (Kimmins, 1992; 2006; Rosser, 2005). While a healthy productive forest is dependent on patch disturbance, there are critical thresholds that must be respected in order to sustain regeneration capacity and long-term forest condition. For example, a spatial threshold exists in terms of maintaining sufficient forest connectivity for wildlife populations such as bear and elk. A temporal threshold exists with respect to maintaining landscape-level natural disturbance patterns over time. Controlling natural disturbance (such as fire and pest outbreaks) may result in an increased potential for catastrophic disruption. For example, the build-up of fuel in the forest understory caused by the suppression of small fires can fuel larger and more devastating fires. Spraying for pests can result in the disruption of non-target species such as insect and bird populations which normally help to contain widespread outbreaks (Rosser, 2005).

The reality is that healthy, productive forests are dynamic, with multiple equilibria that reflect forest succession and spatial variability. Management strategies that attempt to suppress this variability are therefore inherently unsustainable. A key SFM principle emergent from this reality is that forest management (of timber and non-timber values) must be continually adaptive to changing forest conditions and natural disturbance patterns.

2. Timber Supply and Local Economic Prosperity

Further to the mistaken assumption that forests can and should be 'normalized', as noted by Dellert (1998) and Marchak et al. (1999), it has been widely and incorrectly assumed that a constant, non-declining, annual timber supply to local communities will stabilize employment and sustain local economic prosperity.

These assumptions are misguided for several reasons. As previously described, forests are diverse, dynamic ecological communities subject to unpredictable natural disturbance, not crops that can or should be stabilized to provide non-declining annual harvest flows. Basing local social goals on maximizing 'stabilized' timber returns creates a goal that is ecologically unsustainable and opposed to the multiple benefit considerations of SFM.

Secondly, levels of forest employment relate more closely to technological change than to changes in timber supply (Adamowicz et al., 2003, p. 191). For example, in British Columbia in the last 30 years, the volume of timber logged increased from approximately 43 million m^3 to close to over 90 million m^3 but the number of jobs generated per unit of wood was cut in half (Marchak et al., 1999). In western Washington and Oregon between 1970 and 1988, total lumber and plywood production was constant at approximately 13 billion board feet while total employment dropped by 13 000 jobs (Booth, 1994, p. 235). Modern mills consume wood at roughly twice the rate of traditional sawmills but use approximately half the labour to produce the same volume (Marchak et al., 1999). Ultimately, capital will continue to substitute for labour as long as the marginal cost of capital is less than the marginal cost of labour (Adamowicz et al., 2003, p. 191).

Finally, it is the fluctuating demand and supply of timber in the global market that determines the price of wood products and, consequently, the level of economic prosperity of forestry-dependent communities (Adamowicz et al., 2003, p. 191). A non-declining timber supply does not guarantee local economic well-being. In fact, in periods of unfavourable market conditions, minimum annual harvest volume requirements may jeopardize the economic viability of local forestry operations forced to accumulate inventory.

The SFM reality is that the employment levels and prosperity of forest-based communities are determined by technological change, fluctuating global forest product markets and the extent of local economic diversity, and not by merely guaranteeing a maximum, non-declining timber supply. The SFM principle emerging from this reality is the need to encourage economic diversity beyond timber production in order to provide local economic and social adaptive capacity to continual changes in forest ecology, markets and technology.

3. Financial Decisions and Sustainable Forestry

It is a myth that a forest company operating on its privately held land will necessarily have a financial incentive to consider the long-term sustainable management of the forest. The reality is that unless the tree growth rate is greater than the market rate of interest, or there is forest management regulation to ensure long-term stewardship, the financial imperative is to maximize net present value through harvesting as soon and as quickly as possible in order to convert the forested land to a higher yielding 'better use' (for example, tree plantation, real estate, and so on).

Forest companies can be expected to make financial, not economic decisions. Economic concerns of social opportunity costs and/or other non-market environmental impacts are not a financial manager's principal consideration.[2] Rather, their focus is on maximizing the net present value of their capital investment – the timber resource and the land (Adamowicz et al., 2003, p. 187). Instead of sustainably managing to maintain a non-declining range of forest benefits and opportunities for present and future generations, financial forest management decisions assume and apply a discounted future forest value.

Holding trees represents a loss of alternative investment and, therefore, the principal financial forestry concern is with determining the optimal time to harvest the trees (Van Kooten, 1993, p. 335). Assuming a relatively constant timber market price, harvest is ideally when the growth rate of the forest is equivalent to the market rate of interest. Because there is a cost to holding forest 'capital', the commercial forester must also consider the net present value of future harvests or alternative uses for the land (Faustmann, 1849; Van Kooten, 1993, p. 335). Given that many forests grow at a rate slower than the market rate of interest (for example, boreal forest) and can take up to 90 years to reach a mature, harvestable age, and because future harvest value is discounted, the financially optimal decision in most instances is to harvest immediately, invest the capital in a faster growing alternative investment and convert the land, where possible, to a higher yielding alternative use such as a timber plantation or real estate development (Adamowicz et al., 2003, p. 188). For example, many forest companies operating on private land in the United States (for example, Plum Creek Timber and Boise Cascade) have real estate divisions to encourage the sale and conversion of their forested lands to higher investment-yielding uses.

Financial decisions are also concerned with reducing harvest costs. Unless the forest is rapidly growing, silviculture expenses are not financially justifiable (Van Kooten, 1993, p. 334; Adamowicz et al., 2003, p. 189). In addition, there is a financial incentive to achieve economies of scale by maximizing the size of the harvest. As the size of cut increases, the harvest costs per hectare decrease. Clear cut harvesting, where permitted, is financially optimal (Rosser, 2005). Financial decisions do not consider 'unpriced', non-market values, so the social and ecological costs of forest deterioration (and disappearance) are largely ignored (FAO, 1995).

The SFM principle emerging from the reality of financial (not economic) interests is that for the long-term sustainable management of the forest to be achieved on privately held forest land, the discount rate of future harvests needs to be lower, the rate and scale of harvest regulated, and/or the flow value of ecological goods and services priced so as to increase the 'holding value' and future return on the forest capital investment. The feasibility and appropriateness of pricing non-timber forest values is addressed in the next section.

4. Forest Value and Price

There is a long history of attempts to price non-timber flow values such as recreation, tourism and flood control (Hartman, 1976; Adamowicz et al., 2003, p. 191; Rosser, 2005). Through various methods such as contingent valuation, travel cost, hedonic pricing, shadow pricing, and so on the approach has been to estimate the revealed or stated preference monetary value of forest benefits, add them together and then factor them as a cost component into the traditional cost–benefit calculation to maximize the efficiency of timber production (FAO, 1995).

It has been assumed that non-timber forest values 'grow back' following harvest and that these values can be priced and, therefore, exchanged with other value preferences. It has been accepted that individuals have a 'willingness to pay' (WTP) or a 'willingness to accept payment' (WTA) as a substitute for their forest values. Because forest values are assumed reducible to a common unit of exchange (for example, dollars), it is further accepted that the consumption of these 'commodities' is consistent with neo-classical economic consumer theory (fixed preferences, indifference between values, no level of satiation, and so on) (Kant, 2003).

The reality is that the forest incorporates a wide and varied tapestry of values[3] that provide numerous benefits. Many of these benefits are not necessarily amenable to traditional neo-classical valuation approaches of monetary estimation, aggregation and substitution between values (Peterson and Brown, 1999; Rees and Wackernagel, 1999; Vatn and Bromley, 1994; Kant, 2003).

Ecological goods and services are inherently difficult and costly to price because, as discussed in section 1, the forest is a non-linear, discontinuous ecosystem with multiple equilibria and critical, potentially irreversible, biological thresholds (Rees and Wackernagel, 1999; Farber et al., 2002). Ecological functions are generally essential and therefore inappropriate to price (for example, watershed functions) (Lavoie, 2005; Rees and Wackernagel, 1999; Rosser, 2005). Forest values can be complementary (for example, recreation and old growth), competing (for example, timber harvest vs. scenic beauty), of infinite value (for example, spiritual value) or uncertain (for example, biodiversity vs. carbon sequestration) so treating all forest values as substitutable and additive under a single currency and a smooth indifference curve is inappropriate (Kant, 2003; Rosser, 2005; Lavoie, 2005).

Traditional methods of valuation are fraught with difficulty and uncertainty. Subjectivity and inconsistency are frequently observed in individual stated preference for both consumptive and non-consumptive uses (Tversky and Kahneman, 1981). As well, the measurement of forest uses is often incomplete as subsistence non-timber products are rarely traded (Kant, 2003).

Indirect passive-use and existence values are difficult to measure as there is no observable consumer behaviour – individuals are unwilling to trade these values, yet they are willing to pay for their continued existence (for example, biodiversity). As individuals often do not understand the functional relationship between forest values (for example, soil conservation and fisheries), answers to valuation surveys will express moral rather than consumptive preferences for these values (Peterson and Brown, 1999).

Individual utility preference curves will be discontinuous as certain forest values will increase as the forest ages (for example, timber production, tourism) and others will vary or decrease (for example, carbon sequestration, hunting) (Lavoie, 2005).

New valuation methods such as the choice method, which provides individuals with scenarios for ranking and determining value are attempting to overcome some of the traditional challenges of valuation. Unfortunately, these methods can be extremely time consuming and, hence, prohibitively costly to develop and implement (Secretariat of the Convention on Biological Diversity, 2001).

Recent valuation efforts to determine the income flow value of market credits for ecological services such as carbon sequestration and biodiversity are encouraging, as they are creating greater financial incentive for maintaining standing natural forests (Adamowicz et al., 2003, p. 188). However, the inherently high investment risk rooted in the unpredictability of forest disturbance (fire, pest outbreak, harvest) will need to be offset with a sufficiently high market rate of return on the ecological credits.

Thus, the SFM principle which emerges concerning forest value and price is the need for forest managers to recognize that forest valuation is partial and, therefore, to include along with consideration of market price, an appreciation of forest ecology and acknowledgement of non-linear, non-market forest values and preferences. The challenge to SFM of incorporating the uncertain variability in forest value preferences is discussed in the next section.

5. Forest Value and Social Preference

Traditional forest valuation approaches incorrectly assume, based on neo-classical economic theory, that individuals have fixed forest value preferences and will make consistent trade-offs among forest goods and attributes so as to maximize their individual utility (Baron, 2002; Lavoie, 2005; Kant, 2003). Further to this, it is mistakenly assumed that by calculating individual utilities and aggregating their sum, society's forest preference will be revealed and can be generalized into forest management decisions (Adamowicz and Veeman, 1998).

The reality is that individuals are inconsistent in both their revealed and stated preferences, so attempts to measure individual utility often fail (Vatn and Bromley, 1994; Farber et al., 2002; Tversky and Kahneman, 1981). The ordering of utility can reverse depending upon the measurement method (for example, WTP vs. WTA). There are cases where individual utilities are absolute (for example, protection of the spotted owl) and preferences can be lexicographic – that is clustered so that there is an unwillingness to substitute between categories (for example, disposable income versus habitat protection below a certain income level) (Lavoie, 2005; Farber et al., 2002).

Not only are individual tastes and preferences inconsistent, but they also vary over time as a result of education, advertising and changing cultural assumptions. Also, they can change as a reflection of the relative abundance and scarcity of the forest amenity (Farber et al., 2002; Kant, 2003).

The other misconception that builds on the assumption of fixed individual preferences concerns the desire to aggregate individual forest value preferences to reveal overall societal SFM preference. It is incorrectly assumed that the sum of individual utilities equates to a societal forest value-preference. As Arrow's impossibility theorem (1966) describes, unless individuals share the same information, and rank and order their utility preferences consistently, it is not possible to convert individual preference into a general set of societal preferences.

Further, even if individual forest value preferences could be aggregated for a particular community, it is not necessarily appropriate to extrapolate this result to other forest communities. The reality is that every forest community is unique in terms of forest type, ecosystem resilience and provision of forest goods and services, as well as the panoply of individual-weighted forest preferences (Kimmins, 1992, p. 49).

However, sustainable forest management is not only community-specific. Unique forest communities also share similar SFM challenges in terms of the increasingly interconnected external pressures of the global marketplace. For example, pressures from the broader society (for example, European interests in preserving Canadian old growth forests) can strongly influence local forest management decisions through the competitiveness and market access effects of locally targeted international boycotts (Adamowicz and Veeman, 1998).

In summary, it is a significant SFM challenge to determine and steer a course towards diverse, continuously dynamic and emergent societal forest value preference. If individual preferences are inconsistent, variable and hard to measure; if societal preference cannot be revealed from the sum of individual preference; and if every forest community is different, yet influenced by similar external market forces, it is difficult to decipher a general SFM solution (Farber et al., 2002). Rather than the traditional approach of maximizing a single fixed criterion of timber value, SFM is concerned with optimizing dynamic, multi-attribute individual local preferences and external interests, many of which are not accounted for by the market. Social dialogue is therefore an essential element of SFM as a crucial means to inform and reveal shared societal forest value goals (Farber et al., 2002; Adamowicz and Veeman, 1998; Kant, 2003; Peterson and Brown, 1999). In addition, ongoing forest science research is imperative in order to increase our understanding of critical ecological thresholds. Educational efforts based on sound forest science are essential to guiding our social dialogue and contributing towards optimum sustainable forest management decisions that will be ecologically appropriate, socially acceptable and economically viable.

The central principle emerging from this reality is that an SFM approach is not defined by the pursuit of a single, predictive outcome solution but rather by an ongoing process of social dialogue guided by sound forest science and education. In other words, effective SFM will require participatory, adaptive management processes that encourage meaningful dialogue amongst key parties, particularly at the forest planning and evaluation stages. The incorporation of up-to-date scientific understanding and the promotion of continual learning will be essential ingredients to defining and realizing successful SFM outcome.

CONCLUSION

In summary, key sustainable forest management principles emerge from the examination of several myths of the traditional timber management paradigm:

- Adaptively manage the forest to recognize natural disturbance patterns.
- Encourage regional economic diversity beyond timber production in order to provide local adaptive capacity to respond to global forest product market fluctuations, increasing technological efficiency and unpredictable forest disturbance.
- Encourage an appropriate financial rationale for the maintenance of future forest values through a lower forest discount rate, regulation of harvest cut, and/or fuller pricing of ecological goods and services.
- Recognize that monetary forest valuation is partial and include an appreciation of the intrinsic value of ecological functions and an acknowledgement of non-linear, non-market forest values and preferences in addition to market-based exchange value.
- Acknowledge that shared societal forest value preferences are emergent through social dialogue guided by sound forest science research and ongoing education.

Sustainable forest management concerns the optimization of ecological, economic and social considerations – specifically, the integration of scientific knowledge of forest ecological processes and capacities with market valuation of forest amenities and weighted individual and emergent societal forest value preferences. The SFM challenge is great and ongoing as society and the forest landscape change over time. Although, in theory, forest management has moved well beyond the traditional myths described in this paper, in practice, forest management continues to be influenced by many of these misconceptions. Hopefully, the recognition of these myths and the nature of their essential 'sticking point' in theoretical neoclassical economic assumptions will facilitate a gradual release from their institutionalized hold, thus enabling the sustainable management of forests to become a demonstrated reality.

NOTES

1. Maximum sustained yield is defined as the maximum possible annual output of commercial timber that can be maintained in perpetuity (Van Kooten, 1993, p. 335).
2. Triple bottom line accounting of financial, social and ecological considerations is only beginning to emerge in the financial world.
3. The range of forest values include direct consumptive (for example, fuel, food, medicinal products) and non-consumptive uses (for example, recreation, tourism), option values related to future uses and indirect, passive-use values (for example, watershed functions, carbon sequestration, biodiversity) and existence values pertaining to the intrinsic properties of the forest ecology (for example, scenic beauty, wilderness, spiritual values) (Secretariat of the Convention on Biological Diversity, 2001; FAO, 1995).

REFERENCES

Adamowicz, W.L. and T.S. Veeman (1998), 'Forest policy and the environment: changing paradigms', *Canadian Public Policy*, Vol. **XXIV**, Supplement 2.

Adamowicz, W.L., Glen W. Armstrong and Mark J. Messmer (2003), 'The economics of boreal forest management', in Philip J. Burton et al. (eds), *Towards Sustainable Management of the Boreal Forest*, Ottawa: NRC Research Press.

Arrow, Kenneth J. (1966), *Social Choice and Individual Values*, 2nd edn, Cowles Foundation for Research in Economics at Yale University, New York: John Wiley & Sons Inc.

Baron, Jonathon (2002), 'Value trade-offs and the nature of utility: bias, inconsistency, protected values and other problems', Conference on Behavioral Economics and Neoclassical Economics, American Institute for Economic Research, July 2002, Massachusetts.

Booth, Douglas, E. (1994), *Valuing Nature: The Decline and Preservation of Old-Growth Forests*, Maryland, USA: Rowman & Littlefield Publishers, Inc.

CCFM (Canadian Council of Forest Ministers) (1995), *Defining Sustainable Forest Management: A Canadian Approach to Criteria and Indicators*, Canadian Forest Service, Natural Resources Canada.

Dellert, Lois, H. (1998), 'Sustained yield: why has it failed to achieve sustainability?', in Chris Tollefson (ed.), *The Wealth of Forests*, Vancouver: UBC Press.

FAO (Food and Agriculture Organization of the United Nations) (1995), *Valuing Forests: Context, Issues and Guidelines*, FAO Forestry Paper 127, Rome.

Farber, Stephen C., Robert Costanza and Matthew A. Wilson (2002), 'Economic and ecological concepts for valuing ecosystem services', *Ecological Economics*, **41**, 375–92.

Faustmann, M. (1849), 'Calculation of the value which forest land and immature stands possess for forestry', reprinted in *Journal of Forest Economics* (1995), **1**(1), 7–44.

Hartman, Richard (1976), 'The harvesting decision when a standing forest has value', *Economic Inquiry*, **XIV**, March.

Kant, Shashi (2003), 'Extending the boundaries of forest economics', *Forest Policy and Economics*, **5**, 39–56.

Kimmins, H. (1992), *Balancing Act: Environmental Issues in Forestry*, Vancouver: UBC Press.

Kimmins, H. (2006), 'Sustainability: a focus on forests and forestry' (Chapter 10, this volume).

Lavoie, Marc (2005), 'Post-Keynesian consumer choice theory for the economics of sustainable forest management', in Shashi Kant and Albert R. Berry (eds), *Economics, Sustainability and Natural Resources: Economics of Sustainable Forest Management, Vol. 1*, Dordrecht: Springer Publishers.

Marchak, M. Patricia, Scott L. Aycock and Deborah M. Herbert (1999), *Falldown: Forest Policy in British Columbia*, Vancouver: David Suzuki Foundation and Ecotrust Canada.

Pearse, P.H. (1967), 'The optimum rotation period', *Forestry Chronicle*, June, 178–95.

Peterson, George and Thomas, Brown (1999), 'The application of information about non-market outputs to forest management decisions', in Charles S. Roper and Andy Park (eds), *The Living Forest: Non-market Benefits of Forestry*, London: The Stationery Office.

Rees, W.E. and M. Wackernagel (1999), 'Monetary analysis: turning a blind eye on sustainability', *Ecological Economics*, **29**, 47–52.

Rosser, J.B. Jr (2005), 'Complexities of dynamic forestry management policies', in Shashi Kant and Albert R. Berry (eds), *Economics, Sustainability and Natural Resources: Economics of Sustainable Forest Management, Vol. 1*, Dordrecht: Springer Publishers.

Secretariat of the Convention on Biological Diversity (2001), *The Value of Forest Ecosystems*, Montreal, Canada.

Toman, Michael A. and Mark S. Ashton (1996), 'Sustainable forest ecosystems and management: a review article', *Forest Science*, **43**(3), 366–77.

Tversky, A. and D. Kahneman (1981), 'The framing of decisions and the psychology of choice', *Science*, **211**, 453–8.

Van Kooten, G.C. (1993), *Land Resource Economics and Sustainable Development – Economic Policies and the Common Good*, Vancouver: UBC Press.

Vatn, Arild and Daniel W. Bromley (1994), 'Choice without prices without apologies', *Journal of Environmental Economics and Management*, **26**, 129–48.

10. Sustainability: a focus on forests and forestry

J.P. (Hamish) Kimmins

INTRODUCTION

Occam's razor: '*Pluralitas non est ponenda sine neccesitate*'
(William of Occam (1284–1347), an English philosopher and theologian)
  Occam's razor is the basis for the law of parsimony and the rule of simplicity: *do not posit complexity more than necessary*. However, Occam's razor has two 'edges': it says as simple as possible but as complex as necessary.
  A problem is an issue that does not get solved. An issue that gets solved quickly is not a problem. Problem issues often persist because they are complex and only simple solutions are offered. Complexity must be addressed, as required by Occam's razor.

There are few issues that have united the nations of the world more than concern over the environment and sustainability. Although there are still some countries which have not yet given environmental issues a high priority, their number is declining. Important contributions to this growing international unity over the environment include the report of the World Commission on Environment and Development (*Our Common Future*) which promoted the concept of 'sustainable development', and the Rio Summit on the Environment (UNCED) that produced Agenda 21.
  There is widespread support for the principle of sustainable development, but not everyone agrees with it. Some consider that the term is an oxymoron: that 'sustainable' and 'development' are incompatible concepts, and point to the numerous examples in which past industrial development and the application of technology have resulted in environmental damage: deforestation in the tropics, non-sustainable agriculture, over-exploitation of marine resources, air and water pollution, and the alteration of the earth's atmosphere. Many environmentalists have challenged the claim made by foresters that forests are being managed in a sustainable manner; they assert that industrial utilization of forest resources is not sustainable. The current public criticism of forestry demands a careful analysis of what is meant by sustainable use or development of forests. The question, 'can

we use and sustain our forests', which must be answered by those who manage public forests, transcends the traditional concern over sustaining the supply of timber products, important though this is. Today's society is demanding that a wide range of values be sustained.

A 2006 world human population of about 6.5 billion, with the prospect of another 3 to 4 billion by the end of the century (Lutz et al., 2001), requires that humans learn to live sustainably with their environment and with each other. The 'human footprint' per capita (Wackernagel and Rees, 1996) must be reduced as the abundance of our species continues to rise if we wish to bequeath to our great grandchildren the future that we think they and their grandchildren will want. Few would disagree with this inter-generational ethical imperative. Equally few appear to agree on what we have to do to achieve this.

There are many reasons for the difficulty. One of the most fundamental is the diversity of definitions of what sustainability is. Another is the dichotomy between the fundamentals of biophysical sustainability and the ideals of social and economic sustainability, a dichotomy that we will see shortly is more apparent than real.

While societies and their economies are certainly dynamic, many of the contemporary goals of society imply the stability of human economies and communities. Continued growth in economic activity and improvement in human well-being is currently a fundamental pillar of most western soci-eties, but this is considered by many to be non-sustainable, and basic principles suggest that eventually humans will have to develop stable econo-mies, communities and lifestyles. In contrast to contemporary social goals, one of the key characteristics of ecosystems, especially terrestrial ecosys-tems, is that they change over time, and it is widely accepted by forest ecol-ogists that shorter-term change is a necessary prerequisite for longer-term constancy in forests. The structure, function, complexity, diversity and the interconnections between components of an ecosystem are undergoing periodic natural[1] disturbance, leading to change and recovery as internal processes return the ecosystem towards the pre-disturbance condition or some new condition. Maintenance of the historical character, the biodi-versity and other values of forests, if this is our objective, requires that we sustain, or emulate the effects of, historical ecosystem disturbance regimes.

The utopian ideal of social stability ignores the continuing momentum of human population growth, international migration, the omnipresent tendency towards urbanization of the world's population (3 per cent in 1800, 30 per cent in 1950, 40 per cent in 2000, and predicted to be 60 per cent in 2030; UN, 2002), and our current addiction to non-renewable energy and material resources. Because humans are ultimately as depen-dent on their environment and other species as are those other organisms, there is ultimately less difference between social and biophysical sustainability than suggested above. Human societies are a subset of the global biophysical system, and we must not permit social and cultural considerations to blind us to the ultimate biophysical constraints on our endeavors. People must adapt to environmental change, not ignore it.

The purpose of this chapter is to draw attention to the complexity of the sustainability issue and the many dimensions of sustainability in forest management. The assessment of sustainability of biophysical systems is both time and space dependent. Whether or not one concludes that a forest is being sustained depends as much or more on the spatial scale at which the assessment is made and on the time period that is included as it does on the actual trends in forest values. Unless the full complexity of the question is explicitly recognized in policy, regulation and practice, it is unlikely that we will achieve our forest sustainability goals, whatever we decide they are. William of Occam was right – we should keep our definitions of sustainability and our actions to achieve this as simple as possible, but as complex as necessary to honor our ethical and intergenerational obligations.

SUSTAINABILITY AND THE ORIGINS OF FORESTRY[2]

Forestry is a human activity that has developed at various times and places around the world, but always in response to the same need: to sustain some forest-related condition or resource value. The desire to maintain wildlife for hunting, strategic supplies of timber to support armies and navies, supplies of fuel wood for domestic or industrial use, or forest cover to protect villages or roads from avalanche are among the many reasons why governments or land owners acted at various times over the past millennium to restrict unregulated forest exploitation. Forestry and the modern forest preservation movements thus share a common ultimate objective and spring from common roots: the desire for conservation and sustainability.

Environmentalists can be forgiven for a moment of incredulity when it is suggested that they share much in common with foresters. Forestry normally evolves through a series of rather predictable stages. The first stage generally fails to achieve its goal of sustaining particular forest values, and the results have often differed little from unregulated exploitation. This is because this early stage is usually characterized more by legal restrictions and an administrative, bureaucratic approach to resource use and renewal than by regulations that reflect the needs and desires of the local people and the spatially and temporally variable ecological character of the forest. One cannot successfully manage a complex, living, changing ecological system such as a forest as though it was coal in the ground or a manufactured commodity. Nor can one expect simple regulations that ignore existing and traditional uses of the forest by local communities, the needs of these people, and their increase in numbers and impacts on the forest over time, to conserve forest values effectively. Most of the early attempts to establish sustainable forestry failed either because of the lack of a sound ecological foundation, or because of the failure to recognize existing and changing social and political conditions, or both.

Because the failure of the first ('Administrative') stage of forestry to achieve sustainability has often resulted from a lack of a sound ecological foundation, the second stage of forestry has been characterized by the development of such a foundation. This ('Ecologically-based') stage has generally focused on the sustained renewal of timber and associated values, and there are many examples where this silvicultural stage of forestry has been successful in maintaining the growth and harvest of tree crops. However, sustainable silviculture does not necessarily satisfy all of the desires of a 'post-industrial' society. It may not conserve adequate areas of old-growth forest, and associated wilderness and spiritual values. Depending on how it is done, it may not sustain some aspects of biodiversity, and it may fail to satisfy requirements for landscape aesthetics, wildlife habitat and various other non-timber values. Consequently, the affluent, post-industrial societies of western countries are now requiring that forestry evolve to a third stage ('Social Forestry') in which the requirement for sustainable tree crops is accompanied by the demand that a variety of other resource values, both social and environmental, be maintained.

Canadian forestry only emerged from the exploitative, pre-forestry stage relatively recently – in the middle of the last century. The administrative stage of forestry was put in place in most parts of Canada in the first half of the century or soon thereafter. The subsequent two or three decades confirmed what was already well known in countries with a longer history of forestry: that the administrative approach is not an adequate basis for sustainable development of forests. There was a steady transition to the second (ecologically-based silvicultural) stage over the last three decades of the twentieth century, although in many parts of the country this transition is not yet complete. However, the public now expects that forestry will operate according to the objectives and policies of the third (social forestry) stage and will achieve the results expected of this stage. Herein lies much of the current conflict between forestry and the public.

In comparison to the development of forestry in Europe or Scandinavia, forestry in much of Canada is being expected by the public to skip a stage – to go directly from the administrative stage to the social stage. Some of the results of forestry practices that the Canadian public can still observe on the landscape represent predictably unacceptable consequences of the administrative stage of forestry, or even a 'leftover' from the days of unregulated exploitation. In other cases, what the public sees may actually be 'good' silviculture – it may sustain timber production but may not satisfy the expectations of 'social forestry' – the aesthetic, spiritual, biodiversity and various other demands of an increasingly urban society. The Canadian public expects the standards of the most advanced stage of forestry from a resource sector that has only recently begun to emerge from an early stage in its evolution. The rate of change in the public's expectations of forestry has outstripped the rate of change in forestry, and this has resulted in a classical example of what Alvin Toffler called *Future Shock* (Toffler, 1970; Kimmins, 2002).

The challenge to Canadian forestry is to make the change to social forestry in a fraction of the time that was available to their European and Scandinavian predecessors, and to make the change without threatening the sustainability of any resource values.

DEFINITION OF FORESTRY AND THE TWO RESPONSIBILITIES

Forestry is defined as the art (skill), practice, science and business of managing a forested landscape to sustain the ecologically possible balance of values desired by the landowner. In the case of publicly owned forests, the landowner is society. On private forest land, there is a balance of ownership between public and private ownership because forests always support a variety of private (for example, timber) and public values (for example, air, water, and either all or at least the migratory species of fish and wildlife).

Sustainability thus lies at the heart of forestry. However, many people find that hard to believe. This may be because they are concerned about the sustainability of different values than the forest landowners, or because they are evaluating the issue at different spatial and temporal scales. Sustainability must be evaluated at both the stand and the landscape, and over time scales that are ecologically appropriate for the ecosystems and values in question. This disbelief may also relate to the two responsibilities of foresters that are implicit in the above definition of the profession:

- To change how forests are managed as the balance of values and environmental services desired by society from forests changes, and to reject current practices that are not consistent with the desired balance, but
- To resist suggested changes in management that are incompatible with the known ecology and sociology of the desired values.

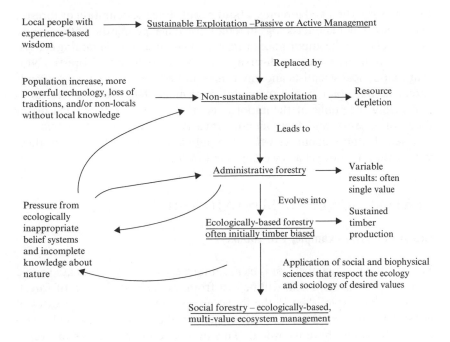

Figure 10.1 The evolution of forestry

This dual responsibility for sometimes conflicting directions in management creates a tension in forestry that is poorly understood by many people. It creates a case of Alvin Toffler's *future shock*. It poses a challenge to foresters to find the right balance between changing their plans and practices to honor their primary responsibility of being prepared to change, and respectfully rejecting suggested changes that in their experience and knowledge will not deliver to present and future generations the values and ecosystem conditions they are asking for or we think they will want, respectively. The need to resist public demands may be because the suggested changes are ecologically inappropriate for the forests in question; because they are socially unacceptable over various time scales; or because they are incompatible with management and economic considerations, including worker safety. This second (but not secondary) responsibility is vital to prevent public pressure from pushing forestry back in its development sequence rather than forward (Figure 10.1).

Because my background is in forest ecology, I will focus for the rest of the chapter on the biophysical aspects of sustainability. I recognize, however, that forestry is first and foremost about people (see the definition of forestry given above), not about ecology and biology. When people did not recognize and understand the importance of respecting nature, of maintaining ecosystem function and biological diversity, these were not a part of forestry. Now that biophysical scientists and environmental education (to a considerable extent because of the environmental movement) have been successful in convincing the public of the importance of these values, they are a major focus of forestry and their maintenance is now a key responsibility of foresters. In those countries where the public has not yet focused on these values, they are not yet a key component of forestry.

SPATIAL SCALE OF SUSTAINABILITY

Stand Level (for example, 1 to 100 ha)

When a 100 ha area of forest is clearcut harvested, many values associated with the pre-harvest stand will be lost from the harvested patch of forest, but will be re-established as the forest grows back unless the processes of ecosystem recovery have been damaged or the area is harvested again before the values have recovered. This may take many decades or even a century or more, which is beyond the time scale considered by most people but is well within the time scale of a 'healthy' and sustained ecosystem. Adjectives such as *lost forever*, *destroyed* and *degraded* are common responses when people see such changes. However, if considered in the context of a 12 000 ha forest managed on a 100-year cycle with 1000 ha of un-harvested reserves and the retention of features of older forests scattered throughout ('variable retention' logging, or 'structure retention silviculture'; Franklin et al., 1997; 2002), such stand-level disturbance may not only sustain local human communities (the local employment and economy), but may be essential to sustain a landscape that offers the full range of wildlife habitat values, ecological conditions, maintains an acceptable balance between trees and their diseases, and sustains ecosystem productivity and various measures of biological diversity.

Where it is desired to sustain a relatively constant supply of a variety of social and environmental values from a small area – say, for example, a 100 ha woodlot – a 100 ha clearcut is clearly inappropriate and would not constitute sustainable management. Frequent, much smaller scale harvesting – 'continuous forest cover silviculture', 'partial harvesting' or small patch harvesting – would be needed to sustain a variety of values for the landowner of a small 'woodlot'. However, in some types of forest, such 'soft-touch' silviculture may not provide sufficient ecosystem disturbance to sustain all the desired values into the future (Attiwill, 1994; Kimmins, 2004b). Where there is a mismatch between the ecological characteristics and disturbance requirements of the values that are to be sustained and the spatial scale, severity and frequency of disturbance that the public, or a particular woodlot owner, will accept, sustainability will not be achieved. In such cases, sustainability may have to be evaluated over larger spatial scales. The concept may simply be inappropriate at small spatial scales.

Landscape Scale (for example, 1000 to millions of ha)

Many aspects of forest sustainability cannot be judged at the stand level because in many healthy, sustained forests, conditions at the stand scale involve non-declining patterns of change over time rather than constant conditions. Unlike diamonds, any particular forest condition is not 'for ever'. As in any biological system, there is continuing change. Assessment of sustainability in the face of this inevitable and, frequently, essential change (Attiwill, 1994) cannot be made on the basis of 'snapshot' evaluations. It must involve assessment of the temporal patterns of change to see if they are sustained. Sustainability can, however, be assessed at the landscape scale.

This assertion invites the question: what is a landscape? From an ecological perspective it is a geographical area that is large enough to encompass the spatial scale and frequency of ecosystem disturbance events, 'natural' or human-caused[2]. An ecological landscape is that area that incorporates the full range of ecological effects of historical disturbance regimes on ecosystem structure and function so that the full cycle of ecosystem disturbance and recovery is represented. Obviously, for areas affected by very large fires, insect outbreaks, vertebrate animals that range very widely or other disturbances, a landscape will be very large – tens of millions of hectares in the boreal forests of British Columbia. Where natural disturbance is generally small scale and the key native fauna have small home ranges, a landscape may be only a few thousand hectares.

At the landscape scale, sustainability involves a shifting mosaic of stand level conditions that are undergoing non-declining patterns of change. While any particular ecosystem condition or value will not be available at any particular place all the time, all values will be available somewhere in the landscape all of the time. If this is not true, then the area being considered is not large enough to be a truly sustainable landscape. In fact, in many of the world's forests it may never be possible to identify landscapes large enough to satisfy the definition of true sustainability. By the time the area approaches adequate size you are already into a different type of ecosystem, and factors such as climatic differences and post-glacial species migrations become an issue. This emphasizes the complexity and somewhat theoretical nature of the concept of sustainability. Just as the world faced with human population growth cannot be considered sustainable, many forests may simply have to be considered as continuously changing systems.

Areas that are larger than stands but too small to be true ecological landscapes are often referred to as *local landscapes*. This is an important scale in forestry, but is usually too small for the assessment of sustainability of a variety of values. Because they are generally too small, the overall character of the shifting mosaic of stand conditions will exhibit considerable variation over time.

TEMPORAL SCALES OF SUSTAINABILITY

The importance of the temporal scale of sustainability was introduced above. Stand-level sustainability cannot be judged outside of its temporal context.

If one observed a decline in agricultural soil fertility and annual crop production over five successive growing seasons, it would be reasonable to conclude that the farm was not being managed sustainably. In contrast, five years of declining soil organic matter and nutrient availability in forests following disturbance does not necessarily indicate non-sustainability. Temporary declines in various ecosystem characteristics are a common phenomenon in both sustainably-managed and unmanaged forests after either natural or human-caused disturbance. In some types of forests, periods of decline in certain ecosystem characteristics may be essential for the longer term maintenance of 'normal' ecosystem function.

Just as the farmer must judge the consequences of his or her actions over several successive (annual) crop rotations, the sustainability of forest values can only be assessed by comparing several successive complete management cycles, or from a knowledge of the expected variation in ecosystem processes and conditions over the rotation in a forest that is being managed sustainably (sometimes called the 'temporal fingerprint' of the forest in question; Kimmins, 1990a; 1990b).

Judging the sustainability of forest values should not be based on whether or not there is any change in forest conditions over time, but whether the combined frequency and intensity of human-caused or natural disturbance exceeds the capacity of the ecosystem to recover between successive disturbances. The concept of *ecological rotations* (Kimmins, 1974) can be used to evaluate this temporal aspect of sustainability. An ecological rotation is the time taken for a given ecosystem to recover back to some original condition, or to some desired new condition, following a particular intensity of disturbance. Some ecosystems recover slowly. Some recover rapidly. Others are intermediate. As long as a particular ecosystem is managed on its ecological rotation, always returning to some particular condition, the values associated with that condition would be renewed in successive rotations. However, if the rotation is shortened (the frequency of disturbance is increased), the level of disturbance must be reduced if ecosystem processes and conditions are to be sustained in successive rotations. Similarly, if the intensity of disturbance is increased, a longer rotation will be needed to renew the values. If this is not done, there may be a progressive decline in ecosystem conditions in successive rotations. This is illustrated in Figure 10.2.

The conditions of, and values provided by, a particular natural or managed even-aged forest stand will vary over time because of natural or human-caused disturbance and ecosystem recovery. However, if there is a mosaic of stands of different age distributed across the landscape, it will be possible to find some area in any particular forest condition at any particular time. Thus, if an area of forest is managed to provide a mosaic of stand ages and conditions, a wide range of values will be continuously available within the landscape. This will only be true, however, if the mosaic includes the appropriate range in size of patches of forest of different ages distributed in a spatial pattern across the landscape that satisfies wildlife habitat, hydrological, aesthetic and other considerations. Like any ornamental mosaic, sustaining forest values at the landscape level requires more than merely having all the correct pieces of the mosaic; they must also be arranged in the correct pattern (Perera et al., 2004).

Assessing whether or not sustainable forestry is being practiced involves comparing the 'temporal fingerprint' of change in a particular ecosystem with the expected pattern of change in a 'healthy' ecosystem of comparable ecological character (c.f. adaptive management; Walters, 1986). It also involves comparing the existing landscape mosaic (the 'spatial fingerprint') with the ideal mosaic that would sustain all desired landscape-level values. Where we have several rotations of experience of the effects of management, we can use this experience to design and establish these temporal and spatial 'fingerprints' for a particular forest. Where we lack such experience, we must harness our knowledge of ecosystem function, change over time and species ecology into computer-based management decision support tools (Messier et al., 2003). Where we lack the knowledge needed to develop and use these tools, it is the responsibility of foresters and forest scientists to ensure that appropriate research is undertaken to fill the knowledge gaps. Imperfect though they are, in the absence of appropriate long-term experience such computer-based decision aids are often the only way of assessing sustainability.

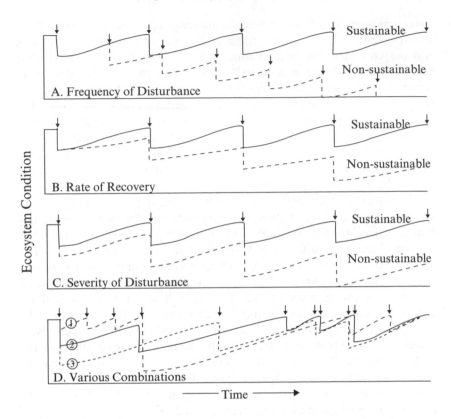

Note: *Sustainability* at the stand spatial scale results from combinations of severity (degree of ecosystem change) and frequency of ecosystem disturbance, and the resilience (rate of recovery) of the ecosystem or value in question that produce a non-declining pattern of change. The difference between sustainable and non-sustainable may be a factor of (A) frequency of disturbance, (B) ecosystem resilience, and (C) severity of disturbance. Many different combinations of disturbance over time can all result in the same long-term level of sustainability, but with different levels of various values at any one time (D).

Figure 10.2   Concept of ecological rotations and stand level sustainability

SUSTAINABILITY OF TIMBER VALUES

It is an article of faith for most foresters that they are practicing sustainable timber management. Assessment of whether or not this is true requires analysis at two different spatial scales: the local site or stand level, and the regional or whole forest estate (landscape?) level.

1. Stand-level Site Productivity; Potential vs. Achieved

Sustainable timber management at the stand level involves two separate issues: sustaining the potential productivity of the site, and achieving this potential.

The potential productivity of a particular forest site is determined first by the regional climate, and secondly by the soil conditions on the site. Climate is determined largely by latitude, longitude, elevation, aspect, distance from the ocean or large lakes, and position (leeward or windward) relative to mountain ranges. Soil conditions of importance include soil moisture, aeration and fertility. These are often closely related to the quantity and quality of soil organic matter, and the activity of soil organisms.

Forest management can significantly affect microclimate for the period between harvest and canopy closure. However, sustained yield forestry is not believed to affect regional climate. In contrast the large-scale deforestation that accompanies major land use changes has the potential to alter regional climatic conditions significantly in some parts of the world (for example, the tropics).

Forestry often has a significant effect on soil conditions. It can either increase or decrease soil organic matter levels, and either improve or impair the moisture, aeration and fertility of the soil. It can alter the community of soil organisms.

Achievement of the biological potential set by regional climate and soil conditions requires a community of locally-adapted plants, animals and microbes developing through the sequence of stages of ecological succession that is characteristic for the site. Attainment of the full potential production of specific plants (for example, crop trees) or animals (for example, game species) requires that the processes of ecological succession are managed to favor these particular species by maintaining the ecosystem in a particular seral stage or sequence of stages, or a mosaic of seral stages across the landscape.

Achievement of the potential of the site to produce timber values also requires that the forest is protected from natural risks such as fire, insects, diseases or wind. Maintaining potential site productivity and ensuring that an appropriate biological community occupies the site will not ensure sustained economic stand-level production and various other social values if these risk factors cannot be controlled.

Sustaining stand-level timber productivity is thus the combined result of conserving soil resources, managing the processes of natural succession through silvicultural interventions, and protecting the forest from natural risks. In areas of severe climates, the maintenance of a modified microclimate may also be important. However, sustaining timber production at maximum levels may impair certain other values, and the prevention of natural disturbance (for example, fire) that may threaten timber production can increase the risks of insects, diseases and more destructive fire. These may threaten timber production more than the disturbances that have been prevented. Consequently, assessment of sustainability cannot be undertaken by considering one value at a time. There will be tradeoffs between the sustainability of different values, which requires multi-value scenario and tradeoff analysis, something that is best done with the aid of ecosystem management models, as discussed later.

2.   Forest-level Productivity

Sustaining stand-level productivity does not ensure a sustainable supply of all desired resource values in a major valley or large forest management unit. Forest-level (or landscape-level) issues are also important.

A sustained supply of timber products over time from a particular valley, forest management unit or region depends on having even-aged stands of commercial tree species of all ages up to the age of final harvest, or a large enough area of uneven-aged forest with an appropriate range of tree age and size classes to permit continuous harvesting of wood products at a desired level. In both cases, there is the requirement for a particular age and size class distribution, and a sufficient area of economically operable (that is harvestable) forest available each year to sustain the harvest. If the age and size class distribution is not 'normal', or if the area of economically-harvestable stands available each year is not fairly even, there will not be an even flow of wood products and related social and environmental values over time. This can result from a history of natural losses due to fire, wind, insects, and so on, or excessive rates of logging, that has produced an unbalanced age class structure. It is also a common feature of forests as they are being converted from an unmanaged to a managed condition (for example, conversion of 'old-growth' to second growth forest). Failure to sustain the whole-forest level of timber supply and associated social values can thus occur as a result of an inappropriate age class structure or lack of economic operability, even though the site production potential of individual stands has been sustained. Age class and operability problems are often a far greater short-term and medium-term threat to sustainability of timber and related social values in western Canadian forests than problems of damage to potential site productivity. However, long-term sustainability involves both issues.

An uneven distribution of forest age classes also has sustainability implications for wildlife and various biodiversity values. Unless there is a continuing supply of all ages and forest conditions across the landscape, the wildlife populations that depend on them will not be sustained at constant levels. Such fluctuations may or may not be consistent with wildlife sustainability. Wildlife populations naturally undergo fluctuations in abundance, and local reductions or even extirpations of subpopulations are sometimes a component of the sustainability of the larger 'metapopulation'. It may prevent the build-up of diseases and predators to debilitating levels.

The discussion in this section so far has focused on potential forest-level production. Achievement of this potential depends upon economics, technology, human resources and the existing land-use strategy. As the national and international prices of timber, pulp and other wood products fluctuate, the area of forest that can be harvested economically will change. Sustained directional changes in log values or the competitive status of forest companies may reduce or expand the area of forest managed for timber, thereby affecting the level of sustainable harvest and the supply of certain types of wildlife habitat. Changes in technology may increase the area of forest that can be harvested economically, or the area that can be harvested without unacceptable environmental impact. Technological change thus influences forest-level timber supply and the sustainability of employment; as harvesting methods and manufacturing equipment and processes change, there is often a loss of jobs. Conversely, the availability of an appropriately trained skilled workforce determines the technologies and management methods that can be used. Strikes or lockouts may influence whether the annual allowable cut is achieved or not, and wage rates will affect the silvicultural techniques that can be employed and the marketability of the harvested products.

Failure to sustain the landscape-level of timber supply can also result from land-use allocation changes that reduce the area of forest to be harvested. The creation of new parks, wilderness or ecological reserves is a valid land-use decision, but it can have significant consequences for the sustainability of timber production and associated social values in the region where they are created. Similarly, restriction on silvicultural techniques such as slashburning, herbicide use or clearcutting may sometimes reduce the success of reforestation efforts. If this results in significant delays in reforestation, it will influence the level of the annual allowable timber harvest. Such restrictions on silviculture may affect the species of tree that can be grown and thus the sustainability of particular types of wood products.

The ability to sustain forest-level timber yields is obviously the combined result of a complex of factors, from risk factors to changing social and cultural conditions.

SUSTAINING NON-TIMBER VALUES

Forests are much more than an industrial timber resource. They are complex ecosystems that provide a wide range of non-timber values and environmental services desired by our post-industrial society, including: wildlife, hunting and trapping, range, watershed, fish, biodiversity, recreation, aesthetics, spiritual values, and the traditional cultural values of forests to Canada's forest-dependent indigenous peoples. It is both a requirement and an ethical responsibility of today's foresters to sustain a balance of these values across the landscape, with due regard to the consequences for economics, employment and community stability of the change from a focus on timber.

1.   Wildlife, Hunting and Trapping

Sustaining wildlife populations involves the maintenance of both appropriate habitat values and populations of animals to utilize these habitats. According to how it is practiced and the wildlife species you are considering, forest management may either improve or deplete the supply of habitat. However, the availability of habitat will have little influence on the actual abundance of wildlife if over-hunting and trapping, high populations of natural predators, or other mortality factors are maintaining populations of the species in question below the level which could be supported by the available habitat. Sustaining the trapping industry is closely related to sustaining the populations of their target species, which is the combined result of the availability of habitat, the pressure of hunting and trapping on the population, and the effects of natural mortality agents. The availability of markets is also important. The recent rejection by many in society of animal furs as a form of fashion clothing has had a major impact on the sustainability of the social values created in the past by indigenous peoples by trapping.

2.   Range

Range values are closely related to factors that determine the growth of herbs and shrubs. These include the duration of early seral conditions following harvesting, fire or other types of disturbance, the structure of mature forests, and silvicultural operations that maintain a partially open tree canopy. Delayed reforestation may benefit range values, whereas sustaining timber values at maximum levels will usually impact negatively on range values.

3. Watershed Values

Questions about sustaining watershed values require that the impacts of forest management be considered at different 'watershed orders'. A small, unbranched stream draining a few hectares is a first-order stream; it drains a first-order watershed. Where two or more first-order streams join, they form a second-order stream, their combined drainage areas forming a second-order watershed. The joining of two second-order streams forms a third-order stream, and so on. Clearcut harvesting generally has a significant short-term impact on the quality, quantity and flow regime in first-order streams. This impact will persist until the harvested area is hydrologically recovered, which normally occurs when a closed-canopy forest cover has been re-established over the area. Where less than 25 to 30 per cent of a third- (or higher) order watershed is in the hydrologically-altered, post-harvest (or post-natural disturbance) recovery stage, it is usually difficult or impossible to detect differences in stream chemistry or flow regimes at the outflow of this watershed. However, significant stream sedimentation or debris avalanche events in first-order watersheds can cause episodic turbidity or stream bed instability problems that are detectable at the outflow of second or third-order watersheds. If roads are well constructed, maintained and provided with adequate drainage and culverts, if harvesting is done without roads (helicopter or skyline cable logging), if logged areas are carefully harvested, if unstable slopes are left unharvested, and if second- and third-order streams are appropriately protected by buffer strips, such problems should not occur.

4. Fish Habitat

Sustaining fish habitat over the short to medium term is closely related to maintaining the integrity and stability of streambanks and their vegetation, the stability and diversity of the stream channel, and the quality, quantity and flow regime of streamwater. Leaving appropriate riparian buffer strips (but careful removal of large trees that will be susceptible to windthrow may sometimes be better for fish habitat in the short run than leaving them to blow down), prevention of debris avalanche and sedimentation events, and restriction of the proportion of the watershed in a hydrologically altered condition at any one time should ensure that fish habitat is sustained over periods of decades. This will not ensure that fish populations are sustained, however. Over-fishing at sea, in lakes and in rivers, or environmental pollution such as acid rain, acid mine drainage or other forms of water pollution that are unrelated to forest management can reduce or eliminate fish populations even if habitat is protected. In the long run, prevention of all debris avalanches and landslides (including naturally-occurring ones) and a reduction of large dead trees falling into streams may have a very detrimental effect on fish habitat and fish abundance. Periodic input of coarse woody debris and gravel (by erosion) is an essential component of sustaining the fish resource over the long term in many forest streams and rivers, even though in the short term (years to a few decades) the effects on fish may be negative (Kimmins, 2004c).

5. Biodiversity

After millennia of expropriating the ecological niches of other species, of overhunting, and of promoting the abundance of a small number of desired plant and animal species for food and fiber, the human race is finally beginning to recognize the need to conserve the globe's genetic inheritance. Sustaining biodiversity has become one of the cornerstones of both the environmental movement and the activities of a rapidly increasing number of concerned scientists. However, it is one thing to say 'let's conserve bio-diversity'. It is another to decide how best to achieve it. This is to a great extent because there is a diversity of biodiversities.

Perhaps the most fundamental dimension of biodiversity is genetic diversity. As a species, we limit the genetic diversity of our food and fiber crops at our peril, and conserving species sometimes has as much to do with conserving the genetic variation in their populations as with conserving their habitat.

A second and closely related dimension of biodiversity is the number of species to be found in a particular ecosystem. Unmanaged ecosystems that have not been significantly affected by humans come in a wide range of species diversity. Some (for example, mature tropical humid forests, especially those on fertile soils), can have an extraordinary number of species in a given hectare. Others (for example, fire origin forests in many parts of the world) may naturally have but one species of tree, a handful of shrub, moss and lichen species, and, with the possible exception of soil animals, a small number of bird and animal species. The diversity of soil microbes is not nearly as well described as the diversity of plants and animals. This is partly because of the difficulty of applying conventional species taxonomy to the below ground microbial world, and partly because relatively little work has been done to inventory the genetic and species variation of microbes in forest soils. Thus, most statements about the species diversity of ecosystems refer to plants and animals rather than to total species diversity. Most of the work on animals has referred to the larger animals, and the full diversity of forest insects has not been described for many of the world's forests.

In addition to species diversity, ecosystems vary in their structure: the number of different plant life forms, (for example, trees, shrubs, herbs, mosses and lichens) and their arrangement into different vertical layers in the plant community. Forests that have low plant species diversity will usually have greater total biodiversity if the plants form a multi-canopied community than if they are structurally very simple and uniform: a multi-layered, multi-aged, climax monoculture hemlock stand will generally be more biologically diverse than an even-aged, single layered monoculture hemlock forest.

The species and structural diversity in the local ecosystem or forest stand constitute *alpha diversity*. Reflecting local variations in soil and past disturbance, the species list and structure of forests vary across the local landscape in what is called *beta diversity*. There is also variation in the species list and in the plant community structure at different locations across the larger landscape – *gamma diversity*. This is largely a consequence of diversity of climate that results from latitude, longitude, elevation, aspect and slope, as well as major variations in soils resulting from variations in geology, glacial history and the origin of soil-forming materials. The physical and chemical diversity that constitutes *ecological diversity* forms a mosaic of habitat or site conditions that is largely independent of natural or human-caused disturbance. It constitutes the framework within which biodiversity develops as a result of ecological processes. These processes involve the combination of both natural and human-caused disturbance and successional recovery on these different ecological site types.

The discussion so far has treated biodiversity as though it was constant over time. Nothing could be further from reality. One of the relatively few attributes shared by all forest ecosystems is that they change over time. In some climax 'old-growth' or mature forests, change may be slow, and it may occur as a mosaic of small gaps (5–50 m across) that are created when individual large trees die or are blown over. In most young forests (for example, less than 100 years since the last major disturbance) change occurs more rapidly, and if major disturbance occurs it usually affects patches that range from 1 hectare to many thousands or even tens of thousands of hectares.

As forests are disturbed and recover from disturbance, there are characteristic temporal patterns of change in both alpha and beta diversity. Both species and structural diversity undergo such change over time. Where disturbance occurs at the individual tree or small patch scale, there may be little apparent change in biodiversity over time in areas as small as several hectares. Where disturbance operates at a larger spatial scale, observable changes in alpha and beta species and structural diversity occur continually across local landscape units as large as hundreds or thousands of hectares.

Sustaining biodiversity requires different strategies for the different aspects of biodiversity. Maintaining temporal diversity is not compatible with constant levels of other measures of alpha diversity. Maintaining those aspects of beta diversity that depend on periodic ecosystem disturbance is also not compatible with the concept of unchanging species and structural alpha diversity.

Silvicultural strategies of site preparation, regeneration, weeding, spacing and thinning have certainly reduced both species and structural diversity in some forests. There is also concern that some modern forest nursery techniques and regeneration strategies may be lowering the genetic diversity of planted tree crops. However, appropriately distributed harvesting and regeneration of unmanaged mature or climax forests can increase landscape (beta) diversity, and forest regeneration practices designed with genetic diversity in mind can maintain or increase the genetic diversity of second growth forests in comparison with the mature forest. There is, therefore, no simple relationship between forest management and biodiversity. Specific biodiversity goals that are appropriate for different ecological zones and forest site types must be identified. Specific management regimes can then be designed to achieve these goals.

6.   Recreation, Aesthetics and Spiritual Values

Sustaining aesthetic and spiritual values and certain types of recreational activities will certainly require a different approach to forest management than that which has occurred in many forests in the past. These values are often associated with large trees, mature stand structure, and vistas of forest that provide a pleasing mosaic of colour and texture that blend in with the form of the local landscape. These values have often been damaged in the past by management (especially by timber harvesting) that was not designed to sustain them. When a society has both the desire and the affluence to conserve these values, they can and will be sustained. Similarly, where these values have been damaged in the past, future management should be designed to ensure their renewal and future maintenance. Sustaining these values may involve a significant economic and social cost. Consequently, they will not be managed and sustained at the same level in all forests. The balance between timber and these non-timber values will vary from location to location according to both their absolute and relative values, and the willingness of society to invest in maintaining them.

7.   Traditional Values for Forests for Indigenous Peoples

Forests have many values for modern industrial societies, ranging from industrial raw materials and employment, to recreational and spiritual values. But for millennia, forests have had values for the indigenous people who used the forest before the coming of European and other settlers. Sustaining these traditional values sometimes conflicts with sustaining the values desired by other sectors of western societies. In other cases, careful planning of management or appropriate changes in land-use allocation may resolve these conflicts. Direct involvement of forest-dependent indigenous peoples in the management of forest resources may be the best way to resolve conflicts between traditional and other forest values.

8. Miscellaneous Other Values

Harvesting berries, nuts, foliage, honey and mushrooms are some of the other consumptive activities that may be important in particular forests, both by indigenous and non-indigenous people. Sustaining these values may require a modification of traditional silvicultural practices. In other cases, these values depend upon, or are compatible with, sustainable management and harvesting of timber.

THREATS TO SUSTAINABILITY

1. Population Growth

As Pogo said in what is probably one of the most significant cartoon strips of our time: 'We have met the enemy and he is us'. The greatest single threat to sustainability on earth is the vast and rapidly increasing number of humans. Simple numbers of humans is not the whole story, of course. The earth is a bountiful place. If all the agricultural land and all the forest land were well protected and the areas dedicated to food and fiber crop production were well managed, all the present population, and a considerable expansion thereof, could be provided with the basic necessities of life from a relatively modest proportion of the earth's land surface (Binkley, 1997). However, given the disproportionate allocation of resources between rich and poor countries and between rich and poor within a country, and given the waste of resources on war, the mismanagement of soil, the pollution of air, soil and water, and the wasteful, materialistic life styles of the affluent people of the world, our planet is almost certainly overpopulated. We cannot sustain the present number of people under the present circumstances indefinitely, let alone the expected increase in human numbers.

It was a major conclusion of the World Commission on Environment and Development that the greatest long-term threat to the global environment is poverty. The key ingredients for long-term global sustainability are thus arresting human population growth and raising the standard of living in the world's poor nations to the point at which protection of the environment can become the primary objective of all governments. As long as extreme poverty and rapid population growth continue, there is little hope for global sustainability.

2.   Climate Change

The global patterns of vegetation, soil, land productivity and 'traditional' human settlements are largely a reflection of climate. Climates have always been changing as glacial periods have come and gone and as continents have drifted, but the time scales of these changes have been so long that the climate and the consequent vegetation potential of an area have been thought of as fairly constant. However, if the global climate change that is predicted as a result of the 'greenhouse effect' does occur, there are expected to be significant changes in the geographical location of the major climatic and vegetation zones of the earth within the next century. Caused largely by human alteration of atmospheric chemistry, this poses the greatest single potential threat to a wide variety of forest values. Although there is still much controversy about whether or not it has already begun, and even if it will occur at all, many scientists believe that the evidence supports the claim that human-induced, accelerated global climate change will occur and will have significant effects on forest ecosystems (Watson et al., 2001; Houghton and Hackler, 2002).

3.   Soil Damage

Within a climatic area, the potential productivity of the land is closely related to the soil: its fertility, moisture condition, physical structure organisms and aeration. Soils have been mistreated and mismanaged around the world, and this threatens the sustainability of many resource values, even if human-caused climatic change is averted. Reduction in soil organic matter, loss of soil nutrients, compaction, exposure to wind and water erosion, and the loss of soil stability on steep slopes have been much too common in both agriculture and forestry, and much more respect for these soil values is required. However, this does not imply that soils should never be altered. Some soils degrade naturally if they remain undisturbed for very long periods of time, and all soils have a natural rate of recovery from disturbance. It does imply that the disturbance regimes that we apply to agricultural and forest soils must be of a character, intensity and frequency that result in the maintenance of desirable soil conditions over multiple crop rotations.

4. Loss of Genetic Variation

The ecosystem potential set by the climate and soil can only be achieved if there is an appropriate community of plants, animals and microbes that are adapted to the local ecological conditions. Evolution has provided a wide range of genetic variation that equips organisms to survive and function under a variety of environmental conditions. Faced with actual or potential human-caused changes in climate and soil conditions, it is extremely important that we conserve genetic diversity. Foresters must always be aware of the need to maintain genetic variation and ensure that their actions do not cause unacceptable genetic simplification of forests.

5. Natural Risks

Fire, insects, diseases and wind can all threaten the sustainability of a wide range of forest values. If global climates are significantly altered by human activity, it is probable that all these natural risks will increase in severity. Indeed, this may be one of the major negative impacts of global climate change. Foresters must give considerable thought to how these risks could be reduced if the global climate change that is predicted for the next 50 years does occur. But they must also consider the ecological consequences of, and threats to sustainability posed by, management-induced alteration of historical natural disturbance regimes.

6. Lack of Investment and Loss of Confidence in Forestry

High quality, sustainable resource management costs money. Forest companies that are at the 'economic brink' are rarely able to practice forestry to the same environmental standards as a company with a satisfactory bank balance. Just as global poverty is a major threat to the sustainable global use and development of resources, so corporate or government poverty is a major threat to the quality of forest management. Confidence in the long-term future of forestry is also very important. Unless forest managers are encouraged to take a long-term view, decisions will become short-term and focus on immediate economic rewards rather than on stewardship. The current climate of public concern about the environment has led to a feeling of insecurity amongst many forest companies and individual foresters. Insecurity of land tenure, uncertainty about who will benefit in the long run from voluntary investments in forest management, and the loss of self-esteem and confidence amongst some foresters after repeated and often highly critical attacks by the media and the environmental movement are having a significant negative effect. Some large forest companies are reviewing their investment in forest management and some are reducing their involvement in growing forests in favor of being processing industries. In some cases, they may be replaced by companies that do not have nearly such a good environmental 'track record'. Other companies are limiting their investments in forest renewal, silviculture and management to the minimum that is required by law.

Unless the current crisis of confidence and the growing reluctance to invest in long-term forestry can be reversed, there is a risk that the quality of forest management will decline. In particular, the public antipathy against clearcutting and disturbance to forest ecosystems is leading to a style of forestry that in some forests may be closer to exploitation than to sustainable forestry. In some cases, this could become a major threat to sustainability (c.f. Figure 10.1).

7. Lack of Secure Long-Term Tenure

One of the most important ways of building confidence in the future and promoting stewardship in forestry is to assign long-term responsibility and accountability for resource management. Long-term tenures, albeit with tough performance standards, are an essential ingredient of forest stewardship. In British Columbia, the public distaste for the concept of long-term tenures by timber companies is a significant threat to the practice of the type of multi-resource management that is required for sustainable use and management in the forests of the province. Steps must be taken to develop socially-acceptable tenure arrangements that will encourage stewardship and sustainable management. In particular, there is an urgent need to switch from timber management tenure to ecosystem management tenure. This complex topic is beyond the scope of this paper, but is explored in Kimmins (2003b).

ESSENTIALS FOR SUSTAINABLE USE AND DEVELOPMENT OF FORESTS

Defined as the use of forests that satisfies present demands for a wide variety of values, but which does not reduce the options and the values available to future generations, sustainable forests must involve the following essentials.

1. A Sound Ecological Foundation

Although sustainable forestry involves much more than just science and, within the realm of science, much more than just ecological science, forestry is unlikely to be sustainable unless it is soundly based on ecology. Just as a well-designed building may collapse if it is erected on an inadequate foundation, sustainable use of forests requires a solid foundation in knowledge of ecosystem function, change over time and spatial variability, and the ecological requirements and tolerances of forest organisms. The single most important component of this foundation is an ecological classification and stratification of the landscape. However, this is not enough. Site classification must be accompanied by knowledge of the functional processes of forest ecosystems, their resilience, the processes that allow ecosystems to recover from disturbance, the ecological role of disturbance, and how characteristics vary from one type of ecosystem to another. The ecology and ecological role of crop and non-crop species must be understood and respected.

2.   An Accurate Inventory of Major Resource Values

Sustainable management is impossible in the absence of an adequate inventory of the extent and location of the values that are to be sustained. The best quantified forest resource in Canada is the timber, but even this inventory is inadequate to meet the demands of today's society. Improved inventories of wildlife, fish and streams, aesthetic, old-growth, cultural and spiritual values, and so on, are necessary if plans to sustain them are to be successful.

Immediate development of all the inventories required to meet the public's current expectations of forestry and foresters is beyond the economic capabilities of the government agencies responsible for the management of public forests. This means that management will have to proceed in the absence of adequate inventories. However, a clear message must be sent to governments that if they intend to respond to public demands for changed levels of forest management, adequate funding of accelerated inventory activities is essential.

3.   Ecosystem Prediction Tools

'If in doubt, ask a tree or read the landscape'. This adage suggests that experience is generally the best guide for the management of our complex forest ecosystems. However, we often lack the appropriate experience. Either we are still logging mature, unmanaged or old-growth forests, and therefore do not have multi-rotation experience of the consequences of our management, or the experience we do have may be valid only for the management practices of the past, many of which have been rejected by the public. Frequently, experience-based decisions must be replaced by knowledge-based decisions.

Unfortunately, we generally lack the decision support tools that can effectively integrate all the relevant knowledge that exists.

There is an urgent need to develop such tools. Geographic Information Systems, computer simulation models, computerized 'expert systems', and maps and field manuals are some examples of the kinds of integrative decision support tools that must be developed where they are lacking. The ability to rank the probable future consequence for a wide variety of resource values of the resource management decisions we make today is one of the most critical needs. Such tools must be developed and used if we are to make management decisions that will sustain resource values. Figure 10.3 presents a summary of a system of ecosystem management decision support tools being developed at the University of British Columbia. A review of computer tools in sustainable forest management is provided by Messier et al. (2003).

4.   Stable Land-Use Strategy

Long-term planning and stewardship require a stable land-use strategy and tenure system. There is no point in having long-term ecosystem prediction tools if there is no incentive to consider anything more than the short term. Society must decide, and rather quickly, how much forest land should be assigned to different intensities and strategies of timber management, how much land should be used for the harvesting of non-timber resources, and how much should be allocated to non-extractive uses such as parks and wilderness. Society must also decide where the different land uses should occur. The 'shifting goalpost' problem, in which land managers do not know the size of the area they will be managing in the long-term, or which forests they will be harvesting in the future, is very damaging to efforts to develop a stewardship ethic and sustainable management.

5.   Integrated Planning

Much lip service has been paid over the years to 'multiple use' of forests. Many foresters now subscribe to 'the best use' concept: a zoning of land into intensive fiber production lands, land for non-consumptive uses, and multiple use lands on which the relative priorities of the different resource values varies from place to place and from time to time.

Much of the conflict in forestry might be avoided if forests were planned in a more integrated manner, rather than assigning the planning and management for timber production to one agency or government or industry, with other values managed by other agencies acting as constraints on timber management (Kimmins, 2003). Management of entire blocks of

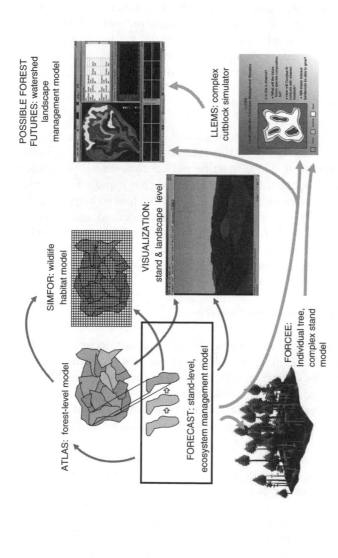

Note: Driven by the stand-level ecosystem management model FORECAST, these models include landscape-level timber and wildlife habitat supply models, an individual tree model, and complex antiblock and small watershed management models.

Source: Reproduced from Kimmins (2003a), with permission of Prentice Hall Inc.

Figure 10.3 Meta-modeling framework of ecosystem management models at various spatial scales

landscape for all resource values by one agency, company or collective, with firmly applied contracts to ensure that an appropriate balance of values is sustained, can offer a much more successful system of land management than the present administrative separation of management for different values; the latter has proven to be a recipe for conflict. Public attitudes towards such a management system will probably prevent it being used in public forests in the foreseeable future, but it is difficult to see how we will ever get truly integrated planning where responsibilities for different ecosystem values are divided amongst so many agencies.

6. Accountable, Well Informed Public

The public owns most of the forests of Canada, especially in the west. The public therefore has the right, and the obligation, to have a choice in how their forests are managed. There must be public involvement in decisions concerning the way public forests are managed, but it must be informed involvement. The forestry profession has the obligation to help the public understand the forestry-related issues they are concerned about and the public has the responsibility to seek such knowledge. There must also be a mechanism by which there is sharing of responsibility and accountability for the consequences of forest management decisions between all those who make the decisions.

7. A Commitment to Sustainable Forestry

In spite of good planning, sustainable forestry will not occur unless there is a commitment to make it happen. Foresters must work with concerned citizens to achieve the changes needed to manage forests sustainably. They must have the knowledge and confidence to resist public pressures to manage forests in ways that are counter to the principles of long-term resource sustainability, but must not hang on to traditional attitudes and methods where these are no longer appropriate.

For their part, concerned citizens must leave behind the rhetoric and confrontation tactics that have contributed so positively to creating the awareness of environmental problems and the need for improved resource management. It is time for concerned members of the public to sit down with government agencies and resource managers to decide exactly what sustainable forestry means in the fullest sense of this term, and how to achieve it. Unless there is a commitment by all parties to move away from polarization, confrontation and rhetoric, to embrace positive change, and to proceed to find ways of achieving sustainable forestry, it is doubtful that we will achieve it.

CONCLUSION

Sustainable forestry is an imperative, not a choice. The need is driven by the inexorable growth in human numbers and deterioration of the global environment. However, it is much easier to talk about it than to achieve it. This is largely because it is such a multi-dimensional concept. There are so many values to be sustained at so many different temporal and spatial scales.

Sustainability does not imply constancy over time, and the metaphor of 'ecological theater', with ecological 'stages', 'plays' and 'actors' could usefully become a foundational paradigm for forestry (Kimmins, 2005). The challenge is to decide at what spatial and temporal scales we will evaluate sustainability, what balance of values is to be sustained in any particular forest, and what pattern of variation in values over time is consistent with the concept of sustainability.

Sustainable forestry is not simply a technical and scientific issue; although to be sustainable, forestry must be well founded in science and use appropriate technologies. Sustainable forestry is also a political, social, cultural and economic issue. Only if all the dimensions of sustainability are considered will we be able to develop land-use plans and management methods that achieve this laudable but often elusive goal.

Returning to the wisdom of William of Occam, we must strive to keep issues as simple as possible, but we must make our approach to understanding, defining and solving them as complex as is necessary. Much of the conflict over the concept of sustainability and how to achieve it relates to a failure to understand the multifaceted nature of the concept, and that there are no simple answers. As Bunnell said in 1999: 'forestry is not rocket science – it's much more complex'.

NOTES

1. Humans are natural and consequently their effects on forests are natural, but I am using the common convention here (see Peterken, 1996).
2. This and other topics in the chapter are discussed in Kimmins (1997, 2003a).

REFERENCES

Attiwill, P.M. (1994), 'The disturbance of forest ecosystems: the ecological basis for conservation management', *Forest Ecology and Management*, **63**, 247–300.
Binkley, C.S. (1997), 'Preserving nature through intensive plantation forestry: the case for forestland allocation with illustrations from British Columbia', *Forestry Chronicle*, **73**, 533–59.

Bunnell, F. (1999), 'Forestry isn't rocket science – it's much more complex', *Forum* (Publication of the Association of British Columbia Professional Foresters), **6**(1), 7.

Franklin, J.F., T.A. Spies, R. Van Pelt, A.B. Carey, D.A. Thornburgh, et al. (2002), 'Disturbances and structural development of natural forest ecosystems with silvicultural implications, using Douglas-fir forests as an example', *Forest Ecology and Management*, **155**, 399–423.

Franklin, J.F., D.R. Berg, D.A. Thornberg and J. Tappeiner (1997), 'Alternative silviculture approaches to timber harvesting: variable retention harvesting systems', in K.A. Kohm and J.F. Franklin (eds), *Creating a Forestry for the 21st Century. The Science of Ecosystem Management*, Washington, DC: Island Press, pp. 11–139.

Houghton, R.A. and J.L. Hackler (2002), 'Carbon flux to the atmosphere from land-use changes', in *Trends: A Compendium of Data on Global Change*, Carbon Dioxide Information Analysis Centre, Oak Ridge National Laboratory, US Dept. of Energy, Oak Ridge, Tenn., US.

Kimmins, H. (1997), *Balancing Act*, 2nd edn, Vancouver, BC: UBC Press, University of British Columbia.

Kimmins, J.P. (1974), 'Sustained yield, timber mining, and the concept of ecological rotation: a British Columbian view', *Forestry Chronicle*, **50**, 27–31.

Kimmins, J.P. (1990a), 'Monitoring the condition of the Canadian forest environment: the relevance of the concept of "ecological indicators"', *Environmental Monitoring and Assessment*, **15**, 231–40.

Kimmins, J.P. (1990b), Workgroup issue paper: 'Indicators and assessments of the state of forests', *Environmental Monitoring and Assessment*, **15**, 297–9.

Kimmins, J.P. (2002), 'Future shock in forestry. Where have we come from; where are we going; is there a right way to manage forests? Lessons from Thoreau, Leopold, Toffler, Botkin and Nature', *Forestry Chronicle*, **78**, 263–71.

Kimmins, J.P. (2003), 'Forest ecosystem management: an environmental necessity, but is it a practical reality or simply an ecotopian ideal?', Proceedings, World Forestry Congress, Quebec City, Quebec.

Kimmins, J.P. (2004a), *Forest Ecology. A Foundation for Sustainable Forest Management and Environmental Ethics in Forestry*, 3rd edn, Upper Saddle River, NJ: Prentice Hall, 610 pp.

Kimmins, J.P. (2004b), 'Emulation of natural forest disturbance. What does this mean?', in A.H. Perera, L.J. Buse and M. Weber (eds), *Emulating Natural Forest Landscape Disturbances: Concepts and Applications*, New York: Columbia University Press, pp. 8–28.

Kimmins, J.P. (2004c), 'Forest ecology: the study of the ecological (spatial) biological and temporal diversity of forest ecosystems', in T.G. Northcote and G.F. Hartman (eds), *Fishes and Forestry. Worldwide Watershed Interactions and Management*, Oxford: Blackwell Publishing, pp. 19–43.

Kimmins, J.P. (2005), 'Forest Ecology', in S.B. Watts and L. Tolland (eds), *Forestry Handbook for British Columbia*, 5th edn, Vancouver, BC: University of British Columbia Forestry Undergraduate Society, pp. 433–71.

Lutz, W., W. Sanderson and S. Scherbov (2001), 'The end of world population growth', *Nature*, **412**, 543–5.

Messier, C., M.J. Fortin, F. Schmiegelow, F. Doyon, S.G. Cumming, J.P. Kimmins, B. Seely, C. Welham and J. Nelson (2003), 'Modeling tools to assess the sustainability of forest management scenarios' Chapter 14, in P.J. Burton, C. Messier,

D.W. Smith and W.L. Adamowicz (eds), *Towards Sustainable Management of the Boreal Forest*, Ottawa, Ontario: NRC Research Press, pp. 531–80.

Perera, A.H., L.J. Buse and M. Weber (eds) (2004), *Emulating Natural Forest Landscape Disturbances: Concepts and Applications*, New York: Columbia University Press, 315 pp.

Peterken, G.F. (1996), *Natural Woodland. Ecology and Conservation in Northern Temperate Regions*, Cambridge: Cambridge University Press.

Toffler, A. (1970), *Future Shock*, Toronto: Bantam.

UN (2002), *World Urbanization Prospects. The 2001 Revision*, New York: Population Division, Dept. Economic and Social Affairs, United Nations.

Wackernagel, M. and W.E. Rees (1996), *Our Ecological Footprint: Reducing Human Impact on Earth*, Gabriola Island, BC: New Society Publishers.

Walters, C.J. (1986), *Adaptive Management of Renewable Resources*, New York: MacMillan.

Watson, R.E. et al (eds) (2001), *Climate Change 2001: Synthesis Report*, Intergovernmental Panel on Climate Change, Cambridge, UK: Cambridge University Press.

11. Tropical forest management systems as economic and sustainable

Roger A. Sedjo

The conventional wisdom among foresters and development economists has been that natural tropical forests do not generate sufficient economic returns to justify management activities (for example, Richardson, 1970; Spears, 1979; FAO, 1983). For example, Leslie (1987, p. 178) states that 'the magnitude of the factors needed to make natural management profitable is unrealistically great.' Recently this view has been reinforced by Rice et al. (1997) and Hardner and Rice (2002).

Lacking acceptable economic returns to natural forest management, the emphasis has been to move towards the substitution of plantation forests, which are generally believed to have higher economic returns and to meet the bulk of industrial and fuelwood needs (for example, Spears, 1984). An inference sometimes drawn from this view is that economic considerations suggest that natural tropical forest systems should be replaced by plantation forests, to which the financial returns are more favorable.

This chapter compares the financial returns to two hypothetical forest management regimes undertaken on the same site in the dipterocarp Asia-Pacific region. Financial returns differ from economic returns to the extent that some returns/costs are 'external' and, therefore, are not captured/borne by the investor. Since the 'external' outputs of the natural forest are believed to be generally greater than they are for plantations (that is both provide watershed protection, but natural forests almost always provide more wildlife and biodiversity), considerations of the values of external outputs would strengthen the arguments of this chapter that tropical forest management is more favorable than is usually believed.

An area is assumed to have been recently harvested of all merchantable trees. One investment possibility is that of the establishment of a plantation forest using *Albizza falcaiaria* on a twenty-year sawtimber rotation (Table 11.1). An alternative possibility is investment in natural tropical forest management in which a lightly managed stand receives only modest

Table 11.1   *Twenty-year plantation sawtimber rotation:* Albizza falcataria

Year	Harvest volume (m³ha)	Harvest cost ($/m³)	Establish costs ($/ha)	Harvest price ($/m³)	Total costs ($/ha)	Total revenues ($/ha)	Net revenues ($/ha)	DPV (6%)
0			350		350	0	−350	−350
1			11		11		−11	−11
2			48		48		−48	−43
3			28		28		−28	−23
.								
.								
.								
10	Thin to waste						−100	−56
.								
.								
.								
15	Thinning (return = cost)						0	0
.								
.								
.								
20	250(a)	20		25	5000	6250	1250	390
						DPV (20 years)		−93
20–60						DPV (20–60)		−29
						Total DPV		−131

Note: (a) sawtimber volume.

Source: Sedjo (1988).

management, with enrichment planting being undertaken where natural regeneration is insufficient. A rotation of sixty years is assumed (Table 11.2). The cost, price and growth data used are drawn largely from Indonesian experience (Sedjo, 1988).

This chapter finds that under the reasonable set of conditions presented, the financial returns to natural forest management systems can be more favorable than is commonly believed, and that financial returns to natural forest management are comparable to those likely to accrue to plantation forests in many situations that are common in the Asia-Pacific region. In addressing these issues, this chapter (1) discusses some broad locational considerations that suggest a potential role for both plantation and natural tropical forest management, (2) addresses the current condition and

Table 11.2   Natural tropical forest management

Year	Harvest volume (m³ha)	Harvest cost ($/m³)	Establish costs ($/ha)	Harvest price ($/m³)	Total costs ($/ha)	Total revenues ($/ha)	Net revenues ($/ha)	DPV (6%)
0			50		50	0	−50	−50
.								
.								
.								
60	60 (b)	35		70	2100	4200	2100	58
							DPV	8

Notes:
(a) costs and revenues from Sedjo (1988).
(b) incremental volume associated with silviculture and management.

regeneration potential of the tropical forest, (3) compares the economic returns to plantation and natural forest management for a prototype situation in the Asia-Pacific region and, finally, (4) speculates as to why plantations appear to be preferred over natural tropical forest management.

FINANCIAL RETURNS AND LOCATIONAL CONSIDERATIONS

Forestry has often been viewed as the land use of last resort. The nineteenth century German economist Von Thunen developed a concentric-zone theory of land use occurring around a village center. In this view, there was a place for forests, agriculture and urban land uses. The forest was typically reserved for lands that are most distant, with the more accessible lands available for cropping and other agricultural uses. Forests could not compete with agriculture in the area closest to the village. However, this view also implied that agriculture would not compete with forests in the more distant locations. Location was important, and accessibility and nearness to market were of differential importance for the various economic activities. To this perspective must be added further considerations that affect land-use decisions, such as soil type, topography, and so forth.

This simple view has much to commend it even today. It suggests that location bestows a comparative advantage on activities that are best suited to a location and that these activities will displace other, less well-suited activities. In forestry and agriculture, locational considerations must be integrated with concerns about soils and moisture. Three activities that often compete for a location are agricultural cropping, plantation forestry and natural forest management. Forestry has traditionally been viewed as uneconomic when pitted against other land uses (Waggener, 1985). On fertile lands, where agricultural cropping is viable, forestry is unlikely to be financially viable. Plantation forestry, which is really a form of agriculture that involves tree cropping, can flourish in advantageous locations (Sedjo, 2001). However, although plantation forestry has demonstrated substantial returns under favorable conditions, such conditions are absent in many tropical locations, and plantations often generate low financial returns (Sedjo, 1988). Requisite conditions include locations having low-cost access to major markets and a scale of operations that allows for complete utilization of all or most of the raw wood. To achieve this, it is often necessary for plantations to be situated with favorable access to a pulpmill.

There are large areas of the tropics that do not have the requisite conditions to allow either sustainable agriculture cropping or large-scale integrated forest plantations. It is in these areas that natural forest management – typically, extensive forestry with modest investments per unit of land area – is likely to generate the highest financial returns.

If this view is correct, however, why do we find plantation forests often displacing natural tropical forests in any situations where large-scale integrated operations are not feasible? The answer is found largely in the wide array of financial incentives provided to plantation forestry and agricultural cropping that are not available to natural forest management. A major problem with the economic evaluation of natural forestry projects is that often they do not compare favorably with the alternative activities because they are being compared on locations where other land uses have an inherent advantage. In addition, there is a tendency for foresters to prefer to manage intensively, when financial considerations will allow only low-cost extensive management. Exacerbating this situation is the tendency of governments directly and indirectly to subsidize cropping and plantation activities while ignoring natural forest management. Hence, natural forests appear to be non-competitive because often they are competing where they, in fact, have a disadvantage; or, when they have an economic advantage, this advantage is negated by subsidies that shift the financial advantage to the cropping or forest plantation modes. Repetto and Gillis (1988), for example, have demonstrated that Third World countries have supported a host of policies which promote activities that are both ecologically destructive and economically undesirable.

Furthermore, in some instances forest plantations are not the viable financial investments they are commonly believed to be. Often, it is only the effects of direct and indirect subsidies that make the financial returns to plantations appealing. Furthermore, the prevalent view that sustainable natural tropical forestry is not economically or financially feasible, together with the unqualified view that plantation forests generally provide high economic returns, has been detrimental to both economic and environmental values. Such a view promotes acquiescence in the conversion of tropical forests to other uses, including agricultural cropping and plantation forestry when, in fact, these uses may be ecologically destructive and financially and economically unjustified. Finally, since it is generally agreed that native forests provide a larger volume of environmental services and non-timber values than do plantation forests, natural forest management should be preferred when the financial returns are roughly similar.

FORESTS IN THE TROPICS

Timber interests are active in many areas of the globe, including West Africa, much of South America (including the Amazon) and the Asia-Pacific region, which includes Malaysia, Indonesia, the Philippines, and the island of New Guinea. About 80 per cent of the world supply of tropical timber exports comes from the Asia-Pacific region. Today, much of what is called tropical forestry is simply logging in the tropical forest. The economics of logging the tropical forests depend on the accessibility of the site and the availability of merchantable size and species of trees. It is this consideration that accounts for the dominance of the Asia-Pacific region as a tropical wood supplier. The dipterocarp forests of the region provide a family of species, many of which can be used interchangeably as industrial wood and that have wide commercial acceptance. By contrast, the tropical forests of the neotropics (for example, the Amazon Basin) exhibit a much greater degree of heterogeneity, with a much smaller fraction of the forest trees being species that are readily accepted by the markets. This feature has resulted in high costs and a relative lack of interest by major commercial logging interests in many parts of the neotropics as a source of industrial wood.

REGENERATION

Intensive high-cost forestry is generally not required to maintain tropical forest systems. If the land is not used for non-forested purposes, tropical forests usually regenerate in a short time, although the species may differ from those harvested. Rapid reforestation is particularly true where the harvests consist of the selective logging of desired species. For example, where the lands have not been converted, the areas of southeast Asia that were logged a few decades ago are again heavily forested. Even where the disturbance was dramatic, or near catastrophic, tropical forests have shown great ability to regenerate. An example of such regeneration is found in areas adjacent to the Panama Canal that were denuded in the early 1900s but now have regenerated naturally to a lush tropical forest.

Other evidence also indicates that the forest has substantial regenerative capacity if the land use is not permanently changed. Of the 2345 million hectares of tropical forests that existed in 1980, the area of potentially productive secondary forest – area that had been disturbed and then refor-ested – was about 896 million ha. Some 280 million ha were non-productive because of poor growth or inoperable terrain, and another 455 million ha were non-productive because of legal constraints such as being declared a reservation (FAO, 1983). The area of secondary forest is increasing – the result of fellings in primary and old-growth forests that are producing new cutover lands. However, conversion to other uses had resulted in a small net reduction for the five years prior to 1980.

Two categories of secondary forest are distinguished in the FAO inventory. One is residual forest cutover in the past 60 to 80 years which has never been completely felled. These forests may rapidly recover their former physiog-nomy, systemic processes, tree species, and other organisms. The other cate-gory of secondary forest, termed 'fallow', is volunteer forest that invades after periodic cultivation. This forest typically lacks both the structure and composition of the mature forest, being usually composed of a large number of species that decrease rapidly as the girth increases (Wadsworth, 1982, pp. 5–6). The FAO estimates that about 55 per cent of the secondary forest is cutover and that 4 per cent is fallow. Years ago Wadsworth (1982, p. 70) stated that the data 'suggest that the potential productivity of the present area of cutover secondary forest [without fallow forest] is, in the aggregate, more than adequate to meet the wood requirements anticipated for the year 2000 [for the tropical countries].' This expectation was, in fact, realized.

Although much is made of the purported lack of regenerative capacity by the tropical forest, there is a host of evidence that regeneration is adequate in the highly valued dipterocarp forest of the Asia-Pacific for most low and medium elevation sites (for example, Proceedings, 1980; Weideft and Banaag, 1982; Whitmore, 1984; Wyatt-Smith, 1987). Dipterocarp forests, due to the relative homogeneity of the stands, offer the best prospects for sustainable timber production with acceptable financial returns.

ECONOMICS OF PLANTATION FORESTS

Over the past several decades, plantation forests have established themselves as a viable economic activity in some places and under some conditions.

Perhaps the most active region of tree-growing worldwide is the US South, where about 1 million hectares of forest plantation have been planted annually for several decades (USDA FS, 2004). Although some subsidies do apply to some tree planters (for example, an assistance program to small non-industrial forest ownerships), the large majority of the plantations are established with minimal or no subsidies. Even in the US, tree-planting must compete for land with agriculture which, as in most countries of the world, receives special concession and subsidies.

In much of the other areas of the world where tree-planting is common, various types of incentives and subsidies were once applied, but have become increasingly rare. This is true also for the tropics and the subtropics. The fiscal incentive programs in Brazil, Chile and elsewhere have largely lapsed as have incentive programs in which most of the costs of establishing the plantation forest are borne by the state.

Studies initially suggested that the underlying economics of plantation forestry can be favorable in many places. One study (Sedjo, 1983) examined the comparative economics of plantation forests for twelve regions around the world. The viability of plantations no longer needs an abstract rationale. Plantations have proved themselves in that they now account for roughly one-third of the world's industrial wood harvest (Carle et al., 2002). Important regions that produce wood from planted forests included the Nordic region of Europe, the US South and Pacific Northwest, the Amazon, central and southern regions of Brazil, Chile, New Zealand, South Africa and Australia. This outcome suggests that for most of these regions the economic and financial returns to plantation forestry have been sufficiently favorable to generate the large investments required for huge volumes of industrial wood.

Plantations efficiently established on accessible sites with relatively high growth rates in sufficient volumes to allow integrated wood processing activities to be undertaken provide for maximum utilization of the wood produced. Furthermore, the favorable returns required that the wood-processing activities (as distinguished from wood-growing) were economically efficient. Also, the mills needed to be well situated with respect to their cost of access to major wood-consuming markets. Finally, the alternative uses of the land had to generate less value than did the production of industrial wood. The absence of a single critical ingredient could compromise the economic viability of the entire activity.

In many regions in the tropics, forest plantations are being suggested to replace, either directly or indirectly, natural tropical forests. The rationale is often expressed in terms of wood volume rather than wood value. Plantation forests make sensible investments in many situations. However, the plantation holdings are often fragmented, poorly located, and with no obvious accessible markets. Furthermore, in the absence of integrated operations, there is no market for much or all of the wood, especially for the residuals from saw milling operations. The financial returns to these types of operations are likely to be quite low (Sedjo, 1988) and even well-run, private plantations in the tropics may generate only barely acceptable returns (Golokin and Cassels, 1987). Governments sometimes will introduce subsidies and, in such circumstances, it is the policy of subsidization that makes the project financially viable. An unfortunate side-effect of a policy to subsidize the establishment of inherently uneconomic plantations is that natural forest management is often a casualty. Given the subsidies to plantations, even economical, viable natural forest management might well be replaced by costly, inherently uneconomic plantation forestry.

ECONOMICS OF NATURAL TROPICAL FOREST MANAGEMENT SYSTEMS

The natural resilience of the tropical forests, their ability under many conditions to achieve acceptable natural regeneration and to generate acceptable economic returns suggests that natural forest management regimes that are characterized as 'extensive management' are preferable under many conditions. A major objective of these regimes is to ensure that regeneration is adequate and to provide forest protection. Although the species mix is important for preservation and biodiversity purposes, the ability of mill technology to utilize more species systematically over time suggests that biodiversity need not be a casualty of natural forestry provided that some long-term flexibility in species use is feasible.

The financial advantages of natural management systems are that: (1) the initial and management costs are low, and (2) the tree species typically harvested are of higher value than those from plantation forests. In addition, the environmental services and non-market outputs of the forest can be largely maintained under a management regime that provides for natural regeneration. Native species are maintained and natural ecosystems are only modestly disturbed. Wildlife, water protection erosion control, non-forest products, and so forth are all maintained. A disadvantage of the system is that the biological growth rate of commercial wood is modest. Also, longer harvest rotations are disadvantaged as a result of the discounting of forestry projects.

COMPARISON OF THE FINANCIAL RETURNS

Tables 11.1 and 11.2 present the financial returns to two alternative forest management systems. These prototypes represent conditions that existed in Kalimantan, Indonesia, in the late 1980s. The analysis is conducted for a representative site after an initial harvest of an old-growth tropical forest. Table 11.1 presents the costs, volumes and returns for a plantation system that introduced *albizza falcataria* on a 20-year sawtimber rotation. The plantation forest required some additional clearing costs and site preparation, planting, weeding for four years, thinning, and harvest of sawtimber at age 20. This cycle is repeated to year 60. Given the absence of pulpmills in the region, small stems, thinnings, and waste from the sawmill had no value. In addition, the prices paid for the sawtimber are assumed to be low (at $25 per cubic meter), because plantation timbers had to compete in the local market with timbers provided by the native forest. Such a situation with low local prices for the plantation sawtimbers and little or no market for pulpwood is common in the region. An evaluation of the financial returns to the forest plantation regime using a 6 per cent discount rate gives a discounted present value (DPV) per hectare of -$122. An alternative investment criterion, the financial internal rate of return (IRR), is also calculated. The IRR for the plantation regime is calculated to be about 4 per cent.

Table 11.2 presents the costs, volumes and returns to a hypothetical lightly managed natural forest that relies to a high degree on natural regeneration. Using experience from Indonesia (Sedjo, 1988), the natural tropical forest management system requires no additional investment inputs beyond the first year, after the initial logging. Although natural regeneration is usually very adequate, initial management costs of $50 per hectare are assumed to enhance natural re-generation. Although some harvesting systems in this region aim towards a 35-year selective harvest cycle, this analysis uses a 60-year period of growth since the large- and medium-sized trees were logged in the initial harvest. The annual growth of commercial species in an unmanaged stand is assumed to be only 1.0 cubic meter per hectare per year. However, modest management and silviculture are estimated to increase the growth of commercial species in that stand to 2.0 cubic meters per year (FAO, 1980). At recent prices, this approach generates additional net revenues of $2100 per hectare. Applying a 6 per cent discount rate over the 60-year project gives a DPV of $58 additional net revenues in the initial year. When the initial costs of $50 are subtracted, the DPV of the investment is $8. Using a financial IRR on natural tropical forest management yields an inflation-free IRR of 6.2 per cent, or about two percentage points better than a plantation forest on the same site.

It is well known that different assumptions can yield different results using these two standard investment criteria. The purpose of this comparison is not to provide definitive estimates but, rather, to demonstrate that under reasonable assumptions the returns on natural tropical forest management can be as good as or better than the returns to plantation forests that are in some cases replacing the native forest.

WHY ISN'T NATURAL FORESTRY PRACTICED MORE OFTEN?

The above suggests that in many places in the tropics natural forestry management is preferable to plantation forestry for ecological purposes and roughly comparable for economic returns. If this is correct, why isn't more natural tropical forestry management practiced? One reason is that the analysis presented is appropriate to the dipterocarp forests of Southeast Asia. In their analysis of the neotropics, Rice et al. (1997) argue that natural forest management is unlikely to be economically viable. This conclusion is not surprising as the tropical forests of the neotropics are highly heterogeneous with far fewer commercial trees found in limited areas. Another reason is that even poor investments may generate substantial future economic activity and, therefore, receive major government subsidies – perhaps under the guise of regional development. In the example above, the total revenues per land unit generated by an extensive natural forest management system are far less than those generated by intensively managed forest plantations. In addition, the plantation will require considerably larger investments, larger start-up costs, more employees, and so forth, which may appear to be desirable from the point of view of the regional economy. However, this perception is flawed since the greater economic activity generated by the inefficient plantations is unsustainable in the absence of large external subsidies, in addition to being a drain on the financial resources of struggling Third World countries.

By contrast, the natural forest regime generates far less revenue and employment. However, given a sufficiently higher rate of return, the private sector might undertake the activity without a subsidy and, even if a subsidy is required, the total expenditure will be far less. In addition, such activity is consistent with the continued production of a higher level of environmental and non-market goods and services.

It has also been well documented that governments frequently undertake inappropriate policies related to their natural resources, often, in effect, promoting economically and ecologically inferior projects (Repetto and Gillis, 1988). These policies fail to value properly the timber resource as well as the environmental and other non-timber benefits provided by the forest. The policy followed by some countries, of fully subsidizing the costs of establishing a plantation forest in an effort to avoid deforestation, has had the reverse effect of inducing the conversion of natural forests to plantations, even when the underlying economics of natural management are superior to those of plantation forestry.

Furthermore, with institutional arrangements whereby firms are granted rights to harvest timber, concession agreements typically are provided for too short a period of time to provide the firms with incentives to take a long-term view towards the management and sustainability of the resource. In many tropical countries, for example, much of the natural tropical hardwood forest is currently being harvested on a selective cutting regime that anticipates a periodic and sustained year harvesting cycle. However, under the current concession system, loggers are limited in their harvesting rights to periods that are shorter than the harvesting cycle. In such a system, firms have no serious expectations of harvests beyond the initial logging and, therefore, no incentive to undertake natural forest management practices aimed at long-term forest improvements or sustainability which extend beyond the period of their harvesting rights.

A final speculation as to the apparent preference of non-economic plantation forestry over natural tropical forest management is consistent with the well-known preference of the large international development banks for large over smaller projects. Planting trees is considered desirable almost in itself, and large forest plantation projects require rather large amounts of financing. By contrast, extensive natural forest management is, as we have seen, an inherently modest operation. There is very little in such projects that would require the types of financing that the development banks find interesting.

CONCLUSIONS

The foregoing proposal argues that forestry projects, as with other investment, may generate competitive returns under some conditions but not under others. The specifics of the project become very important and locational considerations play an important role in determining the financial viability of forestry projects.

This chapter suggests that in places in the tropics, and particularly in the dipterocarpus forests of the Asia-Pacific region, the financial returns to natural tropical forest management are much better than is generally recognized. This challenges the conventional wisdom that natural tropical forest management is inherently financially inferior to forest plantations. The study further suggests that plantation forestry can generate low economic returns in the absence of a set of favorable conditions, and that these favorable conditions are often not present in real world projects. In many cases, plantation forestry is undertaken only because of subsidies to plantation management built into the system as the result of public policies. Finally, the chapter demonstrates that under reasonable assumptions, the financial returns to natural forest management are often comparable or superior to the returns to plantation forests.

REFERENCES

Carle, J., P. Vuorinen and A. Del Lungo (2002), 'Status and trends in global forest plantation development', *Forest Products Journal*, July/August, **52**(7), 1–13.

Food and Agriculture Organization (FAO) (1980), *Tropical Forest Growth*, FAO Consultancy Study.

Food and Agriculture Organization (FAO) (1983), *Management of Tropical Mixed Forests: Preliminary Assessment of Present Status*, FO:MISC/83/17, December, Rome.

Golokin, Stan L. and Patrick K. Cassels (1987), 'An appraisal of Sabah Softwoods Sdn. Bhd. 12 Years After Establishment', presented to Seminar of the Future Role of Forest Plantations in the National Economy, Kota Kinibalu, Sabah, 30 November–4 December.

Hardner, Jared and Richard Rice (2002), 'Rethinking green consumerism', *Scientific American*, **286**(5), 88–97.

Leslie, A.J. (1987), 'The economic feasibility of natural management of tropical forests', in Francois Mergen and Jeffrey R. Vincent (eds), *Natural Management of Tropical Moist Forests*. Yale School of Forestry, New Haven, pp. 177–98.

Proceedings of the Seminar on Selective Cuts in Indonesia (1980), Jogakarta Faculty of Forestry, University of Gajah Mada, 23–14 July. As reported in *Final Report: Wood Raw Material Supply*. P.T. Inproma Engineering, 1985, 62–65.

Repetto, Robert and Malcolm Gillis (1988), *Public Policies and the Misuse of Forest Resources*, Cambridge: Cambridge University Press.

Rice, Richard E., Raymond E. Gullison and John E. Reid (1997), 'Can sustainable management save tropical forests?', *Scientific American*, **276**(4), 44–9.

Richardson, S. Dennis (1970), 'The future availability of tropical hardwoods', *Commonwealth Forestry Review*, **49**(1), 24–9.

Sedjo, Roger A. (1988), *The Economics of Natural and Plantation Forestry in Indonesia*, Field Documents No. 2, FAO Project INS/83/019, Assistance to Forest Sector Development Planning, January.

Sedjo, Roger A. (2001), 'From foraging to cropping: the transition to plantation forestry, and implications for wood supply and demand', *Unasylva*, **52**(204).

Spears, John S. (1979), 'Can wet tropical forest survive?', *Commonwealth Forestry Review*, **58**(3), 165–80.

Spears, John S. (1984), 'Role of forestation as a sustainable land use and strategy option for tropical forest management and conversion and as a source of supply for developing country wood needs', in K.F. Wiesum (ed.), *Strategies and Designs for Afforestation, Reforestation and Tree Planting*, Pudoc Wageningen.

USDA Forest Service (1988), *The South's Fourth Forest: Alternatives for the Future*, Forest Resource Report No. 24, Washington, DC.

USDA Forest Service (2004), *National Report on Sustainable Forests – 2003*, FS 766, February. www.fs.fed.us/research/sustain/.

Wadsworth, Frank H. (1982), 'Secondary forest management and plantation forestry technologies to improve the use of converted Tropical Lands', Unpublished draft, submitted to US OTA.

Waggener, Thomas R. (1985), 'The economics of shifting land use margins', in R.A. Sedjo (ed.), *Investments in Forestry*, Boulder: Westview Press.

Weideft, Hans Joachim and Valeriano Banaag (1982), *Aspects of Management and Silviculture of Philippine Dipterocarp Forests*, German Agency for Technical Cooperation, eschborn.

Whitmore, T.C. (1984), *Tropical Rain Forest of the Far East*, Oxford: Clarendon Press.

Wyatt-Smith, John (1987), 'Problems and prospects for natural management of tropical moist forests', in F. Mergen and J.R. Vincent (eds), *Natural Management of Tropical Moist Forests*, New Haven: Yale School of Forestry, pp. 2–22.

PART IV

The conceptual challenges

Introduction

The management of natural resources is ultimately a function of both governmental and corporate decision-making, mediated by organizational structure and process, legislative and regulatory mandates, and social and legal organization of resource ownership and control. Much of the challenge to achieve sustainable development ultimately faces the private sector – insofar as it is this sector which largely extracts, processes and markets natural resources. Regardless of the role of government, it is incumbent upon the corporate sector to seek new business models incorporating innovative analytical methodologies and strategic solutions which advance the cause of sustainable development while maintaining or enhancing their own profitability.

In a seminal work on 'Natural Capitalism', Amory Lovins, L. Hunter Lovins and Paul Hawken (Lovins et al., 1999) have identified a critical challenge facing the corporate sector:

> The real trouble with our economic compass is that it points in exactly the wrong direction. Most businesses are behaving as if people were still scarce and nature still abundant – the conditions that helped to fuel the first Industrial Revolution. . . . The logic of economizing on the scarcest resource, because it limits progress, remains correct. But the pattern of scarcity is shifting: now people aren't scarce but nature is. This shows up first in industries that depend directly on ecological health. Here, production is increasingly constrained by fish rather than by boats and nets, by forests rather than by chain saws, by fertile topsoil rather than by plows. Moreover, unlike the traditional factors of industrial production – capital and labor – the biological limiting factors cannot be substituted for one other. In the industrial system, we can easily exchange machinery for labor. But no technology or amount of money can substitute for a stable climate and a productive biosphere. Even proper pricing can't replace the priceless (Lovins et al., 1999, pp. 157–58).

In a similar vein, William Smith argues in Chapter 12 that the essential prerequisite to aligning corporate and social issues within the domain of sustainability is a fundamental transformation in the way information is arrayed and processed within the corporation. Accounting concepts and practices play a crucial role in the corporate sector's drive for sustainability (see, for example, Rubenstein, 1994; US EPA, 1995; Bennett and James, 1998).

One of the earliest and most insightful reports on this subject was produced by the World Resources Institute and authored by Ditz et al. (1995) under the title *Green Ledgers: Case Studies in Corporate Environmental Accounting*. The basic theme of this book is that the lack of recognition of the true magnitude and location of all environmental costs in a corporation prevents it from making intelligent resource allocation decisions. Most importantly, lack of information about these costs forecloses important strategic opportunities for the firm. One major consequence of a firm's ignorance of the extent and location of environmental costs borne by the company is that 'products with relatively higher environmental costs are often subsidized by those with lower ones'. Products which may appear profitable may impose significant environmental costs on other parts of the business and such costs are not attributed to their original source. This introduces a major distortion in the process of profit maximization through efficient resource allocation decisions at the margin. Certain products or processes may be encouraged/discouraged on the basis of such incorrect price signals within the corporation. Remedying this costly pathology requires a fundamental reconceptualization of the flows of goods and service through an organization and the costs associated therewith (see, for example, NRTEE, 1999). In this volume, Smith outlines several approaches, known as 'eco-accounting' and 'industrial ecology', which can be undertaken to address these complex issues. He concludes that:

> There is a need to rethink industrialism. Our prosperity and future depend upon it. Industrial ecology provides a useful way of thinking about the challenges that lie ahead. The blueprint and tools needed to build an industrial ecosystem need further work. Industrial ecology has the potential to succeed in the marketplace. It links environmental protection to other strategic management concerns such as increasing business value, reducing risk, and increasing productivity. Industrial ecology provides the means of testing hypotheses about how things work – a reality check – to help us learn from experience and transform the marketplace.

Not only must the modern corporation understand and identify the true costs, risks and opportunities afforded by environmental issues, they must be able and willing to transmit this information to the broad range of stakeholders who rely on accurate data on which to form investment decisions. In Chapter 13, Robert Repetto outlines how better financial disclosure protects both investors and the environment. Using case studies from four major industries, including pulp and paper, oil and gas, electric utilities and hard rock mining, the author demonstrates how exposure to environmental risk varies significantly across companies. Only recently have government regulatory agencies, suggested, if not required, that such risk exposure be signaled to the market. To quote:

> For corporations in environmentally sensitive industries the message is clear. Shareholders are demanding and governments are requiring more transparency regarding the ways in which environmental costs, risks and liabilities are affecting their financial conditions and prospects. There is no reason to believe that these demands will weaken. Well-managed companies will realize that they can benefit from this trend because financial markets clearly reward good corporate governance and public trust is a valuable business asset.

The final three papers of this volume are devoted to broader conceptual issues of sustainable development at the societal level. Few people have done more to advance the cause of sustainable development than David Suzuki, a zoologist and ecologist, who has written and broadcast extensively on the need to replace our prevailing, and what he views as our destructive world view. In Chapter 14, Suzuki challenges our embrace of scientific reductionism, and principles of modern economics and management. He even challenges the dominant paradigm of sustainable development itself. To quote:

> Some people say that the concept of sustainable development is like a stool that rests on three legs: the economy, environment and society. I totally disagree with that. I think that what we rest on is a three-tiered foundation. The first foundation is defined by the fact that we are animals. And as animals we have an absolute need for clean air, clean water, clean soil that gives us our food, and clean energy that comes from the sun. Biodiversity, the web of living things, cleanses, replenishes and creates the four sacred elements. Our basic needs: earth, air, fire and water, are defined by our animal nature. But we are also social animals and we must deal with social issues. A starving man who comes across an edible plant or animal is not going to first ask, 'Is this on the endangered list?' He's going to kill it and eat it. So if we don't deal with hunger and poverty, then forget the environment. If you live in communities that have chronic high levels of unemployment, then they've got more urgent priorities than protecting the environment. If we live in communities in which there's no equity, justice or security, where there's constant threat of genocide, war or terror – the environment is not an issue. There are social needs that people have: strong communities with full, meaningful employment – that have equity, justice and security and are free of war, genocide or terror – that is what I define as the second level of the foundation of sustainable development. And finally, we are spiritual beings, and never was there a time when we needed spirit more than now. We've become carried away with how clever we are and need a huge dollop of humility. We need to know that we are deeply embedded in nature, that we arose out of nature, and when we die we will return to nature. We need to know that there are forces impinging on our lives that lie beyond our understanding or control. And we need sacred places. If we don't have sacred groves, then they just become trees that are ready to be cut down as commodities or resources. We need places that

humans come to with great respect. We need to rediscover our place on this planet. That's the challenge of the twenty-first century, to rediscover our place in nature, our relatives who are all the other species that sustain us. The challenge of our time is to find a way to live in balance with the factors that make our lives and economies possible.

William Rees (co-inventor of the ecological footprint), in Chapter 15, joins David Suzuki in attempting to reformulate the currently accepted paradigm of sustainable development and understand what motivates human behavior at the most basic of cognitive and emotional levels. To quote:

the sustainability dilemma is not merely an ecological or technical or economic crisis as is usually assumed, but rather it is a crisis rooted in fundamental human nature. More specifically, it is a crisis of human evolutionary success – indeed, we have reached the point where our success is killing us! This interpretation is not part of the conventional sustainability debate for a very simple reason. We human beings – for all that we suppose ourselves to be evidence of intelligent life on earth – really fail to understand who we are. We have a very limited understanding of what motivates us, why it is we do certain things that we do. Little wonder that human nature is hardly on the sustainability radar. At the heart of this problem is the fact that people today rarely think of themselves as biological beings. It comes to mind from time to time if one has heart palpitations or some other illness but, on the whole, we moderns don't like to think of ourselves as biological entities. But indeed we are – we are products of evolution, and our behaviour both as individuals and as society represents a delicate dialectic between self-conscious reasoning and deeper and sometimes darker unconscious urges and predispositions. The fact is that we humans have a long evolutionary history and many of the traits that we've acquired along the way, traits that were adaptive 50 000 years ago, are with us still. But now some of these once-desirable qualities may threaten humanity's future prospects. That is, some characteristic human qualities and behaviours may well now be maladaptive. I will try to make the case that these ancient traits are such that techno-industrial society *in particular* is inherently unsustainable. The world is ecologically full – but evolution has not provided us with inhibitions against extinguishing other species, against eliminating competing human groups or, indeed, against destroying our earthly habitat(s).

Here, in a nutshell, is the essence of the extraordinary challenge which faces humanity. On the face of it, the prospects for achieving sustainability – economic, ecologic and social – seem monumental and potentially insurmountable. We live in a society which celebrates and thrives on economic growth and greets with dismay any news than such growth is waning. As Ronald Colman states in Chapter 16 on the Genuine Progress Indicator:

The costs of holding on to the illusion that 'more' is 'better' are frightening. Scientists recognize that the only biological organism that has unlimited growth as its dogma is the cancer cell, the apparent model for our conventional economic theory. By contrast, the natural world thrives on balance and equilibrium, and recognizes inherent limits to growth. The cancer analogy is apt, because the path of limitless growth is profoundly self-destructive. No matter how many cars we have in the driveway or how many possessions we accumulate, the environment will not tolerate the growth illusion even if we fail to see through it.

REFERENCES

Bennett, Martin and Peter James (eds) (1998), *The Green Bottom Line. Environmental Accounting for Management*, Sheffield: Greenleaf Publishing.

Ditz, Daryl, Janet Ranganathan and R. Darryl Banks (1995), *Green Ledgers: Case Studies in Corporate Environmental Accounting*, Washington, DC: World Resources Institute.

Lovins, Amory B., L. Hunter Lovins and Paul Hawken (1999), 'A road map for natural capitalism', *Harvard Business Review*, May–June, pp. 145–58.

National Round Table on the Environment and the Economy (NRTEE) (1999), *Measuring Eco-efficiency in Business: Feasibility of a Core Set of Indicators*, Ottawa, Canada.

Rubenstein, Daniel Blake (1994), *Environmental Accounting for the Sustainable Corporation. Strategies and Techniques*, Westport, CT: Quorom Books.

US Environmental Protection Agency (EPA) (1995), 'An introduction to environmental accounting as a business management tool: key concepts and terms', Washington, DC, EPA 742-R-95-001, June.

12. Accounting for the environment: can industrial ecology pay double dividends for business?

W.G.B. Smith

THE PROBLEM

A growing sense of frustration and social injustice, and the inevitability of the coming environmental crisis have led to speculation about how the modern industrial system might be transformed to better meet the needs of human society. Human population growth and consumption now place unprecedented demands on the environment. Faced with these challenges, the Brundtland Commission recognized that the only way we would be able to continue to meet human needs was 'by steadily reducing the energy and resource content of future economic growth' (WCED, 1987, p. 213). In particular, Brundtland recommended that industrial operations should be encouraged 'that are more efficient in terms of resource use, that generate less pollution and waste, that are based on the use of renewable rather than non-renewable resources, and that minimise irreversible adverse impacts on human health and the environment' (WCED, 1987, p. 219).

Population and economic growth and, now more than ever, the lifestyles and consumption habits of more wealthy industrialized nations draw massive amounts of energy and materials into the industrial system (Wernick et al., 1996). Studies show in North America that only 7 per cent of industrial throughput winds up as product and only 1.4 per cent is still product after 6 months (Friend, 1996). The waste generated per capita is now more than double that of the preceding generation (Davies and Mazurek, 1997). Urban and industrial wastes are rapidly becoming potentially richer and more reliable material sources than naturally occurring ores and harvested fibres.

In nature, waste is the key to renewal. If we want to meet human needs and at the same time minimize the damage we do to the environment, then we will have to accept two challenges. We must steadily reduce the energy and material content of industrial production. At the same time, we must increase our reliance on the use of industrial and post-consumer waste as the primary feedstock of future economic growth.

It is also time that we examined the problem of the environment as a business problem. Environmental management that is not economically sustainable will fail. Since Mike Royston published *Pollution Prevention Pays* (1979) managers and investors have wondered: does it pay to be green? (Hart and Ahuja, 1996). Many believe that business won't act without a regulatory push (Ashford, 2002). A common line of reasoning is that better environmental performance will inevitably translate into higher product prices, a competitive disadvantage, and lower profitability (Walley and Whitehead, 1994). Others believe that improved environmental performance can enhance a company's efficiency and productivity, and also generate new market opportunities (Porter and van der Linde, 1995).

Although there may have been some doubt at the outset, current research reviews generally confirm that improved environmental performance contributes to the financial bottom line. In 85 per cent of the studies assessed by White and Kiernan (2004), there was a positive correlation between environmental and financial performance. Murphy (2002) found in his literature review that companies that scored well on environmental criteria realized stronger financial returns than the market as a whole. He also concluded that environmental investment funds have above-average returns. In addition, companies that go beyond compliance realize stronger stock price gains. However, inadequate disclosure of environmental liabilities appears to have a compounding negative effect on the financial results of poorly performing companies.

Derwall and his associates (2005) conducted an experiment where they evaluated investment portfolios to determine whether there is a long-run premium or penalty for investing primarily in environmentally responsible companies. They controlled for other factors known to influence stock performance because there is mounting evidence that environmentally and socially screened portfolios tend to be biased toward large capitalization, low-risk growth stocks. They showed that a portfolio comprised of stocks of highly eco-efficient companies outperformed its counterpart after adjusting financial returns for market risk, investment style and industry effects. Earle's (2000) review of nine investment funds yielded a similar conclusion.

Cap Gemini Ernst and Young's 1999 survey found that 81 per cent of Global 500 executives rate environment, health and safety (EHS) among the top ten issues driving value in their businesses (GEMI, 2004). Soyka and Feldman (2000) also surveyed institutional investors and fund managers to gather their opinions about the impact of EHS issues on corporate financial performance. They found that managers and investors recognize that EHS improvements can contribute to firm value, and that they are willing to pay a premium for the equity and debt of firms for which this value has been convincingly demonstrated.

Industry sector studies have mirrored many of these findings. Blaconniere and Northcut (1997) showed that chemical companies which were likely to be impacted by adverse environmental legislation suffered collectively negative stock price returns while the legislation was being debated and enacted, and that firms with the largest potential liabilities suffered the greatest share price declines. Christman (2000) found the chemical companies that employed innovative proprietary pollution prevention technology enjoyed significant cost savings over those who merely relied on industry best practices. Units employing innovative proprietary technologies realized the strongest gains when they acted before their competitors. In an earlier study of the impact of the Bhopal leak on chemical sector share prices, Blaconniere and Patten (1994) found that the incident had a significant negative impact on the entire sector. However, they found that firms with more extensive environmental disclosure prior to the accident experienced a less negative reaction from financial markets.

No one will dispute that there is a need for improvement or the potential for profit. However, there is a pressing need to transform business thinking about the environment. Business has ignored its major product lines: pollution and waste. Why would anyone set out to produce something, which it cannot sell, for which it has no conceivable use, and for which it might be held potentially liable? Regulation is forcing business to take responsibility for the environmental effects of its activities and to internalize these costs. Increasing energy costs and supply issues will further discipline its operations. A worldwide demographic transition is reshaping tomorrow's markets. How will we serve them?

THE TRADITIONAL INDUSTRIAL PRODUCTION AND MARKETING MODEL

In the nineteenth and early twentieth centuries, we managed industry as if we had unlimited resources and could produce unlimited waste without doing any harm. The traditional once-through model of industrial production depended on cheap abundant resources and waste disposal. Most industrial processes were fossil-fuelled, made intensive use of energy and materials, involved high temperature and pressures, and contained multiple steps where harmful substances could be discharged to the environment. Products were mass-produced, had limited useful lives, were not easily repaired and were cheaply discarded. Producers' responsibility for their products ended at the plant gate.

Since the 1970s, governments have forced industry to respond to growing public concern, one pollutant at a time, by imposing 'command and control' regulations. Command and control regulations specify the allowable rates of discharge based on the use of a particular technology. To comply with these regulations, most companies have installed add-on pollution control devices. By definition, these control devices cannot reduce risks to zero and may produce waste requiring safe disposal. As the stringency of control increases, the use of pollution control devices is sharply limited by rising costs. Moreover, the further removed from source, the more costly and less feasible pollution control and remediation options become. By relying on add-on control devices, increased economic activity invariably leads to decreased environmental quality. The command and control approach to regulation has diminished industry's capacity for adaptive learning and response. Industry has no incentive to innovate or to exceed the standards imposed by government.

WHAT IS INDUSTRIAL ECOLOGY?

More recently, public attention has shifted to more global concerns about the environmental effects of industrialization and consumerism. We are entering a period where industry will have to make limited use of energy and resource inputs and to produce limited waste as an output. Industrial ecology has emerged over the last ten years as a distinct response to these concerns. It has been described as everything from a 'metaphor' for looking at our society (Ehrenfield, 1997; Socolow, 1994) to 'an agenda for management' (Tibbs, 1992). The basic premise of industrial ecology is that the only way we can achieve a sustainable society is to redesign industrial production so that it emulates the workings of natural ecosystems. Industrial ecology suggests two lines of corporate self-improvement, centred on either the industrial plant or the products it produces.

Using nature as a model, industrial ecology views the industrial plant or system as an integrated set of cyclical processes in which the consumption of energy and materials is optimized, waste generation is minimized, and wastes from one process serve as feedstock for other production processes (Frosch and Gallopoulus, 1989). Industrial ecology draws heavily on the work of Robert Ayres (1993) which views industrial production as a 'metabolic' process. It attempts to close the 'open materials cycle' characteristic of industrial society, whereby materials and energy are lost to economic use, and harmful toxic substances are released to the environment. Industrial ecology tries to 'close the loop' in two ways: by eliminating waste from production processes, and by redesigning wastes as useful by-products that can be used in other processes.

Until recently, product design emphasized ease of manufacture and disposal over ease of repair and recycling. Stahel and Jackson (1993) felt that designing durable and upgraded products with a longer useful life could further reduce the demand for energy and materials. Further, progress could also be made in closing the loop if producers developed customer service networks to support their products and to take back products at the end of their useful life.

The critical barrier to the internalization of environmental costs and considerations by the firm is the lack of an all-inclusive environmental accounting system (Todd, 1994). Moreover, managers lack the necessary market information about opportunities to turn waste into profit. In order to find new uses for waste or changing processes, so that the waste generated has some value to customers elsewhere in the industrial system, managers have to know who has what (supply), who needs what (market), who could use what (potential market) and who could produce something if somebody else wanted it (potential supply). Without a management information system functioning as a control feedback loop, we will be unable to identify the need for improvement in environmental performance or to assign the responsibility for change.

Industrial ecology asserts that an industrial system can be made to emulate a natural ecosystem through progressive modification of inputs, product design, production processes and plant infrastructure. An agenda for action could include the following steps. First, products and production processes can be reformulated, through input substitution, so that scarce and harmful substances are replaced with plentiful and more benign substances. Second, production processes can be restructured so that waste is recycled and reused within the plant. Third, open production processes can be closed, so that harmful substances can be contained or reprocessed on-site. Fourth, infrastructure can be redesigned, so that waste from one process can be used either as feedstock in another process or as a saleable by-product. (An example of the application of this step would be co-generation.) Fifth, products can be reformulated and redesigned for decreased weight/mass and energy use as well as for disassembly and recycling after use. Sixth, product life can be extended by improving durability and by redesigning for easy repair, part replacement and reassembly. Seventh, products can be marketed as services with lease and take-back provisions. Any of these actions would progressively reduce, but not completely eliminate, the throughput of energy and materials associated with economic growth.

Another development that will likely have a significant impact on the future of industrial ecology is the Zero Emission Research Initiative

(ZERI) of the United Nations University in Tokyo (Heden, 1995). ZERI was inspired by Gunter Pauli, a Belgian entrepreneur, who found that in his own line of business he could reduce waste but not completely eliminate it. The trick in his view was to find the 'missing links' to complete the cycle so that waste from one plant or process could be used as input to another. His vision was to establish multi-industry clusters of factories based on careful assessment of the missing links in their production processes. There are broad ranges of 'symbiotic' linkages that are only feasible now with government intervention in the marketplace in the form of regulations or price adjustments. However, Pauli (1997) thinks that increasing demand for scarce commodities will ensure that in the near future, zero emissions will be beneficial from the firm's perspective even without public policy intervention. Pauli sees the elimination of waste solely as a way of obtaining maximum value from one's resources. If 'zero inventory' (just-in-time delivery) or 'zero defects' (total quality management) is possible, then 'zero emissions' should also be possible. Pauli places zero emissions squarely in the realm of corporate strategy, and would clearly like to take the industrial system the next step to where virtually all material used or released by the industrial system would be cycled (Pauli, 1997).

DO WE HAVE THE BLUEPRINT FOR DESIGNING AN INDUSTRIAL ECOSYSTEM?

Life Cycle Thinking

Industrial ecology entails a considerably broader conception of industrial production than has been previously held by managers. It incorporates a life cycle approach to management and a precautionary approach to decision making.

Life cycle thinking recognizes that managers' responsibilities no longer end at the plant gate. Their responsibilities now extend upstream and downstream from the plant gate, encompassing a web of new relationships with suppliers and consumers. For example, through supply chain management, producers may try to make their purchasing habits more environmentally friendly. Lenders and insurers may force producers to incorporate the environmental liabilities associated with the construction, operation and closure of plants (that is brownfield sites) in their business financial plans. Moreover, government authorities may force producers to take back discarded or spent products at the end of their useful life. Generally speaking, life cycle thinking emphasizes that the feasibility and benefit of environmental measures is greater, and the cost is less, when these measures are taken earlier in the life cycle. For example, in-plant recycling is more cost effective and has a greater environmental benefit than post-consumer recycling. Moreover, the positive effects of management actions taken early in the life cycle are cumulative throughout the remaining phases of the product life cycle.

As a strategy, the precautionary approach tries to act on the sources of potential harm or hazards rather than trying to determine acceptable or unacceptable levels of risk. The precautionary approach to decision making is imprecise about how to identify an adequate level of investment in technical or social change to prevent further environmental harm (Wynne, 1993). The challenge is to provide a justification for policy decisions requiring efficiency gains (reduction in resource use and waste outputs). What the precautionary approach must provide are the motivation and incentives to seek out 'no-regrets' solutions that are currently passed over under existing regulatory and profit-making regimes.

Industrial Metabolism

Every industry, regardless of sector or scale, can be characterized by its 'metabolic processes' – a complex web of chemical, physical and biological processes that convert energy, raw materials, and labour into finished products and wastes. Industrial ecology tries to minimize total industrial throughput and waste, and to find beneficial uses for the by-products of industrial production in the metabolic processes of other industrial or living systems.

Managers face the daunting challenge of striking an optimum balance among improving process efficiency to minimize use of energy and natural resources; recovering waste created during production processes; re-using wastes created as by-products in other processes; and recycling materials from spent products at the end of their useful lives. Industrial metabolic efficiency can be measured through the reduction in material input per unit of economic output. Dissipative usage by which energy and resources are lost to economic uses is also a good measure of unsustainable consumption. By implication, this approach suggests that a 'steady state' industrial economy would be characterized by near-total recycling of toxic or hazardous substances as well as a significant degree of recycling of materials whose disposal poses environmental problems.

Product Life Extension

Product life, the period over which goods are typically used, governs the demand for replacement goods, natural resource depletion and waste generation rates (Stahel, 1986). For example, a product that lasts twice as long as a comparable alternative effectively uses only half the natural resources and creates only half the waste of more quickly discarded goods. Consumer choice has as much influence on the product's useful life as does the producer's design decisions.

Contemporary consumers often appear to be looking for bigger-better-faster-newer models, and many production managers are still preoccupied with capacity utilization, economies of scale, fast depreciation and quick replacement. Modern society is a far cry from the old English maxim: 'use it up, wear it out, make it do or do without'.

Used and repaired goods in our consumer society are no longer a sign of good stewardship but have become a sign of poverty and inferior status. However, consumers in developing nations and the rapidly ageing populations of more developed nations who have less purchasing power may become a viable market for long-life goods.

Replacement part prices for mass produced goods can be prohibitive compared to the overall price of the product, and second-hand spares can be difficult to obtain. Consumers in industrial society are fast becoming technological illiterates incapable of performing even minor repairs. Modular designs using standardized components with an option to upgrade may become one possible solution to this problem. It is not always cheaper to produce new goods. Rebuilt parts do not last as long but they often cost much less. Reconditioning, with the option to customize or upgrade technologically, leaves room for innovation.

Materials choice has often been influenced by commodity prices and ease of transformation, rather than by the material's inherent properties or suitability. However, increasing scarcity, cost, and consumer concern may help make material recycling a viable option.

Industrial mass production, standardized designs, and rapid depreciation of easily replaced goods have increased pollution and waste in modern society. Product life extension could be the first step in reducing the throughput of modern industrial economies because it does not unnecessarily restrict economic growth or technological progress. An increase in transformation-type activities, such as repairs and reconditioning, substitutes labour for energy and scarce materials, and may increase local employment. Further energy savings and reductions in waste and pollution may come from reductions in transportation and infrastructure requirements.

Closing the Loop – From Product to Service

To 'close the loop' industrial ecology must replace linear, once-through, industrial processes with cyclical processes that reduce the throughput of energy and materials and the use of the environment as a sink for pollution

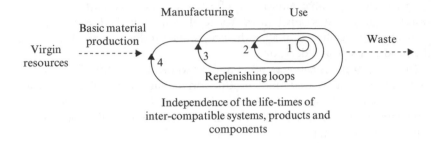

Loop 1: Re-use of goods   Loop 3: Reconditioning/rebuilding of goods
Loop 2: Repairs of goods   Loop 4: Recycling of raw materials

Source: Stahel and Jackson (1993, Figure 4.1).

Figure 12.1   Product life cycle

and waste. Through 'energy and material cascades' and 'away grading', wastes become feed stocks for other processes. This strategy also calls for the production of more durable products, using recyclable materials and replaceable components. These products would be designed to be reusable, possibly reconditioned, upgraded and eventually recycled. The Four R's of appropriate technology (see Figure 12.1) include:

1. Reuse of products that are discarded;
2. Repair of goods that are malfunctioning, under-performing or broken;
3. Reconditioning or updating of products with new or second-hand components; and
4. Recovery of raw materials from durable products for local use in other goods.

At the bottom end of the service hierarchy (Loop 1), products may be sold as second-hand goods in lower value markets. The next grade of products (Loop 2), may be reused after tune-up or cleaning. Minor damage may be repaired. At the next service level (Loop 3), products could potentially be restored to their original functionality by a complete overhaul and the replacement of component parts. At the highest service level, over grading, the product would be adapted or updated to incorporate the latest techno-logical advances or to meet current standards. Ultimately, the raw materials from discarded products and components would be recovered and recycled for use in the manufacture of similar or lower grade products (Loop 4).

Although energy/material cascades will reduce the rate of industrial throughput, they are still open, non-cyclical flows (O'Rourke et al., 1996).

So far, industrial ecology has paid more attention to options such as co-generation – the use of low-grade excess energy for heating, cooling or refrigeration – which presents limited opportunities for dissipating energy flows. The switch to renewable forms of energy should receive greater attention because the use of fossil fuels imposes a far greater burden on the environment than other energy sources. Hydrocarbons account for 86.8 per cent of the pollution released to the environment (Wernick et al., 1996). Another consideration is that the transition from open to closed material cycles is often accompanied by significant shifts in energy consumption. For example, recycling aluminum cans results in significant energy savings; whereas recycling solvents from industrial waste streams will increase energy use. Finding sinks for existing waste streams will not be enough. Significant investments in separating and reprocessing technologies will be required to close material cycles.

Closing the loop also implies phasing out the use, large-scale production, and on-site storage of toxic or hazardous substances. Less harmful inputs would have to be substituted wherever possible. If toxic substances are used, they could be locally produced in small quantities on demand, rather than transported long distances and stored in large quantities on-site for future use. For example, Mitchel (1992) suggested that where toxic substances must be used in a process, we could rely on the dynamic reaction of less hazardous precursors to create toxic substances that would be immediately transformed into benign final products. Another possibility is to produce waste streams from these processes in concentrated rather than dilute form, so that toxic substances may be reused. Closed-loop recycling and on-site containment may also be viable options for achieving zero-discharge.

Economies of scale discourage the design of products for long life and low maintenance, and make it uneconomical to repair broken or to upgrade worn out products. Demand for any product tends to increase as real prices fall due to economies of scale. Firms are thereby encouraged to increase sales and maximize profits by increasing output and capacity.

In the future, products would have to be positioned on service for industrial ecology to succeed in the marketplace. Growth could occur through finding new applications for current products or diversifying the product line. Extended producer responsibility and product take-back policies would have to become the norm.

Manufacturers would have to be willing to help develop the necessary local infrastructure and service networks necessary to recuperate and refurbish their own products. This network of local collection and recovery agencies could also become the source of new sales. In addition, they could become service centres for the maintenance and repair of existing units.

Product life extension will inevitably lead to the replacement of relatively few large-scale, capital-intensive industrial plants with smaller-scale, labour- and skill-intensive production units. Any profits on the service component of the product line would have to more than offset the associated increase in overhead and labour to succeed. By implication, profit margins would come to depend not on the volume of sales but on the value of the services sold to the consumer.

Machines and durable goods may be treated as capital assets rather than as consumables – rented or leased but not sold. The producer retains the installed base of the product as an asset. This strategy makes it more costly for customers to switch to competitors, especially when the service offered is not standard. It works well with high-cost physical products. Customers may find this sales strategy attractive because it will free up their capital for other investments that may have potentially greater return or strategic value for their enterprise.

Building an Industrial Ecosystem

Industries tend to form spatial clusters in specific geographical regions. Their decision on where to locate is based on a combination of factors such as access to raw materials, convenient transportation, and markets. In addition, firms have to consider the environmental constraints of various building sites.

Recent attempts to develop eco-industrial parks have shifted attention from product policy to a system-wide review of industrial production processes, and resulted in a growing realization that, in many instances, greater economic and environmental gains can be made through collaboration than competition (Lowe et al., 1995; Côte et al., 1994). In an ideal industrial system, all material inputs go into products and all energy is used to do work. Individual firms cannot 'close the loop' on their own; that is to say, they can reduce but not completely eliminate pollution and waste. The trick is to find the 'missing links' in their production processes to complete the cycle so that the waste from one plant or process can be used as input to another. An industrial complex could be built that would function as a virtual ecosystem, and would make use of the resulting waste by-products.

Eco-industrial parks are characterized by symbiotic relations between dissimilar firms. Industrial facilities can be clustered to minimize energy and material wastes through internal bartering and local sales of by-products. The total environmental impact of all the firms participating in an eco-industrial park should be less than the sum of the firms' individual impacts. The park infrastructure itself could also incorporate the best environmental practices in the choice of materials, energy use, waste reduction and water management.

The strategy used to recruit new firms to the park should also reflect the potential for by-product exchange among the participants. Often the by-product from one firm and the input required by another firm are not a perfect match. Changes in process or technology used by the firms may have to be considered to make the match. Excess waste, heat and energy from one process may be used as feedstock in other processes. This may involve open loop or partial recycling where energy and waste is only partially recovered; closed loop recycling with near complete recovery; or synergistic relationships such as co-generation, where one process is dependent on the by-products of another. The success of these relationships depends on the scale of local demand, the efficiency of the conversion of waste to useable by-product, and the dependability of supply.

By establishing a waste exchange, eco-industrial parks help overcome informational barriers to transactions between firms. Firms may still face regulatory barriers and liability considerations. By becoming linked to other firms by means of resource recovery loops, a firm's survival, growth and expansion may become tied to the fate of other firms in the industrial ecosystem. Therefore, the long-term reliability of these symbiotic supply relationships must be assured. Standby capabilities may have to be developed with other suppliers.

The creation of eco-industrial parks also creates many opportunities for partnering and networking. In a knowledge-based economy, small firms may not be able to achieve the critical mass of skills required to achieve breakthrough performance. Small- and medium-sized firms can achieve a competitive advantage over larger firms through their ability to create and explore new solutions by working together with other small firms. Networks of small- and medium-sized firms may also be more able to quickly reorganize the entire production cycle and value chain. A firm may obtain a competitive advantage by sharing common services or by technology transfers within the industrial park. Several types of networks could also emerge in response to other needs of the participants, including co-operative purchasing, production, marketing and learning networks. Factors influencing the development of networks include a common challenge, the benefits of collaboration, personal rapport or strong local community ties, and geographic proximity (Gertler, 1995).

Waiting for the Next Industrial Revolution

Industrial production and mass consumption are still largely linear processes. Production, use and disposal often occur without substantial reuse or recovery of energy or materials. The industrial system is still driven by inputs of virgin materials, and waste continues to be generated and disposed of outside the economic system. As internal recycling is incorporated into production processes, the throughput of materials and energy will decrease. By integrating the lifecycles of diverse processes and products so that the waste streams from some become the feedstock for others, the materials and energy cycle may also be extended.

> If every factory in the world shifted to the cleanest production available (or even the cleanest plausible technology), the larger environmental crises would at best be deferred a few years. . . . As long as the material component of products is still largely based on the use of virgin resources, while the energy is largely derived from fossil fuels, clean is an impossible dream . . . indeed sustainability will be a distant receding goal (Ayres, 1993).

Much of the debate about sustainability obscures the fact that corporations, not individuals and households, are responsible for most of the decisions about energy and material use, waste disposal and pollution released to the environment. Industrial ecology allows us to focus on the role of technology, something we ignore at our peril. By helping to introduce more benign and less wasteful products and processes, industrial ecology could make a major contribution to reducing the flow of matter and energy per unit of economic activity. Short product life cycles with limited functional end-of-life value are also incompatible with sustainability. Moreover, the scale of industrial production must receive due consideration in the calculus of sustainability.

The transition from an industrial to a service-oriented economy will be difficult. This transition will be further complicated by our lifestyle and consumption habits. If we accept Ayres' (1995a) premise that 'human welfare depends on the service, not the material content of production', it follows that the technological transformation of the economy promised by industrial ecology could allow us to increase human welfare without limits. The challenge to business is no more than 'Find pollution and waste and you've found something you have paid for but can't sell. . . . By striving to eliminate it we can grow a more efficient, competitive economy' (Lowe, 1992).

CAN INDUSTRIAL ECOLOGY SUCCEED IN THE MARKETPLACE?

Current environmental rhetoric claims that win–win solutions should be the foundation of management strategy and that trade-offs can largely be avoided through smart decision-making and technological innovation. Although there are many instances where managers have overlooked win–win solutions, they more commonly face decisions where there are trade-offs. The environmental 'value chain' (Porter, 1986) includes activities that occur throughout the whole product life cycle: out-sourcing ('supply chain' management), research and development ('green' design), manufacturing operations (industrial 'symbiosis'), sales (service marketing, eco-labelling), packaging and waste disposal (extended producer responsibility). By improving their knowledge of the value-creating potential of efforts to improve their environmental performance, managers can strategically position their firms in the marketplace and differentiate their products from those of their competitors.

Corporate Buy-In

Although waste reduction and energy efficiency improvements are low risk, overhead-reducing investments, they often receive scant attention from managers. When pollution prevention opportunities are found, corporate business priorities and decision-making processes can pose significant barriers to acting on these opportunities (Porter and Van der Linde, 1995; Denton, 1994; A.D. Little, 1991). Managers are more likely to be rewarded for increasing revenue than cutting costs. Up to now, decisions about where to invest capital, what products to provide, and where to sell them have been considered to be the most important determinants of long-term business success. Eco-efficiency projects have to compete with proposals to increase production capacity and sales.

A 1996 case study of Dow's Laporte facility provides a typical illustration of these problems (Greer and van Löben Sels, 1997). An environmental audit revealed an opportunity to recycle half a ton of chlorinated hydrocarbons, and thereby shut down the on-site waste incinerator and avoid the cost of re-permitting the facility. Plant managers were already aware of this opportunity. However, the returns from this pollution prevention project needed to be superior to all of Dow's other opportunities for capital investment. Moreover, the existing structure of incentives rewarded plant managers and engineers for expanding capacity and sales, not for reducing waste and saving money.

Demand for energy and other inputs are a function of price. Raw materials are still so cheap that suppliers can often undercut the price of recycled materials. Even where waste disposal is problematic, disposal costs may be still too low to matter. Energy costs are routinely lumped together with other overhead costs and may be inconsequential relative to overall costs. As a result, energy conservation projects usually do not call for fundamental changes in production processes. Because waste disposal costs, energy and resource prices are too low, they fail to induce input substitution, or technological innovation.

To an increasing extent, firms' access to investment capital, debt refinancing and insurance now requires the full disclosure of their environmental liabilities. Only rarely are environmental issues associated with other business concerns such as loss of market share or damage to their corporate image and reputation. Under existing business conditions, firms are more likely to consider pollution prevention strategies when:

- Costs of regulatory compliance and exposure to liability can be reduced;
- Cost increases cannot be passed on to the consumer;
- Thresholds of risk are very large;
- Exact location of risk thresholds are unknown;
- Potential damage is not reversible; or
- The magnitude of the possible losses is unknown.

Managers also have many incentives to conceal poor environmental performance and liabilities. For example, the perceived risk to managers or the firm would outweigh possible long-term benefits in all the following situations:

- After all the associated environmental costs are attributed to the product, it is found to be unprofitable to produce;
- The product accounts for a large percentage of the firm's revenue and its discontinuance would mean loss of market share; or
- The mere existence of this highly sensitive information could result in potential contingent liabilities or the threat of regulatory restraints.

Consumer Demand

Green consumerism uses individual preferences to promote less environmentally damaging goods and services (Smith, 1998). It is based on the belief that individuals in their everyday lives should help to save the planet. Although eco-labelling helps consumers make informed choices and verify product claims more cheaply than a comparable regulatory program, the very notion of green consumerism is itself problematic. Since the 1960s, the amount of solid waste disposed of per capita in North America has doubled (Davies and Mazurek, 1997). The environmental loading from consumer use of goods and services exceeds that from manufacturing processes in most advanced economies (Ayres, 1993). This means that people are simply buying, consuming and disposing of more things. Uncoupling material wants from affluence may prove to be more difficult than reducing energy/material used to meet human needs (Wernick et al.,

1996). Our goal should be to reduce consumption, not to redefine it according to consumer preferences or market forces.

'Green' consumer products typically are niche market products that have improved their performance in relation to one or more environmental attributes. Most green consumer products are the 'less from less' variety. Their claim to environmental soundness is usually based on what they do not contain. They rarely generate significant market share because they simply do not do a good enough job – such products must have a lower overall environmental impact than alternatives and sell in place of products that have a greater environmental impact. Business is not fundamentally interested in increasing the physical volume of goods it makes and sells – its real interest is in profit. Business would be more than happy to increase its profit, while making and selling less tonnage of product. Focusing efforts on product usage is the key to achieving more profit from fewer resources; that is provide a product that yields better results at lower cost than the competition (Hindle et al., 1993).

Typically when firms develop environmentally sound products, the newer speciality product is sold in upscale markets to discriminating consumers who can afford to pay for it. Existing polluting products continue to be sold in mass markets at a discount. Experience has shown that except in narrow market segments, environmental soundness is not a substitute for basic product performance and quality, but only an additional benefit (see Fischer and Schot, 1993).

Regulatory and market pressures to adopt eco-design and clean production practices are generally weak. Life cycle impacts, with the exception of packaging or waste disposal, are difficult to regulate. Other than in a few European countries, consumer demand for green products is generally weak. The experience of most firms to date has been that customers are not willing to trade off performance or to pay more for green products (Centre for Clean Design, 1997; Hindle et al., 1993). Few firms have been active in this domain for more than three to five years. Most of the active firms are larger multinationals in the telecommunications and electronics sectors (Centre for Clean Design, 1997) or specialized firms serving niche markets. Eco-design and clean production practices can improve a firm's productivity and reduce the cost of compliance with environmental regulations. They could also be a significant source of competitive advantage. The real challenge to firms, however, is to get more value and performance in products that use fewer resources and produce less waste.

Tomorrow's markets will be very different from today's (Doering et al., 2002). The world's population, even at replacement levels, is likely to increase by at least 50 per cent within the next 50 years. Rapid population growth in low and medium income countries will contribute a large number of

potential workers and consumers to the world economy. Currently, purchases by consumers in these nations represent less than 4 per cent of all
private consumption. High levels of income inequality inhibit the poverty-
reducing effects of economic growth. To build developing country markets,
large and small national and international enterprises will have to provide
stable employment, and supply people with products and services that are
culturally appealing, affordable, and meet their basic needs.

While overall industrial efficiency is improving, total materials throughput and waste generation continue to grow. The world's food system is not
sustainable, and does not meet the basic needs of the poor. However, the
economic value of goods and services created can increase, even as the
throughput of national economies decreases (Matthews et al., 2000).
Industrial activity will have to undergo a transformation on a scale never
before imagined in order to meet the needs of tomorrow's markets.

Investor Response

Research to date suggests that although environmental performance and
financial performance appear to be correlated, not all firms or industrial
sectors are equally well positioned to take advantage of environmental
opportunities (Reed, 1998; WBCSD, 1997). For some industrial sectors
such as forestry, mining and utilities, environmental performance is a core
business concern because they need to protect their licences to operate. For
others, headline risk may play a larger role in investment decisions. Event
studies show that the market punishes negative headlines and disclosures
(Reed, 1998). Lending institutions also have a strong interest in performing
extensive due diligence reviews of the environmental performance of
prospective borrowers (Bisset, 1995; Robbins and Bisset, 1994). They are
likely to be concerned about potential lender liability (for example, for
clean-up costs), possible sudden drops in the firm's capitalized value, and
the risk of loan default due to cash flow problems because of falling sales,
litigation, insurance claims, fines or penalties (Weiler et al., 1997).

A more recent phenomenon is the emergence of ethical investment funds.
Traditionally these funds have been considered 'green' because of what they
do not contain. Portfolio studies show that these funds outperform the
market. Nonetheless, it is not possible to say at this time whether these
favourable preliminary findings are a function of low risk investments or
better-managed investments (Reed, 1998; Adams, 1997; WBCSD, 1997).
Portfolio managers have a fiduciary duty to maximize returns, minimize
risks and conserve capital/assets for the beneficiary. Only when the linkage
between environmental and financial performance is accepted will environmental considerations become a routine part of the selection process

that any prudent investor would normally follow (Reed, 1998). However, corporate managers would be foolhardy not to take action now to position themselves to take advantage of the increasing public and shareholder interest in the environmental performance of their firms.

Institutional investors (for example, pension funds) own an increasing share of equity markets, and an increasing share of investor assets are held in professionally screened portfolios. Investors and fund managers who want to use corporate environmental performance as a criterion for selecting or screening stocks are often at a disadvantage because of corporations' failure to disclose materially relevant data on environmental, health and safety risks (Franco, 2001). However, low cost media such as the Internet have to some extent offset this difficulty by greatly facilitating risk communication. For example, a group of Dupont shareholders established their own website (www.dupontshareholdersalert.org) when Dupont was fined by the US EPA for failing to disclose findings about the potential risks of Teflon-related chemicals (PFOA). This diverse group of shareholders is not only concerned about their investments but also concerned about the impact of these chemicals on worker health and the safety of community drinking water supplies. The EPA fines resulted in a short-term drop in Dupont's stock price, and exposed the company to future lawsuits and the threat of regulatory action. Dupont entered this market after its competitor 3M stopped producing this family of chemicals. 3M withdrew Scotchgard, its own brand name product, from the market because of concerns about the product's potential health and environmental risks. Analysts estimate that annual production of these chemicals is now worth $1.23 billion in sales and $100 million in profit to Dupont.

The Commission on Environmental Cooperation (CEC, 2003) is examining ways and means of improving corporate environmental disclosure in North America. The US Senate has also asked the General Accounting Office (GAO) to investigate the adequacy of corporate disclosure after a 1998 US Environmental Protection Agency study (US EPA, 2001) found that 74 per cent of the publicly traded companies subject to environmental legal proceedings had failed to disclose the proceedings adequately in either their annual report or filings with the Securities and Exchange Commission (SEC). US companies are required to disclose contingent environmental liabilities affecting their future earnings in their annual report, and the impact of compliance costs and potential sanctions in their SEC 10-K report.

Many lenders, such as leading investment banks, have adopted common principles for managing their environmental risk exposures (for example, Equator Principles, 2003). Corporate borrowers who do not comply with these principles are considered to have defaulted on their loans.

Environmental investment criteria are increasingly an important factor in prospective assessments of companies' earning potential. For example, Innovest (2004) is a leading industry strategic investment analyst. Over the years, Dow has consistently ranked highly in Innovest's assessments of the chemical sector, (8th out of 30 competitors in a recent industry survey). This was largely due to Dow's eco-efficiency initiatives that made it more cost competitive. However, by 2003 Dow had accrued environmental liabilities of $381 million (for example, Agent Orange and Bhopal, inherited from the takeover of Union Carbide) equal to 22.02 per cent of its net income after taxes. In other words, Dow Chemical needed over $2 billion in sales to cover its accrued environmental liabilities. Innovest's analysis of Dow's business plan and goals for future growth and development also showed that these environmental risks might even increase over time. It thought that Dow's core business, organochlorine chemicals, and many of the chemicals in its product portfolio could be threatened by changing market demands and possible regulatory action. As a result, it concluded that Dow's eco-efficiency efforts alone would be inadequate to cope with changing public policy priorities and emerging risk factors. Because Innovest thought Dow would be likely to under-perform in the stock market over the medium to long term, it downgraded Dow's investment rating (it now ranks 47th out of 68 competitors).

Regulation

Companies that have to undertake projects to comply with environmental regulations don't usually scrutinize them as much as other capital projects, believing that they have no choice but to comply, regardless of whether or not the project is financially sound. By requiring extremely short payback periods, not using the typical investment screens, and ignoring future cash flows, companies often make the wrong capital investment decisions (Epstein and Young, 1999).

The belief that companies will act on profitable environmental opportunities without a regulatory push may be based on false assumptions: companies often have limited time and attention, and lack basic information and the incentive to act. Regulation may be needed to level the playing field and to force action when the cost of compliance is not offset by other advantages (Porter and van der Linde, 1995). A firm has an incentive to go 'beyond compliance' when it thinks it can improve its financial bottom line or more appropriately manage business risk (Reinhardt, 1999; Estey and Porter, 1998). The firm may be able to reduce the cost or quantities of inputs it must purchase, or capture a price premium for its products. It may also seek to minimize the risk of accidental failure and product liabilities, thereby reducing the threat of future litigation and government intervention. Through strategic interaction with regulators, a firm may obtain government sanction for a business solution in which they have a competitive advantage. For example, Dow exited from the CFC business prior to the phase out of ozone-depleting substances because they had patented a more profitable substitute. Internationally coordinated regulatory action prevented Dow from being undercut in the marketplace.

Market-based approaches have become the default option for modern environmental regulation (Portney, 2003). Traditional command and control approaches to regulation often freeze existing control technology in place, and deny companies the flexibility needed to modify their production processes or reformulate their products. Performance-based regulations, in contrast to prescriptive, standards-based regulations, set goals and priorities for improvements. They are designed to provide information needed to drive public and private decision-making. The choice of how to comply is often left up to the companies themselves.

Environmental regulations can be conceived as industrial policy instruments designed to increase the competitiveness of firms by forcing them to innovate in a way that could turn out to be both privately and socially profitable. Companies in high impact industries, such as chemicals, may face a competitive disadvantage if stringent environmental regulations burden them with higher environmental compliance costs than other firms in the industry. Firms facing higher compliance costs have an incentive to research new technologies and production approaches to reduce their costs of compliance. They can gain 'first mover advantages' by selling their innovative solutions to other firms (Esty and Porter, 1998). Environmental performance can be a potential source of competitive advantage when it results in the development of more efficient processes, improves productivity, lowers compliance costs, or creates new market opportunities (Wagner and Schaltegger, 2003; Porter and van der Linde, 1995).

Value Creation – The Key to Breakthrough Performance

For industrial ecology to succeed in the marketplace as a business strategy, it must contribute to the financial success of the firm. Industrial ecology contributes to the financial success of the firm by reducing costs, improving asset usage, increasing productivity, diversifying revenue growth, and reducing risk (see Table 12.1). Better environmental performance helps contain a firm's cost of doing business. For example, process improvements reduce resource input, overhead, operating, waste treatment and disposal costs, yielding many small earning improvements that may not appear to be significant unless aggregated. Improved environmental

Table 12.1   Value-added environmental strategies

Environmental strategy	Improve production processes	Redesign or upgrade products	Diversify product lines
Focus	Efficiency gains / Pollution prevention	Improved product quality	Increased service / Product stewardship
Business value	Reduce costs and exposure to liability	Command a price premium or increase market share	Develop new products or lock-in customer base
Financial impact	Increased profit margin and return on equity	Increased competitive advantage	Increased revenue

performance could also improve a firm's competitiveness by creating new product opportunities from waste by-products and new revenue from recycling. Product improvements may increase a firm's market share and pricing power by building retailer and customer loyalty. The firm must be able to protect itself from imitators long enough to recoup its investment or be able to target customers who are willing to pay more for a better product. A firm may diversify its product lines by increasing the service content of its offering, or by locking in its customer base through extended product stewardship. However, the revenues from diversification must more than offset increased overhead and labour costs associated with this strategy. Environmental strategies that are not value-added are unlikely to be sustainable in the marketplace (Arnold and Day, 1998; Reed, 1998).

The goal of Porter's value chain analysis (Porter, 1986) is to identify the drivers of shareholder value by understanding how each of the firm's activities creates value for its customers. An equally important aspect of the analysis is identifying where one can prevent the destruction of value. Adopting a value-creating environmental strategy is analogous to changing the justification for a company's existence (Figge and Schaltegger, 2000). All the enterprise's business systems (for example, planning, target setting, performance measurement and incentive systems) must work together to effectively link value creation with environmental strategy.

Rappaport (1996) and Copeland (1990) have shown that business decisions can be assessed on the basis of value drivers (see Table 12.2). These include strategic, operating, investment and financing decisions.

Strategic value drivers include anticipated future costs and earnings potential. These drivers include opportunity costs and how long a better-

Table 12.2   Shareholder value

Free Cash Flow			Discount Rate
Strategic	Operating	Investment	Financing
Value growth	Sales growth	Working capital	Cost of capital (debt & equity)
Opportunity costs	Profit margin Tax rate	Fixed capital	

Source: Adapted from Rappaport (1996, Figure 3.1)

than-market-average return can be sustained. For example, products that have earned above-average returns can adversely impact shareholder value if they suddenly become environmentally problematic, prices and sales fall, and the firm has to exit the market.

Operating value drivers focus on profit per unit sales. By increasing the product benefit or quality for the consumer (price leadership or product differentiation) and lowering costs of production through reduced use of inputs and waste, managers should be able to increase their profit margins. In recent years, the chemical industry has cut costs (and its exposure to liability) through waste minimization and energy and water savings, to name just a few general examples. Greener products can also boost sales and widen profit margins.

Investment value drivers stress the ratio of sales to fixed assets. If business investments are not capital-intensive, or do increase efficiency or productivity or create other savings, they will have a positive effect on the corporate bottom line. End-of-pipe technologies are generally more capital-intensive and usually incur higher operating costs than cleaner technologies (for example, reducing energy and material consumption, emissions, waste disposal and treatment costs) or pollution prevention measures (such as the substitution of safer inputs).

The financial value drivers of concern are borrowing and insurance costs. Environmental risks are implicitly taken into account when the interest rates on borrowed capital and the costs of equity are calculated. Unsystematic risks affect only one company (for example, accidental spills), while systematic risks (for example, rising energy costs) affect the industry as a whole. Investors can protect themselves from unsystematic financial risks by a diversified portfolio of investments and by the accumulation of sufficiently large capital reserves to defray the costs of compensation for damages, when these events occur. However, often the only way to reduce the associated costs or liabilities of a systematic environmental risk is to reduce the risk itself.

Banks are concerned about systematic environmental risks because they may lose the money they invested, and could become liable for the environmental damage these companies have caused. Insurance companies face even greater problems dealing with unsystematic environmental risks, such as natural disasters. Investments in global financial markets were once adequate to cope with unsystematic risks. However, if insurance companies have underestimated the frequency or severity of these events (for example, climate-related natural disasters), and these events are now more systematic than was once thought, insurance companies could be facing everything from wholesale premium increases to financial failure (see Figge, 1997).

The economic success of any environmental strategy can be assessed on the basis of shareholder value – the net present value of a company's future earnings (Melchiorsen and Mogensen, 2005; Schaltegger and Figge, 1997). Current accounting practices reflect past performance, and are of little help in envisioning a company's future business success (Figge et al., 2001; Schaltegger and Burritt, 2000). Environmental costs are either not measured at all or are hidden away in various administrative and overhead accounts, and very rarely reported (Epstein and Young, 1999). General accounting principles allow for more than 150 adjustments to be made to traditional business accounts, where fewer than five adjustments need to be made in calculating shareholder value. The shareholder value approach in comparison has the advantage of transparency and simplicity (Epstein and Young, 1999). It is much more manageable since only a few variables need to be calculated (for example, forecast free cash flow, discount factor). Critics think that shareholder value analysis allows no more environmental protection than the market conditions permit, and its use of discounting is unethical because discounting assigns lower values to the needs of future generations (Schaltegger and Burritt, 2000). However, traditional accounting schemes ignore the level of investment required, the opportunity costs, and the risks involved. If we ask the question: 'does a particular environmental strategy pay and will it contribute to our business success?' then environmental shareholder value analysis is the answer.

DO WE HAVE THE TOOLS TO DO THE JOB?

Industrial ecology currently relies upon stand-alone decision tools such as Life-Cycle Analysis (LCA), Design for the Environment (DfE) and an assortment of environmental indicators. These tools have been developed to support product-oriented environmental policies and corporate reporting requirements.

Life Cycle Analysis

LCA is used to evaluate the environmental burdens associated with all phases of a product's production, use and disposal. LCA has mainly been applied to simple, low design, resource-intensive products. The materials in these products may be recycled as bulk commodities or may place excessive demands on waste disposal facilities. LCA has also been used to rate potential hazards and the impact of input substitution on the performance of products such as detergents.

The most telling criticism of LCA has been that when different LCA methods are used to evaluate the same product, substance or material, they often give inconsistent results (Ayres, 1995b). LCA has failed to provide conclusive results because there are no commonly agreed-upon methods for comparing, valuing or weighting different environmental impacts. Moreover, use of LCA methods is often limited by cost or unreliable data. LCA tools rely on aggregated inventory data. This data is often of low relevance and precision, not representative, and consolidated in a way that ignores spatial and time differences. As industry averages are used, companies performing better than the industry average are penalized, and those performing below the industry average benefit as free riders (Schaltegger and Burritt, 2000). Although LCA does not provide a common denominator or bottom line for comparisons of different product claims, it has been extensively used within firms to evaluate corporate progress towards environmental targets. (For examples, see Nortel, 1996; Kortman et al., 1994; Adriaanse, 1993; Steen and Ryding, 1992; Braunschweig, 1991).

Design for the Environment

DfE first emerged in the 1980s as a generic response to concerns about the scale of technology, incineration and the amount of waste going to landfills. It deals with the potential environmental impacts of industrial processes and consumer products in a completely different way. It introduces the principles of pollution prevention into the design process before non-reversible choices have been made and while the selection of alternatives is still feasible and not cost prohibitive. DfE has been applied to structurally complex, high design products (for example, electronics). These products usually contain valuable components or rare materials that are worth recovering.

DfE is a rule-based design system. First, the number of parts and assembly steps should be drastically reduced. Process chains should be shortened, bypassing as many intermediate steps as possible. These changes will reduce production, scrap and rework costs. By reorganizing production, there will also be savings in space, heating and lighting costs. Second, products and packaging should be redesigned to reduce their material content, size and weight. Third, the use of toxic and hazardous substances should be discontinued because of inherent dangers-in-use and potential liabilities. Fourth, products should also be reformulated for durability, easy repair, eventual disassembly and recycling. This change can be achieved through modular design, standardization and the use of materials that are easily machined or reprocessed. The bottom line is the reduction or elimination of potential hazards and waste: anything that does not add value to the product (Graedel and Allenby, 1995). Although eco-design and clean production practices work well with heavily engineered products, they do not provide easily understood metrics that can be used in strategic business decision making.

Both LCA and DfE are product-oriented methods. They do not address production issues directly. Strategic opportunities for waste minimization and pollution prevention arise throughout the production process. Figure 12.2 (Ciambrone, 1996) illustrates the range of decision possibilities.

Eco-Efficiency

Even though environmental reporting is based on the adage, 'what gets measured gets done', no one has yet agreed on a common set of bench-

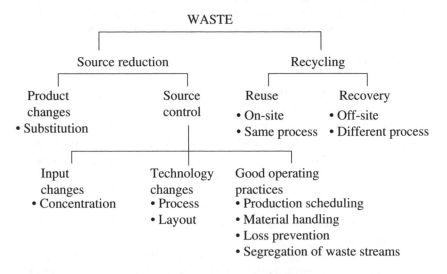

Source: Adapted from Ciambrone (1996, Figure 1, p. 10).

Figure 12.2   Waste decision tree

marks or performance indicators that firms can use in decision making. Moreover, existing indicators generally do not clarify the relationship between the value of goods and services created and their associated environmental impacts. The recent Global Reporting Initiative (1999) has not materially advanced the state-of-the-art of corporate environmental reporting. Its primary concern has been the audit and verification of the facts and figures disclosed in the reports, not their usefulness in corporate decision making. Many critics feel that corporate environmental reporting is nothing more than a public relations exercise.

The World Business Council (WBCSD, 1999) has been actively trying to promote the concept of eco-efficiency and to develop mutually agreed upon eco-efficiency indicators. In a recent survey of Canadian business, Vrooman and Beillard (2000) found that 'eco-efficiency is recognized by some, endorsed by a few and not widely promoted'. They encountered a general resistance by business to the use of 'one-size-fits-all' environmental indicators that could be used to compare different businesses lines, products or services. Their survey found that the four most important priorities for Canadian business were to reduce energy intensity (75 per cent), material use (60 per cent) and toxic dispersion (50 per cent) and to improve material recyclability (36 per cent).

Business is always interested in improving productivity. Efficiency is the ratio of a desired output to the resources used. Eco-efficiency indicators link environmental and financial performance (Müller and Sturm, 2002). Eco-efficient enterprises waste fewer resources, and release fewer emissions to air, soil and water, while producing the same output as their competitors. Eco-efficiency is relevant to the financial valuation of an enterprise because it often results in:

- Higher margins due to lower operating costs;
- Higher sales where the value of product to consumers or the company's public image improves;
- Lower capital requirements when integrated solutions are found or because of better supply management;
- Lower discount (financial risk) factors and fewer contingent liabilities.

Eco-efficiency analysis is a systematic approach to incorporating a broad range of environmental impacts and costs into decisions regarding processes and products. Rather than basing a decision on a single criterion (for example, toxicity), the approach uses multiple criteria. For example BASF (Shonnard et al., 2003), uses five reference categories in calculating the 'ecological fingerprint' of their products:

- Consumption of raw materials;
- Consumption of energy;
- Emissions into air water and soil (wastes);
- Inherent toxicity of the substances employed and released, and
- Potential hazards and misuse.

The results of eco-efficiency analyses have been used in strategic decisions about whether or not to improve a product, substitute an alternative, or bring a product to market. Eco-efficiency analysis has also improved the competitiveness of BASF's products. In a recent study, they found that their eco-efficient products performed much better in the marketplace than their non-eco-efficient products.

Eco-Effectiveness

Is eco-efficiency – doing more with less – enough? It is not a new idea. Business has always been interested in productivity. Henry Ford built and operated an eco-efficient factory. He saved his company money by recycling and re-using materials, reduced the use of natural resources, minimized packaging, and set new standards of productivity with his timesaving assembly line. Contemporary consumers often practise the three Rs – reduce, re-use, recycle. Reduction, re-use and recycling slow down the rates of contamination and resource depletion but do not stop these processes. McDonough and Braungart (2001) think that eco-efficiency is not enough. Instead they think that we should start thinking in terms of eco-effectiveness. Effectiveness poses the question: are we doing the right thing?

McDonough and Braungart (2001) look at environmental management as a design question. They think we should be creating eco-effective rather than eco-efficient products. They criticise eco-efficiency because it does not go far enough, and feel that we should simply design out waste, and make reusable products instead of short-lived discards. McDonough has added three principles to the traditional design criteria of cost, performance and aesthetics (Can I afford it? Will it work? and Do I like it?)

- **Waste equals food**. Every material used must be designed so that other living systems' metabolism can use or decompose it. Alternatively the material must be contained within a closed-loop industrial system.
- **Use current solar income**. Nature does not mine the past nor borrow from the future, but lives on current income. Passive solar and benign renewable forms of energy production should replace fossil fuels.

- **Respect diversity**. Instead of the one-size-fits-all, designs should be adapted to local conditions.

For example, McDonough-Braungart Design Chemistry (www.mbdc. com/) designed a fabric (Climatex Lifecycle www.climatex.com) for a Swiss textile company that was suitable for use in the upholstery of office chairs. The company's weaving mill is located next to a historic conservation area. The manager had systematically improved the energy and water efficiency of his plant over time. However, Swiss regulators thought fabric remnants from his plant were hazardous waste. MBDC used their Sustainable Design Protocol to assess the fabric, dyes and fixatives. They chose wool because it absorbs moisture, and ramie, a plant similar to nettles, because it provides a strong structural fibre that wicks water away. Combining these two fibres kept the chairs' occupants cool in summer and warm in winter. Only one out of 60 chemical companies (Ciba-Geigy, now Novartis) was prepared to participate in the project. MBDC reviewed 8000 chemicals and rejected 7962, finding only 38 suitable for use in the product. After production runs of the fabric, the water coming out of the process is cleaner than the water going in because the fabric acts as a filter. The fabric safely decomposes and can be used as mulch. The richly coloured and textured fabrics of the collection have won several design awards, and have been so popular that other companies have been licensed to manufacture them.

MBDC describe three types of products: consumption, service and unmarketable products. Consumption products, such as the Climatex fabric, can safely be returned to nature through open-loop organic life cycles. Service products are synthetic materials designed solely for use within closed-loop industrial life cycles. These products should never be released to the environment. Finally unmarketable products are hazardous and cannot be recycled. The goal of sustainable design is to eliminate unmarketable products entirely.

Design innovation starts with the professional education of tomorrow's chemists and engineers (Shonnard et al., 2003; Kirchoff, 2003; Hjeresen et al., 2000; Anastas and Warner, 1998). Green chemistry, for example, is the use of chemistry for pollution prevention. More specifically, it is the design of chemical substances and processes that are environmentally benign. Examples include the development of renewable feedstocks, safer reagents, alternatives to solvents, and more efficient syntheses. Green chemistry provides the foundation for green engineering technologies needed to build sustainable products, processes and systems. Using inherently safer materials eliminates the need to engineer out environmental risks later in the process.

ECO-ACCOUNTING FOR DOUBLE DIVIDENDS – THE NEXT STEP

What gets measured gets managed. Industrial ecology provides a coherent framework for strategic thinking about and testing of management options for the whole spectrum of environmental issues confronting an industry. Industrial ecology goes beyond mere efficiency improvements. By conceiving of environmental liabilities as potential assets and waste as potentially valuable products, industrial ecology could contribute a value-added perspective to environmental management. The value of an end-product can be defined by the sum of the processes needed to make it, its properties in use and the possibilities of the end-product being reused and recycled. For example, the 'greenness' of consumer products could be determined from the percentage of inputs that are derived from recycled energy, materials and waste by-products. Industrial processes could be reassessed on the basis of the proportion of the inputs that wind up in useful products. Substitution of plentiful (renewable) for scarce resources and benign for harmful substances would also be an important consideration. Industrial ecology could guide the transition from fragmented and costly compliance with environmental regulations to more proactive programs yielding cost savings and new sources of revenue. It links the achievement of environmental quality objectives with continuous technological improvement and wealth creation.

It is no longer possible to ignore environmental costs and damages that fall outside the production process and to allow them to be borne by third parties, nature and future generations. Industrial processes and products must now start to incorporate environmental costs and damages in their financing, cost allocation and pricing structures. The problem is how to do it.

There is no consensus about what constitutes an environmental cost or expenditure. Accounting systems often do not identify or assign environmental expenditures to corporate responsibility centres. Environmental costs are often lumped into overhead. In a recent Tellus survey (US PCSD, 1995) over 55 per cent of the firms allocated environmental expenditures to overhead. In allocating overhead costs, firms used labour hours (58 per cent), production volume (53 per cent), and material use (27 per cent). If environmental costs are ignored, left in a common pool or allocated incorrectly (say on a fixed percentage basis) to the various product lines, product managers do not have incentives to make improvements. An effort has to be made to capture the environmental cost elements associated with each activity or process and to use this information in business decision making. Managers need a coherent accounting framework to guide environmental

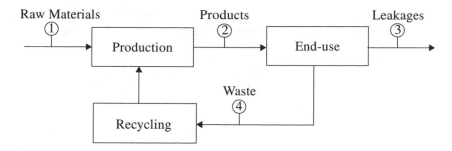

Source: Adapted from Winsemius and Hahn (1992)

Figure 12.3 Option analysis

decision making because they lack the means of assessing the contribution of improvements in environmental performance to the financial success of the firm. It will help them direct their attention to high impact and high opportunity business units. Conventional bookkeeping systems do not track the environmental costs of their decisions. These decisions include: (1) the selection of raw materials and process technology; (2) product design and marketing; (3) pollution control (reducing leakages from the system); and (4) recycling of waste by-products (see Figure 12.3). To achieve minimum waste at minimum cost, managers must strike an optimum balance among decisions to:

- Reduce the use of inputs
- Limit the creation of wastes during production
- Reuse wastes produced during production as raw materials in other processes, and
- Recover wastes from products at the end of their useful lives (Frosch, 1996).

The first step in creating suitable environmental accounts is to implement activity- or transaction-based costing. Activity-based accounting provides the missing link between the demand for resources and value creation (Cooper and Kaplan, 1991; 1988). Many important cost categories are not driven by short-term changes in output but vary over a period of years with changes in plant layout and design, production process, product mix and client services. Costs must be allocated to products/processes in order to ensure that the responsible managers have the necessary incentives to make needed improvements or to find creative alternatives. Then activity drivers (for example, increased sales) and cost

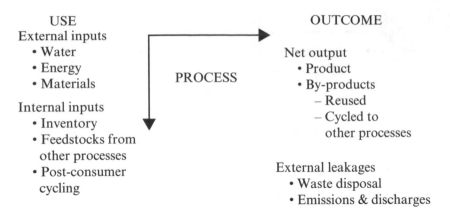

Figure 12.4   Product-by-process matrix

drivers (for example, energy and materials used, waste disposal) must be identified for each product/process. Managers must account for conventional costs (such as increased use and more waste), for potentially hidden costs (such as siting and design, inspections, eventual plant closure and site decommissioning), and for contingent liabilities (such as potential claims, fines and penalties).

A product-by-process matrix could be created (see Figure 12.4) from the same information. As long as the units are consistent along rows, inputs and outputs may be measured in any convenient physical unit. The aggregate net resource requirements, direct and indirect outputs (including leakages) of a series of linked processes, may be determined by the application of matrix algebra. This would simplify the task of developing a process-based map linking activities, inputs, costs, revenues, impacts and effects.

The next step would be to develop environmental performance indicators (see Table 12.3) that would be based on the product-by-process matrix, and could be incorporated into financial spreadsheets. It is not necessary to construct a mass balance sheet of company operations. Activity based accounting systems already track cost and quantity. What are needed are performance indicators that show how environmental management decisions impact net discounted cash flows and debt repayment. Management decisions about the use of inputs are operating value drivers. Decisions affecting throughput, increasing cycling and reducing leakages, are often investment value drivers. Design decisions, and those affecting product offerings are strategic value drivers. Anything that improves the economy with which resources are acquired, the efficiency or productivity of company operations and sales will affect the

Table 12.3   Inputs, throughputs, outputs, leakages

INPUTS:	• Water: freshwater intake
	• Energy: renewable/fossil/nuclear
	• Raw material: renewable/non-renewable
	• Toxic or hazardous substances
	• Recycling
	– On-site recovery (waste water, energy, materials)
	– Feedstocks (by-products from other processes)
	– Post-consumer recycling (components and materials)
THROUGHPUTS:	• Extractive waste or recovery ratio
	• Renewables: regrowth, restocking ratios
	• Process efficiency: (Products+Leakages-Recycled by-products/$_{New + Recycled inputs}$)*100
	• Cycle time (similar to inventory turnover)
	• Recovery rate: by-products and useable waste
OUTPUTS:	• Product: decreased weight/mass and energy use
	• Service life (% of output that is replacement demand)
	• Packaging
LEAKAGES:	• Onsite storage/treatment: toxic/hazardous/radioactive
	• Other emissions and discharges to air or water
	• Waste disposal: landfills/incineration

cost of capital (debt and equity). Samples of potential performance measures are described in Table 12.3.

Industrial ecology simplifies environmental accounting considerably. By clarifying the relationship between the stocks and flows of resources required and identifying their fate in the environment, industrial ecology makes it much easier to quantify the costs, revenues and potential liabilities associated with any product or process. Industrial ecology provides a framework for conducting a corporate financial assessment of the net impact of environmental management efforts on their business bottom line. Eco-accounting would also facilitate the analysis of policies and market constraints limiting corporate environmental performance.

CONCLUSIONS

There is a need to rethink industrialism. Our prosperity and future depend upon it. Industrial ecology provides a useful way of thinking about the challenges that lie ahead. The blueprint and tools needed to build an industrial ecosystem need further work. Industrial ecology has the potential to succeed in the marketplace. It links environmental protection to other strategic management concerns such as increasing business value, reducing risk and increasing productivity. Industrial ecology provides the means of testing hypotheses about how things work – a reality check – to help us learn from experience and transform the marketplace.

NOTE

The views expressed in this chapter are those of the author and not necessarily those of Environment Canada.

REFERENCES

Adams, Roger (1997), 'Linking financial and environmental performance', *Environmental Accounting and Auditing Reporter*, **2**(10).

Adriaanse, Albert (1993), *Environmental Policy Performance Indicators – a Study on the Development of Indicators for Environmental Policy in the Netherlands*, The Hague: Netherlands Ministry of Housing, Spatial Planning and the Environment.

Anastas, P.T. and J.C. Warner (1998), *Green Chemistry: Theory and Practice*, New York: Oxford University Press.

Arnold, Matthew B. and Robert M. Day (1998), *The Next Bottom Line: Making Sustainable Development Tangible*, Washington DC: World Resources Institute.

Ashford, N.A. (2002), 'Government and environmental innovation in Europe and North America', *American Behavioral Scientist*, **45**(9), 1417–34.

Ayres, Robert U. (1993), 'Industrial metabolism – closing the materials cycle', in T. Jackson (ed.), *Clean Production Strategies: Developing Preventive Environmental Management in the Industrial Economy*, Boca Raton, Florida: Lewis Publishers.

Ayres, Robert U. (1995a), 'Economic growth: politically necessary but not environmentally friendly', *Ecological Economics*, **15**, 97–9.

Ayres, R.U. (1995b), 'Life cycle analysis: a critique', *Resource Conservation and Recycling*, **14**, 199–223.

Bisset, Doug (1995), 'Managing risk: a new responsibility for banks', *The Bankers Magazine*, **178**(2), 55–9.

Blacconiere, W.G. and D.W. Northcut (1997), 'Environmental information and market reactions to environmental legislation', *Journal of Accounting, Auditing and Finance*, **12**(2), 149–78.

Blacconiere, W.G. and D. Patten (1994), 'Environmental disclosures, regulatory costs, and changes in firm value', *Journal of Accounting and Economics*, **18**(December), 357–77.

Braunschweig, A. (1991), 'The new ecological valuation method based on ecological scarcity and its application to Switzerland', paper read at SETAC – Europe Workshop on Environmental Life-Cycle Analysis of Products, December, at Leiden.

Centre for Clean Design (1997), *Identification of Research Agenda and Issues in Relation to Clean Design (Eco-Design)*, Farnham, Surrey: Surrey Institute of Art and Design.

CEC (Commission on Environmental Cooperation) (2003), *Environmental Disclosure Requirements in the Securities Regulations and Financial Accounting Standards of Mexico, Canada and the United States Update and Recommendations*, Montreal.

Christmann, P. (2000), 'Effects of "Best practices of environmental management on cost"', *Academy of Management Journal*, **43**(4), 663–80.

Ciambrone, David F. (1996), *Waste Minimization as a Strategic Weapon*, Boca Raton, Florida: Lewis Publishers.

Cooper, Robin and Robert S. Kaplan (1988), 'How cost accounting distorts product costs', *Management Accounting*, **LXIX**(10), 20–27.

Cooper, Robin and Robert S. Kaplan (1991), 'Profit priorities from activity based costing', *Harvard Business Review*, No. 3, 130–35.

Copeland, T. (1990), *Valuation: Measuring and Managing the Value of Companies*, New York: John Wiley and Sons.

Côte, Raymond, Robert Ellison, Jill Grant, Jeremy Hall, Peter Klynstra, Michael Martin and Peter Wade (1994), *Designing and Operating Industrial Parks as Ecosystems*, Halifax, Nova Scotia: Dalhousie, School for Resource and Environmental Studies.

Davies, J. Clarence (Terry) and Jan Mazurek (1997), *Regulating Pollution: Does the US System Work?*, Washington DC: Resources for the Future.

Denton, Keith (1994), *Enviro-Management: How Smart Companies Turn Environmental Costs into Profits*, Englewood Cliffs NJ: Prentice Hall.

Derwall, Jeroen, Nadja Guesnter, Rob Bauer and Kees Koedijk (2005), 'The eco-efficiency premium puzzle', *Financial Analysts Journal*, **61**(2).

Doering, Don S., Amy Cassara, Christian Layke, Janet Ranganathan, Carmen Revenga, Dan Tunstall and Wendy Vanasselt (2002), *Tomorrow's Markets – Global Trends and Their Implications for Business*, Washington DC: A collaboration of the World Resources Institute, United Nations Environment Programme, and World Business Council for Sustainable Development.

Earle, R. (2000), *The Emerging Relationship between Environmental Performance and Shareholder Wealth*, Concord, MA: Assabet Group.

Ehrenfield, John R. (1997), *Industrial Ecology: A Framework for Product and Process Design*, Cambridge MA: MIT Program on Technology, Business and the Environment.

Epstein, M.J. and D.S. Young (1999), 'Greening with EVA', *Management Accounting*, **80**(7), 45–9.

Equator Principles (2003), 'The equator principles: A benchmark for the financial industry to manage social and environmental issues in project financing', available online at http://www.equator-principles.com/principles.shtml.

Estey, D.C. and M.E. Porter (1998), 'Industrial ecology and competitiveness: Strategic implications for the firm', *Journal of Industrial Ecology*, **2**(1), 35–43.

Figge, F. (1997), *Systematisation of Economic Risks through Global Environmental Problems*, Lüneburg, Germany: University of Lüneburg/Bank Picte & Cie/UNEP.

Figge, F. and S. Schaltegger (2000), *What is 'Stakeholder Value'? Developing a Catch Phrase into a Benchmarking Tool*, Nairobi Kenya: UNEP.

Figge, F., T. Hahn and S. Schaltegger (2001), *Environmental Shareholder Value. International Workshop on Improved Investment Analysis Tools*, Lisbon, Portugal:

United Nations Department of Economic and Social Affairs, Division for Sustainable Development.

Fischer, Kurt and Johan Schot (1993), *Environmental Strategies for Business: International Perspectives on Research Needs and Policy Implications*, Washington DC: Island Press.

Franco, N.C. (2001), *Corporate Environmental Disclosure: Opportunities to Harness Market Forces to Improve Corporate Environmental Performance*, Conference on Environmental Law, Keystone Colorado: American Bar Association.

Friend, Gil (1996), 'A cyclical materials economy: what goes around comes around . . . or does it?', *New Bottom Line*, March 12.

Frosch, Robert A. (1996), 'Towards the end of waste: reflections on a new ecology of industry', *Daedalus*, **125**(3), 199–211.

Frosch, R.A. and N.E. Gallopoulus (1989), 'Strategies for manufacturing', *Scientific American*, **261**(3), 144–52.

GEMI (2004), *Clear Advantage: Building Shareholder Value – Environmental Value to the Investor*, Washington DC: Global Environmental Initiative.

Gertler, Nicholas (1995), *Industrial Ecosystems: Developing Sustainable Industrial Structures*, Masters, Civil and Environmental Engineering, Technology and Policy Program, Massachusetts Institute of Technology, Boston.

Global Reporting Initiative (1999), *Sustainability Reporting Guidelines – Exposure Draft for Public Comment and Pilot Testing*, Boston: CERES.

Graedel, T.E. and B.A. Allenby (1995), *Industrial Ecology*, Englewood Cliffs, New Jersey: Prentice Hall.

Greer, L. and C. Van Löben Sels (1997), 'When pollution prevention meets the bottom line', *Environmental Science and Technology* (September).

Hart, S. and G. Ahuja (1996), 'Does it pay to be green?', *Business Strategy and the Environment*, **5**, 30–37.

Heden, Carl-Goran (1995), *The Zero Emissions Research Initiative*, Tokyo: United Nations University.

Hindle, Peter, Peter White and Kate Minion (1993), 'Achieving real environmental improvements using value impact assessment', *Long Range Planning*, **26**(3), 36–48.

Hjeresen, D.L., D.L. Schutt and J.M. Boese (2000), 'Green chemistry and education', *Journal of Chemical Education*, **77**(12), 1543–47.

Innovest (2004), *Dow Chemical: Risks for Investors*, New York: Innovest Strategic Value Advisors.

Kirchoff, M.M. (2003), 'Promoting green engineering through green chemistry', *Environmental Science and Technology*, **37**, 5349–53.

Kortman, J.G.M., E.W. Lindeijer, H. Sas and M. Spengers (1994), *Towards a single indicator for emissions – an exercise in aggregating environmental effects*, no. 1994/2, The Hague: VROM.

Lewis, S. (2005), *The Shareholder's Right to Know More: E.I. du Pont de Nemours and the Growing Financial Challenges of PFOA*, Dupont Shareholders for Fair Value.

Little, Arthur D. (1991), *Seizing Strategic Environmental Advantage: A Life Cycle Approach*, Cambridge, MA: Center for Environmental Assurance – Arthur D. Little Inc.

Lowe, Ernest (1992), *Discovering Industrial Ecology: An Overview and Strategies for Implementation*, Oakland, California: Change Management Centre.

Lowe, Ernest A., Steven R. Moran and Douglas B. Holmes (1995), *Fieldbook for the Development of Eco-Industrial Parks V. II, Final Report, Indigo Development*, Research Triangle Park NC: Research Triangle Institute.

Matthews, Emily et al. (2000), *The Weight of Nations: Material Outflows from Industrial Economies*, Washington, DC: World Resources Institute.

McDonough, W. and M. Braungart (2001), 'The next industrial revolution', in P. Allen, C. Bonazzi and D. Gee (eds), *Metaphors for Change – Partnerships, Tools and Civic Action for Sustainability*, London: Greenleaf Publishing, pp. 66–75.

Melchiorsen, A.S. and B. Mogensen (2005), *Environmental Shareholder Value – Understanding the Value of Environmental Performance*, Copenhagen: Danish Environmental Protection Agency.

Mitchel, James W. (1992), 'Alternative starting materials for industrial processes', *Proceedings of the National Academy of Sciences*, **29** (February), 821–6.

Müller, K. and A. Sturm (2002), *Standardized Eco-Efficiency Indicators*, Basel, Switzerland: Ellipson Ltd.

Murphy, C.J. (2002), *The Profitable Correlation between Environmental and Financial Performance: A Review of the Research*, Seattle WA: Light Green Advisors, Inc.

Nortel (1996), 'Northern Telecom Environmental Performance Index (EPI)', (www.nortel.com/cool/environ/epi): Northern Telecom.

O'Rourke, Dana, Lloyd Connelly and Catherine P. Koshland (1996), 'Industrial ecology: a critical review', *International Journal of Environment and Pollution*, **6**(2/3), 89–112.

Pauli, Gunter (1997), *The Second Green Revolution*, Tokyo, Japan: United Nations University, Zero Emissions Research Initiative.

Porter, Michael (1986), *Competitive Advantage: Creating and Sustaining Superior Performance*, New York: Free Press.

Porter, M.E. and C. van der Linde (1995), 'Green and competitive: ending the stalemate', *Harvard Business Review*, **73**(5), 120–34.

Portney, P.R. (2003), 'Market-based approaches to environmental policy', *Resources* (Summer), pp. 15–18.

Rappaport, Alfred (1996), *Creating Shareholder Value: The New Standard for Business Performance*, 2nd edn, New York: Free Press.

Reed, Donald J. (1998), *Green Shareholder Value, Hype or Hit – Sustainable Enterprise Perspectives*, Washington DC: World Resources Institute.

Reinhardt, Forest L. (1999), 'Market failure and the environmental policies of firms: economic rationales for "beyond compliance behavior"', *Journal of Industrial Ecology*, **3**(1), 9–21.

Repetto, R. and D. Austin (2001), 'Quantifying the impact of corporate environmental performance on shareholder value', *Environmental Quality Management* (Summer), pp. 33–44.

Robbins, Lorne and Doug Bisset (1994), 'The role of environmental risk management in the credit process', *Journal of Commercial Lending*, **76**(10), 18–25.

Royston, M.G. (1979), *Pollution Prevention Pays*, Oxford: Pergamon Press.

Schaltegger, Stefan and Frank Figge (1997), *Environmental Shareholder Value*, Basel: University of Basel, Center of Economics and Business Administration (WWZ), and Bank Sarisin & Co.

Schaltegger, S. and R. Burritt (2000), *Contemporary Environmental Accounting: Issues, Concepts, and Practice*, Sheffield UK: Greenleaf Publishing Ltd.

Shonnard, David R., Andreas Kicherer and Peter Saling (2003), 'Industrial applications using BASF eco-efficiency analysis', *Environmental Science, and Technology*, **37**, 5340–48.

Smith, Toby M. (1998), *The Myth Of Green Marketing*, Toronto: University of Toronto Press.

Socolow, Robert (1994), 'Six perspectives from industrial ecology', in R. Socolow, C. Andrews, F. Berkhout and V. Thomas (eds), *Industrial Ecology and Global Change*, New York: Cambridge University Press.

Soyka, P.A. and S.J. Feldman (2000), 'Investor attitudes toward the value of corporate environmentalism: new survey findings', *Environmental Quality Management*, **8**(1), 1–10.

Stahel, W. (1986), 'Product life as a variable: the notion of utilization', *Science and Public Policy*, **13**(4), 196–203.

Stahel, W.R. and T. Jackson (1993), 'Optimal utilization and durability: towards a new definition of a service economy', in T. Jackson (ed.), *Clean Production Strategies: Developing Preventive Environmental Management in the Industrial Economy*, Boca Raton, Florida: Lewis Publishers.

Steen, Bengt and Sven-Olof Ryding (1992), *The EPS Enviro-Accounting Method: An Application of Environmental Accounting Principles for Evaluation and Valuation of Environmental Impact on Product Design*, Goteborg: Swedish Environmental Research Institute (IVL).

Tibbs, Hardin B.C. (1992), 'Industrial ecology – an agenda for environmental management', *Pollution Prevention Review*, **2**(2), 167–80.

Todd, Rebecca (1994), 'Zero-loss environmental accounting systems', in B.R. Allenby and D.J. Richards (eds), *The Greening of Industrial Ecosystems*, Washington, DC: National Academy Press.

US EPA (2001), *Enforcement Alert*, Washington DC: United States Environmental Protection Agency, Office of Enforcement and Compliance Assurance, 4.

US President's Council on Sustainable Development (US PCSD) (1995), *Environmental Cost Accounting for Capital Budgeting: A Benchmark Survey of Management Accountants*, Boston, Massachusetts: Environmental Protection Agency, Pollution Prevention Division, Office of Pollution Prevention and Toxics – Tellus Institute.

Vrooman, Wally and Cheryl Beillard (2000), *The Status Of Eco-efficiency and Indicator Development in Canadian Industry – A Report on Industry Perceptions and Practices*, Ottawa: Industry Canada.

Wagner, M. and S. Schaltegger (2003), 'How does sustainability performance relate to business competitiveness?', *Greener Management International*, **44**(Winter), 5–16.

Walley, N. and B. Whitehead (1994), 'It's not easy being green', *Harvard Business Review*, (May–June), pp. 46–52.

WBCSD (World Business Council for Sustainable Development) (1997), *Environmental Performance and Shareholder Value*, Geneva, Switzerland.

WBCSD (World Business Council for Sustainable Development) (1999), *Eco-Efficiency Indicators and Reporting*, Working Group on Ecoefficiency Metrics and Reporting, Geneva, Switzerland.

WCED (World Commission on Environment and Development) (1987), *Our Common Future – The Brundtland Report*: Oxford University Press.

Weiler, Edward, Brian C. Murray, Sheryl J. Kelley and John T. Ganzi (1997), *Report on Environmental Risk Management at Banking Institutions and the Potential Relevance of ISO 14000*, Research Triangle Park, North Carolina: Research Triangle Institute.

Wernick, Iddo, Robert Herman, Shekar Govind and Jesse H. Ausubel (1996), 'Materialization and dematerialization: measures and trends', *Daedalus*, **125**(3), 171–97.

White, A. and M. Kiernan (2004), *Corporate Environmental Governance: A Study into the Influence of Environmental Governance and Financial Performance*, Bristol, UK: Environment Agency.

Winsemius, P. and W. Hahn (1992), 'Environmental option analysis', *Columbia Journal of World Business*, **27**(3–4), 248–66.

Wynne, Brian (1993), 'Uncertainty and environmental learning', in T. Jackson (ed.), *Clean Production Strategies: Developing Preventive Environmental Management in the Industrial Economy*, Boca Raton, Florida: Lewis Publishers.

13. Better financial disclosure protects investors and the environment

Robert Repetto

INTRODUCTION: INCREASING CAPITAL MARKET ATTENTION TO ENVIRONMENTAL ISSUES

Throughout financial markets, attention to environmental issues has increased rapidly over the past two decades (Labatt and White, 2002). Some believe this trend merely reflects underlying fundamentals. Expanding economic output and population have over-stressed environmental quality while rising incomes have strengthened public demands for environmental amenities (Hawken et al., 1999). Inevitably this conflict has raised environmental issues to greater prominence in the business world and will continue to do so. Leaders in many industries already cite them as important management concerns (Schmidheiny and Zorraquin, 1996).

Asset Managers

Among institutional asset managers these trends are reflected in the rapid growth and proliferation of environmentally screened or 'socially responsible' mutual funds and other managed investment portfolios. Such portfolios now hold more than 2.1 trillion dollars in assets (Social Investment Forum, 2003). This growth has been stimulated by the proliferation of defined-contribution plans in which beneficiaries have greater control over asset allocation, which has led money management firms to create and offer at least 175 different screened funds as an investment choice. The demonstration in recent years that such screened portfolios often provide risk-adjusted returns superior or equal to unscreened benchmarks has encouraged investors to allocate at least a portion of their assets to the environmentally screened portfolios (Labatt and White, 2002, pp. 151–4).

Many managers of pension funds and other endowments have evolved a heightened interest in the sustainability of entire communities and economies because of their long-term obligations to beneficiaries and the size and breadth of their asset holdings. A recent report under United

Nations sponsorship by a coalition of funds managing $1.6 trillion in assets asserted that environmental issues are increasingly material to their investment choices and outcomes (United Nations Environmental Program, 2004). This trend has been reinforced by government regulations in many countries requiring fund managers to report publicly on the way that they take environmental and social issues into account in their financial decisions. A by-product has been the growth of new financial research firms such as Trucost, Innovest, SERM and others that analyze the financial implications of companies' environmental exposures.

Broader concerns about sustainability have led managers of large US pension funds such as Calpers and TIAA-CREF to take active interest in corporate governance, including environmental governance. In April 2004 a group of 14 large institutional investors, including eight state treasurers or comptrollers, four union pension fund managers, a foundation president and the New York City comptroller, called on the chairman of the Securities & Exchange Commission (SEC) to issue a clarifying statement that publicly traded corporations must disclose the financial risks that exposure to the climate issue presents to their companies. The Connecticut State Employee's Pension Fund had previously led a coalition of investors in presenting shareholders' resolutions calling on companies to reveal and address the financial risks arising from their greenhouse gas emissions. These resolutions were endorsed by Institutional Shareholder Services, an important source of advice to institutional investors in voting their proxies. The resolutions captured impressive shares of the votes, leading several large electric utilities, including American Electric Power, the Southern Company, TXU, Reliant and Cinergy, to agree to make such disclosures. An Investor Network on Climate Risk has expanded to file 30 more climate-related resolutions in 2004, with the support of a widening group of institutional investors (CERES, 2004).

Insurance Markets

For good reason, environmental issues became embedded earliest and most deeply in property and casualty insurance markets. As early as 1980, the passage of Superfund legislation (CERCLA) in the United States mandating the clean-up of thousands of badly contaminated industrial sites alerted insurers to the possibility that despite policies written to cover only 'sudden and accidental' releases, they could be financially liable for huge clean-up costs on policies that had been written decades ago when such coverage was never anticipated. Despite enormous litigation costs, insurance companies have paid out billions of dollars in such claims. Equally large claims have been upheld related to asbestos liabilities.

As a result, property and casualty insurers as well as commercial banks, the other deeply involved financial institutions, have invested heavily to inform themselves about contamination risks in order to define and limit their liabilities. In response to demands from financial institutions, the Environmental Protection Agency, the Securities and Exchange Commission, the Accounting Standards Board and other oversight bodies have placed heavy emphasis on disclosure and proper recognition of these environmental liabilities. As a result, industrial companies have been forced into much fuller disclosure. Using newly available databases, financial institutions and their consultants now routinely evaluate sites and entire neighborhoods for potential contamination. Such evaluations now are important elements in insurance underwriting, mortgage lending and project finance. Consequently, contamination risks are priced much more efficiently in insurance and other financial markets. New financial products have even been developed to handle such risks. For example, insurance against the discovery of contamination is again available, as is insurance against cost overruns in site remediation. Such insurance is becoming increasingly popular as companies guard themselves against inaccurate reporting of environmental liabilities, which could lead to problems with auditors and regulators, even though insurers have become more demanding in underwriting and limiting their exposures (Katz, 2004).

Another environmental alarm for the property and casualty insurance industry was triggered when Hurricane Andrew hit the Florida Coast in 1992, causing $16 billion in insured losses, a sum almost 50 per cent larger than the premiums collected in Florida over the preceding 20 years. Confronted with a geometrically rising trajectory of insured and total losses from catastrophic natural disasters, the insurance and reinsurance industries came to grips with climate change. They have responded vigorously on several fronts, one of which has been an intensive effort to improve their modeling and estimation of catastrophic risks (Froot, 1999). In addition, the insurance industry, particularly European reinsurance companies such as Munich Re and Swiss Re, has taken an active role advocating government and industrial actions to reduce the risk of natural disasters by curtailing greenhouse gas emissions. Swiss Re has let it be known that it now is prepared to discuss companies' exposures to climate risks in renewing their policies.

Increased Recognition of Environmental Issues by Mainstream Investors

More slowly but with increasing momentum, mainstream securities markets have begun to incorporate environmental factors into considerations of risk and return. Mainstream investors and analysts have become aware that environmental factors are financially relevant through experience, often painful. Investors have suffered severe and abrupt losses when environmental disasters occurred or news of such situations became public. In addition to such notorious calamities as the Exxon Valdez Alaskan oil spill or the Union Carbide toxic release in Bhopal, many other such events have caused investors pain. For example, the stock of Solutia, a company formed when Monsanto spun off its chemical division, plunged by almost 60 per cent within a few weeks when an article in the *Washington Post* revealed that Monsanto had dumped tons of PCBs in a poor community in Anniston, Alabama and had covered up its behavior for decades. The company's behavior was deemed to be 'outrageous' by an Alabama jury that held the company liable for negligence, suppression of truth, and nuisance, opening Solutia to further lawsuits. In another well-known case, the stock of US Liquids, a Houston waste-management firm, fell 58 per cent in one week when employees revealed to government authorities that the company had illegally dumped hazardous wastes and falsified records. Consequently, shareholders filed suit against the company for violation of securities law by issuing false and misleading reports and failing to disclose material information. In the mining sector, the stock of Manhattan Minerals fell 30 per cent in a few days following a referendum in which 93 per cent of the voters in a local referendum voted against the company's proposed gold mining project in Peru for environmental reasons (Repetto, 2004).

Many studies have demonstrated that environmental events can have material financial consequences. Repeatedly, so-called 'event studies' have found that stock prices have been affected, often by substantial amounts, by spills and accidents, announcements of new environmental regulations, initiation or settlement of environmental litigation, and other environmental matters. Thus for example, in the five trading days following the 1986 explosion at Union Carbide's Bhopal, India plant, Union Carbide's common stock price lost approximately $1 billion or 27.9 per cent in value (Blacconiere and Patten, 1994). After the Valdez accident, Exxon's stock was depressed for six months (Jones, Jones et al., 1994), with a value loss ranging from $4.7 billion to $11.3 billion. When Toxic Release Inventory data was first published in 1989 the stock value of TRI-reporting firms dropped by an *average* of $4.1 million (Hamilton, 1995; Konar and Cohen, 1997; Khanna, Quimio et al., 1998). Most environmental event studies to date find a significant negative impact of pollution news on stock prices.

Balancing these negative experiences, investors have found that companies with good environmental performance often outperform others in their industries (Dowell, Hart et al., 2000). Such companies may be more efficient in their use of materials and energy and more technologically advanced, leading to higher operating margins, but are also likely to have better management systems in place. Superior environmental management may signal superior overall management efficiency. A recent study commissioned by Morgan Stanley Dean Witter found that an equity portfolio of companies that were 'best-in-class' on environmental sustainability issues outperformed a comparable portfolio of environmental laggards by a substantial margin (Baue, 2003).

In addition, companies that develop and commercialize solutions to environmental problems have found favor with investors, especially venture capitalists. For example, two highly successful companies in the rapidly growing organic foods sector have been Horizon Dairy, which supplies organic dairy products throughout the United States, in Europe and Japan, and Whole Foods Market, which has achieved a commanding presence as an organic foods retailer. Many other 'solution-oriented' firms have been successfully established and brought to market in the energy sector, including firms dedicated to wind energy and waste-to-energy converters. The pool of venture capital available for such companies has expanded rapidly. Large and successful companies such as General Electric have also greatly expanded their involvements in these industries, recognizing their growth potential.

New Financial Products to Manage Environmental Exposures

Increasing attention from financial institutions has led to innovative financial products with which to allocate environmental risks efficiently. In order to distribute catastrophic risks to broader capital markets, the insurance sector has successfully marketed catastrophe bonds, which have variable returns linked to the occurrence of extreme weather events. Because of their high expected yield and low risk correlation with economic variables, these have found buyers among large portfolio managers.

An even more revolutionary innovation has been the emergence of financial markets on which emission permits can be traded. Beginning in pilot markets in the United States in the 1980s, emission trading emerged nationwide with the passage of the 1990 Clean Air Amendments mandating trading of permits to emit sulfur oxides. The notable success of that initiative in containing costs while accelerating the schedule for reducing pollution has led to the adoption of emission trading as a policy tool in other countries and for other pollutants. Notably, it has become a crucial feature of the Kyoto Protocol on reducing greenhouse gas emissions. An entire industry of brokers, exchanges and market makers has grown up to facilitate emission trading. Emission futures, options, swaps and other derivatives are now regularly traded on the Chicago Board of Trade and over the counter. The accounting profession in Europe has had to decide how valuable emissions permits should be treated on companies' balance sheets.

THE KEY ROLE OF INFORMATION DISCLOSURE

Mandatory Disclosure of Environmental Information

These developments have underscored the key role of informational transparency in bringing financial markets to bear on industry's environmental performance. When environmental risks could be hidden behind a veil of corporate secrecy until unfortunate occurrences revealed their extent, investors incurred significant unforeseen losses. When mandatory reporting and disclosure rules required companies to reveal to the public and to investors the extent of their environmental exposures, financial markets reacted in ways that priced those risks more efficiently and allocated them to willing, rather than unwitting, risk-bearers.

Mandatory disclosure has become a widespread public policy instrument to protect the public and to improve the performance of businesses and government in fields as diverse as food safety, fuel efficiency, management of toxic substances and sales of financial securities (Graham, 2002). Disclosure is a policy tool that appeals to liberals and conservatives alike because it relies on informed public choice rather than direct regulation. Disclosure typically increases market efficiency by eliminating informational asymmetries between sellers and potential buyers. Such asymmetries often distort market prices and sometimes deter market transactions altogether (Akerlof, 1970; Grossman and Stiglitz, 1976). Publicity provides strong incentives for business and government managers to improve performance by eliminating the possibility of shielding inferior or excessively risky products and services behind a veil of secrecy.

Mandatory disclosure has become a more effective policy instrument in recent decades. Citizens and consumers can now use the Internet to diffuse information across the globe within minutes. Moreover, in many industries a company's market value increasingly consists of intangible assets, such as its brands and business reputation. Since strategic alliances, supplier networks, complex chains of financial relationships and other networks have become an increasingly prominent aspect of the business world, impairment of a firm's reputation can be a devastating loss. Reputational losses can also undermine consumers' brand loyalty and make it more difficult for a company to recruit and retain high-quality employees.

In the environmental realm, mandatory disclosure programs have been notably successful as tools to promote environmental protection. In the

United Sates, the EPA's Toxic Release Inventory (TRI) has not only informed the public about potential hazards in their communities, it has also provided a strong stimulus to companies generating toxic substances to reduce the amounts they produce or release (Fung and O'Rourke, 2000). After TRI data was first published and shocked public and investor opinion, prominent companies such as Dupont and Dow Chemicals made voluntary commitments to achieve major reductions, largely through pollution prevention initiatives. In Canada, the National Pollution Release Inventory (NPRI) has had a similar success, prompting many companies to embark on accelerated pollution prevention and reduction programs, especially when also under some regulatory threat (Harrison and Antweiler, 2003). The TRI and NPRI stimulated managers in some companies to quantify emissions on a plant and company-wide basis for the first time. On the principle that 'You manage what you measure', this expanded measurement by itself encouraged better environmental control. In addition, greater transparency discouraged management from pursuing unduly risky environmental policies that might save money in the short-run but would expose the company and the public to excessive potential damages in the longer run.

European countries have typically taken a broader view of corporate social responsibility than has the United States. Consequently, a large number and variety of corporate reporting systems are in place, most of them voluntary. To make such reports more comparable across companies, the Global Reporting Initiative and other programs are attempting to achieve more standardized reporting frameworks. However, since these are not integrated with financial accounting and reporting systems, they have so far been of limited usefulness to investors and financial analysts.

Mandatory Disclosure in Financial Markets

Disclosure of all financially material information is essential for the protection of investors against fraud and for the efficient functioning of financial markets. When the Securities and Exchange Acts of 1933 and 1934 enshrined disclosure as the principal means for regulating financial markets in the United States, Justice Brandeis said, 'Sunlight is the best disinfectant'. Disclosure is the dominant regulatory mechanism underlying the Securities Act to promote capital market efficiency, as emphasized in a recent law review article (Williams, 1999). Williams quotes the House Report on the Securities Act of 1933:

> The idea of a free and open public market is built upon the theory that competing judgements of buyers and sellers as to the fair price of a security brings about

a situation where the market price reflects as nearly as possible a just price. Just as artificial manipulation tends to upset the true function of an open market, so the hiding and secreting of important information obstructs the operation of the markets as indices of real value (Williams, 1999; note 59, p. 1210).

Reinforcing this perspective, a leading scholar of securities law states: 'At its core, the primary policy of the federal securities laws today involves the remediation of information asymmetries' (Seligman, 1995; p. 604). The recent revelations in the United States of accounting irregularities, executive self-dealing, and other corporate scandals dramatically revealed the financial risks of informational asymmetries between insiders and outside investors. These scandals have reduced investor confidence in corporate management and have increased the potential damages to companies and investors when hidden information becomes public.

To ensure sufficient disclosure by companies, the SEC has established a comprehensive set of guidelines and rules governing what companies should report. In addition to rigorous accounting rules for reporting financial results, SEC rules demand disclosure of qualitative non-financial information that is needed lest current financial statements be misleading. These requirements include not only information about current conditions affecting the firm that investors would consider relevant but also any known risks and uncertainties that might have future material financial effects.

In general, in addition to disclosures specifically required, registrants must disclose any material information needed to prevent statements from misleading investors (17CFR.240.10b-5(b) 1998; SEC Release Nos. 33-6130, 34-16224, Sept. 27, 1979; 44FR56924-56925). The SEC and the courts have eschewed any numerical measure of materiality, instead defining it as information that a reasonable investor would be likely to consider important in the context of all the information available. Moreover, SEC guidance states that facts can be considered material if they bear on the ethics of management, its integrity, or its law compliance record, irrespective of the financial sums involved (SEC Staff Accounting Bulletin 99). Omitting to disclose material information is equivalent to making false or misleading statements and is subject to serious penalties. These disclosure requirements explicitly include forward-looking statements.

The emphasis on transparency in financial markets is by no means restricted to the United States, of course, although disclosure requirements are more detailed in the US than in most other major financial markets. The principle that all material information should be promptly disclosed is widespread in countries with developed financial markets, including Canada, Australia and the UK.

Disclosing Environmental Information in Financial Reporting

The requirement that companies disclose to the investment community the material financial implications of their environmental exposures has become increasingly important. Unless financial market valuations of risk and return accurately reflect the financial risks that companies incur through their environmental management decisions, investors will be endangered and an important market incentive for prudent environmental management will be lacking. Rational investments to reduce future environmental costs, liabilities or risks may be undervalued in the capital markets and thus discouraged. Because managers who position their companies to gain competitive advantage by virtue of their superior ability to cope with impending environmental challenges might not be rewarded by investors, such strategies might be discouraged. If external investors cannot accurately value companies' investments in pollution control, managers may have an incentive to inflate stock prices for short-run gain by neglecting such investments. As managers' compensation is more closely tied to stock market performance through stock options and performance-linked bonuses and as financial analysts focus ever more closely on quarter-by-quarter earnings, the temptation to manage earnings through short-sighted strategies has become more powerful. Recently this has been demonstrated most dramatically by such companies as Enron and Worldcom but the temptation to pursue short-sighted environmental practices may be no less strong. The Solutia and US Liquids experiences illustrate the dramatic damages that can be suffered by companies and investors through lack of transparency regarding environmental risks and exposures.

A case has been made by corporate activists and some academics that the SEC should require disclosure of information on environmental performance and other social issues – irrespective of financial materiality (Williams, 1999). The Securities and Exchange Acts were designed to influence corporate governance by increasing management accountability to other stakeholders and the general public as well as to shareholders. Section 14(a) of the Securities Exchange Act empowers the SEC to issue necessary or appropriate rules regulating proxy solicitations 'in the public interest or for the protection of investors' (Exchange Act 14(a), 15U.S.C. 78n (1994)). Similar language pervades the acts. Moreover, the National Environmental Protection Act (NEPA) authorizes all federal agencies, including the SEC, to include environmental protection as a policy objective when not inconsistent with their primary missions.

This case was first put forward in a petition to the SEC by the Natural Resources Defense Council (NRDC) in the early 1970s, shortly after NEPA was enacted, proposing that listed companies should have to report on pollution, environmental practices and the environmental impacts of their products and operations (NRDC v. SEC, 389 F. Supp. 689, 693-94 (DDC 1974)). After lengthy hearings, appeals and reconsiderations, the SEC decided, with judicial concurrence, that it would continue to rely on an economic criterion of materiality in judging environmental disclosure requirements. The SEC determined that, to the extent that environmental issues are economically material, they must be disclosed under existing disclosure requirements. At the time, Harvey Pitt, who later became Chairman of the SEC, argued that much environmental information would be material under a strict definition and would have to be disclosed (Sonde and Pitt, 1971).

In those proceedings, the SEC argued that its enforcement activities would be applied to elicit disclosure of environmental information in specific cases when appropriate on materiality grounds (Williams, 1999). Thus, as far back as the 1970s, the SEC has committed itself to active enforcement of its general and specific disclosure requirements concerning financially material environmental information. That commitment has not yet been fulfilled. Disclosure remains incomplete despite considerable evidence that the materiality of environmental information has increased substantially since the early 1970s. For example:

- Companies have to spend more and more to comply with environmental regulations. Between 1972 and 1994, expenditures by business on pollution abatement and control more than doubled in real terms (Vogan, 1996).
- In the NRDC proceedings, the SEC demonstrated that only a trivial fraction of institutionally managed assets were in socially screened funds or portfolios. By 2003, the asset base had grown to $2.1 trillion. Socially responsible investing can no longer be considered a negligible phenomenon.
- It has been demonstrated repeatedly that companies' stock prices have been influenced by disclosure of information regarding emissions (even if legal) or failure to comply with environmental regulations or potential liability to environmental remediation requirements.
- Several financial research services that sell environmental performance information to investors have emerged. Most large investment houses also employ environmental managers and undertake in-house research on environmental issues affecting companies. The fact that the generation and sale of environmental information has become an economic activity in the investment community indicates that professional investors consider such information relevant to their decisions – and thus financially material.

However, the availability of information on environmental issues has not kept pace with this growing materiality. Many EPA and state government databases, even those theoretically in the public domain, are hard to access, often inaccurate, inconsistent, or out of date, and not formatted in useful ways for financial or company-specific analysis. Moreover, companies' own environmental reports are typically selective, unstandardized, and unrelated to financial statements (Birchard, 1996). Therefore, the information available through stand-alone environmental reports, from government agencies, or from environmental research services is not a substitute for adequate disclosure by companies of financially material environmental information.

Specific Requirements in the United States

Disclosure of environmental exposures is governed both by the SEC's core rules on materiality and by specific requirements regarding environmental liabilities and compliance with federal and state environmental regulations. General disclosure requirements explicitly include forward-looking statements. Item 303 of Regulation S-K requires a Management Discussion and Analysis (MD&A) of 'material events and uncertainties known to management that would cause reported financial information not to be necessarily indicative of future operating results or future financial condition' (17 CFR 229.303). The firm shall disclose 'where a trend, demand, commitment, event or uncertainty is both presently known to management and reasonably likely to have material effects on the registrant's financial condition or results of operations' (SEC Release Nos. 33-6835, 34-26831, May 24, 1989; 54FR22427). Disclosure of known trends, risks and other uncertainties affecting future business results is particularly important to investors because asset markets are themselves inherently forward-looking. The value of any financial security is derived from the stream of returns it is expected to bring and the riskiness of those returns.

The SEC has strengthened these requirements by narrowing a company's ability to avoid disclosure on grounds of uncertainty. In its release on MD&A requirements, the SEC indicated that disclosure of uncertain events is necessary unless the registrant 'determines that a material effect on the registrant's financial condition or results of operations is not reasonably likely to occur' (54FR22427). In the same release, the SEC warned companies that, if a registrant's future filings reveal a material effect from an event that was a known uncertainty in a prior period, the SEC enforcement staff will 'inquire as to circumstances existing at the time of the earlier filings to determine whether the registrant failed to disclose a known . . . uncertainty' (54FR22427, n.28). Moreover, forward-looking disclosure is further encouraged by a 'safe harbor' rule that protects companies from applicable liability provisions of federal securities laws that might otherwise be relevant (SEC Release Nos. 33-6084; 34-15944). Companies cannot be penalized for making 'reasonably based and adequately presented' projections that subsequently fail to materialize.

Disclosure requirements of known uncertainties under Item 303 of Regulation S-K apply to environmental uncertainties. While the SEC has recognized Superfund liabilities as known uncertainties requiring disclosure, the requirements of Item 303 of Regulation S-K could reasonably apply to many other environmental uncertainties:

- Many firms own contaminated industrial sites that have not yet been identified for mandatory remediation, although contamination might well be discovered through future investigation, particularly if the site is transferred to another owner. Ownership of such contaminated sites might be considered a known uncertainty.
- EPA regulations are first issued in proposed forms before final promulgation. Affected industries typically submit extensive comments on proposed regulations through their industry associations or sometimes individual companies submit comments directly. Not infrequently, these submissions complain of financial impacts ranging from serious to dire. Many final regulations are challenged in court, with billions of dollars in compliance costs resting on the judicial outcome. Thus, many proposed environmental regulations are known uncertainties with potentially material financial consequences.
- The Kyoto Protocol to the United Nations Framework Convention on Climate Change is now in force and its possible economic impacts should be considered a known uncertainty, especially for multinational companies. The European Union has developed an emission trading system that will begin operations in 2005, with possible material financial effects on companies operating in or competing with Europe.

In addition to these general requirements, SEC rules and Generally Accepted Accounting Practice (GAAP) impose specific requirements on companies for environmental disclosure. Item 101 of Regulation S-K, governing the general description of the business, states:

> Appropriate disclosure shall be made as to the material effects that compliance with Federal, State, or local provisions which have been enacted or adopted regulating the discharge of materials into the environment may have on the capital expenditures, earnings, and competitive position of the registrant and its subsidiaries. The registrant shall disclose any material capital expenditures for environmental control facilities for the remainder of the current fiscal year and its

succeeding fiscal year and for such future periods as the registrant may deem material [17 C.F.R. 229.101 (c) (xii)].

This requirement evidently covers regulations that have been enacted but not yet adopted because of court challenge. It requires that the registrant apply existing materiality guidelines to financial impacts beyond the one- or two-year expenditure horizon. Many regulations include compliance deadlines several years in the future, such that planned capital expenditures to comply with them are initiated only after considerable time has elapsed.

Item 103 of Regulation S-K, governing disclosure of legal proceedings (civil and criminal suits), requires reporting of 'any material pending legal proceedings, other than ordinary routine litigation incidental to the business, to which the registrant or any of its subsidiaries is a party or of which any of their property is subject' (17 C.F.R. 229.103). Environmentally related proceedings must be disclosed if: they are material; they involve a claim for more than 10 per cent of current assets; or they involve the government and potential monetary sanctions greater than $100 000.

During the 1980s, the discovery of many contaminated industrial sites requiring remediation under the Comprehensive Environmental Response, Compensation and Liability Act (CERCLA) – the 'Superfund' statute – or under the Resource Conservation and Recovery Act (RCRA), and the rapid escalation of clean-up costs, led to an elaboration of disclosure requirements for contingent liabilities. GAAP, as enunciated by the Financial Accounting Standards Board (FASB), requires companies to accrue a contingent liability for future remediation costs if the loss is probable and reasonably estimable (SFAS 5). SEC and FASB guidance added clarification that if a loss is probable, the firm must recognize its best estimate of the loss, despite uncertainty, and cannot wait until only one estimate is likely. New information should be recognized in later disclosures (SEC Staff Accounting Bulletin 92, June 1993; FASB Interpretation 14). Together, these rules impose extensive obligations on corporate management to disclose financially material environmental costs, liabilities and future risks.

A recent interpretative release by the Financial Accounting Standards Board limits companies' ability to delay recognizing and disclosing closure and remediation costs for industrial sites by 'mothballing' them. It requires companies to estimate and disclose such costs as soon as the fair value of the liability can be determined, even though the future date of closure and remediation remains uncertain (Financial Accounting Standards Board, 2005).

Beginning in the 1980s, financial reporting of Superfund liabilities attracted the SEC's enforcement attention, in part because of attention drawn to the issue by public interest groups and shareholders. A 1998 report revealed that Phelps Dodge had estimated clean-up costs at a contaminated site to be 10 to 30 times smaller than had a federal court, and also questioned the company's disclosure of remedial costs at 39 of its other sites (Lewis, 1998). A coalition of public interest groups drew the SEC's attention to the fact that Viacom had stated in a filing that it did not believe its clean-up obligations were financially material even though it had been identified as a Potentially Responsible Party at dozens of Superfund sites, implying a total liability of more than $300 million as against a 1995 total profit of $165 million (Friends of the Earth, 1997).

In addition to accounting guidances and releases mentioned above and a flurry of articles by environmental lawyers, it became known that the EPA was sharing information with the SEC about companies' potential liabilities. Consequently, a few SEC letters of enquiry were sufficient to put companies on notice that improved disclosure of site remediation liabilities was expected. By and large, US corporations have responded. Disclosure of potential Superfund liabilities is by far the most complete and detailed of all environmental information to be found in corporate financial reports. As a result, banks, insurance companies and other financial sector actors can now evaluate such risks more accurately. This experience indicates that a modicum of enforcement attention is sufficient to produce a fairly high degree of compliance with disclosure obligations.

UNREALIZED OPPORTUNITIES TO MAKE USE OF FINANCIAL DISCLOSURE

Inadequate Disclosure of Known Environmental Exposures

Despite this success in stimulating improved disclosure of material site clean-up costs and the constructive results in financial markets, until now there has been little effort to enforce disclosure of other financially material environmental information. In the United States, over the period 1975–2000, the SEC initiated only three administrative proceedings and one civil action over inadequate environmental disclosures. In other countries, the enforcement record is even scantier. Enforcement has not been vigorous in years past because environmental issues were not salient among all the securities regulatory issues facing the regulatory agencies. Moreover, at least in the United States, those agencies have typically been understaffed and under-funded to the extent that they were able to deal with only the most urgent and egregious issues (US General Accountability Office, 2002). In addition, the securities and accounting supervisory bodies have resisted attempts to enlist them in environmental causes, seeing their sole mission as the protection of investors and financial markets.

In the absence of enforcement efforts, corporate compliance with existing disclosure requirements has been scanty. Many companies have not even complied with the letter of the law, failing to reveal environmental legal proceedings or failing to disclose an accurate estimate of their environmental obligations and liabilities. A 1998 study by EPA that found that 74 per cent of the companies subject to environmental legal proceedings that should have been disclosed under SEC rules had failed to do so (US Environmental Protection Agency, 2001). More conscientious companies have typically complied with the letter of the law but have revealed as little as possible. Very few companies have complied with the spirit of existing securities laws that require disclosure of all material information and material risks known to management that would significantly affect the financial conditions or results of the enterprise (Repetto and Austin, 2000). Reports typically discuss in any detail only those regulations that have already been issued in final form and have survived court challenges, while mentioning legal actions in which the reporting companies are involved. If companies mention other pending environmental regulations, legislation, litigation or other issues at all, they usually take refuge in uncertainty, claiming inability to estimate likely or possible financial outcomes, even within a range.

Case Study: the US Pulp and Paper Industry

Recent research has provided strong evidence that US corporations in environmentally sensitive industries have not been adequately disclosing known financially material environmental exposures and risks in their Management Discussion and Analysis, as required by Item 303d of Regulation S-K. The first of these studies examined 13 of the largest publicly listed companies in the US pulp and paper industry, a sector with a wide range of environmental issues, including air and water pollution, toxic releases and land use practices. The study estimated the impacts of known, impending environmental issues on the capital expenditures and future earnings (Repetto and Austin, 2002). It found that those impacts were likely to materially affect the value of stockholder equity, the firms' competitive position within the industry and their financial risks. The study found that these exposures and financial impacts were not disclosed or adequately discussed in the firms' financial reports. The study was unique in that the companies themselves participated in identifying important impending environmental issues affecting the industry and in estimating probable outcomes of those issues.

The methodology of the study involved the following steps:

1. Impending environmental issues affecting companies in the industry were identified and categorized with respect to their potential financial impacts on those companies.
2. For issues deemed to have potentially significant financial impacts, scenarios were developed regarding their evolution and outcomes. For impending regulatory issues, for example, scenarios were developed regarding final regulatory designs.
3. Through consultation with industry and environmental experts, likelihoods were estimated and assigned to each scenario.
4. Each company's exposure to each scenario was assessed through a facility-by-facility investigation of location, product mix, installed technology, input use, emission rates and other relevant parameters.
5. The financial impact of each scenario on each company was estimated by applying estimates of regulatory compliance costs, impacts on input prices, site remediation costs and the ability of firms in the industry to pass along higher costs through output price increases.
6. The likelihoods previously estimated were applied to all scenarios in order to construct a probability distribution of potential financial outcomes for each firm, including the mean impact on the discounted present value of earnings over a 10-year horizon and the variance of discounted future earnings.
7. Those measures of financial impact for each company were normalized by dividing the change in the discounted present value of future earnings by the market value of stockholder equity.
8. The financial statements of companies whose material financial impacts were estimated from known, impending environmental issues were examined to see whether such impacts had been disclosed in the Management Discussion and Analysis (MD&A).

This methodology is particularly revealing of the inadequacy of MD&A disclosure of known, financially material environmental information, because senior representatives of the sample companies participated in identifying environmental issues with potentially significant environmental impacts, through the cooperation of the American Forests and Paper Association's Regulatory Policy Committee. Company representatives also reviewed scenarios for plausibility and provided their estimates of the probabilities that should be assigned to each scenario.

The study found that companies in the industry were differentially exposed to most of the environmental issues. Differences among companies in exposure stemmed from many causes: the location of their facilities, the extent of their present and past pollution releases, the technologies installed in their mills, their energy and fiber sources, and other factors. As a result, the issues impinging on the industry are likely to create competitive advantages and disadvantages that should be discussed as known risk factors.

Overall financial risks across all issues were estimated by weighting each scenario by the likelihood assigned to it by industry representatives and other experts. These probabilities were used to estimate the joint probability of a 'worst case' outcome, in which all the most costly scenarios for a company would come about, and the probability of a 'best case' outcome, in which all the least costly scenarios would come about. Other scenario combinations were used to generate the probabilities of all intermediate outcomes. In this way, probability distributions of financial outcomes were generated for all companies in the study.

A summary of these findings, comparing the financial exposures of all companies in the study, shows material financial risks. The mean values indicate that at least half the companies in the group face expected financial impacts of at least 5 per cent of shareholder equity and that several face expected impacts approaching or exceeding 10 per cent. These magnitudes are impressive because the expected effects of environmental issues on earnings in the pulp and paper segment are being compared to the total market value of the companies, which for many firms includes the value of their other business segments, including wood products and converted paper products. Even relying on the most likely outcomes, estimates show that companies' environmental exposures involve them in significant financial risks.

The estimated variances of financial outcomes tell an even stronger story. Several companies are virtually immune to environmental risk: their earnings will be relatively unaffected, whatever the outcome of the salient impending issues. At the other extreme, other companies face significant probabilities that impending environmental issues will be resolved in ways that will reduce the value of their companies by as much as 15 or 20 per cent. Table 13.1 shows the estimated probabilities from the study that each company's shareholder value will be reduced by 10 per cent or more. Three companies are more likely than not to suffer a 10 per cent loss. In total, 7 of the 13 companies have a greater than 20 per cent chance of experiencing a loss of this magnitude.

The environmental statutes and regulations analyzed in the study would be likely to have quite different financial impacts, individually and collectively, across companies in the same industry and these differential impacts can have material consequences on firms' competitive positions. They should have been disclosed in Management's Discussion and Analysis. However, only three of 13 companies even mentioned in their SEC filings

Table 13.1   *Probability of a reduction in company shareholder value by more than 10 per cent or 5 per cent*

Firm	Expected (mean) impact (percentage of market value)	Variance of expected impact (percentage of market value)	Probability of loss greater than 10% of market value	Probability of loss greater than 5% of market value
A	−10.2	3.6	64	90
B	−0.6	0.5	0	0
C	−3.4	0.8	0	37
D	−2.7	4.4	0	33
E	−6.9	2.8	24	87
F	−10.8	9.3	63	86
G	−8.4	6.1	44	88
H	−0.9	0.8	0	0
I	−6.8	6.9	34	69
J	−4.2	3.4	0	60
K	−10.8	9.1	61	80
L	−6.3	2.4	24	79
M	2.9	3.2	0	0

Source: Repetto and Austin (2002).

any of the issues that were deemed significant by their senior environmental officers.

Some companies, while disclosing little information about the financial impacts of impending regulations, minimized their likely effects on their own competitive positions. For example, according to one company: 'In the opinion of . . . management, environmental protection requirements are not likely to adversely affect the company's competitive industry position since other domestic companies are subject to similar requirements.' Or, according to another company, '[Company X] does not anticipate that compliance with environmental statutes and regulations will have a material effect on its competitive position since its competitors are subject to the same statutes and regulations to a relatively similar degree.' A third company stated: '[S]ince other paper and forest product companies also are subject to environmental laws and regulations, the company does not believe that compliance with such laws and regulations will have a material adverse effect on its competitive positioning.' In view of the differences revealed in Table 13.1, these statements are quite inaccurate and could be considered misleading. According to the results of the study, all three of these companies have above-average financial exposure to pending environmental issues and will probably suffer adverse competitive impacts.

Case Study: the Oil and Gas Producing Industry

A second recent study used a similar methodology to examine the exposures of 16 oil and gas producing companies to policies to reduce greenhouse gas emissions and to potential future restrictions on access to areas holding petroleum resources (Austin and Sauer, 2002). Climate policy scenarios assumed either ratification of the Kyoto Protocol, alternatively with and without US participation, or non-ratification of the Protocol, alternatively with and without other restrictions on the use of carbon fuels. Sub-scenarios explored alternative approaches to implementation, especially with regard to the disposition of 'rents' arising from restrictions on fossil fuel availability.

The results of the analysis are strikingly similar to those found in the pulp and paper study. Companies differed widely in their financial exposures to these environmentally related risks. Exposures varied due to differences among companies in the composition and geographical location of their reserves, their reliance on earnings from exploration and production, vs. earnings from refining and distribution, and other factors. For the most exposed firms, the most likely financial impacts were found to be highly material.

Figure 13.1 plots these impacts for all 16 companies. The central 'dot' for each company represents the probability-weighted mean, or expected, financial impact across all scenarios, expressed as a percentage of share-

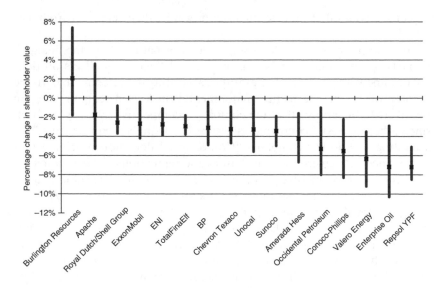

Source: Based on Figure 2 from Austin and Sauer (2002).

Figure 13.1   Oil and gas company exposures

holders' equity in the company. The vertical lines represent the range of outcomes, from worst-case to best-case. For seven companies, expected impacts exceed 5 per cent of shareholder value and for four companies, worst-case impacts approach 10 per cent.

As in the pulp and paper industry, few companies made any reference to these financial exposures in their SEC filings. Only two of the 16 mentioned climate change as a known risk to future operations or financial conditions, indicating that the financial impacts could be substantial. Three others mentioned the issue in their annual reports but did not elaborate on any possible financial implications. The other 11 made no mention of the issues.

Case Study: the Electricity Generating Industry

A more recent study of a third environmentally-sensitive industry, the electric power generating sector, strongly confirmed the findings of these two earlier reports (Repetto and Henderson, 2003). Forty-seven of the largest investor-owned electric utility holding companies in the United States were analyzed to estimate the potential financial impacts of environmental legislation pending in the US Congress.

The methodology followed the same approach used in the two studies described above. It estimated the least-cost option to comply with pending air quality regulations for each of the companies. The least-cost option was defined as the minimized, discounted present value of adopting least-cost controls on all generating units owned by each utility holding company to bring them into compliance. The compliance options include a suite of combustion controls, post-combustion pollution controls and permit trading. Available compliance options and associated costs were tailored to the specific technological characteristics of each generating unit and took into account pollution control equipment already installed. Least-cost combinations of emissions controls and permit trading were derived by minimizing discounted estimated capital and operating costs over a 25-year horizon.

This methodology was used to analyze the following scenarios:

- the financial impacts of a three-pollutant cap and trade bill that imposes stricter future controls on emissions of nitrogen oxides, sulfur oxides and mercury;
- a four-pollutant cap and trade bill that adds restrictions on future emissions of carbon dioxide to the preceding environmental requirements;
- a third hybrid scenario constructed on the assumption that controls on carbon emissions would be announced belatedly, after decisions

to comply with the three-pollutant caps had been finalized, with a later compliance deadline.

These policy scenarios were chosen to resemble proposed legislation submitted to the then current and the previous Congresses but do not exactly replicate these bills' provisions. Under one set of scenarios, financial impacts were estimated under the assumption that permits would initially be grandfathered to utilities in proportion to their historical 1998 emissions, the most likely outcome.

In order to facilitate comparison of environmental exposures among companies, the present value of future compliance costs in constant year 2000 prices, discounted at 8 per cent per year to the year 2000, were benchmarked to each company's revenues in the year 2000. These benchmarks indicate the financial materiality of the companies' environmental exposures to pending environmental issues and allow their exposures to be compared.

The approach did not allow for adjustments by companies in the dispatch of their various generating units in order to achieve compliance, although companies may reduce the hours operated by particular units rather than installing pollution control equipment if the former is the least-cost option. Nor did the calculation allow for the fact that companies may recover some or all of their environmental costs if market or regulatory processes pass through these cost increases to electricity product prices. However, under current securities laws financially material costs of compliance with environmental regulations, such as those estimated through this methodology, must be disclosed in financial statements without netting these costs against possible future cost recovery.

If a three-pollutant cap and trade policy similar to that endorsed by the current US administration and submitted in proposed legislation is adopted, many large US electric utility holding companies will face significant financial impacts. The required cuts in emissions would ensure that utilities would be forced to install expensive internal controls and that permit prices in an allowance trading market would remain high.

Figure 13.2 illustrates the finding that more than half of the 47 major utility holding companies included in the study would face compliance costs with a discounted present value greater than 10 per cent of their total year 2000 revenues. Over a quarter would face costs in excess of 20 per cent of year 2000 revenues. Total revenues include not only revenues from sales of generated electricity, but also revenues from distribution, transmission and unrelated business activities. To put these magnitudes into perspective, operating profits among these companies average only 4 or 5 per cent of operating revenues.

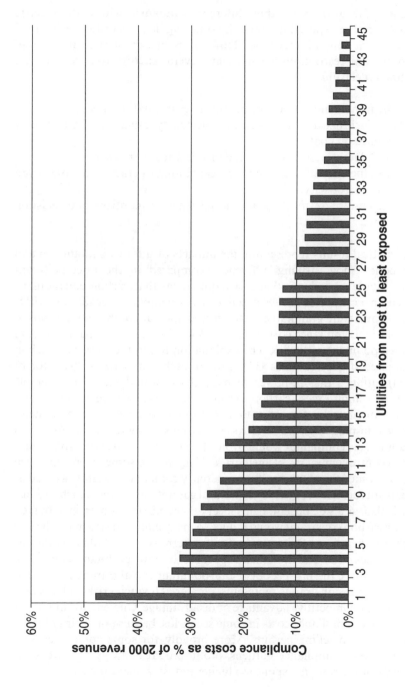

Figure 13.2 Three-pollutant cap and trade, permits grandfathered

Figure 13.2 also shows that different companies within the electric power sector are exposed in markedly differing degrees to future environmental restrictions of this kind. Differences in exposure to impending environmental restrictions stems from several factors that reflect past investment decisions:

- The importance of generating revenues in total revenues;
- The fuel mix used in generating electricity, especially the degree of reliance on coal;
- The effectiveness of emission controls already in place;
- The efficiency of the company's generating operations in converting fuel to electricity;
- The ease of retrofitting additional emission controls onto existing plants.

The analytical results representing the impacts of a four-pollutant cap and trade policy show striking differences compared to the three-pollutant results. Figure 13.3 shows that if a requirement that carbon emissions be reduced 7 per cent below a 1990 baseline, with a compliance deadline of 2015, and if permits were grandfathered to utilities, then under the assumptions of the scenario, compliance costs would be *lower* for many companies than in the three-pollutant scenarios. The explanation lies in the projected carbon permit price. If it is as high as $32 per ton of carbon dioxide ($100 per ton of carbon), utilities that re-power to natural gas would make considerable money by selling excess carbon permits, since re-powering would reduce carbon emissions by far more than necessary to meet the requirement. Moreover, in reducing carbon dioxide emissions by switching plants to run on natural gas, companies would avoid the need to install expensive equipment to control emissions of mercury, sulfur, and (to some extent) nitrogen emissions. Since the natural sulfur or mercury content of natural gas used as power plant fuel is low, switching to natural gas not only reduces carbon emissions, it also, as a side benefit, helps meet other emission constraints. In fact, adding a carbon constraint would induce so many companies to make the fuel switch that the prices of nitrogen and sulfur permits would fall precipitously.

Companies differ greatly in their exposures to a four-pollutant regime. For most companies, the prospect of a four-pollutant cap and trade policy that includes carbon constraints represents a material financial risk and a potential source of competitive advantage or disadvantage. One or two companies face negative compliance costs in some scenarios, because of their potential revenue gains in selling permits. More broadly, for some companies with relatively small compliance burdens, profits would be likely to increase as electricity prices rose in response to higher industry operating costs.

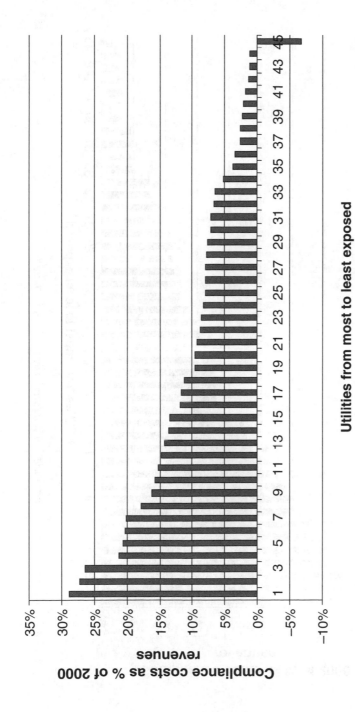

Figure 13.3   Four-pollutant cap and trade, announced carbon, permits grandfathered

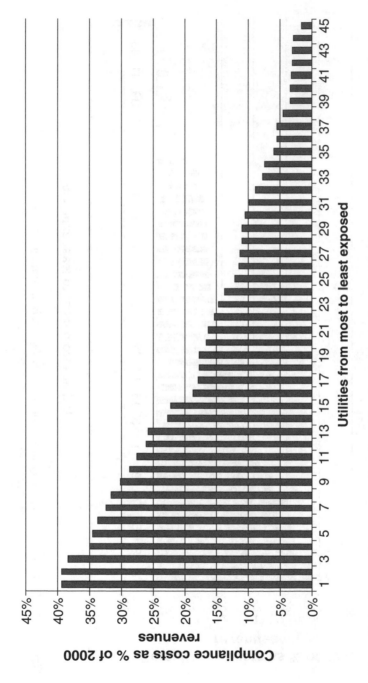

Figure 13.4　Four-pollutant cap and trade, carbon later, permits grandfathered

Figure 13.4 shows that for most companies, the worst of all worlds would be one in which they make least-cost decisions to comply with a three-pollutant cap and trade policy regime but are then faced, a few years later, with a new carbon reduction requirement. The ability to defer carbon control expenditures would not make up for the wasted costs of pollution control equipment for the other three pollutants and the loss of potential revenues from selling excess carbon permits. The costs of dealing with this situation would be higher for most companies than the costs of dealing with an integrated four-pollutant cap and trade regime.

At this point few companies among the 47 large investor-owned electricity-generating companies have disclosed in their financial reports the implications of proposed three-pollutant or four-pollutant cap and trade policies, particularly in any quantitative detail. An exception is the American Electric Power Company, which in response to a shareholders' resolution commissioned a consultant's study similar to that described above for its own generating facilities and has disclosed the results (American Electric Power, 2004). Interestingly, this response shows the complexity of the financial implications of potential air quality restrictions and also shows that AEP, one of the largest US electric utilities, had not carried out such a study internally prior to the shareholder resolution.

Unless companies can determine that the known risks are unlikely to be material or would not be material, they are obliged to provide a Management Discussion and Analysis. Facing potential new air quality regulations, most firms in the electric utility sector would find it difficult to reach the latter conclusion. Nonetheless, there is currently little information in many companies' financial reports regarding these issues. Though some companies have provided fuller disclosure than others, a perusal of SEC filings would be of little help to investors and analysts in understanding the distribution of exposures of electric utility companies to these environmental risks. This situation has prompted the shareholder resolutions directed at electric utilities that were mentioned above and the letter to the SEC demanding clarification of disclosure requirements.

Case Study: the Hard Rock Mining Industry

A third study reviewed past disclosures of financially material environmental information by companies in the North American hard rock mining sector (Repetto, 2004). Its approach took up a promise made years ago by the Securities and Exchange Commission, which said that when a material event occurred that had not been disclosed in earlier filings, the SEC staff would inquire whether the risks of that event had been a known uncertainty in earlier periods that should have been discussed in the MD&A. The SEC has rarely, if ever, done so. However, in this research ten recent environmentally-related events were identified that had highly material consequences for investors in the companies involved, including bankruptcies for several companies. The events also had severe environmental consequences, such as toxic spills or the abandonment of badly contaminated mine sites.

In all ten of these cases, the study found that the companies did know of the risks well before the events occurred. However, in nine of the ten cases, the companies made inadequate disclosures of those risks, if any. In most instances, in the financial reports, particularly the Management Discussion and Analysis section in which such disclosures are required, no mention at all was made of those known uncertainties. Three of the most egregious instances are briefly summarized below:

- After the Hecla Mining Company was ruled to have a 31 per cent liability for natural resource damages and remediation costs at a huge Superfund site in the Coeur d'Alene Basin in Idaho, it disclosed a liability of $18 to $58 million, deeming the lower figure as likely as any other, even though the government had already spent $212 million on remediation and the EPA's Record of Decision called for further remedial action costing an estimated $359 million more in discounted present values and the company's liabilities included natural resource damages over an area of 1500 square miles and over a period of decades into the past and decades into the future.
- For years the Royal Oak Mining Company used a roasting process to refine ore in its Giant gold mine in Canada, which eventually produced 240 000 tons of highly lethal, water-soluble arsenic trioxide wastes that the company blew into underground tunnels and vaults, from whence it began leaching into a major watershed. Though the company had legal liability for remediation, it disclosed no financial liability prior to declaring bankruptcy in 1999, leaving the government with a $200 million clean-up.
- In August 1995 the stock of Cambior, a Canadian mining company, fell 23 per cent over a weekend when a tailings dam failed at its Omai mine in Guyana, sending 4 million cubic meters of cyanide wastes into rivers flowing through the capital city. A Commission of Enquiry found that the company had known of flaws in dam construction that had led to the failure and that the company had filled the reservoir behind the dam to eight times its designed capacity with excessively toxic wastes. Prior to the disaster, the company had not disclosed these problems as a known material risk.

These findings provided further evidence of the inadequacy of environmental disclosures by companies in environmentally sensitive industries.

Growing Shareholder Demand for Environmental Information

Financial markets are now asserting a growing demand for transparency, in part because of these experiences. According to a recent Standard & Poor's Transparency and Disclosure Study (Standard & Poors, 2003), 'Public companies around the world are increasingly under pressure from the ongoing "corporate governance revolution" in which large institutional investors are intensifying the pressure on management to disclose all material information.' A corroborating study by the accounting and consulting firm Ernst and Young found, after a study of share performance in 1000 largest global companies, that poor investor relations was the third most frequent cause of sudden and major drops in share value. Companies that are lax on disclosure are more vulnerable to share price volatility than those that provide qualitatively good information. Moreover, investors have shown that they are willing to pay a premium for companies with superior disclosure records (Investor Relations on the Net, 2002).

The demand for more disclosure extends to environmental information. The initiatives discussed above demonstrate increased concern and activism with regard to environmental risks and particularly climate risks. Electric utilities have been prominent targets (Ball, 2003). However, other industries have also been targeted. In the oil and gas sector, a similar climate resolution submitted to Exxon Mobil captured 20 per cent of the vote. Resolutions have also been directed toward ChevronTexaco, Anadarko, Marathon and other large producers. In Canada, shareholders of Imperial Oil recently submitted a resolution requiring the company to spell out potential financial liabilities associated with its greenhouse gas emissions and to put in place a plan to reduce those liabilities. The Carbon Disclosure Project, an even larger initiative backed by 35 of the world's largest institutional investors, has been urging companies to disclose their greenhouse gas emissions and the risks they pose to the companies, and the extent of their emission reduction programs. The demand for environmental disclosure has been gathering force.

Government Responses

In the United States, in the wake of corporate scandals, new requirements have been adopted in the Sarbanes-Oxley Bill requiring CEOs and CFOs to certify the accuracy and completeness of their financial statements. Section 302 requires certifying officers to certify that financial filings contain no untrue statements or omissions of material facts and that reports fairly present financial results and conditions. Fair presentation includes critical accounting estimates of material environmental liabilities and environmental loss contingencies. Sections 302 and 404 of the Act also require top management to certify their responsibility for maintaining internal control systems to assure accurate financial reporting and to disclose any material weaknesses in those controls. Audit reports must assess these controls and report on material weaknesses as well as provide an opinion on the fair presentation of material information. These certification requirement will elevate compliance with environmental disclosure requirements to top management attention (Rogers, 2005). Other provisions have been adopted requiring more independence of corporate directors from management, requiring corporation lawyers to take action if accounting or reporting irregularities are discovered and not corrected, and requiring separation of auditing and advisory functions. In addition, the Administration and Congress have markedly increased appropriations of funds to strengthen the enforcement capabilities of the SEC, which itself has taken steps to tighten disclosure standards, particularly of off-balance sheet arrangements and contingent liabilities.

In 2002 the US Senate requested the General Accountability Office to investigate the adequacy of environmental disclosure by corporations publicly listed on US securities markets and of the SEC's enforcement of its own requirements (SriMedia, 2003). In 2003 several Democratic Senators introduced the 'Global Climate Security Act', which included a resolution calling on the SEC to clarify that existing regulations require publicly traded companies to inform shareholders of the financial risks that might be incurred on account of greenhouse gas emissions. In addition, the administration and Congress have markedly increased appropriations of funds to strengthen the enforcement capabilities of the Securities and Exchange Commission.

A report made public in 2003 by the Securities and Exchange Commission on their review of financial statements filed by the Fortune 500 largest US companies stated:

> We found that we issued more comments on the MD&A discussions of the Fortune 500 companies than any other topic. Item 303 of Regulation S-K requires . . . [a discussion of] known material events and uncertainties that would cause reported financial information not to be necessarily indicative of future operating results or of future financial conditions. . . . Our comments addressed situations where companies simply recited financial statement information without analysis or presented boilerplate analysis that did not provide any insight into the companies' past performance or business prospects as understood by management.

The SEC review of Fortune 500 company disclosures found specifically that information on environmental exposures and liabilities was frequently deficient (US Securities and Exchange Commission, 2003). The SEC has set up a telephone helpline in the Office of Senior Special Counsel for Disclosure Operations to answer questions about environmental disclosure issues.

The GAO report was released in July 2004. Despite such findings and the testimony and evidence from a large majority of experts consulted in the course of the study that environmental disclosures have been inadequate, the report concluded that too little evidence is available to make that determination. Nonetheless, it recommended closer cooperation and information sharing between the SEC and the EPA (US Government Accountability Office, 2004). So far, neither has the SEC shown much enthusiasm for any more formal cooperation (Inside EPA, 2004), nor has it shown itself sympathetic to shareholder resolutions on environmental disclosure matters, allowing companies to block several such resolutions as relating to ordinary business matters. However, the SEC has implemented a GAO recommendation by beginning to make public its comment letters on company filings and company responses, including comments on environmental disclosures. These materials are available on the commission's 'Edgar' website. Public posting allows analysts and activists to scrutinize what the SEC has noted in companies' financial reports and what it has not, increasing transparency and accountability.

In Europe as well, steps have been taken to improve environmental disclosure. The UK government has required that UK listed companies begin filing in 2005 a new Operating and Financial Review (OFR), similar to the Management Discussion and Analysis in the US system. The OFR must provide management's overview of the company's strategy, performance and prospects and must include information regarding its environmental exposures when material to an understanding of the business. Directors are responsible for appropriate OFR reporting and auditors must provide an opinion whether the OFR has been prepared after 'due and careful enquiry'. The European Commission issued stricter non-binding guidelines in 2001 for disclosure of environmental costs and liabilities, in response to a finding that unreliable and inadequate information about environmental performance 'makes it difficult for investors . . . to form a clear and accurate picture of the impact of environmental factors on a company's performance or to make comparisons between companies.' The recommendation stated that 'environmental issues should be disclosed to the extent that they are material to the financial performance or the financial position of the reporting entity' (European Commission, 2001; Sutherland, 2001).

In addition, many European governments require companies to report on their environmental impacts and also require pension and savings funds to report on the way in which environmental and social concerns enter into their portfolio management decisions. Such requirements now exist in Belgium, France, Germany, Italy, Sweden and the United Kingdom, among others.

In Canada, the Canadian Institute of Chartered Accountants has issued new guidelines on the preparation and content of the Management Discussion and Analysis portion of the financial reports. The guidelines reiterate that the purpose of the MD&A is to enable investors to understand the company's business and prospects through the eyes of management and should state clearly the factors that drive performance as well as the risks that may affect results. These factors and risks may include environmental matters (CICA, 2002).

Despite these steps, further governmental action is needed. If financial markets are to evaluate financial risks arising from companies' environmental exposures accurately and thereby to exert a useful influence on corporate management, fuller disclosures of known environmental exposures and resulting financial risks must be encouraged. Fortunately, relatively small actions can bring substantial results. Corporations are advised by lawyers responsible for protecting the company from legal difficulties, prominent among which would be difficulties with securities regulators. If a government notification or an action taken against a single company signals that new emphasis is being placed on environmental disclosure, those signals reverberate powerfully through corporate boardrooms and executive suites. Therefore, a signal from the SEC that environmental disclosures will be scrutinized more carefully would have substantial effects. This might take the form of a speech by an SEC Commissioner or Enforcement Chief, a Staff Release reinforcing existing disclosure obligations, or a well-publicized enforcement action taken against one or a few companies. The increased budget for enforcement should make such an action feasible.

There are also relatively simple and low-cost initiatives that environmental agencies can take. For example, in October 2001, following release of its study showing inadequate compliance, the US EPA issued an enforcement alert emphasizing the obligation of publicly listed companies to disclose environmental legal proceedings and other material environmental information (US Environmental Protection Agency, 2001). In that document the EPA revealed that it had begun notifying companies subject to certain enforcement actions of their potential duty to disclose and had established informational links to the SEC's enforcement division.

In addition to inter-agency cooperation of this kind, environmental agencies can greatly enhance their role as an information resource to investors and investment analysts, thereby using information as an effective non-regulatory policy instrument. At present, investors and analysts typically do not see the environmental agency as a potentially useful source of information, and most within these groups lack any knowledge of how information from the environmental agency might be accessed. To some extent, analysts' perceptions regarding the paucity of useful information available from environmental agencies has been justified. Many databases maintained by these agencies, though ostensibly public, are difficult to access and analyze. On some, the data can be outdated or of questionable accuracy or formatted in ways that are not useful to investors or analysts. For example, data should be readily aggregated by company but often cannot be. To remedy this situation, the environmental agency could review their publicly available data bases and attempt to make them more accessible and more useful. This effort, of course, would be of benefit to many users, not only to the investment community.

For corporations in environmentally sensitive industries the message is clear. Shareholders are demanding and governments are requiring more transparency regarding the ways in which environmental costs, risks and liabilities are affecting their financial conditions and prospects. There is no reason to believe that these demands will weaken. Well-managed companies will realize that they can benefit from this trend because financial markets clearly reward good corporate governance, and public trust is a valuable business asset.

REFERENCES

Akerlof, G. (1970), 'The market for lemons: qualitative uncertainty and the market mechanism', *Quarterly Journal of Economics*, **84**, 488–500.

American Electric Power (2004), 'An assessment of AEP's actions to mitigate the economic impacts of emissions policies', 31 August, Columbus, Ohio.

Austin, D. and A. Sauer (2002), *Changing Oil: Emerging Environmental Issues and Shareholder Value in the Oil and Gas Industry*, Washington, DC: World Resources Institute.

Ball, J. (2003), 'Global warming is a threat to health of corporations', 16 April, *Wall St. Journal*.

Baue, W. (2003), 'Morgan Stanley study correlates sustainability with financial outperformance', *Social Funds News Alert*, Baltimore: SRI World Group, 5 December.

Birchard, W. (1996), 'Make environment reports relevant', *CFO Magazine*, June, p. 79.

Blacconiere, W.G. and D.M. Patten (1994). 'Environmental disclosures, regulatory costs, and changes in firm value', *Journal of Accounting and Economics*, **18**, 357–77.

Canadian Institute of Chartered Accountants (2002), 'Management's discussion and analysis: guidance on preparation and disclosure', Toronto.

CERES: Coalition for Environmentally Responsible Economies (2004), press release online at www.ceres.org/newsroom/main.htm.

Dowell, G., S. Hart et al. (2000), 'Do corporate global environmental standards create or destroy market value?', *Management Science*, **46**(8), 1059–74.

European Commission (2001), 'Commission recommendation of 30 May, 2001 on the recognition, measurement and disclosure of environmental issues in the annual accounts and annual reports of companies', Document C(2001)1495) (2001/453/EC).

Financial Accounting Standards Board (2005), 'Accounting for conditional asset retirement obligations', Interpretation No. 47, Washington, DC, 30 March.

Friends of the Earth, Citizen Action and Sierra Club (1997), 'Viacom, Inc.: a hidden legacy of hazardous waste', Washington, DC: Friends of the Earth.

Froot, K.A. (ed.) (1999), *The Financing of Catastrophe Risk*, Chicago: University of Chicago Press.

Fung, A. and D. O'Rourke (2000), 'Reinventing environmental regulation from the grassroots up: explaining and expanding the success of the toxic release inventory', *Environmental Management*, **25**, 115–27.

Graham, M. (2002), *Democracy by Disclosure: The Rise of Technopopulism*, Washington, DC: The Brookings Institution.

Grossman, G. and J. Stiglitz (1976), 'Information and competitive price systems', *American Economic Review*, **66**, 246–53.

Hamilton, J.T. (1995), 'Pollution as news: media and stock market reactions to the toxics release inventory data', *Journal of Environmental and Economic Management*, **28**, 98–113.

Harrison, K. and W. Antweiler (2003), 'Incentives for pollution abatement: regulation, regulatory threat, and non-governmental pressures', *Journal of Policy Analysis and Management*, **22**(3), 361–82.

Hawken, P., A.B. Lovins and L.H. Lovins (1999), *Natural Capitalism: The Next Industrial Revolution*, London: Earthscan.

Inside EPA (2004), 'SEC downplays call for pact with EPA to improve disclosure scrutiny', 23 July.

Investor Relations on the Net (2002), 'Going with the flow', at www.irmag.com, 15 October.

Jones, J.D., C.L. Jones et al. (1994), 'Estimating the costs of the Exxon Valdez oil spill', *Research in Law and Economics*, **16**, 109–49.

Katz, D. (2004), 'Turning point for pollution insurance', CFO.com. available at www.cfo.com/article.cfm/3148326?f=related, 9 September.

Khanna, M., W.R.H. Quimio et al. (1998), 'Toxics release information: a policy tool for environmental protection', *Journal of Environmental and Economic Management*, **36**, 243–66.

Konar, S. and M.A. Cohen (1997), 'Information as regulation: the effect of community right to know laws on toxic emissions', *Journal of Environmental and Economic Management*, **32**, 109–24.

Labatt, S. and R.R. White (2002), *Environmental Finance*, New York: John Wiley & Sons.

Lewis, S. (1998), 'The investor's right to know less: a case study of environmental reporting to shareholders by Phelps Dodge, Inc.', The United Steelworkers of America, at www.PhelpsDodgeWatch.org.

Repetto, R. (2004), 'Silence is golden, leaden, and copper: financial disclosure of material environmental information in the hard rock mining sector', online at www.yale.edu/fes/publications.htm.

Repetto, R. and D. Austin (2000), *Coming Clean: Corporate Disclosure of Financially Significant Environmental Risks*, Washington, DC: World Resources Institute.

Repetto, R. and D. Austin (2002), 'Quantifying the financial implications of corporate environmental performance', *Journal of Investing*, **11**, 77–85.

Repetto, R. and J. Henderson (2003), 'The complexities of strategic environmental management in the electric utility sector', *Corporate Environmental Strategy*, **10**, 1–15.

Rogers, G. (2005), *Financial Reporting of Environmental Costs, Liabilities and Risks after Sarbanes-Oxley*, New York: John Wiley & Sons.

Schmidheiny, S. and F.J.L. Zorraquin (1996), *Financing Change: The Financial Community, Eco-Efficiency, and Sustainable Development*, Cambridge, MA: MIT Press.

Seligman, J. (1995), *The Transformation of Wall Street*, Boston, MA: Northeastern University Press.

Social Investment Forum (2003), '2003 report on socially responsible investing trends in the United States', SIF Industry Research Program, at www.socialinvest.org.

Sonde, T. and H. Pitt (1971), 'Utilizing the federal securities laws to "Clear the Air! Clean the Sky! Wash the Wind!"', *Howard Law Journal*, **16**, 832–69.

SriMedia (2003), 'Disclosure of potential environmental liabilities in the wake of Sarbanes-Oxley, *SriMedia, Corporate Governance News*, at www.srimedia.com/artman/publish/article_347.shtml, 18 January.

Standard & Poor's (2003), 'Standard and Poor's transparency and disclosure study for international investors', at www.standardandpoors.com.

Sutherland, D. (2001), 'Europe tightens corporate environmental accounting rules', Brussels: *Environmental News Service*, 5 October.

United Nations Environmental Program (2004), *Who Cares Wins*, Geneva: United Nations Environment Program Financial Initiative.

US Environmental Protection Agency (2001), 'US EPA Notifying Defendants of Securities and Exchange Commission's Environmental Disclosure Requirements', *Enforcement Alert*, **4**(3), at www.epa.gov/oeca/ore/enfalert, October.

US Government Accountability Office (2002), *SEC Operations: Increased Workload Creates Challenges*, Washington, DC: Government Printing Office, March.

US Government Accountability Office (2004), *Environmental Disclosure: SEC Should Explore Ways to Improve Tracking and Transparency of Information*, Washington, DC: Government Printing Office, July.

US Securities and Exchange Commission (2003), 'Summary by the Division of Corporate Finance of Significant Issues addressed in the review of the periodic reports of the Fortune 500 companies'; available at www.sec.gov/divisions/corpfin/fortune500rep.htm, 27 February.

Vogan, C. (1996), 'Pollution abatement and control expenditures, 1972–1994', *Survey of Current Business*, **9**, 48.

Williams, C. (1999), 'The Securities and Exchange Commission and corporate social transparency', *Harvard Law Review*, **112**, 1197–31.

14. The challenge of the 21st century: setting the real bottom line

David T. Suzuki

THE ENVIRONMENTAL MOVEMENT

This year is the 40th anniversary of the publication of a book that for many people – certainly for me – was one of the most influential and important works of the twentieth century. In 1962, Rachel Carson published *Silent Spring*, a book that dealt with pesticides, but could have been equally valid for virtually any modern technology. Carson pointed out that in nature, nothing exists in isolation because everything is connected to everything else. Humans invent powerful technologies and we use them for specific purposes, for example DDT is used to kill insect pests. But because everything is interconnected, there are ramifications throughout the web of life that affect fish, birds and mammals, including human beings. Her book was a global call to action, an eloquent look at the natural world and the impacts that human beings are having on it. Her book galvanized millions of people around the world, including me, into becoming part of the modern environmental movement. Within 10 years the movement had grown to such an extent that the United Nations called the first global environmental conference on the Environment and Development in Stockholm. At Stockholm there were eminent scientists – Paul Ehrlich, Barry Commoner, Barbara Ward, Margaret Mead – who discussed many of the issues that remain familiar to us today: population growth, poverty, species extinction and toxic pollution.

Awareness Grows

In the years that followed Stockholm we had constant reminders of the impact of humanity on the environment – names like Exxon Valdez, Bhopal and Chernobyl punctuated the steady increase in environmental awareness. And after Stockholm we learned of new phenomena that Rachel Carson and the Stockholm delegates didn't know about. We learned of the immense scale of destruction of tropical rainforests around the world, the acceleration of loss of species as a result of human activity, the overfishing of marine resources, ozone depletion when most of us didn't even know there was such a thing as the ozone layer, global warming and, more recently, the very worrying phenomenon of endocrine disruptors that leach out of plastics and affect sexual development.

Environmental concern had grown to such an extent, that by 1988 a man ran for President of the United States and said, 'if you vote for me, I will be an environmental president.' He was George Bush and, after being elected, he revealed how shallow promises are when made during the heat of elections. In 1988 Margaret Thatcher was filmed for television picking up litter in London and saying to the camera, 'I'm a greenie too.' In 1988 Brian Mulroney was re-elected for a second term and, to show his born-again environmentalism, he raised the Minister of the Environment into the inner Cabinet and appointed the biggest star of that election, Lucien Bouchard, to the Ministry of the Environment.

All of that awareness and concern peaked in 1992 at the Earth Summit in Rio de Janeiro. At Rio, the largest number of heads of state in human history assembled to signal a fundamental shift: from that point on, whatever humanity did, the ecological implications would have to be considered. The rallying cry in 1992 was 'sustainable development' and at the Earth Summit, Agenda 21, a massive blueprint to get us onto a sustainable path, was signed by most of the leaders at that conference. They also signed Conventions on Biodiversity and Climate that were to be formally ratified in later years.

As if to punctuate the significance of the Earth Summit in Rio, in 1992 the Canadian government finally admitted what fishermen had been warning of for years – the northern cod off Newfoundland were vanishing. This fishery had attracted Europeans for centuries; before Columbus, boats were fishing off the Grand Banks. The entire culture of the province was built on northern cod, and in 1992 the government admitted that they were commercially extinct and called a moratorium. That moratorium was to last for two years. It's now 10 years later and there's no sign that the cod are coming back. So we see the consequences of an ecological disaster in Newfoundland, the loss of a key species in the waters off that island and, as a result, a 500-year-old way of life is now vanishing in that province.

World Scientists' Warning

In November of 1992 a remarkable document called 'World Scientists' Warning to Humanity' was released. Its list of 1600 signators reads like the All-star Hall of Fame of Scientists, including more than half of all living Nobel Prize winners. The introduction reads:

> Human beings and the natural world are on a collision course. Human activities inflict harsh and often irreversible damage on the environment and on critical resources. If not checked, many of our current practices put at serious risk the future we wish for human society and may so alter the living world that it will be unable to sustain life in the manner that we know. Fundamental changes are urgent if we are to avoid the collision our present course will bring about.

Then they go on to document the areas in which that threat is perceived: the atmosphere, water, oceans, soil, forests, species, population. And then the warning grows even more bleak (and I want to remind you that scientists are a very conservative lot; they don't want to say anything that's going to shake people up, so to have such an eminent group signing such a strong document is quite unusual). They go on:

> No more than one or a few decades remain before the chance to avert the threats we now confront will be lost and the prospects for humanity immeasurably diminished. We the undersigned senior members of the world scientific community hereby warn all of humanity of what lies ahead. A great change in our stewardship of the earth and life on it is required if vast human misery is to be avoided and our global home on this planet is not to be irretrievably mutilated.

And then it goes on to describe what we must do.

Media Response

Now what was even more remarkable about this statement was the response of the global media to it. There was no response. The major television networks in the United States didn't bother to report it. Nor did the CBC or the *Globe and Mail*. Both the *Washington Post* and the *New York Times* rejected it as 'not newsworthy'.

So consider this: half of all Nobel Prize winners among 1600 leading scientists of the world tell us we may have as little as 10 years to avoid an absolute catastrophe and this is judged not newsworthy by the media. Now I want you to reflect on what the media *do* consider newsworthy. Do you remember O.J. Simpson? Princess Diana and the car crash? Monica and Bill? The media were obsessed with these stories – not for days or weeks but months and years, and I guarantee you that future historians will look back and not even register those events. Yet that's what the media are preoccupied with; so when half of all Nobel Prize winners give us a timeframe of 10 years, this isn't even worth reporting. That is truly scary.

Climate Change

In 1997 delegates met in Kyoto in an attempt to take the Convention on Climate and make it into a Protocol that people could sign onto. Nobel Prize winner and MIT physicist, Henry Kendall, said:

> Let there be no doubt about the conclusions of the scientific community. The threat of global warming is very real and action is needed immediately. It is a grave error to believe that we can continue to procrastinate. Scientists do not believe this and no one else should either.

Come ahead now five years after Kyoto – we have the Premier of Alberta telling us that it's too costly to ratify Kyoto. We have the Canadian Manufacturers' and Exporters' Association telling us that 450 000 jobs will be lost if Kyoto is implemented. What Ralph Klein and the CMEA are saying is an insult to the scientific community. Scientists, especially those on the IPCC – the Intergovernmental Panel on Climate Change – painstakingly sifted through tens of thousands of papers on climate and weather and cautiously concluded in 1996 that global warming was indeed happening – this was not a part of a natural cycle – and that the human imprint was discernible as one of the factors influencing it. And every year since then reports that have come out from the IPCC have indicated that the warming trend is even more intense than our models had anticipated. To say that there will be a huge loss of jobs and economic disaster is a display of ignorance, because study after study – including studies done by the federal Department of Finance, the CD Howe Institute (hardly known as a radical environmental organization), and many environmental groups – show that the economic costs of implementing Kyoto will be so minor that they will hardly register. The government's study indicated that 0.7 per cent of the GDP would be the cost of implementing Kyoto in a time when the GDP is expected to rise by 30 per cent. So it's a very tiny component or cost. Indeed, cities like Toronto and Regina in their attempts to save money by reducing energy use have demonstrated that they will be able to do better than a 20 per cent reduction target below 1990 levels, and save millions of dollars while creating hundreds of jobs. So what we're actually seeing – and I've documented this in my latest book *Good News for a Change* – is groups and governments putting the lie to the claim that it's impossible to implement Kyoto.

FROM NAKED APE TO SUPERSPECIES

Throughout human history one of the major survival strategies of our species was to marshal the knowledge we had acquired about our surroundings and to use that knowledge and look ahead – to anticipate opportunities or dangers – and consider what the various options were, then to choose the option that gave the greatest chance of survival. It was a strategy that *worked* because it got us to where we are today. But now, with all of the amplified brain power of computers, telecommunication, scientists and engineers, we no longer seem able to look ahead and choose the best survival option.

What has happened to blind us to and immobilize us with respect to some of the hazards that are so obvious now to the scientific community? One of the problems is that in the past century, humanity has undergone an unprecedented transformation into a new kind of force that has never existed on the planet. There has never been, in the 4 billion years that life has existed on earth, a single species capable of altering the chemical, physical and biological features of the planet on the scale that we are now doing. But because it's happened so suddenly, we haven't come to grips with the fact that we now have to concern ourselves not only with our *individual* effects but with the *collective* impact of all humanity. That requires a very different awareness and way of looking at ourselves.

Population Explosion

Our change to a superspecies has resulted from the sudden conjunction of a number of factors. The first and most obvious of course is population. Humans have been around as a distinct species for perhaps 200 000 years, and if you were to plot population over that time, for 99.9 per cent of that time there were never a billion people on earth. The curve of population growth is virtually flat, rising barely perceptibly over the vast bulk of that time. It's only in the last pencil-width of time that the curve suddenly inflects up. When Jesus Christ was born 2000 years ago, it's estimated there were about 200 million human beings on earth. Then it took almost two millennia to reach the first billion, early in the 19th century. When I was born in 1936 there were just over 2 billion people on earth. In my lifetime the population of the planet has tripled. And if I were to live another 40 years we will probably reach 10 billion people; at least that's what all the projections suggest.

On that curve of 200 000 years, in the last brief period of time, the curve suddenly leaps straight off the page. It took 200 000 years for our species to reach a billion people, yet now we're adding a billion people every 12 to 13 years. We are now the most numerous mammal on the planet. There are more of us than all of the rabbits, rats or mice. But of course we're not like rabbits, rats or mice because – as well as numbers – we have amplified enormously our technological muscle power in the last 100 years.

Technological Revolution

A huge amount of technology is now used on behalf of each of us. The entire history of virtually all of modern technology is encompassed within the last 100 years. Suddenly population is skyrocketing, while technological capacity is escalating even more steeply. And that vastly increases our ecological impact.

Hyper-Consumption

It doesn't end there. It's not just our numbers and technology. Each of us, especially since the end of the Second World War, has been afflicted with an incredible appetite for consumption. There was a time when people thought of themselves as parents first, or as churchgoers, businesspeople or teachers. Today our primary identity is consumer. Certainly that's how the government and business look on us. Our consumptive demand compounds our impact on the planet because everything we consume has to come from the earth. One of the most humiliating statistics I know is that in the last 40 years the average size of the Canadian family has decreased by 50 per cent while in that same period, the size of the average home has doubled. If there are half as many people living in twice as much space, that means each of us has an average of four times as much space per person living in the house. Why do we need all that space? Because we've got so much *stuff* to put in it. The average house being built today has at least one bathroom per person living in the house! We are far beyond consuming in order to survive or enjoy a bit of creature comfort. Our hyper-consumption is being driven not by basic human needs but by a globalized economy for which the entire planet is a potential resource for transnational corporations, while all 6 billion people on earth are a potential market for its products.

A SHATTERED WORLD

Taking all of that together then, we have suddenly become a force as has never existed in the history of life on this planet. But we have a very short memory. Most human beings alive today have been born after 1950. That means most people have lived their entire lives in a period of unprecedented growth. If you look over the entire 200 000-year time span, this period is a blip that suddenly appears very, very late. But because this period of spectacular growth is all we've ever known, we think this is normal, and the way it must continue to be.

So we need a mind shift if we're going to recognize the reality of our impact on the planet. For most of human existence, people understood that we are deeply embedded in the natural world, that we are dependent on nature for everything we need, including life itself. That's what many of our prayers, songs and rituals were all about – to affirm our embeddedness in the natural world, give thanks for the abundance, and recommit ourselves to acting in the proper way to make sure that nature would continue to be as generous as it was in the past.

From Agricultural Villages to Megacities

Today we live in a world that has been shattered and so we no longer see the connectedness and our embeddedness in that world, and that's one of the real challenges we face. The sense of connectedness has been shattered by a number of factors. In the last 100 years, humanity has undergone a spectacular shift in the way that we live. In 1900 the vast majority of human beings in the world lived in rural village communities. We were an agrarian species. There were only 14 cities in 1900 with more than 1 million people. The largest was London with a population of 6.5 million. Tokyo was the 7th largest city with 1.5 million people. Today, there are 400 cities of a million or more. The 10 largest cities all have more than 11 million people. Tokyo is the largest city in the world with 26.5 million people. They went from 1.5 million to 26.5 million people in 100 years! We think that growth is everything and this is all wonderful, but we never think about what has been lost for the sake of that growth. With more than half of all humankind dwelling in a human-created world of big cities, it's easy to believe we're not like any other species. We're different. We're smart. We create our own environments. We don't need nature. When you ask children in cities today, 'when you put the garbage on the curb or when you flush the toilet, where does it go?' they don't know. 'When you turn on the lights or a tap, where does the electricity or water come from?' they don't know. And when you know so little about where these things are coming from or going, then it becomes easy to believe what we're told by business people and politicians: 'those are services brought to you by the economy. The economy provides you with garbage collectors, clean water, and food. The economy is the source of all we need in our lives.'

Of course, such thinking is a delusion. Take a look around you – at work, home or play – everything, starting from the air that you can't see to the concrete, wood, glass, metal, plastic, energy, all comes from the biosphere, the zone of air, water and land in which life exists. And when we're done with it, we send it back into the biosphere as garbage. It's the *earth* that makes it possible for us to live this way. But because we live in this human-created environment, it's easy to think that we're in command and the economy is what provides us with all those wonderful things. We don't want to admit that our biological nature as animals makes us as dependent on the world of nature as any other species.

Info-glut

Our urban habitat has led to a profound schism – a disconnect – that blinds us to what people have known since the beginning of time. Today we celebrate the enormous amount of information that floods over us. In fact, we are overwhelmed with information; information that is so devoid of context, history or explanation that it becomes just a little disconnected factoid. Just think of the news that we get on CBC Radio at 6 o'clock. The half hour of news may carry 20 different items, usually between 15 and 40 seconds long. When the announcer says 'tonight I bring you an in-depth report', he's talking about a 2-minute segment usually so devoid of context or history that you have no idea why it is important. And we don't have anything in that report telling us, if we get caught up in it, what we can do about it. It's just a factoid that comes shooting out at us and, for most of us, it simply ends up as entertainment. It's certainly not serious information because it doesn't empower us to be able to do anything.

Too often what becomes a validation of information is simply the statement: 'I saw it on TV' or 'I read it'. When you get to that state we're in deep trouble, because you can find anything you want out there. You want to believe the earth is flat? There's a website. You want to believe that little green men have landed here, raped women and had kids? Check the website. I always get someone at the end of a global warming discussion saying 'You're full of baloney. I found a website that says we're going into an Ice Age.' You can find anything you want. The critical question is: How do you know what to take seriously and what not to? Most of us can't do that today.

I'm always astounded at how the newspapers – often in the same issue – will come out with a report on flooding in this area, very unusual fires in that place, a bleaching of corals in the oceans, but they are never put together so we might conclude 'Perhaps this has to do with the world getting warmer!' We just look at them all as disconnected bits and pieces.

Scientific Reductionism

We in the scientific community also have to take responsibility for the shattering of the world, because the essence of most of modern biology and medicine is based on the Newtonian revolution which was reductionism. If you look at the universe as a giant clockwork mechanism, or a machine, in principle you can pull it apart and analyze the various components, reducing those components to the smallest possible elements. Once you know everything about those pieces you should be able to fit them back together again like a giant jigsaw puzzle and recreate the universe. That's basically how modern medicine and biology continue to run, on the reductionist notion of focus and isolation.

The problem is that it ignores important factors. You can study something – let's take atomic hydrogen and oxygen – and find all there is to learn about them. But then if you ask a physicist what happens when you combine two atoms of hydrogen with one atom of oxygen to make a molecule of water, or what the properties of water are, you find that they have to admit, 'I'll be damned if I know.' Because when you combine those elements, properties emerge from their combination that cannot be anticipated by the properties of the isolated elements. There are synergistic effects that do not allow you simply to add up their properties.

The other problem with reductionism is when you begin to focus, you lose sight of the context – the rhythms, patterns and cycles – within which that element existed that made it interesting in the first place. By focusing on a part of nature, we can learn a great deal about it, manipulate it, and acquire a tremendous amount of power over that fragment. But when something like that is manipulated in the real world, there are ramifications that cannot be anticipated.

Scientific reductionism has allowed us to see the world in fractured bits and pieces, and we've sold the public on the idea that if we look at enough of these fragments we'll be able to fit them back together and explain everything. Well, we won't be able to for the reasons I've just cited.

The great strength of science is that we're making discoveries all the time. Why? Because we know so little about the world around us. We're very good at description. We can describe changes and we can describe new things. That's what scientists do best. Where we're very poor is in prescriptions. Because our knowledge base is so limited, we're not good at answering 'what should we do to get out of the jam that we've now created?'

THE FALLACY OF MANAGEMENT

In many ways, scientists have sold people on the idea that science is so powerful, it confers tremendous insights that enable us to manage the world around us. There are people who claim to manage forests, foresters who tell us, 'yes, we know enough to carry out proper silvicultural practice.' There are experts who manage soil, who manage water, who manage salmon and halibut, who manage the atmosphere and air. To them I say, 'how can you claim to manage *anything* out in the real world?' If you're going to manage something far simpler – let's say a candy store – what would you have to know in order to manage it forever? At a minimum you would need two things: an inventory of everything in your candy store, and a blueprint showing how everything in your inventory interacts. Once you know that, then in principle you may be able to manage it indefinitely. Well, how much of an inventory do we have of life on the planet? There are about 5000 or 6000 species of bacteria that have been classified. Scientists in Norway once took one teaspoon of soil and analyzed it to find about 4000 species – almost all of them completely new to science. And then they went just a half a kilometre down the road to a different area, took a teaspoon of soil, and found another 4000 species, almost all of them also new to science and different from those they found in the first location!

We don't know anything. How many species of large organisms – ignoring microbial organisms – are there? We have no idea. I've seen estimates ranging between 2 million and 100 million. That's quite a range. There are ways of making estimates. The vast majority of the animal species that we do know, for example, are insects. Insects are by far the most abundant, the most diverse and successful group of organisms on the planet. It's estimated that for every human being on earth there are at least 200 million insects.

Knowing that insects are abundant and their proportion among other species, then you can try to make estimates. A few years ago Terry Erwin of the Smithsonian went to the Amazon rainforest in Peru, put plastic sheets on the forest floor and fired a jet of pesticides into the canopy. Insects rained down and virtually every one had never been seen by a human being before. On that basis he estimated there are some 30 million species. So how many do we know? 1.5 to 1.7 million species. (The reason for the uncertainty is that a lot of species have been captured or collected by different people, then classified and reported in the literature as different species when in fact, they're the same species.) So there are about 1.5 million species that have been identified. When I say 'identified', that just means that someone sitting in a lab has given a name to a dead plant or animal. It doesn't mean we know anything about the organism's life cycle, how many there are, their distribution, how they interact with other species, what they eat, how they reproduce – none of that.

So our current inventory may represent 10–15 per cent of all of the species that exist, and of those species that we do claim to know, we know some kind of biological detail for less than 1 per cent. Given that, it's amazing that anyone would claim to be able to 'manage' something as complex as a forest, or a population of animals like halibut and salmon. We ought to be far more humble about the knowledge that we acquire and the powers that accompany such knowledge. Science has fragmented the world that we see.

A DESTRUCTIVE ECONOMY

But I think the big disconnector, the greatest impediment to dealing seriously with our ecological problems around the world today, is economics, the kind of economics that is currently being globalized around the world. I've had many encounters with politicians and businesspeople who say 'we can't afford to protect the environment if we don't have a strong, growing economy. It's the economy that gives us the money that we need to have a clean environment.' I've never really understood that. It is the biosphere that gives us all we need and that makes an economy possible. The biosphere is fixed and finite. The only legitimate question is how big the economy can grow before it hits limits.

There's something so fundamentally flawed in the economic system that we have bought into, that it is invariably destructive. A few years ago I found that when I was giving talks about the environment, I was spending more and more time talking about economics. But I didn't know anything about economics, so I thought I had better sit in on a course. So I did. About halfway through his first lecture, the instructor put up a slide of the economy. It was filled with arrows going from raw materials to extraction, processing, manufacturing, retail, wholesale and so on. The reason economists like to depict the economy this way is because in principle, if you know all the components of the economy, then by tweaking it here with an incentive or a disincentive there, you manage the economy.

But then I asked: 'In that diagram, where do you put the ozone layer? Where do you put deep underground aquifers of fossil water? Or topsoil or biodiversity?' And his answer was: 'Those are externalities. We're talking about the economy. It's got nothing to do with those things.' The environment wasn't even in the diagram of the economy. So that notion of economics is fundamentally disconnected from the real world.

Nature's Services

There are ways of estimating what it would cost for us to replace what nature's doing for us for nothing. Nature performs all kinds of services that we exploit. For example, I always boast that Vancouver has the best water in the world. Why? Because we get our water from three watersheds surrounded by old-growth rainforests. When it rains, the tree roots and other plant roots, the soil fungi and micro organisms filter that water so that we can drink it. Nature filters the water for us. So you could make an estimate of what that service is worth by estimating the cost if humans had to build a factory to filter the water. What would it cost us if we had to replace all the photosynthesizing organisms and make a plant that produced oxygen and sequestered carbon? I don't think we could do it, but suppose we could. How much would it cost? How much would it cost us to take nitrogen out of the atmosphere and fix it as fertilizer in the soil? How much would it cost to pollinate all of the flowering plants around the world?

Using these kinds of crude estimates of the cost of human substitutes for nature's services, Bob Costanza (1997) and a group of ecological economists estimated that the annual economic value of natural services was about $35 trillion. The annual GDPs of all of the countries in the world add up to $18 trillion. So nature is performing twice as much service for us in economic terms as all of the economies of the world, yet conventional economics renders these services 'externalities'.

A Flawed Indicator

To compound this flaw, we allow economists to invent economic indicators that tell us how healthy our economy is and how well we're doing. The current indicator of choice is the GDP. The GDP measures every currency transaction for goods and services. So anything that results in paying money for something is added to the GDP. To calculate GDP, economists never subtract, only add. It doesn't matter why money is spent; any exchange of money is added to the GDP.

Ralph Nader said many years ago, 'every time there's a car accident and someone dies, the GDP goes up.' Consider Canada's biggest nuclear plant, Darlington, that sits next to the biggest city in Canada, Toronto. Suppose that the unthinkable happens and a Darlington reactor vents a huge jet of radioactive material which floats over Toronto, and thousands of people get radiation sickness and get very ill. Well, economically it's a bonanza. You need doctors, nurses, medicines, and no doubt a few people are going to hire lawyers, and flowers – all of that increases the GDP. And if hundreds of people die of radiation sickness, you need funeral parlours, caskets, gravediggers, limousines – all of that adds to the GDP. And then, if the nuclear plant is ordered to clean up the mess, all that also adds to the GDP. Our politicians turn somersaults to keep the GDP growing, without regard to why it's growing. When the Exxon Valdez oil spill happened, the United States' GDP went up by $2 billion that year because that's what was spent to clean it up.

The Myth of Constant Growth

Many economists think that humans are so clever, inventive and productive, that the economy is built on that productivity and inventiveness. Since
there's no limit to human imagination, they suppose then there's no limit to
economic growth. So the economy can grow forever. Indeed, if it doesn't
grow, that is considered to be catastrophic. We believe not only that steady
growth indefinitely is possible (which it is not), but that it's necessary. But
we live in a finite world. The biosphere can't grow. Yet we have created an
economic system that is predicated on the notion that it must keep growing
indefinitely. As Paul Ehrlich says, 'steady growth forever is the creed of the
cancer cell.' The end result of that kind of thinking in a finite world is
exactly the same as with cancer: death. Nevertheless, economists are hell-
bent on keeping the economy growing at all costs.

Anything growing steadily over time – whether it's the number of books
you write, the amount of air you breathe, water you consume, or garbage
you produce – is called exponential growth. Anything growing exponentially will double in a predictable time. If it's growing at 1 per cent a year,
it'll double in 70 years. At 2 per cent per year, it'll double in 35 years. At 3
per cent, in 23 years. Four percent, in 17.5 years. And so on. Imagine a
system analogous to the earth, namely a test tube full of food for bacteria.
One bacterial cell is placed in it and every minute that cell is going to divide;
that's exponential growth. So at time = 0, at the beginning, you've got 1 cell.
At one minute you've got 2 cells, at 2 minutes you've got 4, at 3 minutes
you've got 8. At 60 minutes the test tube is completely full and there's no
food left. So it's a 60-minute cycle.

When is a test tube only half full? Well of course, the answer is at 59
minutes. Even though the culture has been going for 59 minutes, the test
tube is still only half full. But one more minute and it's filled. So at 58
minutes it's 25 per cent full; at 57 minutes it's 12.5 per cent full; at 55
minutes of a 60-minute cycle it's only 3 per cent full. So if at 55 minutes
one of the bacteria said, 'You know, I think we've got a population
problem', the other bacteria would say, 'What the hell are you talking
about? Ninety-seven per cent of the test tube is empty and we've been
around for 55 minutes.' So if we assume bacteria are no smarter than
people, then at 59 minutes they realize 'Oh my God, we've got a problem!'
What do they do? Well they could do what human beings would do.
Megaprojects. Turn the problem over to genetic engineers or computer
experts. And suppose in less than a minute, those bacterial scientists invent
three test tubes full of food. So they quadruple the amount of food and
space. So they're saved, right? Well, what happens? At 60 minutes the first
test tube's full. At 61 minutes the second is full. And at 62 minutes, all four

are full. By quadrupling the amount of food and space, they have bought two extra minutes.

We live in the biosphere and it can't grow. And every biologist I've talked to believes we are long past the 59th minute. What we are doing now is using up our biological capital – forests, fish, topsoil, atmosphere, water – which rightfully belongs to our children and our grandchildren and all future generations. We're using it up now in order to serve an economy that has to be kept growing. So all of this talk by all of the political parties (except the Greens), and all of the businesspeople who talk about the need for growth, are taking us along a suicidal path for future generations.

A NEW PARADIGM

The turning point for me in trying to make sense of what is happening took place in the late 1970s when I went to Haida Gwaii (the Queen Charlotte Islands) to film the battle over logging. I interviewed loggers and forest executives, politicians and government bureaucrats, and environmentalists. And I interviewed Guujaaw, now the President of the Haida Nation, who was a young artist and carver at that time and had led the fight against logging. I reminded him that his community had more than 80 per cent unemployment and many of the loggers were Haida. So logging was giving jobs to Haida. And the forest workers shop in Haida stores and inject money into the community. 'So', I asked him, 'why are you fighting against the logging?' And he said, 'sure they can come and add some value to our communities and, after the trees are gone, we'll still be here. But when that happens, we won't be Haida anymore, we'll be just like everybody clse.'

Only when I came back to Vancouver and starting reflecting on what he had said, did I realize that he had opened a window on a radically different way of looking at the earth. What he was saying was that the Haida don't end at their skin or their fingertips. To a Haida, being Haida means being connected to the land, the air, the water, the soil, the fish, the trees – all of that is what distinguishes the Haida. Their history, culture and very reason why Haida are on this earth is told to them by their connection with the land. And ever since meeting Guujaaw, I've been privileged to travel and meet many aboriginal people around the world – in Australia, New Zealand, Borneo, Japan, Papua New Guinea, the Kalahari Desert, the Amazon, the Arctic – and everywhere it's the same, even in the most dysfunctional, impoverished, oppressed community. Many of you may have heard of Sheshashit in Labrador where Innu kids are sniffing gasoline. I've been to Sheshashit and I've gone out on the land with elders in the middle of winter. And I can tell you that even though the community has incredible problems, there is a profound sense of connectedness to the land. That's why they've been fighting the NATO low-level flights and gone to jail over many years. The land is what makes the Innu different and it's what defines them.

I realized that the problem is that we've defined the environmental issues the wrong way. We've tended to think that the environment is 'out there' and we've got to regulate the way we interact with it. Well, this is the wrong way to look at it. There is no separation. Aboriginal people refer to the earth as our Mother. They say it gives birth to us, and they're right. We literally are the earth because we are made up of the four sacred elements: earth, air, fire and water. It is impossible to distinguish where we end and where air, water, soil or fire begin. There is no separation. So what we do to earth, we do directly to ourselves. That means that we've got to define the environmental issues and our basic needs in a radically different way.

THE FOUNDATIONS OF SUSTAINABILITY

Some people say that the concept of sustainable development is like a stool that rests on three legs: the economy, environment and society. I totally disagree with that. I think that what we rest on is a three-tiered foundation. The first foundation is defined by the fact that we are animals. And as animals we have an absolute need for clean air, clean water, clean soil that gives us our food, and clean energy that comes from the sun. Biodiversity, the web of living things, cleanses, replenishes and creates the four sacred elements. Our basic needs: earth, air, fire, water and biodiversity, are defined by our animal nature. But we are also social animals and we must deal with social issues. A starving man who comes across an edible plant or animal is not going to first ask, 'Is this on the endangered list?' He's going to kill it and eat it. So if we don't deal with hunger and poverty, then forget the environment. If you live in communities that have chronic high levels of unemployment, then they've got more urgent priorities than protecting the environment. If we live in communities in which there's no equity, justice or security, where there's constant threat of genocide, war or terror – the environment is not an issue.

There are social needs that people have: strong communities with full, meaningful employment – that have equity, justice and security and are free of war, genocide or terror – that is what I define as the second level of the foundation of sustainable development.

And finally, we are spiritual beings, and never was there a time when we needed spirit more than now. We've become carried away with how clever we are and need a huge dollop of humility. We need to know that we are deeply embedded in nature, that we arose out of nature, and when we die we will return to nature. We need to know that there are forces impinging on our lives that lie beyond our understanding or control. And we need sacred places. If we don't have sacred groves, then they just become trees that are ready to be cut down as commodities or resources. We need places that humans come to with great respect. We need to rediscover our place on this planet. That's the challenge of the twenty-first century, to rediscover our place in nature, our relatives who are all the other species that sustain us. The challenge of our time is to find a way to live in balance with the factors that make our lives and economies possible.

REFERENCE

Costanza, Robert et al. (1997), 'The value of the world's ecosystem services and natural capital', *Nature*, **387**, 15 May, 253–60.

15. Is humanity fatally successful?

William E. Rees

A framing premise of this chapter is that the sustainability dilemma is not merely an ecological or technical or economic crisis as is usually assumed, but rather it is a crisis rooted in fundamental human nature. More specifically, it is a crisis of human evolutionary success – indeed, we have reached the point where our success is killing us!

This interpretation is not part of the conventional sustainability debate for a very simple reason. We human beings – for all that we suppose ourselves to be evidence of intelligent life on earth – really fail to understand who we are. We have a very limited understanding of what motivates us, why it is we do certain things that we do. Little wonder that human nature is hardly on the sustainability radar.

At the heart of this problem is the fact that people today rarely think of themselves as biological beings. It comes to mind from time to time if one has heart palpitations or some other illness but, on the whole, we moderns don't like to think of ourselves as biological entities. But indeed we are – we are products of evolution, and our behaviour both as individuals and as society represents a delicate dialectic between self-conscious reasoning and deeper and sometimes darker unconscious urges and predispositions.

The fact is that we humans have a long evolutionary history and many of the traits that we've acquired along the way, traits that were adaptive 50 000 years ago, are with us still. But now some of these once-desirable qualities may threaten humanity's future prospects. That is, some characteristic human qualities and behaviours may well now be maladaptive. I will try to make the case that these ancient traits are such that techno-industrial society *in particular* is inherently unsustainable. The world is ecologically full – but evolution has not provided us with inhibitions against extinguishing other species, against eliminating competing human groups or, indeed, against destroying our earthly habitat(s).

In these circumstances, prospects for building civil society, and maintaining the conditions necessary for civilized existence on earth depend mainly on our capacity to devise mutually beneficial cultural constraints on social behaviour that has become maladaptive on a crowded planet. Of course, if we're going to 'fix' ourselves in this way, we need to know more about ourselves.

The notion that we are not sufficiently conscious of our own nature has been a persistent theme in the literature of many countries. Listen to Anton Chekhov: 'Man will become better only when you make him see what he is like.' (A notebook entry). Or perhaps you prefer WH Auden: 'We are lived by forces we can scarcely understand.' (Auden in Hill, 2003). I believe that coming to understand these forces will give us a chance to take a great evolutionary step forward to the point where sound intelligence incorporated into our cultural 'programming' holds sway over more well-tested, biologically-determined, but increasingly dangerous behavioural patterns.

My second major premise should already be obvious, namely that if humans are the product of evolution, we are also the product of Darwinian natural selection. Uniquely, however, human evolution is as much determined by socio-cultural as by biological factors. This means, of course, that both cultural and biological 'mutations' are subject to natural selection. Everyone recognizes that maladaptive physical mutations will be 'selected out' in an environment for which they are unsuitable. It is less well appreciated that, like biological mutations, ill-suited socio-cultural patterns can also be selected out. To reiterate this central idea, culture now as much determines the human future as biology but, like disadvantageous physical characteristics, unfit cultural traits will be eliminated by evolutionary forces.

We can find support for this assertion in both ancient and more recent history. One of the most interesting cases – one that even makes the popular press from time to time – is the story of Easter Island, a small button of land of about 165 square kilometres (65 square miles) in the South Pacific, 2250 kilometres (1400 miles) from the nearest land mass, another smallish island, Pitcairn. Easter was a verdant subtropical island, heavily forested with at least two very important tree species and many plant and animal species useful to humans. It was first inhabited only around the year 450 or 500 AD when probably no more than two or three canoe-loads of Polynesian explorer-sailors landed on its shores. The new colony took hold and grew over the next 10 centuries into a kind of microcosmic culture. Over that period, the Easter Islanders developed class structure, division of labour, a priesthood and religion, agriculture, science and art, including some of the finest stonework – both fitted stones for buildings and platforms, and carvings – known to preindustrial times. In short, Easter Island society had most of the basic manifestations and characteristics of the much grander and earlier human cultures of Europe, Africa, Asia and even the Americas (Incas and Aztecs), with which most people are more familiar.

The population flourished, growing to around 10 000 (perhaps as few as 7000 or many as 20 000) people by AD 1400–1500. But then something rather mystifying happened. Easter Islanders cut down the last palm tree growing on their isolated rock. Easter Island was a culture entirely dependent on the forest for their buildings, for log rollers to move their massive carvings, and, most important, for the dugout canoes by which they obtained most of their animal protein. Easter Islanders ate porpoises and fish that could be obtained only by active pursuit in boats.

How could this have happened? Whatever were they thinking? Easter Island's population was small enough that everyone must have at least recognized just about everyone else. One could walk around the island in about two days, so presumably everyone was aware that the forest was disappearing and that a crisis was upon them. There was probably much discussion of what might happen if the forest disappeared and maybe even heated political debates about what to do. And yet, for whatever reason, any effort to change the established pattern of resource exploitation, any move toward a conservation plan, clearly failed – in the end the last tree was felled.

When Europeans (the Dutch explorer Roggeveen) discovered Easter Island in AD 1722, the population had fallen to something like 2000 sorry souls. These people were living in rude reed huts and caves – houses had been destroyed, and art and science abandoned. The human dregs of the Easter Island culture that had been thriving just 200 years earlier now survived, in part, on cannibalistic raids on each other's encampments.

The secret of Easter Island's implosion has slowly been revealed by mud core samples taken from the swamps in the interior of the island. Paleobotanists have examined the pollen profile laid down through the island's entire 1500-year post-discovery history. What they learned is that, one by one, the important species of resource plants disappeared. The pollen record suggests that the last specimens of the critical palm tree came down around 1400. Meanwhile, Easter Island's midden heaps tell a similar story. Here we can trace the dietary history of Easter Island society, including the disappearance, one after another, of valuable food species. Most critically, around 1500, fish bones and porpoise bones disappear from the record to be replaced a few years or decades later by human bones.

What could possibly be going on if virtually every member of a society is aware of their society's dependence on limited local resources, of their utter isolation from any other sources of supply, and yet the people do nothing to prevent the destruction of their own prospects. Many articles have been written about Easter Island. British public servant and historian Clive Ponting (1991) was mystified that the Easter Islanders seemed 'unable to devise a system that would allow them to find the right balance with their environment.' Most relevant to the present discussion, Jared Diamond (1995) asks 'Are we about to follow their lead?' Think about it. Virtually everyone on earth is aware that we have an ecological crisis and a population problem, and now there is fear of increasing geopolitical strife. We are utterly dependent on the resources of a tiny planet isolated in space with no hope of finding alternative supplies, and, yet, we too seem unable to devise a system that will allow us to find the right balance with our environment.

Ominously, Easter Island is no exception. Joseph Tainter (author of *The Collapse of Complex Societies*, 1988) has observed that 'what is perhaps most intriguing in the evolution of human societies is the regularity with which the pattern of increasing complexity is interrupted by collapse' (Tainter, 1995). Perhaps, then, ignominious collapse is the *norm* for complex societies.

But, surely, you protest, modern society is different. We know better. Our technological prowess and mastery over nature distinguish us from more primitive cultures. We can avoid crises by reading the warnings, by responding positively to data and analysis. Well, this sounds good – certainly one of our most cherished contemporary beliefs is that we are a science-based culture. But what's the de facto modern record? In a controversial paper reviewing the recent record of human exploitation of natural resources, some of my UBC colleagues (Ludwig et al., 1993) concluded that: 'Although there is a considerable variation in detail, there is remarkable consistency in the history of resource exploitation. Resources are invariably or inevitably overexploited, often to the point of collapse or extinction.'

Another UBC colleague, Daniel Pauly, has conducted path-breaking research on the current state of the world's fisheries. Something like 75 per cent of the world's fish stocks have been overexploited by humans. Pauly has demonstrated that although the FAO-measured fish catches each year remain relatively constant, it's not because we're managing well, but rather because we eliminate one species or one stock and simply move on to another. We are literally 'fishing down the food web', sweeping up the ocean's bounty as we go (Pauly et al., 1998; Pauly and MacLean, 2003). More recently, Myers and Worm (2003) and Christensen et al. (2003) report that only 10 per cent of the original biomass of predatory fish remain in the world's oceans after just 50 years of industrial fishing and that remaining specimens are a fraction of the size of their forebears a few decades ago.

The list goes on. A recent article in the *Globe & Mail* described the threat to certain orchids because of human over-harvesting. In some African countries, orchid tubers are a favoured food, and easier trade has opened up wider markets for these tubers. This situation is fairly typical. When any valuable species – particularly rare ones like these orchids – is exposed to a globalizing marketplace, there will always be people willing to pay top dollar to have it, down to the last remaining specimen. And so we see growing international trade in rare and endangered plants and animals (or their parts). Globalization is a major threat to their survival because humans have little inhibition against destroying non-human species if they profit in the short term from doing so.

To summarize, there is evidence enough in both the historical record and present trends to support the assertion that *H. sapiens* is inherently biased against sustainability *by nature*. This socio-behavioural bias has led to frequent societal collapses in the past and modern society is far from being invulnerable. Indeed, I would argue that unsustainability is an *inevitable* emergent property of the interaction of growth-bound, techno-industrial society and the ecosphere. By this I mean that it doesn't much matter how one reconfigures the system at the margins, it won't make much difference. Industrial society is being propelled to the precipice by certain deep-seated (genetically-based) behavioural tendencies that are actually being reinforced by contemporary values and beliefs.

What can we do about our situation? As I stated at the outset, we should begin by coming to know ourselves better. So, with that in mind, let's look at the bio-behavioural factor first.

On one level, our dilemma is by no means unique to humans. All species have an inherent capacity to expand into all the ecological space available to them. Unless there are other constraints on that expansion – negative feedback of one kind or another – all populations grow to the point that they destroy some critical resource and then they collapse. (This was Reverend Malthus' great insight about humans.)

Figure 15.1 illustrates a famous ecological example involving reindeer. A few of these animals were introduced to islands in the Pribilof chain which had previously not had reindeer populations. The islands were therefore free of reindeer parasites and predators and, in each case (although with rather different temporal profiles), the reindeer populations rose exponentially to a peak which was followed by a more rapid collapse. If we relabelled the 'y' axis 'Human Population' and extended the 'x' axis out a thousand years or so, the graph would effectively trace the history of Easter Island's population. The rise and subsequent collapse of the deer populations is fundamentally no different from the rise and fall of the human populations of Easter Island. Even the 'experimental' circumstances are similar: the invader species (reindeer or human) occupies a new, rich environment with no natural or cultural checks on population growth. In each case, the introduced organism inevitably overwhelms its new habitat, destroying its food sources. Subsequent starvation and disease (and a little cannibalism in the human case) leads to population collapse. The main point is that on a very basic level – having an innate propensity to expand into new habitat – humans are no different from any other species.

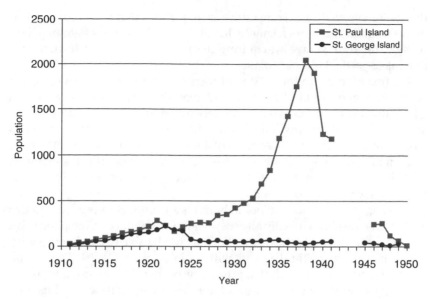

Source: Data provided by Professor Charles Krebs

Figure 15.1   The rise and fall of reindeer population on the Pribilof Islands

On another level, humans differ greatly from other species. One key to understanding this difference was brought to light in the early part of the last century by Ludwig Boltzman, a physicist and one of the fathers of thermodynamic theory. Familiar with Darwinian natural selection, Boltzman recognized the central role played by energy as an evolutionary driver. Boltzman argued that the struggle for life is really a struggle for free energy available to do work. All species have evolved in competition – and cooperation – with each other in ways that tend to maximize their appropriations of the energy and material resources they need to survive and reproduce.[1] By the 1920s, Alfred Lotka, one of the great ecologists of the twentieth century, recognized that successful species (and whole systems) are those that maximize their appropriations of energy from their environment and then secondarily maximize the efficiency with which they convert that energy into offspring. In the case of humans, we use the energy/matter we appropriate from our ecosystems not only to maintain and reproduce ourselves, but also to create and sustain all our so-called economic capital. Humans have both a biological and an industrial metabolism.

The title of this chapter asks whether humans are fatally successful. There can be little question about the 'successful' part and if one accepts that we're engaged in a competitive struggle for energy, it's not hard to derive from the literature a lengthy list of those things about human beings that give us an advantage in acquiring energy. I've boiled these down to four that make particular sense to me.

The first is access to food – don't forget our first source of energy is the basic bio-energy we need to grow and reproduce. Here the advantage is straightforward – humans have uniquely broad or catholic feeding habits. We can eat just about anything. We're omnivorous in the extreme, and this enables us to tap into more sources of bio-energy than virtually any other large mammal of comparable size. Moreover, if we cannot eat something, we'll domesticate an animal that can, and then we will eat the animal or its products such as milk or blood.

This takes us to the second point: humans are uniquely adaptive, and this enables us to exploit virtually all ecosystems and habitats on the planet. We can live in the Arctic or the desert. We may not be able to eat desert plants, but goats will, so we'll take goats with us into the dry-lands. There is no habitat type on planet earth that is not now occupied to some degree (or at least heavily exploited in the case of the sea) by human beings. Since we exploit all major ecosystem types, we have access to the multiple food classes we can digest wherever on earth they occur. Even in pre-agricultural times, this gave humans an advantage far beyond the capacities of any other vertebrate species.

It is interesting that in modern times, many people who are mesmerized by our economic and technological progress see humans as becoming increasingly independent of nature, as moving ever further away from our biological roots. Yet if you look at food sourcing from an ecological perspective, it becomes clear that we have become *increasingly* embedded in the ecosystems that sustain us over time. For example, what is the most ecologically significant marine mammal? The answer is *H. sapiens*. As the dominant macro-consumer species in the marine food web, humans appropriate a larger share of the final products of photosynthesis from the world's oceans than any other marine mammal, probably more than all the others combined. We don't tend to think of ourselves as marine mammals because we don't live *in* the sea like whales or even seals.[2] But in trophic (food web) terms, abetted by increasingly sophisticated fishing technology, we are by far the dominant marine carnivore (see the findings of Myers and Worm, 2003, and Christensen et al., 2003).

The same argument can be made about humanity's place in terrestrial ecosystems. Humans are by far the most ecologically significant herbivore on the plains and grasslands of the world. We are the major exploiter of the productivity of the world's forests. Again, because of our unique capacity to exploit multiple environments and tap into all available sources of energy/matter, no other species comes close to dominating the planet and its eco-processes as do human beings.

However, more important to human success than any of the above is the evolution of intelligence and our acquisition of language, particularly written language. This great leap forward – our third unique quality – made possible the fourth advantage of humans over the competition, the fact that *human knowledge is cumulative*. Not only do we have unique capacities to exploit every nook and cranny of the planet but, because of our ability to communicate within and between generations, we get better and better at doing it. Technological advance piles on technological advance.

Again, it is worth emphasizing that the main ecological effect of technology has not been to disconnect humankind from nature, but rather to extend the scope and the intensity with which we exploit the ecosphere. This is how we have become the dominant consumer organism. The common belief that because of urbanization and technology we have effectively become independent of nature, is one of the great perceptual disconnects of modern times. (As we shall see, it is a fine example of a modern myth.) In reality, we are more *in* nature and as dependent *on* nature as we have ever been.

So far I have emphasized the role of energy in evolutionary success and the special capacities that humans have evolved to acquire it. I want now to underscore the importance of energy by reference to two particularly significant energy-related advances in the human dominance of the earth. The first is the (possibly forced) adoption of agriculture. The estimated average rate of population growth in the 10 000 years since the agricultural revolution has been about 13 times greater than during the previous of 10 000-year period. Agriculture involves a shift from simple hunting-gathering, which had major effects on ecosystems but didn't destroy them, to processes that modify entire landscapes in order to redirect the bio-energy flows from photosynthesis to a single species, namely ourselves. Little wonder there was a 13-fold leap in population growth.

The second great surge in energy availability began only a century and a half ago with the explosive increase in the use of fossil fuels. The significance of this to human 'success' is readily apparent from a look at the human population growth curve over the last two millennia (Figure 15.2). Here we can see a parallel explosion, the fourfold increase in human numbers from about 1.5 billion in 1850 to the present population of over 6 billion, over the same century and a half.

Let's consider the relationship to fossil energy more closely. Figure 15.3 illustrates the displacement of human and animal labour by fossil energy that took place over the century from 1850 to 1950. What it shows is that we are now utterly dependent for most of the work done in our society on a single source of energy. It has truly been said that no resource has changed

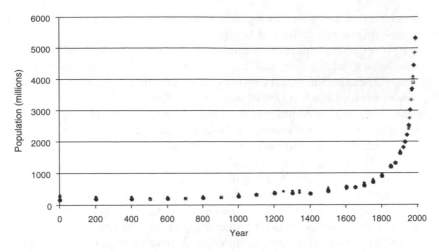

Figure 15.2   Human population growth over the past two millennia

the structure of our economies, the nature of technology, or the balance of geopolitics more than fossil energy. Indeed, the average citizen today in the wealthy industrial countries has between 100 to 200 energy slaves working for him or her. In this sense, each of us is the equivalent of 100 to 200 pre-industrial humans.

Keep in mind that a major human use of energy is to increase our rate of exploitation of everything else. We could not have fished down the seas or deforested the planet without the huge extra-somatic energy 'subsidy' from fossil fuels. It follows that from the perspective of sustainability, human success imposes enormous costs on the rest of the system. The human enterprise is an open, growing subsystem expanding within a materially closed, non-growing ecosphere (Daly, 1992; Rees, 1995). Thus, the extent to which human beings appropriate energy and material from the total flows through ecosystems reduces the quantity of resources available for other consumer species. In short, the growth and maintenance of the human enterprise is necessarily at the expense of biodiversity.

Humans use three main strategies to appropriate the bio-energy that would otherwise be available to other species. The first is simply to displace other species from their natural ecological niches. For example, up to 60 million bison used to migrate annually North and South through the great plains of North America. But humans ploughed under the native prairie and replanted it to wheat, oats, barely, rye, and so on, which we now consume directly or feed to cattle. If one performs an energy accounting of

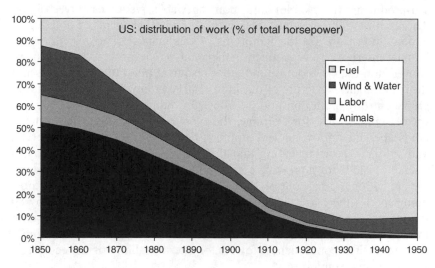

Source: Dewhurst (1955).

Figure 15.3 The fossil fuel subsidy

the former bison habitat and adjusts for the increased production due to artificial fertilizer, irrigation, and so on, the biomass of human beings and domestic livestock currently supported by prairie agriculture is the energetic equivalent of the biomass of the bison and other species (pronghorns, grizzlies, and so on) that once occupied this formerly native grassland. Humans have largely taken over the vertebrate herbivore and carnivore niches of the great plains.

Secondly, we are inclined to eliminate any residual non-human competition. Right now in British Columbia we're debating whether we ought declare open season on wolves – again! Why are we interested in killing wolves? Because they eat *our* deer, moose and caribou (and possibly domestic stock from time to time). We blame wolves for declining wild ungulate numbers in seeming denial that we are often the main predators on these species. If we really want to increase moose populations, we might decide to cut back on hunting licences, but we'd rather blame and eliminate competitors such as wolves. It's also legal for salmon 'farmers' to shoot seals and sea-lions that might steal from their floating salmon net-pens. Finally, humans are unique in that we poison our own food supply with massive applications of pesticides to eliminate insects that would otherwise claim some of our food crops.

The third way in which humans grow at the expense of nature is through sheer over-exploitation – we deplete the earth's finite stocks of both self-producing (renewable) and non-renewable resources. Overfishing, deforestation, falling water-tables, erosion and other forms of soil degradation, and so on, are the symptoms of this malaise. The growth of the human enterprise is very much a thermodynamic process by which we convert non-human biomass and other resources into human biomass and the material infrastructure of our industrial economy at a great increase in global entropy (pollution and disorder). In the process, we destroy other species populations (for example, the North Atlantic cod), deforest the landscape, draw down ancient aquifers, deplete our oil and gas reserves, and so on. It bears repeating that this pattern is an unavoidable consequence of our being a growing component of a finite non-growing system. We are but one species out of 10 to 30 million – we don't really know how many species there are – and not only is our population growing by 80 million per year but, because of our fossil energy subsidy, our per capita impact is also increasing (in effect, we are getting bigger as well as more numerous). The consequences for the long-term stability of the ecosphere are increasingly ominous.

Resource over-exploitation by humans is an ancient story. We now have a fairly good record of the consequences of the spread of human beings over the planet from Africa through Europe, Asia and ultimately Australasia, North America and South America. In every area where the picture is coming into focus, we see that the dispersal of humans over the earth in the last 50 000 years has led to mass extinctions. Large flightless birds, relatively slow-moving, easily-hunted mammals, and other so-called 'low hanging fruit' often disappear completely in the decades or centuries following human invasion of their ecosystems. For example, New Zealand was populated by several endemic species of Moa, large meaty flightless birds that had had no exposure to predators before humans arrived. All were extirpated within a few decades by the ancestors of today's Maori. In short, even in pre-agricultural times, when humans inserted themselves into new habitats and ecosystems, there was a massive shift in the energy and material flows through those systems and in the subsequent distribution of biomass among species, resulting in the extinction of the most vulnerable.

Human displacement of competing species is a variation of what ecologists call the Competitive Exclusion Principle. If there is a limited supply of some critical resource required by two or more species, then species 'a' might abolish species 'b' from the habitat altogether if 'a' is competitively superior. Humans are clearly superior competitors, and bio-energy appropriated by humans from the global total is irreversibly unavailable to competing species – what we get, they don't. Population growth and the massive fossil-energy subsidy has greatly increased the rate of human resource use and expropriation of wildlife habitats and their conversion to production for our use. As a result, the estimated current rate of species extinction (global competitive exclusion) varies from 100 to 10 000 times – the consensus is settling at about 1000 times – higher than in pre-industrial times.

A corollary: if we are interested in conserving non-human life on earth, it might just be that the greatest disaster that could befall the ecosphere is for humans to discover another cheap, super-abundant source of energy to replace fossil fuels. If there's no change in the consumer values and behavioural characteristic of high-income countries – in other words, no change in the ways in which we use energy to exploit nature – then the present pattern of biodiversity loss and ecosystem degradation will continue on an even grander scale. This would spell calamity for the non-human world, whatever short-term good it *might* be for humans.

I have tried to make the case that human beings have an innate propensity to over-exploit their habitats. We are large, warm-blooded social mammals with correspondingly large demands and an inherent tendency to expand. The latter is part of our basic biology but, with the evolution of culture and the cumulative effects of technology, we simply got better and better at doing whatever is necessary to extend our range over the entire earth. I've also made the point in passing that humans have no built-in inhibition against destroying their habitats. It's not hard to imagine why this is so. In pre-culture pre-technology times, humans were simply not capable of destroying whole ecosystems and would simply move on once favoured sites had been hunted out or picked over. In the absence of massive habitat destruction, there was no selection pressure for more moderate behaviour, so modern humans still lack instinctive restraints against doing the massive damage made possible by technology. With the evolution of intelligence and the subsequent rapid development of culture in the last 10 000 years, humans have therefore come to dominate (if not control) the ecosphere, uninhibited by natural constraints.

There is a second factor behind contemporary expansionism that has to do with perception and knowing (epistemology), and their relationship to prevailing cultural values and belief. To understand this factor it helps to recognize that the human brain is fundamentally an 'illusion organ' (Regal, 1990). For example, although we are a visual animal – in other words, our sight is our most important sense – and our vision is our most direct contact with reality, the fact is that what we 'see' (our *perception* of reality) is really a multifaceted yet limited and neurologically altered *model* of the seen object that the brain constructs for our convenience.

Indeed, all perception is a combination of biophysical reality or social construction. If you can accept the argument that you don't 'see' actual physical objects but rather you perceive reconstructed images in the brain, it is no great leap to accept that most of the fundamental beliefs, values and assumptions – the very underpinnings of our culture – are social constructions derived from shared perceptions, experiences and deliberate indoctrination.

A major element in the construction of social belief systems has to do with myth-making, a universal property of human societies which plays a vital role in every culture including our own. Nevertheless, most people today are biased against the concept of myth. We tend to think of myths as fanciful stories or primitive superstitions characteristic of the belief systems of relatively primitive peoples. By contrast, we see ourselves as a science-based, fact-based society that has long since abandoned its need for mythic constructs.

My argument here is that this is, itself, our greatest social myth. The common belief that techno-industrial society generally makes its major decisions based on scientific knowledge, fact and analysis, is simply wrong. We can find myriad examples where factual scientific knowledge has almost no impact on how people think, on popular (group) behaviour, or on the political process. In short, like every culture that has preceded us, we moderns are so embedded in our myths that we don't recognize them as such. Colin Grant, in his book *Myths We Live By* (1998), makes much the same point, that we delude ourselves if we think we are myth-free. He argues the case that even in the modern world, myths play a key role and, therefore, 'Myths should be seen not as mistaken beliefs but as comprehensive visions that give shape and direction to life.'

Like our expansionist tendencies, humanity's myth-making tendency also has a biological basis. The capacity for mass self-delusion, the creation of mutually satisfying stories, was a necessary quality for an intelligent species evolving in a world filled with mysterious and sometimes frightening phenomena. To make sense of their environment, to provide social cohesion and common reference points, human beings created elaborate cultural myths. These became indispensable elements of people's understanding of their place in nature and of their relationships to each other.

For all its positive functions, the human capacity for self delusion does have a perverse side. As Derek Jensen (2000) has argued, there are times such that for us to maintain our way of living, 'we must tell lies to each other and especially to ourselves. These lies act as barriers to truth [and] the barriers are necessary because, without them, many deplorable acts would become impossibilities.' In these circumstances, the power of the myth disallows consideration of contrary evidence, including the best of scientific data.

What I am leading to here is an argument that, first, contemporary global culture is as susceptible to comfortable myths as any other and, second, that today's unwavering commitment to sustained economic growth is the broadest and most widely held cultural mythic story in the history of humankind. In the last 25 years virtually all official international agencies and national governments have come to share a comprehensive vision of global development centred on unlimited economic expansion fuelled by more liberalized trade. At the heart of this vision is a singular belief that has now been raised to primacy in socioeconomic policy circles everywhere: that human welfare, or human well-being, can be all but equated with a single variable: indefinitely rising per capita income (increasing GDP per capita). A corollary to the central myth asserts that, because humans can substitute other factors for natural resources and the life support functions of ecosystems, contemporary species loss and resource depletion is merely of passing interest. As a result, even in already rich countries, we are sacrificing, through globalization, an inordinate array of other values in the name of the growth-inducing properties of economic efficiency and specialization. There is little question that this contemporary myth has been the principal force giving shape and direction to political and civil life in both high income and developing countries on every continent for at least the past quarter century.

There is also little question that this myth has armed the thinking of many against the hard scientific evidence. In fact, today's favoured development model is not even good theory. Sound economic theory recognizes that we ought to maximize human well-being, but also recognizes that many variables and values contribute to this goal. If society wants safe communities, good public education and health care systems, safe cities, and so on, and people are willing to pay taxes (or forego the next increment of income) in exchange for more of these social goods, then well-being would increase despite people's reduced capacity to consume.

With this in mind, consider the argument that globally, with each increase in Gross World Product (GWP), we may well be destroying more value in the form of social and ecological damage than the world is gaining in income. Unfortunately, while we do measure the dollar value of GWP, the damage costs of growth go largely unmonitored because of our inability to measure them (and our lack of interest in doing so). We may well have unwittingly already reached the point in global development where the marginal costs exceed the marginal benefits of further increases in GWP. If so, our modern scientific society is actually guilty of promoting uneconomic growth, growth that impoverishes (Daly, 1999).[3]

Unfortunately the problem is even worse than this because of the grossly inequitable distribution of benefits and costs. The benefits flow mainly to the already rich while the world's poor suffer the largely unaccounted negative consequences. And because this distributional inequity is not generally considered in mainstream economic models – it doesn't show up in the GDP/GWP accounts, for example – it is easy for the beneficiaries to continue perpetuating the growth myth from which they benefit.

Science provides plenty of empirical evidence of other flaws in our prevailing economic myth. Data for most of the world's countries show that once a certain level of income is achieved – about 7500 or 8000 US dollars per capita per year – there's no further positive correlation between various *objective* indicators of population health and income growth. Moreover, in many rich countries today we can find no *subjective* improvement in well-being as incomes increase. Robert Lane's recent book, *The Loss of Happiness in Market Democracies* (2000), actually documents a negative correlation in the United States between rising per capita income and the average numbers of people reporting themselves as happy or very happy in a standardized survey conducted annually over a period of some 50 years. And this American experience is not unique among rich market economies.

In summary, both theory and data reveal a serious disconnect between scientific knowledge and the global growth myth. The popular model represents bad economics to begin with, and the data show it is not achieving its stated goals, yet the delusional power of the myth overwhelms all the contrary evidence to keep us on our present destructive path.

There is yet another problem. The economic models we use to run the planet are structurally incompatible with any complex real world system. Most importantly, neo-liberal models do not incorporate any information about actual ecosystem structure or function. Economist Paul Christensen (1991) is more specific, arguing that economic theory lacks any representation of the time and space-dependent behaviours of real-word ecosystems. Accordingly, the simple reversible mechanistic behaviour of many economic models is inconsistent with the connectivity, irreversibility and complex feedback mechanisms characteristic of ecosystems.

These conceptual flaws imply that the world is currently relying on economic management models whose behaviour is inconsistent at virtually every level with the behaviour of the systems we are trying to control. Of course, our mythic model *is* working at one very basic level – Gross World Product, the mesmerizing single variable on which we've focused is, indeed, growing. The economy has increased 40-fold in the last 150 years, threefold in the last 23 years or so, and we anticipate an additional fivefold expansion of Gross World Output in the next half century. Meanwhile, the population has increased by 30 per cent since 1980, and is still growing at 80 million per year. We expect three billion additions to the human family by the middle of this century.

Little wonder that humanity becomes ever more dominant – half the world's forests have been logged, half the land on earth has been modified for human use, 70 per cent of the fish stocks are in jeopardy, carbon dioxide levels are up by 30 per cent in the past century, and biodiversity loss is accelerating. These are remarkably massive impacts considering they are caused by a species whose mental constructs consider it to be essentially decoupled from 'the environment' and unaffected by the consequences of ecological change. This is no minor cognitive lapse. Once we've separated ourselves mentally from 'the other', then it doesn't much matter to us what happens to the other. But if the separation is only myth (and the empirical data shows that the human enterprise is a fully embedded subsystem of the ecosphere) then what happens to 'the other' becomes absolutely critical to our own future survival.

I want now to examine our predicament using a tool I invented some years ago called 'ecological footprint analysis' (EFA). I devised EFA explicitly to counter the argument that, because of trade and technology, the concept of carrying capacity is irrelevant to modern humans (Rees, 2001; 2002a). EFA estimates the proportion of the earth's surface dedicated to supporting any defined human population. Thus, the ecological footprint of a specified population is *the area of land and water ecosystems required in continuous production to produce the resources that the population consumes and to assimilate the wastes that the population produces, wherever on earth the relevant land and water is located.* We can now estimate the ecological footprint of any human population for which data is available – an individual, a city, a country or the whole human family. The method is fairly conservative and is more likely to under-estimate than over-estimate the human 'load' on the planet (Wackernagel and Rees, 1996).

EFA is now widely used in studies to assess sustainability by, for example, comparing the eco-footprint of a study population against the area of its productive domestic territory. Most recently, the International Union for the Conservation of Nature (the World Wide Fund for Nature), which publishes a biannual report called 'The Living Planet Report', has begun to apply eco-footprint analysis in its assessments of the state of the planet. Figure 15.4 presents WWF's plot of the increase in the human ecological footprint over the past 40 years or so. Compare this with Figure 15.5 which shows the steady decline in the WWF's own Living Planet Index, a measure of species diversity and biomass. This data supports my earlier assertion that the steady increase in human appropriations from the ecosphere (the growing human eco-footprint) is driving the steady decline in non-human biodiversity. The WWF's and other eco-footprint studies suggest that humanity has already overshot the long-term carrying capacity of the earth.

Eco-footprint studies raise a new concern about the nature of sustainability. People are no longer merely displacing other species from their

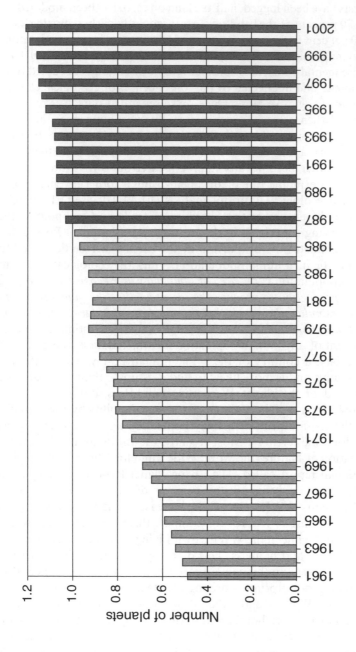

Figure 15.4 World ecological footprint (1961–2001)

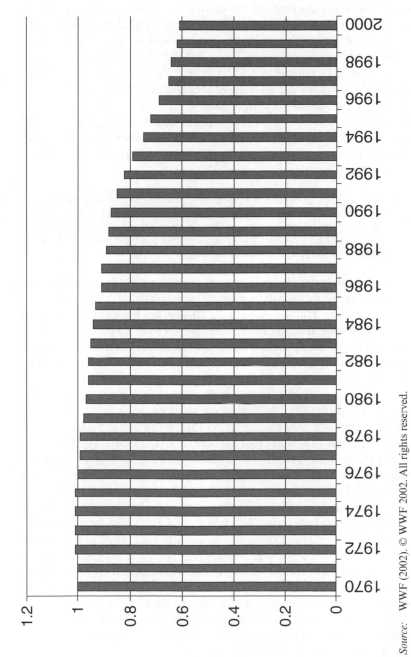

Figure 15.5   Living planet index, 1970–2000

409

habitats; it can be argued that unnecessary consumption by the already rich is already beginning inadvertently to deny other humans the basic requirements for survival (Rees and Westra, 2003). If critical resources (water, petroleum, arable land) become even scarcer, will we extend competitive exclusion to other human groups *with intent*? We may soon have to confront an unprecedented moral and ethical crisis brought on by blind subscription to the global growth myth on a finite planet characterized by an increasing population and a declining resource base.

Certainly, world events in the recent past suggest we may well be entering an era of increasing geopolitical instability, of resource wars that pit the rich against the poor. There should be no surprise here. Political scientist Ted Gurr (1985), found as far back as 1985 that:

> So long as ecological decline is temporary, advantaged groups are likely to accept policies of relief and redistribution as the price of order and the resumption of growth. But once we accept decline as a persistent condition, people will do almost anything to regain their economic and political power and thereby maintain their absolute and relative advantages.

Such overt dominance behaviour may seem abominable to the educated mind. However, as previously suggested, it is arguably a natural human response to scarcity. Human individuals and groups have always competed with each other for the dominance and power that ensure survival in a resource crisis, for example. Such aggressive behaviours are apparently primarily rooted in the limbic system, the older parts of the human brain in evolutionary terms. (Obviously it served our mammalian forebears well.) The more recently-evolved, unique components of the brain – the thinking part, the imaginative part, the creative components such as the neocortex – were added later as a kind of overlay on top of the older mammalian and so-called 'reptilian' brainstem that are central to the limbic system.

All human reasoning, emotions and behaviour result from an exquisitely complicated interplay of influences from all parts of our brain/nervous system and body, but it could be argued that when push comes to shove, the more primitive basic emotions and behaviours tend often to trump the higher rational/contemplative functions. Certainly the innate behavioural repertoire pertaining to dominance and aggression seem to hold sway in the political arena. Politics is all about status, prestige and power which goes a long way toward explaining why the political system seems incapable of responding to real data if necessary actions would challenge vested interests or jeopardize the power or position of the decision-maker. In short, politics is not primarily a rational thinking system oriented to determining the best way to serve the public good. It is mainly an instinctive/emotive system responding to – well, political pressures. Politicians tend to act in ways that enable them to maintain their positions of power and influence within their own group and, if necessary, to ensure that their group (corporation, tribe, nation) is able to assert control and dominance over other groups and communities.

Now, let's try to tie the above to ecological footprint analyses. It turns out that the average eco-footprints of residents of high income countries vary between 4 and 10 hectares (10 and 22 acres). We can then show by simple multiplication that many densely populated, high income countries today effectively 'occupy' more productive land outside their own boundaries than is contained within them. The basis for resource competition and future conflict is thus revealed.

Let me illustrate. I was at a meeting in Europe not long ago where an economist described the miraculous efficiency of Dutch agriculture and held it up as an example for the developing world to follow. The Netherlands is Europe's most densely populated country, with about 450 people per square kilometre, and yet the country has an agricultural surplus. What the economist really should have said is that the monetary value of Dutch agricultural exports exceeds the trade value of Dutch imports. The counter-fact is that the Dutch need to import fodder for their domestic livestock and this fodder is grown on an area several times larger than the productive land base of the country. Dutch 'agriculture' converts that fodder into high value-added cheeses, meats and other processed goods for export. So Holland may have a dollar trade surplus in food products, but even when trade-corrected (exported food is not part of the domestic eco-footprint), this economic surplus turns out to be supported by a massive ecological deficit. In other words, the ecological footprint of Dutch agriculture occurs largely outside the country. And it's not just the agricultural sector. Total consumption of all goods and services by the Dutch increases the nation's overall demand to six times the domestic land base of the country. Clearly not all countries can follow *this* model!

What eco-footprinting shows is that, in ecological terms, the Dutch don't live in Holland. Similarly, urban dwellers don't 'live' in their cities; urbanization simply separates us from the productive ecosystems that sustain us but lie far beyond the urban boundary. An apt analogy is 'the city as human feedlot'. Like the city, a livestock feedlot is an area with an extraordinarily high density of consumer animals and a corresponding major waste management problem. Cities and feedlots are incomplete ecosystems – the productive land component is some distance away. Incidentally, Holland is both a human and a livestock feedlot where the biggest waste management problem is animal manure!

Figure 15.6 provides a multinational comparison of ecological footprints (1999 data from WWF, 2002). Note how ecological inequity parallels the pattern of economic inequity among nations. In the poorest countries in the

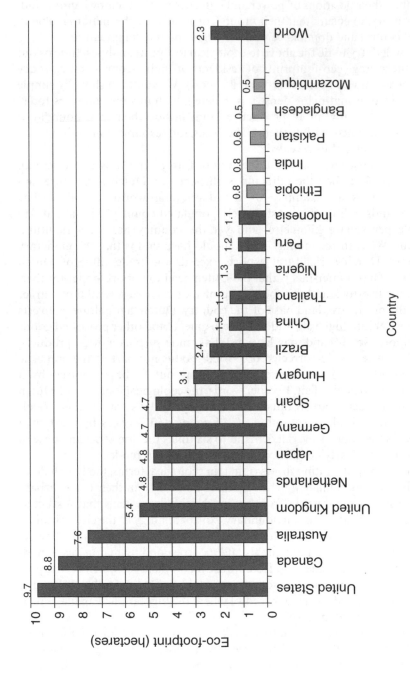

Figure 15.6   Equivalence-adjusted per capita ecological footprints of selected countries

developing world – Ethiopia, India, Pakistan, Bangladesh and Mozambique, for example – people have eco-footprints as little as half a hectare per capita, or one twentieth of the average North American eco-footprint.

In 1999 the global average person required the bioproductivity of almost 2.3 hectares of land and water ecosystems to produce everything he/she consumed and to assimilate/recycle selected wastes. The difficulty is that there were only about 1.9 hectares of productive land- and water-scape per capita on the planet. Multiplying the then human population of 6 billion by the average human footprint gives a global ecological footprint in excess of 13.7 billion hectares, but there are only about 11.4 billion hectares of productive ecosystem on earth. It seems that we actually exceed long-term global human carrying capacity by about 20 per cent (see Figure 15.7).

To recap, high-end consumers 'occupy' ecologically up to 10 hectares each, but there are only 1.9 hectares of productive land per capita on the planet. Arguably the two hectares represents our 'fair earth-share' (Rees, 1996). Where do we get the rest? We get it through so-called trade liberalization. In ecological terms, we can interpret globalization as the socio-cultural process by which wealthy and powerful people and nations extend their ever-expanding eco-footprints into the 'surplus' lands of weaker relatively impoverished countries through trade and into the global commons. In effect, the dominant powers now achieve globally through commerce what used to require territorial occupation.

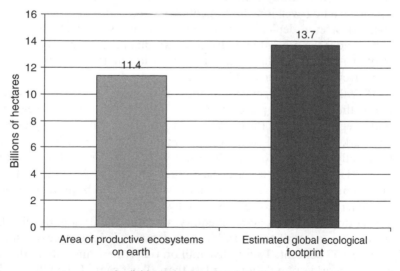

Figure 15.7   Global carrying capacity

Such findings merely confirm a major stated benefit of globalization from the perspective of wealthy consumers – access to cheap resources and commodities from the developing world. However, the dramatic graphics of eco-footprinting sometimes stir political sensitivities. Several years ago the Department of Environment in Britain commissioned the International Institute for Environment and Development to undertake an ecological footprint of Britain (IIED, 1995). Among other things, the IIED study examined significant trade flows and converted them into the area of land in other countries dedicated to sustaining the British population's consumer lifestyle. Almost as soon as it appeared, the study was removed from circulation, apparently because of political uneasiness associated with highlighting the extent to which Britain relies on the rest of the world for critical resources.

To get some measure of that dependence, consider the following: one section of the IIED document showed that to sustain consumption by Londoners alone required an area of bio-productive land equivalent to the entire land-base of the United Kingdom. In other words, were Britain forced to rely on its own bioproductivity – assuming we could convert forest to agriculture and vice versa in the proportions needed – it could barely sustain the population of London at 1995 levels of material consumption. This means, in effect, that most of the UK population is living on carrying capacity imported from other countries and the global commons.

The eco-footprint results for the Netherlands and the UK cited above underscore how, as always, money wealth confers the power to live high on the ecological hog even long after a country's domestic land-base has been over-taxed or even depleted. In these circumstances, it seems fair to ask whether under the present globalization paradigm the poor can claim *any* part of the hog. Or is the competitive exclusion of the poor by the rich already irreversibly underway?

In 1970 the richest 10 per cent of the world's citizens earned 19 times as much as the poorest 10 per cent. After a quarter century of accelerated global integration under the expansionist paradigm, with its emphasis on wider markets, trade and efficiency to stimulate growth in GWP, this ratio had actually increased to 27:1. In other words the very rich are getting rapidly relatively richer leaving the poor even further behind. In many African countries, people are actually worse off in both relative *and* absolute terms. GDP per capita is actually falling.

The bottom line is that global inequity is steadily increasing. By 1977 the wealthiest 1 per cent of the world's people commanded the same income as the poorest 57 per cent. Twenty-five million rich Americans – that's 0.4 per cent of the world's population and less than 10 per cent of the US population – had a combined income greater than the poorest 2 billion people, or 43 per cent of the world's population (UNDP, 2001).

Consider this in the context of international trade and eco-footprint analysis. The United States with less than 5 per cent of the world's population consumes a vastly disproportionate share of the world's resources, including 25 per cent of the world's energy, most of which is imported. The United States may be the world's mightiest military power and most powerful economy, but the country would be paralysed were it not able to extend its eco-footprint into the rest of the world. The same is true of many other densely-populated high-income countries.

This brings us full circle. What is the future for geopolitics if the global development scenario is characterized by growing demand, accelerating eco-degradation, resource scarcities and rapid climate change? Will we on this small blue earth island descend like the Easter Islanders from civilization's peak into the valley of chaos, of tribal factions driven by sheer survival instinct and warring over the last remaining pockets of viable land and resources; or will reason prevail so that we, all members of the human family together, can plan an equitable way to find 'the right balance with our environment'. The contemporary dilemma is that the world is ecologically full – in fact it's full to overflowing. But so far the benefits of the growth that got us to this point are grotesquely inequitably distributed. We cannot grow our way to sustainability, but must instead come to share the world's economic and ecological output.

How we approach this problem will necessarily represent a dialectic between self-conscious reason and unconscious predisposition. It's well known that humans are disinclined to share with strangers, particularly in times of crisis or scarcity. We're not inherently altruistic, except to kin and to people with whom we've developed a reciprocally beneficial relationship. But if we don't learn to distribute the world's economic and ecological output more equitably, even as resource supplies are increasingly strained, we may have to face truly dire consequences. The question is: 'is *H. sapiens* capable of achieving a justly equitable global stability based on a new variant of enlightened self-interest?'

It is often said that those who do not know their history are condemned to repeat it. In present circumstances I would argue that, even if we know our history, we are condemned to repeat it if we are unable to rise above certain primitive forms of survival behaviour. Instead, we must use our much vaunted intelligence and awareness of our predicament collectively to override our baser instincts. The question is: can humanity create the required new forms of social and cultural inhibitions, and will we be able to erect the international legal-institutional framework necessary to constrain the 'rogue within'?

We can obtain some measure of the challenge by reference to the twentieth century. The last century may have been technically and scientifically dazzling but it was also the most destructively bloody century in human history. We may be the most intelligent species on earth, we may be capable of astonishing feats of reason and analysis, but our own history reveals that 'The rise and fall of cultures . . . has always been primarily determined by the tides of human passion not by the ebb and flow of reason' (Morrison, 1999).

The primary goal of all life is to survive, but the self-oriented aggressive-defensive behaviours that served so well for that purpose early in our evolution are maladaptive in the ecologically full world today.[4] The challenge of the twenty-first century is to rise above individual and tribal interests and recognize that our best chance for survival lies in collective self-restraint and mutual commitment to the common good. This is an unaccustomed mode of human political behaviour. As American political scientist Linton Caldwell wrote in 1990:

> The prospect for worldwide cooperation to forestall a disaster seems far less likely where deeply entrenched economic and political interests are involved. . . . Many contemporary values, attitudes, and institutions militate against international altruism. As widely interpreted today, human rights, economic interests, and national sovereignty would be factors in opposition. The cooperative task would require behaviour that humans find most difficult: collective self-discipline in a common effort.

One well-tested and very powerful tool is available to us. We must make deliberate, creative use of humanity's myth-making capacity, our inherent need for unifying stories. Let's frankly acknowledge the weaknesses in the expansionist global development model with its emphasis on efficiency, competition and survival of the few and replace it with a new myth that fosters equity, cooperation and mutual sustainability. The choice is between allowing all our various human 'tribes' to assert their independent self-interests in a global free-for-all, or rising to the challenge of fully exercising the singular human quality that sets us apart from other advanced species, the capacity for rational thought. If enlightened reason does not triumph over violence and aggression as the means of settling our affairs, then we will almost certainly fall back into the ancient patterns that so darkly stained the twentieth century.

At a minimum, and for purely practical reasons, the required new myth must acknowledge the precarious state of both the ecosphere and geopolitics and set as its goal the stabilization of both. But surely we can do better than the bare minimum. The enlightened rationality I am invoking is different from hard, cold, calculating enlightenment rationality. Enlightened rationality incorporates passion for life and compassion for both other humans and non-human nature.

As noted earlier, our evolutionary history has provided us with no inhibitions against destroying our habitats, other species or other human beings, and no such inhibitions will come to us from our biology. We have reached the stage in human evolution where the products of the uniquely human mind, including socially constructed cultural factors, must assume the dominant role. The creation of a grand myth for global survival is a purposeful act of social engineering. And while this might seem a daunting task, is it really that qualitatively different from the social engineering that so effectively entrenched the expansionist globalization model around the world? Once again we must shift our values consciously, but this time away from the narrow focus on individualism, self-interest, competitive relationships, toward a greater emphasis on community/societal values, cooperative institutions, and a sense of participating consciousness in nature.

Certainly humans have all of the qualities necessary in their behavioural kitbag – we can love, we are compassionate, we can show empathy for other people and even other species. Of course, some people are better at these things than others, but these are the human qualities that we must draw out in our schools and universities, in government and the private sector. It is a matter of deliberate social choice whether we stress in all our cultural institutions the darker colours of the human behavioural spectrum or emphasize the brighter shades. The point is that the sustainability crisis may be humanity's final opportunity to rise above mere animal instincts. Can we not elevate the qualities that make *H. sapiens* truly unique to a primary place in determining our species' future? If we succeed, the victory will mark the next great adaptive leap forward in human evolution.

ACKNOWLEDGEMENT

This chapter is based on a lecture delivered by the author to The Vancouver Institute on 15 March, 2003.

NOTES

1. There's a corollary here related to our increasingly competitive global environment: the dynamics of unfettered competition among individuals, corporations and economies in a finite, unregulated environment, will tend to eliminate any restraints on destructive behaviour affecting the global commons that individuals or single entities might have exercised were they the sole exploiters. We call this (somewhat mistakenly) the 'common property problem' or, more accurately, the 'Open Access Problem'.

2. Neither do most sea birds live in the sea – like people, they nest on land and go fishing for food.
3. This is in net terms. Growth is justified in poor countries where the benefits are positive, but not in the rich countries (where most of it is occurring).
4. It is possible that global conflict could leave the most powerful and ruthless to inherit what would be left of the earth, thus satisfying the ancient mission of the genes in a minimalist way. However, the costs in lives and destruction are unfathomable to the civilized mind. Hence the option suggested here.

REFERENCES

Auden, W.H., cited in M.O. Hill (2003), 'Mine eyes have seen the glory: Bush's armageddon obsession, revisited', *Counterpunch*, 4 January.

Caldwell, L.K. (1990), *Between Two Worlds: Science, the Environmental Movement, and Policy Choice*, Cambridge, UK: Cambridge University Press.

Christensen, Paul (1991), 'Driving forces, increasing returns, and ecological sustainability', in Robert Costanza (ed.), *Ecological Economics: The Science and Management of Sustainability*, New York: Columbia University Press, pp. 75–87.

Christensen, V., S. Guénette, J. Heymans, C. Walters, R. Watson, D. Zeller and D. Pauly (2003), 'Hundred-year decline of North Atlantic predatory fishes', *Fish and Fisheries*, **4**, 1–24.

Cohen, Joel E. (1995), *How Many People can the Earth Support?*, New York: W.W. Norton.

Daly, H.E. (1992), 'Steady-state economics: concepts, questions, policies', *Gaia*, **6**, 333–8.

Daly, H.E. (1999), *Ecological Economics and the Ecology of Economics*, Cheltenham, UK and Northampton, MA, USA: Edward Elgar.

Dewhurst, J. Frederic and Associates (1955), *America's Needs and Resources. A New Survey*, New York: Twentieth Century Fund.

Diamond, Jared (1995), 'Easter's end', *Discover*, August, pp. 62–9.

Grant, C. (1998), *Myths We Live By*, Ottawa: University of Ottawa Press.

Gurr, T. (1985), 'On the political consequences of scarcity and economic decline', *International Studies Quarterly*, **29**, 51–75.

IIED (1995), *Citizen Action to Lighten Britain's Ecological Footprints*, London: International Institute for Environment and Development.

Jensen, D. (2000), *A Language Older than Words*, New York: Context Books.

Lane, R. (2000), *The Loss of Happiness in Market Democracies*, New Haven: Yale University Press.

Ludwig, D., R. Hilborn and C. Walters (1993), 'Uncertainty, resource exploitation, and conservation: lessons from history', *Science*, **260**, pp. 17, 36.

Morrison, R. (1999), *The Spirit in the Gene: Humanity's Proud Illusion and the Laws of Nature*, Ithaca, NY: Comstock Publishing Associates (Cornell University Press).

Myers, R. and B. Worm (2003), 'Rapid worldwide depletion of predatory fish communities', *Nature*, **423**, 280–83.

Pauly, D. and J. MacLean (2003), *In a Perfect Ocean*, Washington: Island Press.

Pauly, D. et al. (1998), 'Fishing down marine food webs', *Science*, **279** (5352), 860–63.

Ponting, Clive (1991), *A Green History of the World*, London: Sinclair-Stevenson.

Rees, W.E. (1995), 'Achieving sustainability: reform or transformation', *Journal of Planning Literature*, **9**, 343–61.

Rees, W.E. (1996), 'Revisiting carrying capacity: area-based indicators of sustainability', *Population and Environment*, **17**, 195–215.

Rees, W.E. (2001), 'Human carrying capacity: living within global life support', in Edward Munn (Editor-in-Chief), *Encyclopedia of Global Ecological Change*, London: John Wiley and Sons.

Rees, W.E. (2002a), 'Carrying capacity and sustainability: waking Malthus' ghost', in David V.J. Bell and Y. Annie Cheung (eds), (Theme) 'Introduction to sustainable development', in *Encyclopedia of Life Support Systems* (EOLSS), EOLSS Publishers, Oxford, (www.eolss.net).

Rees, W.E. (2002b), 'Globalization and sustainability: conflict or convergence', *Bulletin of Science, Technology and Society*, **22**, 249–68.

Rees, W.E. and L. Westra (2003), 'When consumption does violence: can there be sustainability and environmental justice in a resource-limited world?', in J. Aygeman, R. Bullard and Bob Evans (eds) *Just Sustainabilities: Development in an Unequal World*, New York: Columbia University Press and London: Earthscan.

Regal, Philip (1990), *The Anatomy of Judgment*, Minneapolis: University of Wisconsin Press.

Tainter, J. (1988), *The Collapse of Complex Societies*, Cambridge: Cambridge University Press.

Tainter, J. (1995), 'Sustainability of complex societies', *Futures*, **27**, 397–404.

UNDP (2001), *Human Development Report*, New York and Oxford: Oxford University Press (for United Nations Development Program).

Wackernagel, M. and W.E. Rees (1996), *Our Ecological Footprint: Reducing Human Impact on the Earth*, Gabriola Island, BC: New Society Publishers.

Watson, Reg and Daniel Pauly (2001), 'Systematic distortions in world fisheries catch trends', *Nature*, **414**, 534–6.

WWF (2002), *Living Planet Report 2002*, Gland, Switzerland: Worldwide Fund for Nature (and others), October 2000.

16. Measuring genuine progress

Ronald Colman

There is a remarkable consensus that crosses all political divisions on the fundamental principles of a decent society and on the benchmarks that would signify genuine progress. We all want to live in a peaceful and safe society without crime. We all value a clean environment with healthy forests, soils, lakes and oceans. We need good health and education, strong and caring communities, and free time to relax and develop our potential. We want economic security and less poverty.

No political party officially favours greater insecurity, a degraded environment, or more stress, crime, poverty and inequality. Why then do we see policies that promote those very outcomes? Why are we unable to create the kind of society we genuinely want to inhabit in the new millennium? Why can we not order our policy priorities to accord with our shared values and human needs?

One reason is that we have all been getting the wrong message from our current measures of progress. All of us – politicians, economists, journalists and the general public – have been completely hooked on the illusion that equates economic growth with well-being and prosperity. Indeed, there is probably no more pervasive and dangerous myth in our society than the materialist assumption that 'more is better'.

Look at the language we use: When our economy is growing rapidly, it is called 'robust', 'dynamic', and 'healthy'. When people spend more money, 'consumer confidence' is 'strong'. By contrast, 'weak' or 'anemic' growth signals 'recession' and even 'depression'. Increased car sales signal a 'buoyant recovery'. 'Free' trade actually means 'more' trade. The more we produce, trade and spend, the more the Gross Domestic Product (GDP) grows and, by implication, the 'better off' we are.

This was not the intention of those who created the GDP. Simon Kuznets (1962), its principal architect, warned 40 years ago: 'The welfare of a nation can scarcely be inferred from a measurement of national income. . . . Goals for 'more' growth should specify of what and for what.'

This chapter was written in 1999 and the trends and other statistics cited therefore refer to the 1990s rather than to the present time.

Our growth statistics were never meant to be used as a measure of progress as they are today. In fact, activities that degrade our quality of life, like crime, pollution and addictive gambling, all make the economy grow. The more fish we sell and the more trees we cut down, the more the economy grows. Working longer hours makes the economy grow. And the economy can grow even if inequality and poverty increase.

ENGINES OF GROWTH

Here in Canada we are currently enamoured with the 'dynamic' American economy and its rapid growth rates. But we do not often ask, as Kuznets counsels, what is driving that growth.

One of the fastest growing sectors of the American economy was imprisonment, at an annual growth rate of 6.2 per cent per year throughout the 1990s. One in every 150 Americans was behind bars, the highest rate in the world along with Russia, compared to one in 900 Canadians and one in 1600 Nova Scotians. The O.J. Simpson trial alone added $200 million to the US economy, and the Oklahoma City explosion and Littleton massacre fueled the booming US security industry, which added $40 billion a year to the economy, with most sales going to schools. Is this our model of a 'robust' and 'healthy' economy?

Gambling was another rapid growth industry – a $50 billion a year business in the US. Divorce added $20 billion a year to the US economy. Car crashes added another $57 billion. Prozac sales quadrupled since 1990 to more than $4 billion – a sign of progress? The more rapidly we deplete our natural resources and the more fossil fuels we burn, the faster the economy grows. Because we assign no value to our natural capital, we actually count its depreciation as gain, like a factory owner selling off his machinery and counting it as profit.

Overeating contributes to economic growth many times over, starting with the value of the excess food consumed and the advertising needed to sell it. Then the diet and weight-loss industries added $32 billion a year more to the US economy, and obesity-related health problems another $50 billion, at the same time that 20 million people, mostly children, die every year from hunger and malnutrition in the world

Similarly, toxic pollution, sickness, stress and war all make the economy grow. The Exxon Valdez contributed far more to the Alaska economy by spilling its oil than if it had delivered the oil safely to port because all the clean-up costs, lawsuits and media coverage added to the growth statistics. The Yugoslav war stimulated the economies of the NATO countries to the tune of $60 million a day, and our economies will benefit even more by rebuilding what we destroy.

Measuring progress by the sum total of economic activity is like a policeman adding up all the street activity he observes. The lady walking her dog, the thief stealing the car, the children playing on the corner, the thug hitting someone with a lead pipe – all are recorded equally. Our growth statistics make no distinction between economic activity that contributes to well-being and that which causes harm. Growth is simply a quantitative increase in the physical scale of the economy, and tells us nothing about our actual well-being.

HAS GROWTH MADE US 'BETTER OFF'?

Are we 'better off' as a result of decades of continuous economic growth? Certainly many of us have bigger houses and more cars, appliances and home entertainment equipment. Are we happier? A US poll found that 72 per cent of Americans had more possessions than their parents, but only 47 per cent said they were happier than their parents.

We are also less peaceful and secure, three times more likely to be victims of crime than our parents a generation ago. We are more time-stressed. Our jobs are more insecure. Our debt levels are higher. The gap between rich and poor is widening. Economists predict that for the first time since the Industrial Revolution, the next generation will be worse off than the present one.

More dangerously, blind growth has undermined our natural resource wealth, produced massive pollution, destroyed plant and animal species at an unprecedented rate, and changed the climate in a way that now threatens the planet.

Ironically, while we are so busy counting everything on which we spend money, we assign no value to vital unpaid activities that really do contribute to our well-being. Voluntary community service, the backbone of civil society, is not counted or valued in our measures of progress because no money is exchanged. If we did measure it, we would know that volunteer services to the elderly, sick, disabled, children and other vulnerable groups have declined throughout Canada during the 1990s at the same time that government has cut social services, leading to a cumulative 30 per cent erosion in the social safety net.

Even though household work and raising children are more essential to basic quality of life than much of the work done in offices, factories and stores, they have no value in the GDP, while every additional lawyer, broker and advertising executive is counted as a contribution to well-being. We value the booming child care industry as a fast growing industry in the country, but we do not count unpaid child care, and so we do not notice that parents are spending less time with their children than ever before – a sign of progress?

If we did count voluntary and household work, we would know that they added $325 billion a year of valuable services to the Canadian economy. If we measured the household not just as a source of consumption, as taught in every economics textbook, but as a productive economic unit, we would also discover that total paid and unpaid work has steadily increased, leading to an overall loss of free time.

In 1900, a single-earner male breadwinner worked a 59-hour week in Canada, while a full-time female homemaker put in an average 56-hour week of household work, for a total household work week of 115 hours. Today the average Canadian dual earner couple puts in 79 hours of paid work and 56 hours of unpaid household work a week, for a total household work week of 135 hours.

All those extra paid hours fuel economic growth and are counted as progress. But the loss of precious free time is invisible and unvalued in our measures of progress. Aristotle recognized 2400 years ago that leisure was a prerequisite for contemplation, informed discussion, participation in political life, and genuine freedom. It is also essential for relaxation and health, for spiritual practice, and for a decent quality of life. In the GDP, time is simply money, and we sacrifice it for material comfort in the name of progress.

WHAT WE COUNT IS WHAT WE VALUE

What we measure and count quite literally tell us what we 'value' as a society. If we do not count our non-monetary and non-material assets, we effectively 'discount' and 'devalue' them. And what we don't measure and value in our central accounting mechanism will be effectively sidelined in the policy arena. If, for example, a teacher tells students that a term paper is very important but worth nothing in the final grade, the real message conveyed is that the paper has no value, and the students will devote their attention to the final exam which 'counts' for something.

Similarly, we may pay pious public homage to environmental quality and to social and spiritual values. But if we count their degradation as progress in our growth measures we will continue to send misleading signals to policy makers and public alike, to blunt effective remedial action, and to distort policy priorities.

Until we explicitly value our free time, voluntary community service, parental time with children, and natural resource wealth, they will never receive adequate attention on the public policy agenda. Similarly, until we assign explicit value to equity in our growth measures, we will continue to give little policy attention to the fact that here in Nova Scotia the poorest 20 per cent of the population had lost 29 per cent of its real income after taxes and transfers between 1990 and 1998.

The obsession with growth and its confusion with genuine development and quality of life have led us down a dangerous and self-destructive path. It is doubtful that we will leave our children a better legacy until we cut through the myth that 'more' means 'better', until we stop gauging our well-being and prosperity by how fast the economy is growing, and until we stop misusing the GDP as a measure of progress.

Thirty years ago, just before he was assassinated, Robert Kennedy (1968) remarked:

> Too much and too long, we seem to have surrendered community excellence and community values in the mere accumulation of material things. . . . The Gross National Product includes air pollution and advertising for cigarettes, and ambulances to clear our highways of carnage. It counts special locks for our doors, and jails for the people who break them. The GNP includes the destruction of the redwoods and the death of Lake Superior. It grows with the production of napalm and missiles and nuclear warheads.
>
> And if GNP includes all this, there is much that it does not comprehend. It does not allow for the health of our families, the quality of their education, or the joy of their play. It is indifferent to the decency of our factories and the safety of our streets alike. It does not include the beauty of our poetry or the strength of our marriages, or the intelligence of our public debate or the integrity of our public officials.
>
> GNP measures neither our wit nor our courage, neither our wisdom nor our learning, neither our compassion nor our devotion to our country. It measures everything, in short, except that which makes life worthwhile.

A BETTER WAY TO MEASURE PROGRESS

What are urgently, indeed desperately, needed are measures of well-being, prosperity and progress that explicitly value the non-material assets that are the true basis of our wealth, including the strength of our communities, our free time, the quality of our environment, the health of our natural resources, and our concern for others. The means to do so exist.

In fact, tremendous progress has been made in the last 20 years in natural resource accounting and in developing good social indicators, time use surveys, environmental quality measures and other means of assessing well-being and quality of life. We are now completely capable of measuring our progress in a better way that accords with our shared values and lets us know whether we are moving towards the society we want to create.

After three California researchers developed a Genuine Progress Indicator in 1995, incorporating 26 social, economic and environmental variables, 400 leading economists, business leaders, and social scientists, including Nobel laureates, jointly stated:

> Since the GDP measures only the quantity of market activity without accounting for the social and ecological costs involved, it is both inadequate and misleading as a measure of true prosperity. Policy-makers, economists, the media, and international agencies should cease using the GDP as a measure of progress and publicly acknowledge its shortcomings. New indicators of progress are urgently needed to guide our society. . . .The GPI is an important step in this direction.[1]

Here in Nova Scotia, GPI Atlantic, a non-profit research group, has developed a Genuine Progress Index for the province, and is participating actively with other government, non-government and academic partners in developing a Canadian Index of wellbeing for the country as a whole – a project that includes Statistics Canada participation. It is designed as a practical, policy-relevant tool that is easy to maintain and replicate, that can accurately measure sustainable development, and that can provide much-needed information to policy makers about issues that are currently hidden and even invisible in our market statistics.

The Nova Scotia GPI assigns explicit value to our natural resources, including our soils, forests, fisheries and non-renewable energy sources and assesses the sustainability of our harvesting practices, consumption habits and transportation systems. It measures and values our unpaid voluntary and household work, and it counts crime, pollution, greenhouse gas emissions, road accidents and other liabilities as economic costs, not gains as at present.

The index goes up if our society is becoming more equal, if we have more free time and if our quality of life is improving. It counts our health, our educational attainment, and our economic security. It attempts, in short, to measure 'that which makes life worthwhile'. It is common-sense economics that corresponds with the realities of our daily lives as we actually experience them.

COSTS AND BENEFITS

Unlike the GDP, the GPI distinguishes economic activities that produce benefit from those that cause harm. For example, more crime makes the economy grow, as more money is spent on prisons, burglar alarms, security guards, lawyers, police and court costs. Having a more peaceful society may actually show up as a disadvantage in the GDP and growth statistics.

By contrast, the GPI regards a peaceful and secure society as a profound social asset, with higher crime rates a sign of depreciation in the value of that asset. Unlike the GDP, lower crime rates make the GPI go up, and crime costs are subtracted rather than added in assessments of prosperity.

GPI Atlantic found that in 1997, crime cost Nova Scotians $1.2 billion a year, or $3500 per household, including $312 million in victim losses, $258 million in public spending on prisons, police and courts, and $46 million in home security expenses. Nova Scotian households pay $800 a year more in higher prices due to in-store retail theft and business crime prevention costs, and $200 more per household in higher insurance premiums due to insurance fraud.

Canadians are three times as likely to be victims of crime as their parents a generation ago. According to the GPI, this is not a sign of progress, even though our economy grows as a result. GPI Atlantic found that if crime were still at 1962 levels, Nova Scotians would be saving about $750 million a year, or $2200 per household, money that would be available for investment in more productive and welfare-enhancing activities.

The GPI takes a similar approach to road accidents, toxic pollution and greenhouse gas emissions, which are also seen as costs rather than benefits. Like crime and resource depletion, they are areas of the economy where more growth is clearly not desirable.

By incorporating 'external' costs directly into the economic accounting structure, the 'full cost accounting' mechanisms in the GPI can also help policy makers to identify investments that produce lower social and environmental costs to society. Gambling, clear-cutting and other growth industries might receive less government support if social costs were counted, and sustainable practices might receive more encouragement.

For example, GPI Atlantic recently found that a 10 per cent shift from truck to rail freight would save Nova Scotian taxpayers $11 million a year when the costs of greenhouse gas emissions, road accidents and road maintenance are included. Telecommuting two days per week would save $2200 annually per employee when travel time, fuel, parking, accident, air pollution and other environmental and social costs are included.

The GPI approach contrasts sharply with conventional accounting methods which value the contribution that commuting makes to economic growth. Canadians spent $102 billion a year on their cars, $11 billion more on highways, $500 million on car advertisements, and billions more on hospital beds, and police, court and funeral costs for the 3000 killed and 25 000 seriously injured car crash victims every year. All this spending counts as 'progress' and 'consumer confidence'. Car-pooling may slow GDP growth. By contrast, full cost–benefit accounting methods would lend more support to taxation policies and subsidy incentives that support mass transit alternatives and other more sustainable practices.

VALUING NATURAL RESOURCES

The costs of holding on to the illusion that 'more' is 'better' are frightening. Scientists recognize that the only biological organism that has unlimited growth as its dogma is the cancer cell, the apparent model for our conventional economic theory. By contrast, the natural world thrives on balance and equilibrium, and recognizes inherent limits to growth. The cancer analogy is apt, because the path of limitless growth is profoundly self-destructive. No matter how many cars we have in the driveway or how many possessions we accumulate, the environment will not tolerate the growth illusion even if we fail to see through it.

Valuing both natural resources and time provides an accounting framework that recognizes inherent limits to our economic activity and values balance and equilibrium. In the Genuine Progress Index, natural resources are valued as finite capital stocks, subject to depreciation like produced capital. Genuine progress is measured by our ability to live off the income, or services, produced by our resources without depleting the capital stock that is the basis of wealth both for our children and ourselves.

The GPI acknowledges the full range of ecological and social services provided by these resources. The GPI forestry account, for example, counts not only timber production, but also the value of forests in protecting watersheds, habitat and biodiversity, guarding against soil erosion, regulating climate and sequestering carbon, and providing for recreation and spiritual enjoyment. Healthy soils and the maintenance of multi-species, multi-aged forests in turn provide multiple economic benefits by enhancing timber productivity, increasing the economic value of forest products, protecting against fire, disease and insects, and supporting the burgeoning eco-tourism industry.

The massive unemployment created by the collapse of the Atlantic ground fishery punctured the conventional illusion that jobs and environmental conservation are in conflict. We now understand that soil erosion today threatens food security for our children and that valuing and protecting our resource wealth is essential to protect the human economy.

VALUING TIME

Like natural resources, time is also finite and similarly limits economic activity. We all have 24 hours a day and a limited life span. How we pass that time, and how we balance our paid and unpaid work, our voluntary service, and our free time, is a measure of our well-being, quality of life and contribution to society. The GPI uses time use surveys to measure and value time over a full 24-hour period and to assess the balance between its alternative uses. Measuring time as time, rather than as money, also cuts through the myth of limitless growth.

According to current accounting methods, the more hours we work for pay, the more the GDP grows, and the more we 'progress'. In an interview, a Fortune 500 Chief Executive Officer stated that he works from 6 am to 10 pm every day and has no time for anything else except sleep. By conventional standards, his $4 million annual income made him rich. According to the GPI, where family time, voluntary service and free time are all measured and valued, the CEO may be leading an impoverished lifestyle.

Here in Nova Scotia the head of the Sobeys empire recently advised aspiring entrepreneurs to think about business 'day and night – when you are walking, driving, eating, shaving' if they want to be successful. By contrast, a more balanced relationship with time may produce a more balanced understanding of the natural world. After all, without the leisure time to enjoy a walk in the forest, it is easy to order it to be cut down.

What happens when we start valuing time? The policy implications are profound. For example, GPI Atlantic found that in 1998, Nova Scotians had the highest rate of voluntary activity in the country, giving 134 million hours a year, the equivalent of 81 000 jobs, or $1.9 billion worth of services, equal to 10 per cent of our GDP – a reservoir of generosity complete invisible in our conventional accounts. Unmeasured and unvalued, the voluntary sector has not received the support it needs to do its work well.

Longer work hours due to downsizing and declining real incomes have squeezed volunteer time, producing a steady decline of 7.2 per cent in voluntary service hours over 10 years. For the first time, claims by the Canadian Finance Minister that volunteers could compensate for government service cuts have been disproved. Without tracking the unpaid volunteer sector, such government statements could never be tested.

Measuring unpaid household work shines the spotlight on the time stress of working parents struggling to juggle job and household responsibilities, and on the need for family-friendly work arrangements and flexible work hours. The modern workplace has not yet adjusted to the reality that women have doubled their rate of participation in the paid workforce. In 1998, working mothers put in an average of 11 hours a day of paid and unpaid work on weekdays, and 15 hours more of unpaid work on weekends.

Measuring housework also raises important pay equity issues. Work traditionally performed by women in the household and regarded as 'free' has been devalued in the market economy, resulting in significant gender pay inequities. Though it is an important investment in our human capital, requires vital skills and continuous alertness, child care workers in Nova Scotia earned an average of only $7.58 an hour.

GPI Atlantic found that single mothers dependent on the household economy put in an average of 50 hours a week of productive household work. If it were replaced for pay in the market economy, this work would be worth $450 a week. Because it is invisible and unvalued, 70 per cent of single mothers in Nova Scotia in 1998 lived below the 'low-income cut-off', the major cause of child poverty in the province. From the GPI perspective, social supports for single mothers are not 'welfare' any more than taxpayer subsidies for job creation in the market economy are 'welfare'. They are seen, instead, as essential social infrastructure for the household economy.

EQUITY AND JOB CREATION

Millions of Americans have been left behind by the growth spurt in that country. The US Census Bureau reports that income inequality has risen dramatically since 1968, by 18 per cent for all US households and by over 23 per cent for families. The richest 1 per cent of American households now owns 40 per cent of the national wealth, while the net worth of middle class families has fallen steadily through the 1990s due to rising indebtedness. Bill Gates alone owns more wealth than the bottom 45 per cent of US households combined. Is this progress?

In 1989 the Canadian House of Commons unanimously vowed to eliminate child poverty by the year 2000. Since 1989 child poverty has increased by 47 per cent. In other words, there is no guarantee that the tide of economic growth lifts all boats, and the evidence indicates that the opposite is frequently the case.

For this reason the GPI explicitly values increased equity and job security as benchmarks of genuine progress. Indeed, Statistics Canada recently recognized that concern for equity is inherent in any measure of sustainable development. Once limits to growth are accepted, the issue is fair distribution rather than increased production. If everyone in the world consumed resources at the Canadian level, we would require four additional planet earths.

Within this country, Statistics Canada points to a growing polarization of hours as the main cause of increased earnings inequality. The growth of insecure, temporary and marginal employment – the engine of employment growth in the 1990s – means that more Canadians cannot get the hours they need to support themselves. At the same time, due to downsizing and declining real incomes, more Canadians are working longer hours.

Interestingly, a recent Japanese study found that the underemployed and the overworked suffer similar stress levels and have the same risk of heart attack.

Measuring and valuing time actually changes our approach to work and job creation. In North America we are completely conditioned to believe that jobs are contingent on more growth, forgetting that the right to work and earn a decent livelihood is a fundamental human right, enshrined in Articles 23 and 25 of the Universal Declaration of Human Rights. 'If' we bring in casinos, 'if' we cut a new deal with China, 'if' we entice another corporation with a tax break or subsidy, it is said, 'then' perhaps we can create or save jobs.

Instead, we might learn from some European countries that have created more jobs by reducing and redistributing the existing workload. The Netherlands, for example, has a 2.7 per cent unemployment rate and also the lowest annual work hours of any industrialized country. In that country, part-time work is legally protected, with equal hourly wages and pro-rated benefits. France has introduced a 35-hour work week. Danes have five weeks of annual vacation.

Sweden has generous parental and educational leave provisions that create job openings for new workers. Phased retirement options gradually reduce the work hours of older workers, who can pass on their skills and expertise to younger workers taking their place. One creative experiment gave parents the option of taking the summer months off to be with their children, with guaranteed re-entry to the workforce in September, thus providing much-needed summer jobs for university students and cost savings to employers.

Reducing and redistributing work hours can also improve the quality of life by creating more free time. Time use surveys show that the Danes average 11 hours more free time per week than Canadians and Americans. But free time has no value in our market statistics, and its loss appears nowhere in our current measures of progress. By counting underemployment and overwork as economic costs, and giving explicit value to equity and free time, the GPI can point to a range of intelligent job creation strategies that are not dependent on more growth.

SHIFTING THE VIEW

None of this means that there should be no growth of any kind. Some types of economic growth clearly enhance well-being, increase equity and protect the environment. There is vital work to be done in our society – raising children, caring for those in need, restoring our forests, providing adequate food and shelter for all, enhancing our knowledge and understanding, and strengthening our communities.

But we will never shift our attention to the work that is needed if we fail to value our natural resources, our voluntary service and our child-rearing, and if we place no value on equity, free time, and the health of our communities. And we will never escape from the materialist illusion that has trapped us for so long, or even know whether we are really better off, if we continue to count costs like crime and pollution as benefits, and if we measure our well-being according to the GDP and economic growth statistics.

We have little time left to abandon the dogma of economic growth and its bankrupt measures of well-being before the environment makes the decision for us at tremendous cost. We can still choose to begin the new millennium sanely, valuing the true strengths that we have in abundance. We can begin to fashion more self-reliant and self-sufficient forms of community economic development that provide a real alternative to the globalization that puts our destiny in the hands of forces beyond our control. Knowing that more possessions are not the key to happiness and well-being, we can still take back our future, and perhaps even live a little more simply.

Nova Scotia seems particularly fertile ground for this experiment, because it has been just far enough removed from the materialist mainstream to preserve its community strength, spiritual values, quality of life, and a strong tradition of generous community service more effectively than many other parts of North America. The province has also experienced first-hand the collapse of a natural resource, and it has not generally been well served by conventional economic theory, thus creating a greater openness to alternatives.

The cusp of the millennium is a rare moment in history when a long-term practical vision can actually overpower our habitual short-term preoccupations. The time has never been better to contemplate the legacy we are leaving our children and the society we want to inhabit in the new millennium. It is a moment that invites us to lay the foundations of a genuinely decent society for the sake of our children and all the world's inhabitants.

NOTES

Editor's Note: The GPI Atlantic website is: www.gpiatlantic.org.

1. The full text and a complete list of signatories is available from *Redefining Progress*, 1904 Franklin St., 6th floor, Oakland, California 94612.

REFERENCES

Kennedy, Robert (1968), 'Recapturing America's moral vision', 18 March, in Edwin O. Guthman, C. Richard Allen and Robert F. Kennedy (1993), *RFK: Collected Speeches*, New York: Viking Press.

Kuznets, Simon (1962), The New Republic, 20 October, cited in Cobb, Clifford, Torn Halstead and Jonathan Rowe (1995), 'If the GDP is up, why is America down?', *The Atlantic Monthly*, October, p. 67.

Concluding comments

This volume has posed the question of whether it is possible to achieve the sustainable management of our global renewable and non-renewable resource base. Part II of this book described three of the more noteworthy achievements in the public and private response to the challenge of sustainable development: marketable pollution permits, ecological tax reform, and competitive advantage build on the emerging reconceptualization of the products of a modern post-industrial economy where the traditional distinction between goods and services has been replaced by an economic model which considers durable and non-durable products not as goods per se, but as vehicles for delivering embodied services.

The third part focused on six critical challenges to sustainable development: the energy–environment nexus, most particularly the impact of energy production and utilization on global climate, the preservation of human health in a rapidly industrializing world, and emerging issues in global fisheries, agriculture, biodiversity and forestry. The results of these analyses are mixed – from serious threats to the maintenance of global fisheries stocks, agricultural output and biodiversity, to the remarkable contrasts in sustainable forest management at the global level.

The fourth and final section addressed two critical meta-issues: how corporations and governments measure their progress toward sustainability, and to what degree corporations and human beings are capable to making fundamental changes in their worldviews, behaviour, short and long-term goals, and cognitive processes. Failing a radical change in our technology of production and the value system which underlies our current 'growth mentality', we must conclude that few business activities can be truly 'sustainable' – only less unsustainable.

So, what is the bottom line? Is global sustainability achievable in the near to mid-term future? The answer is almost certainly no, given the convergence of continued population growth and industrialization, the nature of current technology, the structure of industrial production, market-driven incentives which favour current consumption and profits over long-term investment, and prevailing social values and attitudes. None of these, however, precludes the necessity for individuals, governments and especially corporations from modifying their behaviour in a manner which moves us off, even incrementally, our current path of non-sustainability.

Failure to do so will surely foreclose ecological options, accelerate environmental degradation, and increase the probability of our being faced with a serious and potentially irreversible ecological crisis which threatens the viability of the human endeavour and the planet on which we live.

This conclusion clearly leaves unanswered for now, at least, the central question posed by this volume: is sustainable resource management a reality or an illusion?

Index